C000092647

When a Goddess Dies

WHEN A GODDESS DIES

Worshipping Mā Ānandamayī after
Her Death

———◄◉►———

ORIANNE AYMARD

OXFORD
UNIVERSITY PRESS

OXFORD
UNIVERSITY PRESS

Oxford University Press is a department of the University of
Oxford. It furthers the University's objective of excellence in research,
scholarship, and education by publishing worldwide.

Oxford   New York
Auckland   Cape Town   Dar es Salaam   Hong Kong   Karachi
Kuala Lumpur   Madrid   Melbourne   Mexico City   Nairobi
New Delhi   Shanghai   Taipei   Toronto

With offices in
Argentina   Austria   Brazil   Chile   Czech Republic   France   Greece
Guatemala   Hungary   Italy   Japan   Poland   Portugal   Singapore
South Korea   Switzerland   Thailand   Turkey   Ukraine   Vietnam

Oxford is a registered trademark of Oxford University Press
in the UK and certain other countries.

Published in the United States of America by
Oxford University Press
198 Madison Avenue, New York, NY 10016

© Oxford University Press 2014

All rights reserved. No part of this publication may be reproduced, stored in
a retrieval system, or transmitted, in any form or by any means, without the prior
permission in writing of Oxford University Press, or as expressly permitted by law,
by license, or under terms agreed with the appropriate reproduction rights organization.
Inquiries concerning reproduction outside the scope of the above should be sent to the
Rights Department, Oxford University Press, at the address above.

You must not circulate this work in any other form
and you must impose this same condition on any acquirer.

Library of Congress Cataloging-in-Publication Data
Aymard, Orianne.
When a goddess dies : worshipping Ma Anandamayi after her death / Orianne Aymard.
pages cm
Includes bibliographical references and index.
ISBN 978-0-19-936862-4 (pbk. : alk. paper)—ISBN 978-0-19-936861-7
(cloth : alk. paper)   1. Anandamayi, 1896–1982—Cult.   I. Title.
BL1175.A49A86 2014
294.5'61—dc23
2013037639

1 3 5 7 9 8 6 4 2
Printed in the United States of America
on acid-free paper

A God Died Yesterday

WITH THE PASSING of Ma Anandamayee an era in the annals of Indian culture has come to a close.

Ma, as she was known to Her innumerable devotees in this country and abroad, was a saint in the tradition of the greatest Indian mystics. She had, in her own particular way, stood as a formidable bulwark against the erosion of traditional Indian values and culture at a time when these had come under heavy onslaught from within the nation itself...

For millions of men and women who made the journey to her door Ma had come to crystallize the peace and universality which is so peculiar [particular] to the Indian culture. The Indians, the westerners from wherever they came—the very best minds of nearly four generations—some of them leading writers, philosophers, spiritualists, scientists and politicians—all who flocked to her luminous door were found returning to their respective niches enriched with humanity's rarest and best achievement—love.

That was Ma Anandamayee... Her spirit is as eternal, as everlasting as India herself. She was amongst the finest of Mother's India offspring.

The Himachal Times, August 29, 1982

Contents

Acknowledgments

AS I FIND myself writing my acknowledgments, I think this is probably the most difficult part of my book. How to thank all those who helped me to make this book a reality? Many people have contributed to it in their own ways, and it is not an easy task to express how grateful I am to all of them. The list is long and varied, ranging from academics to neurosurgeons in India and France.

If this book is a great intellectual adventure, it is also much more. Its birth took place on a hospital bed in Dehra Dun, in Northern India. While in a critical medical state, I promised myself to write on Mā Ānandamayī (Mā), if I came through the crisis. Having made this promise, I had no other choice but persevere until I published. This book, then, is a real liberation and represents a true victory of life over death.

My thanks are especially directed to:

Marie-Andrée Roy, also nicknamed Ma, for guiding me on this "pilgrimage on the path of knowledge," to refer to her own words. To me she is a model scholar, an advisor and a friend. I am deeply indebted to her for her enlightened guidance.

Mathieu Boisvert for his great insight and his continuous optimism. Having traveled in India with Mathieu, either at the feet of the Shivling Mountain, the *Ardhakumbhamelā* in Allahabad, or to the sacred place of Hardwar, I thank Mathieu for deepening my understanding of India.

Leslie Orr for having truly enriched my academic reflections and helped me reconnect with the academic sphere after intense humanitarian missions.

John Stratton Hawley for his encouragements and inspiring advice for the publication and beyond. I am deeply impressed at how such a great scholar can be so humble and humane at the same time. This publication could hardly have taken place without his help.

Lisa Hallstrom, who greatly helped me improve this book. When asked at the Apollo Hospital in Delhi what would please me while waiting for my medical evacuation to France, my first answer was the book of Lisa. I have to admit now this was a big challenge to write after her wonderful book on Mā, *Mother of Bliss.*

Oxford University Press (New York), for making this publication happen. I would like to especially thank Theo Calderara and Marcela Maxfield.

The anonymous reviewers who read my manuscript for Oxford University Press.

The South Asia Institute at Columbia University, for welcoming me and giving me the chance to again be part of an academic community. A special thanks to Philip Oldenburg at Columbia for his generous advice, as well as Rachel McDermott for her guidance.

Sarah Myers, from the French Department at Columbia University, for having translated large parts of this work from French to English.

The department of Religious Studies at the University of Quebec in Montreal (UQAM), especially Jean-Jacques Lavoie, Guy Ménard, Paul Leslie, Mark Bradley, and Genevieve Pigeon.

Anne Power, from the London School of Ecocomics, for supporting my decision to redirect my Ph.D. studies from Social Policy in Tibet to Religious Studies in India.

All of my friends, especially Laurence, Genevieve Meera, Juliette, Tarik, Firas, and my "Quebecois godfather," Michel. A special thank to Dinesh, Joe, as well as Pascale, who looked after me at the hospital in Dehra Dun as if I were her own daughter.

My neurosurgeon, Fabrice Parker, without whom I would certainly not have been able to write this book!

The community of Ānandamayī Mā, for trusting me and sharing their most intimate experiences of Mā. Special thanks to Caroline and Izou, who maintain the *samādhi* (tomb) of Swami Vijayānanda at the Père Lachaise cemetery almost daily. I also would like to thank the following people for helping me with the publication of pictures, among other things: Béatrice Abitbol, Christopher Pegler, Pushpraj, Richard Lannoy, Swami Nityānanda (Neeta Mehta), and Swami Mangalananda.

Dr. Jacques Vigne (Vigyānānanda) for his valuable advice to write my Ph.D. thesis and his attention when I was extremely sick in India.

My brother and sister for making me smile even when the situation looks desperate!

My parents for having always supported my decisions, however unexpected and inconsistent they were. Words are missing to express my love and gratitude to them.

In memoriam, Swami Vijayānanda, the greatest magician I have ever met, for teaching me the "Gai Savoir," the path of Joy, and for caring after me in certainly the most critical moment of my life.

And finally, the Supreme Divine Mother, to Mā Ānandamayī, without whom none of this would be possible.

O.A.

When a Goddess Dies

Introduction

NOT FAR FROM the city of Hardwar, one of the most famous pilgrimage sites in India, where millions of pilgrims flock every year to worship Ganga Mā, the Mother Goddess incarnated as the Ganges River, and where every twelve years the largest pilgrimage in the world, the *Kumbhamelā*, is held, lies the town of Kankhal. Described by Mircea Eliade in his writings,[1] this small town on the banks of a tributary of the Ganges at the borders of the Himalayas is host to the mythical site of *Dakṣinesvāra*, where Satī, in a spirit of devotion and sacrifice for her husband Śiva, threw herself into the fire. Only a few steps away from this site, in this atmosphere permeated with the sacred, pilgrims, both Indians and Westerners, come to pray at the tomb of a holy woman whom they simply call Mā.

Further South in Central India, the small island of Omkareshwar, surrounded by the majestic river Narmada, welcomes another ancient pilgrimage place, one that is dedicated to Śiva and that shelters a *jyoti liṅgam* (pillar of light), Śiva's manifestation. On the very same island, every day in a school overlooking the Narmada, hundreds of children sing with devotion and faith the name of the Divine Mother, the name of Mā.

A few thousand miles away, in the heart of the 20th arrondissement of Paris, is the Père Lachaise cemetery, known worldwide for hosting the graves of hundreds of personalities from Jim Morrison to Edith Piaf to Frédéric Chopin and Oscar Wilde. In the Division 41, near the corner of the cross Avenue No. 2 and Avenue Greffülhe, drifts a sweet scent of incense from one of the tombs. On this tomb an inscription is engraved: OM MĀ.

This woman venerated in Kankhal, sung to in Omkareshwar, and honored in a Parisian cemetery, is none other than Mā Ānandamayī (1896–1982). In her lifetime Mā Ānandamayī became arguably the most famous female religious leader in India, counting hundreds of thousands of followers, including personalities like Kamala Nehru, wife of the prime Minister Jawaharlal Nehru, and their daughter Indira Gandhi, and was venerated in turn as guru and avatar, incarnation of the Divine on Earth.[2] Born in East Bengal (now Bangladesh) in 1896 to poor brahmin parents, Mā Ānandamayī, also known as "Mā" (Mother) or in Bengal as Manush Kālī (the "Human Kālī"), to refer to her status as Goddess, as Divine Mother, was at the origin of a religious movement and a vast network of ashrams, something never seen before for a woman in India, as well as reforms seeking to promote gender equality. All this was in a society where women gurus were rarely recognized. Because of her great influence on all layers of society in India, she now represents one of the few Hindu female gurus to be worshiped after her death, and especially in a cult at her tomb, in spite of the fact that tombs of holy women are virtually nonexistent in India.

Omkareshwar is home to the ashram of one of Mā's close disciples, Swami Kedarnath, also called Baba (Father). Swami Kedarnath met Mā in 1976, six years before her *mahāsamādhi* (death of the saint, of the guru), and received guidance directly from her. In the 1990s, after the passing of Mā, he established two ashrams independent of the Shree Shree Anandamayee Sangha, Ānandamayī Mā's official organization, and created his own institution dedicated to spreading Mā's teaching. Today, his organization runs a school, where hundreds of children receive a K–12 education as well as an education in the life and teachings of Mā.

Among the very close disciples that Mā also counted was a Jewish doctor, a native of Metz, France, and son of the greatest Rabbi of that city. In 1950, Dr. Abraham Jacob Weintrob left France for Sri Lanka and India with the intention of staying only two months to meet with spiritual masters, in particular with Ramana Maharshi and Sri Aurobindo. As fate would have it, he met Mā Ānandamayī soon after his arrival. Following this meeting, he decided to follow the holy woman and later became a monk or swami in Mā's organization, taking the name of Swami Vijayānanda (the Victory of Bliss). Swami Vijayānanda never returned to France and spent nearly sixty years in India, including seventeen years as a hermit in the mountains of the Himalayas. This "gentil grand-père" (or "sweet grandfather") as some French followers liked to call him, emphasizing anything but a naïve quality of this man with an exceptional destiny, welcomed Westerners to Mā's ashram in Kankhal, where the tomb of Mā is located, until his death on April 5, 2010, at the age of 95. Today Swami Vijayānanda is an object of veneration for Christians, Jews, Buddhists, Hindus, and others at his grave in Père Lachaise, serving as a bridge between East and West, as well as a central element to the worship of Mā.

While the veneration of a deceased person, especially at his or her grave, is common in the West, especially in the Catholic tradition, it is less developed in the Hindu tradition, where preference is given to the devotion of beings during their lifetime and where death is normally associated with the idea of pollution and impurity, and the corpse synonymous with contamination. With the exception of *satīs*, wives sacrificed in fire by love or by force to follow their deceased husbands, the very idea of worshipping a woman after her death, or even when she is alive until the advent of Mā, is something even more exceptional in India. How does the postmortem worship of Mā then fall within the Indian religious landscape?

The study presented here investigates the postmortem cult of gurus in the Hindu tradition, specifically the Bengali cult of Mā Ānandamayī as it has been expressed since 1982, that is to say since she has "left her body," to use an expression in Indian English designating the death of a guru. The fundamental question of this study is that of the impact of the guru's death on his or her cult. What are the resulting transformations in the guru's cult after his or her death and the origins thereof? Is the cult of the guru, in this case that of Mā Ānandamayī, affected or strengthened by the death of the guru? Does it decline, stagnate, or grow? Or rather does it undergo a redefinition? What are the conditions under which the cult of a Hindu religious figure thrives after his or her death?

This study describes, through the life of Mā Ānandamayī, the consequences of the guru's death on his or her cult, not only from an institutional but also from an experiential point of view, since the institutional and the experiential are closely related and are actually two facets of the same phenomenon. As a result, my research situates itself around these two aspects of the religious, that of actual experience and that of the institution. These two features of the religious refer to the distinction made by William James in *The Varieties of Religious Experience* between "first hand religion," namely the religious experience of the individual, and "second hand religion," the institution, which is only a secondary expression of the religious. The institutional aspect, though secondary for James, is nevertheless indispensable to a transmission of religious experience, although it is often influential in the process. As such this study organizes itself around these two important features, as the postmortem cult of Hindu gurus is examined not only in its institutional but also in its experiential dimension.

In addition of being one of the rare women to be venerated at a tomb, Mā Ānandamayī is a particularly interesting figure for study due to her recent "departure" only thirty years ago. Her cult today is at a crossroads, as it now consists of devotees who knew Mā during her lifetime, those whom I call "early devotees," and of devotees who did not, called here "new devotees." Due to the extent of her influence in her lifetime and her recent death, Mā Ānandamayī then is a noteworthy illustration of a posthumous cult of a Hindu guru.

Research Contribution

This study then explores the devotional movement of the enduring religious figure, Ānandamayī Mā, through the compelling question of what happens to a charismatic movement after the death of the guru. There have been previous studies on gurus, such as Shirdi Sai Baba or Ramana Maharshi, but they have tended to focus more on the life and teachings of the masters, rather than the postcharismatic fate of gurus. As such, this study brings a significant contribution to the field of understanding a community's attempt in modern (and postmodern) times to sustain and enliven the worship of a renowned guru.

Through the iconic figure of Mā, who, paradoxically always denied her status as a guru while fulfilling that role,[3] this study introduces in an interdisciplinary manner the guru's role in society and beyond and affords important insights into the explorations of gurus and devotion. Although an in-depth review of the history of studies on the guru would certainly be of great value here, such an extensive review, however, is beyond the scope of this study. It seems nevertheless essential to situate this work within the state of scholarship on the guru—primarily anthropology, sociology, and religious studies—so as to develop a line of questioning with regard to the role of the guru after his or her death. The more theoretical elements will be provided as they apply throughout this research.

In the past two decades, there has been an explosion of studies on the Hindu guru. Most recently, scholarly works have focused on "middle-class" gurus such as Mā Amṛtānandamayī (or Amma) and Sathya Sai Baba, considered today as the most popular gurus in India. Sathya Sai Baba himself passed away in 2011. Tulasi Srivinas, *Winged Faith* (2010), for example, studies the Sathya Sai Baba transnational movement, arguing for a rethinking of globalization, and suggesting new approaches for discussing religion in a plural world. Smriti Srivinas, in her book, *In the Presence of Sai Baba* (2008), conducts an investigation into the configurations of spatiality and religiosity within the Sathya Sai Baba movement. While giving an account of urban middle-class devotees of Sathya Sai Baba and the proliferation of his presence through diverse physical and virtual channels, she shows ways in which devotees and religious movements engage with global processes. Maya Warrier, *Hindu Selves in a Modern World* (2005), for her part, focuses on Amma's devotional movement, exploring the relationship between religion and modernity in contemporary India, and arguing that Amma's spiritual enterprise responds to the needs of devotees' modern lifestyles. Jacob Copeman and Aya Ikegame, "The Multifarious Guru" (2012), discuss the phenomenon of guruship through an interdisciplinary approach, drawing attention to the guru's "uncontainability" (i.e., the guru's capacity to move between various spheres). While defining the term "guru" broadly, Copeman and Ikegame explore different kinds of gurus, "the governing guru," "the cosmopolitan guru," and "the political guru," for example.

From a gender perspective, much work has also been done on female guruship in recent years. Among the key writings that inspired me, of course, we find Lisa Hallstrom's *Mother of Bliss* (1999), which discusses Ānandamayī Mā as a woman, saint, guru, and avatar. Karen Pechilis's "Gurumayi, the Play of Sakti and Guru" (2004) and the accompanying authors of *The Graceful Guru* are of great value too, as different profiles of female gurus are described and then analyzed, such as Ānandamayī Mā (Lisa Hallstrom) and Mā Amṛtānandamayī (Selva Raj), Śrī Mā of Kāmakkhya (Loriliai Biernacki) and Jaya Ma (June McDaniel), or Mother Meera (Catherine Cornille). While discussing the figure of Mā, one cannot avoid a comparison with Amma, the hugging Mother from Kerala. Of great interest is Warrier's approach to Amma's movement through an examination of secularization, a term she identifies as a "conscious choosing," where religion is not taken for granted but is seen more as an option. Other authors that broadened my understanding of female gurus include June McDaniel, *The Madness of the Saints* (1989), who discusses within a Hindu Bengali context the intimate religious life, or what she calls "madness," of five women, including Ānandamayī Mā, through their visions and ecstasy states. My attention also turned to scholars such as Catherine Clémentin-Ojha, *La Divinité conquise* (1990), who studied the life of a female guru, Shoba Mā, in Benares, and Marie-Thérèse Charpentier, *Indian Female Gurus in Contemporary Hinduism* (2010), who investigated the phenomenon of contemporary female guruship within the framework of the spiritual careers of seventy gurus.[4]

This book then is aligned with an enormous corpus of literature on guruship and contemporary global religious movements from different fields of studies. It is surprising, however, that among the vast majority of these scholarly works, the relationship between guruship and death has been mostly overlooked by both the Indian and Western scholars. There are writings, for example, on the masters' teaching on death or on the preservation of their postmortem memory, as evidenced lately by Christian Lee Novetzke's *Religion and Public Memory* (2008), on the maintenance of saint Namdev's memory through multiple "historical publics," but there is generally a lack of in-depth studies surrounding postmortem guruship.

Indeed, the masters' death and its reception by devotees are rarely addressed in scholarly writings, other than very indirectly. We encounter studies on the self-cremation of sages and their entombment (Charles Malamoud, *Cooking the World* (1996); Marcelle Saindon, "Le Rituel hindou de la cremation" (2000), among other authors), but devotional practices surrounding postmortem cults, more specifically at the tomb, are not addressed. It is often necessary to turn to Sufi studies (to name a few, Pnina Werbner and Helene Basu, eds., *Embodying Charisma* (1998); Marc Gaborieau, "The Cult of Saints among the Muslims of Nepal and Northern India," "Pouvoir et autorité des soufis dans l'Himalaya," and "A Nineteenth-Century Indian 'Wahhabi' Tract against the Cult of Muslim Saints: *Al-Balagh al-Mubin*") and studies of syncretism (Jackie Assayag, *Au Confluent de deux rivières* (1995); Véronique Bouiller and Catherine Servan-Schreiber, eds., *De l'Arabie à l'Himalaya* [2004], among other studies) to find a discussion of these practices of worship at the tomb. Though the religious affiliation of Sathya Sai Baba is unique, as it is located between Sufism and Hinduism, the latest work of Tulasi Srivinas, "Relics of Faith" (2012) on his relics, however, is quite encouraging, as it may lead to future studies on relics in the field of Hinduism. From the experiential perspective, the devotees' religious experiences of the guru after his or her death have not generated great interest in scholarly circles either. Devotees' experiences of trance, of ecstasies, of the miraculous, or of the master's presence are discussed, but generally in regard to a living guru, not one who has died.

Finally, from a more sociological point of view, there have been sociologically based studies of the continuing cults after the death of a guru, such as the study of Ramakrishna movement (Gwilym Beckerlegge, *The Ramakrishna Mission* (2000)), the Divine Society movement of Shivananda (Timothy Miller, "The Divine Life Society Movement" (2001)), the Krishna Consciousness movement (Irvin Collins, "The 'Routinization of Charisma' and the Charismatic" (2004); Steven Gelberg, "The Call of the Lotus-Eyed Lord" (1991)), the Shree Rajneesh movement (Charles Lindholm, "Culture, Charisma, and Consciousness" (2002)), and the Radhasoami movement (Lawrence Babb, *Redemptive Encounters* (1986)), but they are limited and tend to ignore the experiential aspect of the cult. As such, the following work is valuable in terms of further study of the continuation of guru's cults after death, especially with the recent passing away of gurus such as Sathya Sai Baba and Ma Jaya Sati Bhagavati.

While this book fills an existing lacuna in the field by bringing together different scholarly perspectives into a fruitful dialogue on guruship and death, it acknowledges a lack of scholarly attention on this subject until now. Is this lacuna the result of a lack of interest on the part of scholars? Or might scholars shy away from approaching devotees of a guru who has passed to speak about his or her death for fear of devotees' reaction, given that there is a widely held belief that the guru never dies? This was not my personal experience, but this may be a concern for scholars who might not dare to raise these issues.

This pioneering study also adds to the work on holy women in the Hindu tradition, highlighting a new vision of holiness in revealing a new mode of veneration of female gurus, that of the tomb's cult. Worship at a guru's tomb was hitherto an exclusively male phenomenon, as the sepulchral landscape of Hindu sanctity shows. Mā, then, represents a shift to female leadership in the world of Hindu guruship, and her grave is, in this sense, a symbol of the affirmation of the Divine Feminine. With the growing acceptance of the role of guru for women, it is likely in the near future that we will see a far more significant cult of the tomb of women gurus emerge in the Hindu tradition. This very well may come to pass in the case of the most prominent figures of Hindu spirituality, Amma and Swami Chidvilasananda or Gurumayi. As such, this study represents a true milestone in the field, revealing the deep interconnections between women, guruship, and death.

Finally, from an East–West guruship perspective, this study is a reflection of the globalization of religion. It reflects the growing interest in the West in the holy figures of Hinduism, such as Amma, Mother Meera, and Gurumayi, who travel outside the borders of *Bhārat Mātā* (Mother India). In heralding the internationalization of the cult of Ānandamayī Mā through the figure of Swami Vijayānanda, as well as through the Western tours of Swami Kedarnath's disciples, this work contributes to a better understanding of Hinduism and its relationship to the West. As such, it is an undeniable contribution to the advancement of knowledge for South Asian Studies, representing a renaissance moment in the history of guruship.

Overview and Scope

This book is divided into five chapters. Its structure aims to systematically bring the reader to the main question, what is the postcharismatic fate of the guru's cult after his or her death and what are the conditions for the maintenance of his or her cult. I will now describe the subject of each chapter while enumerating the relevant research and literature therein.

Aspects of the Postmortem Cult of Gurus

So as to understand the evolution of the guru's cult after his or her death, it seems first important to present a detailed picture of the postmortem cult of gurus in the Hindu tradition. In chapter 1, I explore the postmortem cult's organization of Ānandamayī Mā. I consider its sacred spaces, its agents, the community of devotees, its function and manifestations, such as rituals, celebrations and retreats, and the cult of images and statues (*mūrtis*). In this context, I refer to the central concepts of *tīrtha* (place of pilgrimage), of *darśana* (to see and be seen by the divinity), of sacred exchange, and of ritual activity.

The Cult of Relics in Hinduism

Compared to other religions, such as Catholicism or Buddhism, the cult of relics in the Hindu tradition is relatively underdeveloped and, therefore, there are relatively few studies on it. This may due to Hindus' preference for the guru's living presence; within the yogic tradition, to be sure, the necessity of a living guru is affirmed. The fact that a cult of relics does exist and may even be becoming more common testifies however to the importance of studying this significant aspect of Hinduism in order to better understand this religious tradition, particularly its relationship to death, transmission, and the master–disciple relation.

In chapter 2, I describe the cult of relics in Hinduism, first by specifying its origin and place in the sacred geography of India, while considering the burial of gurus and the belief in the incorruptibility of their bodies.

I go on to study the role of the feminine in this cult and I then turn to the sacred function of relics, so as to demonstrate the importance of the cult of relics within the postmortem cult. In this regard, I examine the questions of presence (*sannidhi*) and of the power (*śakti*) attached to relics, and I consider the cult of relics as a form of meditation on death. The tantric aspect, especially with regard to the powerful goddess Kālī, is not to be neglected.

I explore themes related to death—transgression and danger, place and embodiment, agency, and memories—through which the figure of the guru is constructed. While approaching relics as a medium of guruship and the transference of power, "contagion," to use Douglas and Frazer's terms,[5] the notion of agency is particularly powerful in relationship to object analysis and materiality. In this regard, Srinivas's work on the relics of Sathya Sai Baba and its discussion of his body, in which she distinguishes between the *sacra* and *ephemera*, is of great interest.[6]

The influence of Sufism on the Hindu cult of relics is here particularly strong. As such, this study covers a vast terrain of unexplored territory, providing a vital contribution to the field of subcontinental theology, guruship studies, and religious studies.

Death of the Guru

It seems important to return to the guru's physical death and to the devotees' response to it, so as to better understand the devotees' relationship with the guru today and thereby to more fully grasp the evolution of his or her cult since his or her death. As a result, chapter 3 addresses Mā's death in general.

What is the meaning of death in the eyes of the guru, here in Mā's eyes? To answer this question, I refer to Mā's words and the words of other *mahātmas* (great souls), such as Ramana Maharshi, Ramdas, Oupasani Baba, and Vivekananda. I also call on sacred texts of the Hindu tradition, quoting the *Bhagavadgītā*, the *Kathā Upaniṣad*, and the *Bṛhadaranyaka Upaniṣad* to discuss the significance of death for the guru. The concept of non-duality (*Advaita*) is particularly addressed here.

Mā's death itself is then discussed with the aid of writings from the Western disciple Atmananda and the Professor Bithika Mukerji, the main biographer of Mā.[7] I also look at the reception of Mā's death among her devotees, their reaction to her departure, using comparisons with the death of the sage Ramakrishna. Finally, I discuss the devotees' beliefs in an afterlife (i.e., the possible return of the guru on earth), referring notably to the concept of avatar or divine descent, and I address the meaning that death holds for Mā's disciples.

Presence of the Guru

Chapter 4 focuses on the experiential face of the postmortem cult of the guru, or that which James calls "personal religion," as compared to "functional"[8] or institutionalized religion. Here I direct my attention to devotees' religious experience, an experience that would not take place without the affirmation of faith, as faith is the central element through which the subject confers his objectivity, or his true nature, to the religious experience. I turn especially to the commentary of James, for whom the religious experience is found at the heart of religion, as well as to Rudolf Otto, who defines the religious experience as nostalgia for the divine and as the experience of the "wholly other," that is to say that which is completely different.[9]

After addressing the question of whether the physical presence of Mā is necessary for her devotees, and what the drawbacks and advantages of her physical presence are, I then consider the experience itself, which for James represents the very essence of religion. What are the principal characteristics of the devotees' experience? What experience do they have with Mā since her passing? The key concepts of presence, of *ānanda* (supreme beatitude), and of *Advaita* (non-duality) are used to qualify the devotional experience after the death of the guru. This chapter looks then to understand the experiential character of the postmortem cult. It is in fact a real work of anthropology to give voice to Mā's devotees.

Sustainability of the Postmortem Cult

Finally, chapter 5, "Sustainability of the Postmortem Cult," is exclusively interested in the institutional side of the guru's postmortem cult. Here I explore the phenomenon of the routinization of the guru's charisma after his or her death, that is to say the perpetuation of his or her charisma through institutionalization. While developing a discussion with reference to scholars such as Bourdieu, Habermas, Hervieu-Léger, or Lindholm, whose comprehension of charisma in non-Western societies, especially in South Asia, is very useful,[10] I use Max Weber's sociological theories concerning routinization, the process in which extraordinary situations transform themselves in order to endure.[11] Weber's concepts of charismatic and bureaucratic domination, and of routinization here direct my discussion.

With reference to routinization, I also address the problems of maintaining ashrams and the cult's community after Mā's death, as well as the role of brahminical orthodoxy's within Mā's organization, notably vis-à-vis foreigners, who are considered outsiders. I draw the contrast between the Bengali orthodox community's custodianship of the site of Mā's *samādhi* (tomb) in Kankhal and the more relaxed and inclusive *sampradāya* (spiritual lineage) established by one of Mā's special disciples, Swami Kedarnath. While observing internal rifts between Indians and Western devotees, and distinguishing between what Habermas call "representative" communities and "critical" communities,[12] I explore South Asian religious power structures. Finally, the principle ways for the cult to sustain itself, notably through hagiography and initiation, are the object of the last section.

Through exhaustive and interconnected empirical and documentative research, I complete an in-depth examination of all facets of the postmortem cult of the guru, particularly with respect to Mā, and I thus look to describe the development of the guru's cult after his or her death from both an experiential and institutional point of view.

Return to Mā Ānandamayī's Life and Teachings

Born on April 30, 1896, in the small village of Kheora in Eastern Bengal, located in the state of Tripura, to poor Vaiṣṇavite brahmin parents, Mā Ānandamayī was given the name of *Nirmāla Sundari*, which means "immaculate beauty" or "purity." Later the surnames of *Hasi* (smile) and *Khusir* (the joyous) were also given to her. According to her spiritual biographies, especially the writings of Professor Bithika Mukerji, the principal biographer of Mā Ānandamayī with whom I was able to meet in Allahabad, Mā proved from her childhood, to be a detached child who had little interest in the surrounding environment, so much so that many thought that she was intellectually disabled.

At the age of 13, *Nirmāla Sundari* was married to the much older Ramani Mohan Chakravarti, and at 18, she finally went to live with her spouse, whom she later called "Bholanāth," one of Śiva's names. Although Mā went through marriage, contrary to other late female gurus like Amma or Gurumayi, and is described as the exemplary housewife, completely devoted to her husband, she actually never consummated her marriage

FIGURE O.I Mā Ānandamayī and her husband, Bholanāth.

Source: Picture belonging to the collection of the photographer Sadanand; now in the possession of Neeta Mehta, also called Swami Nityānanda.

and gave no children to her spouse. She then distanced herself from the traditional forms of marriage, going against the ideal of *pativrata*, of the perfect Hindu woman. In addition to personal experience, Pechilis considers this refusal of the socially defined role of woman as a key element in the charismatic status of Mā Ānandamayī and other female gurus.[13]

Sādhanā Līlā of Mā

In 1918, Mā and Bholanāth moved to Bajitpur in Eastern Bengal, where Mā initiated an intensive *sādhanā* (spiritual discipline). For six years, she is said to have practiced every type of *sādhanā*. Although she never received any direction or spiritual teaching from a master yogi, she spontaneously was able to perform yogic postures and to perfect *mudrā*s (symbolic or ritual gesture). She called this game her "*līlā* of *sādhanā*" (*līlā* meaning play, game), for, as it has always been the same for her, there was nothing to accomplish spiritually. Thus did Mā affirm that her state had always been one of spiritual realization and that she never had past lives nor would she have future lives, as she specifies here:

> I am what I was and what I shall be; I am whatever you conceive, think or say. But it is a supreme fact that this body has not come into being to reap the fruits of past *karma*. Why don't you take it that this body is the material embodiment of all your thoughts and ideas. You all have wanted it and you have it now. So play with this doll for some time.[14]

Regarding the state of realization of Mā, the famous theologian Gopinath Kaviraj views Mā in the following manner:

> *Samadhi* or no *Samadhi*, She is where She always has been; She knows no change, no modification, no alteration: She is always poised in the selfsame awareness as a Supreme and Integral Universality, transcending all limitations of time, space and personality and yet comprehending them all in a great harmony.[15]

Noting Mā's unconventional, even strange behavior, as Mā would engage during her *sādhanā* in complicated yogic postures and be in a trancelike state, people began to think she was either possessed by spirits or was sick. It was then that her husband had exorcists try to stop his wife's "abnormal" behavior, but these exorcists eventually recognized the saintly character of their patient, seeing in her a goddess, an incarnation of *Devī*, the Divine Mother.

Mā continued to focus on the *sādhanā* that eventually led to an initiation (*dīkṣā*) that she gave to herself August 3, 1922, simultaneously becoming the disciple (*śiṣya*), the guru (*guru*), and the divinity (*iṣṭa*). By this act of self-initiation, Mā distinguished herself from most gurus, making herself an exceptional figure. Later, in December 1922, Bholanāth asked to receive initiation from Mā and thus, became her first true disciple. It was at this time that Mā entered into a period of silence (*mauna*) for three years.

Regarding self-initiation, a certain number of female gurus today are self-initiated. This is the case, for example, of Amma and Karunamayi. As spiritual knowledge for women mostly comes outside of the initiation sphere of an established religious order, legitimation of female gurus does not necessarily require succession from previous gurus, but seems to be more related to personal experience, visions, and mystical states.[16]

Years in Dhaka

In 1924, Bholanāth and Mā left for Dhaka, then the capital of Bangladesh. It is during this period that the first disciples began to flock to Mā, and it is also at Dhaka that one of her closest disciples, Bhaiji, gave her the name of Mā Ānandamayī, which means "Mother Full of Bliss," or "Mother Saturated with Joy." Little by little, people began to hear about Mā and her states of ecstasy, and came to meet her. Some saw her as an incarnation of the Divine Mother, a manifestation of the goddess Kālī, from which came the name "Human Kālī" that was given to her. Others envisaged Mā as a being that had attained the state of perfect realization (*jīvanmukta*) and possessed extraordinary spiritual powers. Among the powers that Mā was credited with are the powers of clairvoyance and of healing, the latter being often at the basis of a saint's reputation.[17] Mā though would never attribute these powers and miracles to herself, as she always spoke of the action of God.[18]

At this time Mā began to take less and less care of her body, and so needed others to look after her. She stated that she could not tell the difference between fire and water and that if others did not take care of her body it would be destroyed. In 1926, at the age of 30, Mā also stopped eating with her own hands and was instead fed by Didi, one of her closest disciples.

Ma's Pilgrimages

In the late 1920s, Mā began to take on the role of guru, or spiritual master, giving *dīkṣā* to a small circle of devotees, even as she still maintained throughout her life that she was not a guru. She affirmed: "Only God is the Guru. It is a sin to regard the Guru as a human being."[19] The numbers of her devotees, mostly male in the beginning, continued to increase and in 1928 they built an ashram at Dhaka. Despite this, Mā did not stay at the ashram and began to make pilgrimages all over India, moving around until her death, like "a bird on the wing," as she liked to call herself. Arnaud Desjardins, a French writer and producer of documentaries for French television, with whom I had the chance to exchange written correspondences, spent several long periods of time around Mā and remarked that one of the difficulties in accessing Mā was due to her innumerable displacements: "Her incessant and unpredictable movements do not make it easy to get close to her. You had to be really set on receiving her *darshan* [to see and be seen by a deity] in order to meet her."[20] This reminds us today of Amma, who, similarly to Mā, travels extensively throughout the world, though in a very predictable way, as her trips are usually organized months in advance.

Mā did not give any indication of where she would be going or when she was going, nor did she ever specify if she would return. She would simply go to the nearest train station, oftentimes in the middle of the night, and would take the first departing train. She would follow, what she called her *kheyāla* or divine inspiration, a term which Arnaud Desjardins also defines as "a thought or an impulse suddenly springing out of her spirit for no apparent reason, a whim or a caprice."[21] He adds that this term, when applied to Mā who was without ego signifies a will identified with the divine will, spontaneous and free. Mā ceaselessly moved around until the end of her life following her *kheyāla*, an inner voice that dictated divine will to her.

In her pilgrimages throughout India, Mā attracted a vast number of followers and, although she never encouraged it, ashrams were constructed to welcome her. An organization was created in 1952, the Shree Shree Anandamayee Sangha, making Mā the first woman in the history of India to be represented by a movement of such size. During her travels, she met people from all backgrounds. Kings, politicians, and prominent gurus and saints alike prostrated themselves in front of her. Among these were the saint Shivananda, the yogi Yogananda, and Mahatma Gandhi, as well as numerous politicians, including the President of the Republic, Dr. Rajendra Prasad, the Vice-President and philosopher Radhakrishnan, and Pandit Nehru.

On August 27, 1982, Mā "left her body," to use her devotees' expression, at the ashram of Kishenpur, in Dehra Dun, north of Delhi. A procession took place during the day from Dehra Dun to Kankhal, close to Hardwar, where Mā's *samādhi* (tomb) is now located, and Mā's body was interred following the rules of interment specific to the Hindu burial of a great spiritual being. Indian dignitaries came to pay tribute to Mā, including Indira Gandhi, one of her disciples, who said this:

Ānandamayī Mā was the living embodiment of devotion and love. Just with a glimpse of Her, countless problems are solved. She considered service to suffering humanity Her true religion. Her spiritually powerful personality was a source of great guidance for all human beings. I offer my homage to Her.[22]

Through her life and her radiance, Mā Ānandamayī, a self-initiated being who defined herself as enlightened from birth, emerges then as an exceptional figure who, in Weber's words, disrupts order and produces a certain dislocation: her role as a woman guru and especially as an avatar and Divine Mother in a patriarchal society;[23] her spiritual status independent from her husband; her refusal to adopt the traditional forms of marriage by following the ideal of *pativrata* (the perfect Hindu woman); and her reforms to promote women's equality (introduction of *upanayana*, or the Vedic ceremony, for women, and the study of Sanskrit) testify to her charisma. Despite her conservative tendencies in relation to certain aspects of the *sanātana dharma* ("the eternal law," the Hindu tradition), especially with regard to marriage (such as her views regarding arranged marriage) and *satīs*, this ambassador of Hinduism can paradoxically be recognized, in the Weberian sense, as a charismatic figure, a figure of rupture who dictates the terms of her own sanctity, and revolutionizes the world of her devotees.

A Teaching "Beyond Words"

For Richard Lannoy, the photographer who published an album on Mā,[24] the doctrine that Mā embodied approached the greatest degree of universality that a singular individual can reach. This, of course, explains why Mā gathered around her individuals of many religious backgrounds (i.e., Hindus, Buddhists, Jains, Christians, Muslims, and Jews) and of all geographical origins (i.e., Indians, Americans, and Europeans). As is the case today with Amma, her teaching suited each individual, but generally limited itself to the ancient Hindu tradition, the *sanātana dharma*. Depending on the situation, she could call on the non-dualism of *Advaita*, the qualified dualism of *viśiṣṭādvaita*, or the dualism of *bhakti*.

Mā compared life in the world to a slow poison and also said this: "This world means the constant change between happiness and pain. There can be no stability here, no '*nitya*' [eternity], no '*sthiti*' [absoluteness]. That is only in Him. There cannot be both '*samsar*' [the world] and God."[25] Thus, for her, renouncing the world is not renunciation: "People talk and marvel about those who renounce the world, but in actual fact it is you yourself

who have renounced everything. What is this 'everything'? God! Leaving
Him aside, everyone is literally practicing supreme renunciation. [laugh-
ter]"[26] Thus, she asked that every day one consecrates a moment to God,
however small it may be.

Due to the complexity and, at the same time, the simplicity of her teaching, it can be difficult to give a philosophical synthesis to Mā Ānandamayī's
teaching, for, as she said, a doctrine expressed in words cannot express the
Absolute.[27] We can however summarize her teaching in the affirmation
that the true goal of life is to realize God, to know Oneself.[28] With regard
to this, she spoke of the quest to find our true identity in order to escape
from *saṃsāra*, to escape from the endless cycle of rebirth that is nothing
but the world of death:

> You study and you pass your exam; you earn money and you enjoy
> the use of it. But all this is in the realm of death in which you go
> on life after life, repeating the same thing over and over again. But
> there is also another path—the path of Immortality, which leads to
> the knowledge of what you are in reality.[29]

Although Mā's teaching was not limited to a specific doctrine, she nevertheless advocated for the monist tradition of *Advaita*,[30] of non-duality.
For her, the true source of suffering (*duḥkha*) essentially resides in a false
belief that there is duality: "The sense of the separation is the root cause of
all sickness. It is founded on a misunderstanding: the belief in duality."[31]
In this context, she declared that *darśana* (to see and be seen by the deity),
that is to say a true revelation of the Divine or *ātma darśana*, cannot exist
as long as there exists an "I": "You have not had real *darshan* as long as the
'I' persists."[32]

Mā's non-dual thought is also shown in the way she referred to herself.
Similarly to other sages such as Ramdas, Swami Ramatirtha, or Sathya
Sai Baba,[33] Mā Ānandamayī spoke of herself in the third person, designating herself as "this body" or *ehi śarira* in Bengali, or also as "this little
girl," "this little baby." As Arnaud Desjardins says, the sage is beyond the
possessive adjective and the possessive pronoun, because there cannot be
possession unless there is a separation. To someone who asked to describe
her own experience, Mā also declared the following: "it would imply that
the experiencer has still remained. This cannot be so here" (she often designated herself using the term 'here').[34] And so Mā's words and movements continually focused on the absence of duality.

But, even if Mā constantly associated herself with the non-dual philosophy of *Advaita*, she actually situated herself beyond it: "A state exists
where the distinction between duality and non-duality has no place.... But
where the Brahman is, the One-without-a-second, nothing else can possibly exist. You separate duality from non-duality because you are identified
with the body."[35]

The theologian Gopinath Kaviraj, a disciple of Mā's, shows that
Advaitic thought, which holds that "everything is one," is actually not cor-
rect, in that the meaning of unity disappears in the same moment that the
True One is revealed: "Everything is one, the one is everything. And even
this statement is not exact, for the True One is there where the meaning
of the Unity no longer exists."[36] Mā also referred to the idea of "totality"
to express this necessity of moving past even these ideas of duality and
non-duality: "You will have to become conscious of your Self in its entirety.
Nay, to become fully conscious is not enough; you will have to rise beyond
consciousness and unconsciousness. The revelation of THAT is what is
wanted."[37] Raimon Panikkar's suggestion that we should speak of "adualism" rather than "non-dualism" seems, in this context, appropriate to
eliminating this idea of oppositions.[38]

Although in her statements, Mā constantly stressed the realization of
God, of the True One, as the only goal in life, she nevertheless admitted that she did not have a message to pass on or a mission to accomplish. In reality, for numerous devotees, such as Arnaud Desjardins, "Mā
Ānandamayī's teaching absolutely goes beyond words."[39]

Portrait of Mā Ānandamayī as a Guru

The guru, literally the being of weight,[40] represents "the third gender" and
is located beyond the feminine and the masculine.[41] Most fundamentally,
however, the guru represents the figure of the master, who brings the disciple from darkness to light. In the Hindu tradition, gurus are generally
considered divine, and, up until a certain point, can be considered to be
divinity itself,[42] for, as Bugault affirms, the guru is the radiating mask that
God takes to come to us.[43]

As Hallstrom notes in her study on Mā,[44] mirroring the work of other
scholars on gurus such as Sathya Sai Baba,[45] Mā is for her devotees beyond
all categorization and exceeds all understanding. Despite this "uncontainability," to refer to Copeman and Ikegame's concept as they speak of the

nature of the guru's participation in diverse spheres,[46] Mā nevertheless illustrates different characteristics that seem to define guruship: Mā as a being of paradox; Mā as a being of divine madness; and Mā as a being of power.

Mā as a Being of Paradox

The guru, often perceived as a liminal figure, on the boundary between life and death, is marked by the presence of extremes. While situated in "morality beyond morality,"[47] to refer to an expression of Hawley, these beings cannot always be models for people of this world. This paradoxical nature of the guru is also observed in his or her nature that is both fascinating and terrifying, that which Otto defined as the "*fascinans*" and the "*tremendum.*" As a result, one may feel both attracted and repulsed by the guru. But, if the guru manifests these apparently contradictory characteristics, he or she also surpasses them. This transcendence of contradictions associated with the figure of the guru is referred to in Yoga with the Hindu concept of *dvandvātīta* (beyond the dualities), a concept that has much in common with the two truths of Buddhism, the relative truth and the absolute truth, the two sides of the same coin of reality. Thus, the guru, by being beyond the concepts of good and evil, beyond purity and impurity, would lead us not to the duality of paradoxes but to non-dualism. Far from letting himself or herself be confused with any sort of uniqueness or with univocity, the guru, this individual who is "outside of the world while remaining in it" to use Padoux's expression,[48] thus acts in complete freedom.

In their study of the sacred biography of Mā Ānandamayī, Katherine Young and Lily Miller observe the paradoxical character associated with Mā,[49] as the following description given by a devotee of Mā's demonstrates:

> She (Ma) can be strong and resolute as well as tender and merciful. She is more impressive than thunder and softer than a flower. She is softer than the greatest softness, more beautiful than the greatest beauty, frightening like thunder, soft like the silver rays of the moon and nevertheless as harsh as severity itself, severe and full of compassion. These aspects, which seem so contradictory, show that she is beyond all human classification.[50]

With such a description, it is not surprising that Mā was recognized by some as an incarnation of Kālī, the goddess of the margins who, even in her totality, represents paradox, who incarnates the union of extremes.[51] And if Bengalis sometimes referred to Mā as the living Kālī, "terrible mother" would also have been a very appropriate name. The life of Mā is full of paradoxes and she described herself in the following words:

> I am conditioned as well as unconditioned
> I am neither infinite nor confined within limits
> I am both at the same time...
> I exist before there is any creation, duration, or dissolution of the world.[52]

The following quote from Mā explains the difficulties one encounters in describing Mā: "One cannot describe Mā. To us, she seems to be a fabric of contradictions but, at a higher level of consciousness, all of these contradictions dissolve."[53]

Thus this woman, who was considered simple-minded in her youth, and who paradoxically later assembled around her some of the greatest Indian philosophers and politicians of her age, represents the sum of her contradictions. She who could respect social convention and violate it the next day, who could sing and cry at the same time, who recommended prayer but did not herself pray, was called by her close Western disciple Atmananda "the supreme paradox":

> This evening it struck me how to entitle my article: "Ma—the supreme paradox." She is the most universal and yet the most orthodox. She affirms all paths and yet She says: *"There is no path as all action, all effort, is done by He alone."* She also says: *"He both is and is not, neither is He not nor is He."*[54]

Atmananda also wondered about this mysterious attraction toward Mā: "Isn't it a paradox to feel this strong attraction to a person so totally beyond the physical."[55] Mā's apparently paradoxical position in reality reflects an encompassing vision of life, this Ultimate Reality that Mā defines as *Yā tā*, meaning "It is what it is." Thus are the problems, as Bharati Dhingra points out, in "understanding a being in which the Impersonal is personified!"[56]

FIGURE 0.2 Mā Ānandamayī was called by her close Western disciple Atmananda "the supreme paradox": "Ma—the supreme paradox. She is the most universal and yet the most orthodox. She affirms all paths and yet She says: '*There is no path as all action, all effort, is done by He alone.*'"

Source: Photograph courtesy of Shree Shree Anandamayee Sangha.

Mā as a Being of Divine Madness

If the guru represents a contradictory figure, he or she is also perceived, in some respects, as possessing a certain madness. In India one often speaks of divine madness that, though surprising and incomprehensible, is one of the characteristics of sanctity in India.[57] This divine madness is recognized as a sort of religious ecstasy, of intoxication with divine love, and should not be confused with ordinary madness, as the Bengali saint Lakṣmī Mā specifies.[58] According to McDaniel, it is one of the criteria of sanctity in the Hindu tradition, and particularly in Bengal, Mā Ānandamayī's birthplace. For McDaniel, there is no doubt that the spiritual status of Mā Ānandamayī is based on her states of ecstasy, some of which, especially during her youth, were considered to be a sign of ordinary madness or of intellectual disability. As a child, Mā Ānandamayī was suspected of being simple-minded due to her frequent periods of mental absence; these periods were only later recognized as manifestations of this ecstasy. Mā Ānandamayī speaks of the divine madness as such:

> Go forth to realize God, try at least. This is the genuine madman. Madman (pagol) means paoya gol (to reach the goal), signifying unlimited Enlightenment. When one becomes obsessed by this madness, the madness for the world of duality takes flight. Some people are crazy over another's body. By this sort of insanity, falling prey to infatuation (mohā), one ruins one's body. Turning into a madman after God will not spoil one's body.[59]

Mā's madness thus is interpreted as a sign of absorption in God and demonstrates her sanctity. Moreover, Catherine Clément and Sudhir Kakar discuss this same madness in their study *La Folle et le saint* (The Mad Woman and the Saint), which draws parallels between the life of Madeleine, a French woman interned for several years in the hospital in Salpêtrière for mental disturbance, and the life of Saint Ramakrishna of Calcutta during the same time. These two figures had the same experiences but never met in their lifetimes. And yet, while one was enlightened and perceived as a saint by his entourage, the other was held in a hospital because of her mystical delirium. The two authors refer to Mā Ānandamayī while discussing Madeleine's case: "In India, she [Madeleine] would have been one of these 'Mothers,' like Mā Ānanda Mayee, recently deceased, who at Varanasi was treated like Ramakrishna was in his own time: as a great yogini, a true guru, one of these exceptional souls that the faithful call *Hamsa*, the swan, and who are destined to guide others."[60] Thus, Mā Ānandamayī's sanctity, as well as that of Ramakrishna's or other Hindu sages, is identifiable by the sort of divine madness that is manifested in the figure of the guru.

Mā as a Being of Power

While gurus possess a large array of powers, giving spiritual seekers a large selection of criteria for choosing their guru,[61] the highest power of the guru is said to lie in his or her ability to transmit power (śakti) through initiation (dikṣa), leading the disciple to a real spiritual transformation.[62] This was reported to be true of Mā as she is said to have routinely transformed a materialist into an authentic spiritual seeker. Arnaud Desjardins, who spent months near Mā, speaks of Mā's miraculous ability to penetrate into our consciousness: "What I found truly miraculous in Mā Ānandamayī is what I would try to call the echo of her consciousness within ours."[63]

Contrary to other religious traditions, though, the spiritual master in the Hindu tradition is perceived not as a channel for this power but as the source of it, for he or she represent to a certain extent the very incarnation of God, as shown by the following comment of Swami Vijayānanda:

> I spent 24 hours a day with Mataji, in the course of innumerable trips across India. And well, if I may permit myself to respond to you on this point in a formal fashion: No, Ma Anandamayi was not a human person. She was not a human being! She was, that is without a doubt, an Incarnation of the Divinity.[64]

In this context, it is interesting to wonder about the future of this "contagious" power after the death of the guru. The Hindu tradition generally accepts the posthumous activity of the guru and, by the same token, recognizes the persistence of his or her power after death. Swami Vijayānanda essentially talks about a "residual power" and compares this to the perfume left by a woman on leaving a room. Like the perfume, the guru is said to continue to act after his or her death. For some, the permanence of the guru's power, of his or her *śakti*, after death even represents an authentic proof of his or her divinity. However, the power of the guru does not necessarily accrue after death, as in the Sufi tradition in India, where the *pir*, the Sufi saint, is said to manifest himself in all his power only after his death.[65] In the Hindu tradition, it is recognized that the posthumous power of the spiritual master remains attached to the very spaces in which he or she lived. The location of his or her tomb, called *samādhi*,[66] constitutes the favored among such spaces, one of the most important loci of this study.

Although it is Mā's devotees who have on the whole constructed and affirmed Mā's guruship, despite her numerous claims that she is not a guru, we can nevertheless conclude that Mā fully incarnates the character of the guru.

Methodology

This book, a development of my doctoral thesis, is based on a comprehensive reading of the current literature on this topic, as well as fieldwork extending throughout India and abroad. Because more than five years have passed since the completion of my doctorate in Montreal in the Fall 2008, this study, originally called "Le Culte postmortem des saints dans la tradition hindoue: Expériences religieuses et institutionnalisation du culte de Mā Ānandamayī (1896–1982),"[67] has been revised, both in its form and content, in response to recent developments in the cult. Here, I refer to new scholarship in the field, but more specifically to the death of key monks within the organization and the internationalization of Mā Ānandamayī's movement. This internationalization can be seen today at the Père Lachaise cemetery in Paris with the development of the cult of her monk of French origin, Swami Vijayānanda, as well as in the European and American tours of Swami Mangalananda and Swami Guruśarānanda of Swami Kedarnath's *sampradāya*.

This study represents the time I spent over the course of four years in India, during which I stayed in most of Mā's ashrams, participated in different celebrations and retreats, and conducted interviews. I also had the opportunity to interact with members of Mā's community abroad, especially in France. This study is the fruition then of a long series of interviews with members of Mā's community as well as observational work. In this sense, Fortin's study concerning participatory observation was of much use to my research.[68]

Observation

Mā's cult is located not only in ashrams and other institutions associated with Mā but also in the houses of her devotees. Although I was invited many times to devotees' homes, I have nevertheless limited my research to the spaces directly associated with Mā's cult. This observational work thus was undertaken in some of the twenty-six ashrams of the Shree Shree Anandamayee Sangha in India. All of these ashrams are concentrated in Northern India, with the exception of two in Bangladesh.

Although I had the opportunity to visit most of these ashrams, my attention nevertheless focused on two of them, the Kankhal ashram, near Hardwar in Uttar Pradesh, and the Bhimpura ashram, next to Baroda (Vadodara) in Gujarat. I chose these two sites because of their prominence to the cult. Mā's ashram at Kankhal is considered by many devotees to be the heart of Mā's cult, as it is at this location that Mā's tomb (*samādhi*) is situated and where every year during November a retreat centered on Mā's cult occurs, the *Samyam Saptah*. The Kankhal ashram is also the seat of Mā's organization and is thus a place for assembly. The Bhimpura ashram also constitutes a major ashram within Mā's *saṅgha*, not only because it was inhabited by Swami Bhaskarānanda, the former secretary general of Mā's organization and according to many devotees a guru and one of Mā's closest disciples, but also because Mā's devotees hold an annual retreat in Bhimpura during the months of January and February. I had the opportunity to participate in this retreat in 2007, during Swami Bhaskarānanda's birthday, as well as to attend the festival of *Mahāśivarātri*, Śiva's principal festival. In addition to these two ashrams, I also visited the ashrams at Agartala, Almora, Calcutta, Dehra Dun, Delhi, Dhaulchina, Uttarkashi, Varanasi,[69] Vindhyachal, as well as Mā's two ashrams in Bangladesh, the Siddheshwari Lane ashram at Dhaka and the Kheora's ashram located at Mā's birthplace (*janmabhūmi*).

These pilgrimages across India and Bangladesh allowed me to become familiar with the specificity of each of the ashrams of Mā's *saṅgha*, their respective vitality or lack thereof, as well as to observe the manner in which Mā's cult is maintained in these ashrams. I also visited institutions connected to Mā's organization, such as Mā's hospital at Varanasi and Mā's schools at Agartala, Kheora, and Varanasi. In addition, I was able to visit Mā's *saṅgha* at the *Kumbhamelā* of Allahabad in January 2007, where I participated, despite some initial resistance from orthodox devotees, in two great ritual baths (*śahisnāna*) in the company of Mā's devotees.

I accompanied observation of Mā's ashrams and other institutions with an examination of a group of spaces sacred to cults of deceased gurus throughout India, so as to better establish the postmortem cult of Mā within the larger framework of Hinduism. I have visited the tombs of many Hindu gurus, such as the tomb of Ramana Maharshi in Tiruvanamalai at the feet of Śiva's sacred mountain, Arunachala, the tomb of Sri Aurobindo in Pondicherry, as well as Belur Math in Calcutta, where relics of Ramakrishna and the Holy Mother, Sarada Devi, are also venerated. I also visited spaces devoted to less famous deceased gurus, such as the sacred tombs of the Kina Ram ashram, an *aghori* center in Varanasi. I traveled to and studied spaces sacred to Sufi cults of saints, such as the *dargahs* of Nizamuddin in the suburbs of Delhi, of Shaikh Salim Chisthi in Fatehpur Sikri, or of Haji Ali Shah Bukhari in Mumbai, looking at Sufi influence on the postmortem cult of Hindu saints in India.

Interviews

In addition to observational work and informal conversations, more than forty interviews were completed with Mā's devotees and agents of her cult. The objective of these interviews was to examine the institutional, as well as the experiential, side of Mā's cult, especially with respect to the impact of Mā's death on her cult. Interviews with devotees were then analyzed qualitatively, referring here to the work of Bardin,[70] and addressed in terms of the following three themes: aspects of the postmortem cult; death and the guru's presence; sustainability of the cult. As the vast majority of Mā's community members come from similarly upper-class, educated backgrounds, English was the language used in these interviews. Some were also conducted in French and others in Bengali and Gujarati, these requiring the aid of an interpreter.

So as to reflect the diversity of Mā's devotees, I conducted interviews with as broad a swath of cult members as possible, and thus not only with Hindus but also with followers of other religions, lay people and clergy, Indians and Westerners, and women and men of all ages and of every social class and caste. In the subjects chosen to interview, I have attempted to respect the composition of Mā's community with regard to the proportions between these different variables. These interviews were mainly conducted at Mā's ashrams in Kankhal and in Bhimpura. The followers interviewed include not only early devotees who joined Mā's cult during her lifetime but also new devotees who joined Mā's community at either a very young age during her lifetime or after her death. Although my desire was to interview as many early devotees as new devotees, I was unable to do so due to the prevalence of early devotees in Mā's ashrams. On the other hand, this does give an indication of the direction that Mā's cult takes after her death. So as to better understand the cult's management, key organizational people were also interviewed, such as the then secretary general of the organization, Swami Bhaskarānanda, and the president of the Kankhal ashram, Swami Vijayānanda. I also spoke to specialists of rituals (pūjāris) at Mā's ashram in Kankhal and the person in charge of Mā's samādhi.

In my thesis work, the totality of the interviews were codified along different matrixes (sex, Western/Indian origin, secular status, early/former devotee), so as to allow readers, if they so desire, to undertake a complementary analysis according to the terms of codification. For the present book, I opted, however, for removing this codification and simply writing, in proper language, some relevant elements for most interviewees. As was the case with my thesis, I also decided to forego a numbering of interviews, so as to completely preserve the anonymity of my collaborators. With the numbered coding, it might be possible for a person in close contact with Mā's community to recognize the identity of a certain collaboration. Due to the large number of interviews, I cited only the most germane extracts from interviews in this work in order to illustrate my arguments, and so, I called on certain interviews more than others.

Because I was not sure if devotees would be willing to engage easily with a Westerner, I admit that the beginning of my research was accompanied by some apprehension. However I was quickly and pleasantly surprised with the openness of the vast majority of devotees in their interactions with me. Far exceeding my expectations, I was able to collect interviews of great value and richness, especially in relation to devotees' articulation of their experiences of Mā. Speaking with confidence, the devotees did not hesitate to tell me about their most intimate and deepest experiences of Mā. Far from being an obstacle, being a foreigner even seemed to arouse among some devotees a certain excitement, as some strongly encouraged me to make my work known abroad and to write more about Mā. I believe that being a woman also helped me in approaching Indian women.

It is however important to qualify these words by mentioning the presence of orthodox brahmins within the community of Mā. Considered primarily as an untouchable in their eyes, access to them was not possible, as they would not speak to me at all. Though they represent a minor part of the community in terms of numbers, they exercise a considerable influence on the development of Mā's cult. Swami Vijayānanda's tomb (*samādhi*) is now in France, for example, and this is directly related to the attitude of certain orthodox brahmins who opposed the construction of a *samādhi* for the French monk at Kankhal. The mistrust of these orthodox devotees, however, was largely offset by the warmth and friendliness of the vast majority of devotees throughout my research.

Literary Research

I have completed an exhaustive and systematic research of literature in the field for this study. In this context, I used a multitude of sources in the field of religious sciences, so as to better understand the long-neglected phenomenon of the postmortem cult of gurus in the Hindu tradition, and notably the cult of relics. Relatedly, I have also attempted to frame my study in a global context, so as to tie it to the larger questions of religious sciences.

Although this study is based on research focusing on the Hindu tradition developed both by Indians and Westerners, I also referred to a number of writings about other religious traditions such as Buddhism, Islam (especially the Sufi tradition), and Catholicism. It must be noted however that my goal was not to conduct a comparative study of postmortem cults of Hindu saints with other religious traditions. My aim has rather been to understand the little-studied phenomenon of postmortem worship of Hindu saints by opposing it with other religious traditions. In this regard, Diderot wrote, "What the mind understands, it understands by assimilation or by comparison, or analogy." I have particularly examined the Sufi tradition in India, which, with the Hindu tradition, presents numerous points of comparison. As Lindholm notes, one of them lies in the notion of hierarchical order common to South Asian Muslims and Hindus, referring here to the idea of transcendentally inspired individuals.[71]

While this research aims to reflect the internal logic of the Hindu tradition, it demonstrates an understanding of holiness and postmortem cults that transcends this religious tradition and expands notions of sainthood in the contemporary world, that is, in a global world. The links made with other religious traditions emphasize the specificity and originality of postmortem worship in Hinduism, while demonstrating the existence of certain similarities and continuities between other traditions.

The diversity of literature available in this sphere is also notable in terms of the variety of fields of study employed. Although my research is essentially sociological, I have also called on texts of an anthropological, philosophical, psychological, and historical nature, and in so doing, I have worked within the broader domain of religious sciences, allowing me to better understand the postmortem cult of gurus in the Hindu tradition, and notably the posthumous cult of Mā.

I have also completed a review of literature concerning Mā Ānandamayī, including the words of Mā, hagiographies, and accounts of people who saw her in life. If my study's subject here is Mā specifically, throughout this study I wished to always take into account the whole of spiritual masters in the Hindu tradition. For this reason, I alternately mentioned gurus in general and Mā in particular, the distinction disappearing continuously throughout this study. In this regard, it is remarkable to see a female religious figure increasing our understanding of the postmortem cult of gurus, both men and women. Within the context of the universalized masculine that leads to generalization, this study succeeds in making a female case explanatory and valid for both genders.

Methodological Problems and Limits

Various issues related to methodology arose in the context of this research. In my view, the first is the use of Western terms to express concepts peculiar to the Hindu tradition (i.e., relics, sainthood, soul).

Westernizing Terms

Faced with the complexity of religious beliefs and the multitude of concepts in Hinduism, I recognize that I have sometimes had to rely on a vocabulary borrowed from the Western world. In my anthropological reflections, for example, the reader may find the use of certain terms confusing. This is especially true of the word "soul," which seems rather unexpected in the context of the Hindu world, as it has a strong Greek or Platonic connotation.

It was sometimes difficult to find the right Sanskrit terms to express the complexity of the beliefs of devotees, vis-à-vis, for example, the posthumous future of Mā. These beliefs range from the identification of Mā with Ultimate Reality to her survival as a subtle body, or to her return in a personal or impersonal way, as suggested by the following terms: mind, body, subtle, light body, body which survives, individual soul, collective soul, spiritual principle, impersonal principle, *jīva*, *ātma*, the Self, the One. The reader should be aware of the difficulty of distinguishing these different types of bodies when the devotee evokes a survival of Mā in the form of a subtle body. For this reason, the vocabulary can sometimes be imprecise.

The same issue applies to the word "saint." Used mostly by Western devotees or Westernized Indians speaking English, this Western term is in fact inappropriate to speak of "sainthood" in Hindu India, and even more for Ānandamayī Mā, who is perceived by her devotees as not merely a "saint" but as a goddess incarnated on earth. "Sainthood" in Hinduism is understood differently than in other religious traditions, such as Catholicism, as the Hindu tradition recognizes the state of perfection of a person *in vita*, in their lifetime, and does not generally consider death as a *sine qua non* condition, as a prerequisite for reaching sanctity.[72] Moreover, the people are the only judge of sanctity and this value is generally revealed through the saint's way of life, his or her teaching and spiritual influence, the importance of his or her community, as well as through the miracles he or she is said to have performed. As such, various scholars warn us of the pitfalls associated with employing such a word without a preliminary reciprocal clarification of the concept.[73]

Because I refer throughout this study to other religious traditions such as Buddhism, Catholicism, and Sufism in order to better understand the postmortem cult of gurus in Hinduism, especially the little-studied Hindu cult of relics, I use in some cases the term "saint." Here, however, "saint" is more a general term which corresponds to a state of wisdom (hence the use of "sage" sometimes), a state of perfection reached by one individual and does not imply, in any way, the imposition of a Western pattern or a diminishment of the divinity of Mā. In this context, Denton's definition of "sainthood" in Hinduism seems to be most appropriate:

> The term saint, which has no indigenous equivalent, refers to someone who is recognized as having attained the highest state of spiritual accomplishment appropriate to her form of religiosity. It is analogous to the Christian notion of a person of extraordinary holiness of life, but this holiness admits of a rather different relationship with divinity than in the Christian world: Hindu saints are themselves divine.[74]

If I had focused on the figure of Mā alone, I would have used the term "avatar" throughout my study. In Bengal, the region where Mā originates from, the term "avatar" seems to be the unique word to connote the saintly character of a person. In her study on the construction of the figure of the godman Chaitanya, a Bengali "saint," France Bhattacharya, who is very familiar with the Bengali language, states very clearly: "The word 'saint' has no equivalent in Bengali, and Caitanya cannot be considered but as an *avatâra*, that is to say a divine incarnation."[75] The term "avatar" however is not appropriate in this study to discuss the whole of gurus and Hindu saints, insofar as they are not all of Bengali origin.

In a more general sense, then, avatar represents the descent of the divine to earth, an incarnation of the divinity. Rivière gives the following definition of these "instruments of deliverance:"

> An Avatar is not a human being who struggles to attain enlightenment, to pass through the veil of illusion in order to reach Reality. It is a divine Being who veils himself or herself temporarily for the good of humanity; it is not the ascension of a human being toward

the Real but the divine descent into a human form so as to uphold or restore the *dharma*.[76]

As all gurus and saints discussed here are not necessarily considered avatars, or incarnations of God on Earth, this also explains why this term could not be applied systematically throughout this study.

Within this apparently overlapping set of terms, guru, saint, avatar, I should specify here that there is no systematic equivalence between guru, avatar, and saint, as many of those liberated beings "saints" stay in solitude and do not necessarily fill the role of master (guru). In the same way, many traditional stories of saints represent them as simply merging in God and they are never seen again, implying that there is no *samādhi* dedicated to them and no postmortem cult in general. Thus, all saints are not gurus. Similarly, all saints and gurus are not perceived as avatars or incarnation of the divinity, though the guru is perceived to some extent as God incarnated.

Defining the Cult in Hinduism

It is important to show some reflexivity around the term "cult" in order to avoid misunderstanding about the appropriation of this potent word. Far from having the pejorative connotation and the strong political ramifications that English speakers ascribe to it, the word "cult" here is very much related to the French term "culte" (i.e., "worship"). It connotes the devotion, or *bhakti* (meaning actually "participation in the divinity"[77]) that the devotee manifests toward the saint or guru (the divinity).

The "cult" in the Hindu tradition is characterized by its lack of exclusivity and freedom of expression. Hindus essentially have the ability to simultaneously join several cults of different religious traditions, as dogma does not constitute the unifying principle of the group.[78] In this regard, Warrier refers to "secularization" to emphasize the multiplicity of religious choices.[79] This freedom is to be found in Mā's community, for, as the vast majority of devotees make clear, Mā does not require any specific religious affiliation or commitment, as this Indian woman, an early devotee of Mā's, specified:

Any person from any faith walks into Mā's vicinity, walks into Mā's ashram, anywhere close to Mā, is accepted. We are seeing Mā like a matchbox. Mā is the universal Mother. She represents *Bhagavan*, whether you call Christ, any God. That is Mā. Mā is

everything...Mā doesn't represent only Buddhism. Mā doesn't represent only Hinduism. Mā doesn't represent only Jainism. Mā represents everything that is.

If the devotional relationship (i.e., *bhakti*) between the saint or guru
and the devotee implies duality (*dvaita*), it can actually lead to a non-dual
experience (*Advaita*). As Swami Vivekananda states, there is no fundamental difference between the path of knowledge, *jñāna*, and the path of
devotion *bhakti* as the two in the end converge.[80] In this regard, Swami
Vijayānanda specifies the following:

> On this path (the path of knowledge or jñāna), the intellectual ele-
> ment is employed only by discriminating between the transitory
> and the real; in the observation of the mental and the ascent back
> to its source—our 'me', or even by our search for 'who am I', as the
> great sage Râmana Mahârshi taught. But limiting ourselves only
> to the intellectual element is false Vedânta, it is wanting to fly with
> only one wing. We need two wings to fly, and the second wing is
> the affective element, it is the *bhakti*. The Vedantic devotee does
> not generally adore a personal God (although there is no limit to
> what he does if he so feels the need). His love is directed at the
> guru, not the physical person of the guru, but towards that which
> is *gyana mûrti*, the incarnation of Knowledge; that which leads
> us towards the Supreme Omnipresent, the Formless, the *akshara
> brahma* which is our Real Self.... In reality, there are not two differ-
> ent paths, that of Knowledge and that of Love. *Gyana* and *bhakti* are
> two aspects of the same *sâdhanâ*; they are inseparable. For some,
> *gyana* is superficial and *bhakti* is profound; for others the reverse
> is true.[81]

One cannot then conceive of *bhakti* without *jñāna*. As Vaudeville specifies on *nirguṇa bhakti*, the devotion to the formless, to the extent that
bhakti implies a duality, *nirguṇa bhakti* represents a contradiction in itself:

> Actually, if we admit that there can be no real bhakti (from *bhaj*,
> 'to participate' or 'to adore') without some distinction between the
> Lord (Bhagvan) and the devotee (bhakta), the very notion of '*nirguṇa
> bhakti*' seems to be a contradiction in terms; if it signifies the aboli-
> tion of all distinctions and the thorough merging of the illusory *jīva*

into the One Reality so that all identity is lost forever, the '*nirguṇa bhakti*' would bring about the abolition of bhakti itself.[82]

According to various writings on *bhakti*, there are five types of relationships with the divinity. Swami Vivekananda however suggests an additional path, the path of non-separability, the path of union with the Divine, for, as he explains, when one is in *samādhi*, it is only then that the idea of duality ceases and that the distinction between the devotee and their God fades away.[83]

Transliteration

As the reader will notice in this work, Indian names (authors or characters) sometimes have diacritics, sometimes not. I am referring here to proper names such as Vijayānanda, Bhaskarānanda, Neem Karoli Baba [Nīma Karoli Bābā], Atma[ā]nanda, Kedarnath [Kedarnātha], and other nath [nātha]. Although it seems logical to systematize everything and put diacritics all along, this did not seem appropriate to me as some characters such as Vivekananda [Vivekānanda], Ramdas [Rāmadāsa], Ramakrishna [Rāmakṛṣṇa], or Ramana Maharshi [Ramaṇa Mahāṛṣi] are known in the West with a spelling that does not meet the standards of transliteration. Names that have been published in English without diacritics have thus been left as printed.

Exploring Mā's Personality and Contextualizing Her Cult

Mā is a fascinating figure who deserves further research, especially to complement the work of Hallstrom, which goes into more detail regarding Mā's personality.[84] The reader might therefore feel frustrated that this book is based on the figure of Mā but does not really explore her. My purpose however is to understand the mechanisms involved in the postmortem cult of gurus. As such it did not seem appropriate to me to dwell on the personality of Mā, though I have given a summary of her life and teachings as well as a portrait of her identity as a guru in this introduction. I also engage her relevant teachings throughout my study and show the centrality of her figure as the originator of a new type of worship among female gurus.

Another issue relates to the contextualization of the subject of my study. I do not situate the rise and perpetuation of the cult of Mā within its broader social, economic, and political context—as has become standard in many religious studies today. I hasten to add that, although a broader contextualization would be of interest, such as considering further the contemporary moment of modernity within which I place guruship,[85] I deliberately chose to leave this one aside, as it does not seem central to addressing the subject of my research, which is an exploration of death and modes of transmission within the postmortem cult of gurus. Far from hampering my study, I believe that this "inward turn" on the contrary strengthens it, as it is more attentive to the particularities and uniqueness of the phenomenon under study.

Analyzing the Experiential Dimension

It also seems important to address the experiential dimension of devotees, including its *Advaitic*, or non-dual aspect. As suggested by my numerous references to the *Upaniṣads*, my interpretation of their experience is influenced by the *Advaitic* perspective, as Mā usually recommended the path of non-duality to Westerners, rather than that of *bhakti*. However, far from implying a solely *Advaitic* interpretation of Mā's teachings, I would affirm rather that her teaching was open and included the non-dualism of *Advaita*, as well as the dualism of *bhakti*, although in reality, her teaching was mainly intended to overcome the very notions of dualism and non-dualism, and relied more on the idea of totality (*Yā tā*).[86]

The experiential dimension, moreover, is a complex and multifaceted one, which therefore deserves much more attention, especially given the breadth and quality of the material present here. The objective here is not to make a phenomenological study of devotee's experiences of Mā, but to highlight the relative sustainability of the cult of Mā after her death, showing especially that there has been a continuity of these experiences since Mā left. I could have, in fact, analyzed the religious experience of the faithful in more depth, and shown how it is universal, special, or both, but this is not my objective. Because of the wealth of devotees' testimonies, this research may therefore serve as a basis for further studies.

As description sometimes speaks for itself, the analytical dimension of this research is reflected somehow in the major role given to empirical data, culling it from a vast corpus of interviews, and its arrangement in concordance with the theory presented here. This is in itself a way to translate the experience of the devotee, the relation to the institution, and thus better understand the processes involved in the postmortem cult of the guru.

Relying mostly on primary sources, such as James on religious experience, or Weber on charisma and routinization, but also calling on critical writings from more contemporary scholars, I should conclude by saying that this book does not aim to create a new theory of religion; I would rather say it utilizes existing theories wisely and efficiently. The major contribution of this study is to have explored and analyzed religious experiences and modes of institutionalization of the cult of gurus after their death, mainly through the figure of Ānandamayī Mā.

The Author

An Unexpected Turn

When I started a Ph.D. in Social Sciences at the London School of Economics and Political Science (LSE) on Tibetan issues as a continuity of my master's thesis on Tibet, there were no signs that I would eventually engage in a "religiological adventure" in the Indian subcontinent. As I look back today, however, it seems that all aspects of my life took me in this direction. My first contact with India and the Hindu tradition goes back to a very brief stay in India at the age of 21. A few months later, I discovered Mā through a picture a friend sent me, that of Mā blessing with her hand. Without even suspecting a future absorption into the study of Mā, although I found to be beautiful and radiant, I started to read her words, which were already translated into French at the time.

Only four years later, in 2004, during my first long stay in India to learn Tibetan language as part of my Ph.D., I discovered the tomb (*samādhi*) of Mā by complete chance, as I had originally no intention of going there. During this same trip, a few weeks apart, I visited the *samādhi* several times, before deciding to stay for a complete week. Without a doubt, the presence of this French monk, Swami Vijayānanda, now deceased, influenced my many visits to Mā's *samādhi*.

It seems to me important today, after obtaining my doctorate, to share a major event that led me toward this research on Mā. The last night of my stay at Mā's ashram in Kankhal (foreigners sleep right next to the ashram, a few meters from Mā's tomb), I experienced a serious neurological event, which manifested in several strong epileptic seizures. After hours of unconsciousness, during which I was under the care of Swami Vijayānanda, a former physician, I was taken to the military hospital in Dehra Dun, where I was diagnosed with a brain hemorrhage in the right frontal lobe. After a farewell to my parents on the phone, I prepared for death, or at least I tried to. Then, thinking that perhaps I might continue living, I promised myself to write a book on Mā if I survived. After a very long journey, which included extensive hospital stays both in India and France and a serious brain surgery, for which a special *pūjā* was performed at Mā's *samādhi* for its success, I can today testify to this event in addition to the body of work presented here.

Nearly five years have passed since I received my Ph.D. and many people I was close to in Mā's organization, like Swami Vijayānanda, have died. My path led me personally to join the International Committee of the Red Cross (ICRC) as a Protection Delegate. After a one-year mission in the Great Lakes Region, I was sent for fourteen months to Haiti, following the earthquake that saw the death of over 200,000 people. Thus, this research, which addresses these fundamental questions about death and the impermanence of life, has taken on even more meaning for me. What attitude would Mā have had, for example, in response to the disastrous earthquake in Haiti, or even in response to the violence in the slums of Port-au-Prince? Coming back to my work after these field experiences only intensified the reflection on death already going on even before the beginning of this research on Mā.

Being an Outcast

Despite my determination to complete my research, its execution has not always been simple. Traveling in India is not easy for a single woman (I have visited fourteen ashrams of Mā in Northern India and Bangladesh, as well as other places of worship), but being the subject of censure by the orthodox brahmins was even more of a challenge. During my research in Mā's ashrams I faced the attitude of orthodox brahmins for whom any foreign presence is a source of pollution. As I wanted to maintain some objectivity, I purposely omitted any mention of my personal experiences vis-à-vis these brahminical rules in this doctoral research, only sharing those of other foreigners.

Today however it seems relevant to mention, even briefly, how these orthodox rules sometimes excluded me. I was constantly separated from Indians during meals, as at the *Kumbhamelā*, where, under the eyes of 200 Indian devotees of Mā sitting a few meters from me, I had to eat alone so as not to "contaminate" them. I was also unable to participate in certain rituals, such as *Mahāśivarātri*, as I was separated from Indians through a curtain so as not to pollute the atmosphere and compromise the effectiveness of the ritual. I was shouted at by a swami because I had penetrated and "dirtied" a place where I should not have ventured. These are just examples, of course, and there are others.

My womanhood only further reinforced this exclusion. The most striking example was the retreat of *Samyam Saptah* in Bhimpura, where I was asked to leave the retreat because I was menstruating and thus impure. A feeling of rejection and humiliation, but also strangely a feeling of guilt for being a woman was aroused in me. It was paradoxically accompanied by a sense of betrayal as the person who had "denounced" me was a woman herself, an Indian lady whom I had asked to lend me hygienic products! Another example is the great bath (*śahisnāna*) of the *Kumbhamelā* in Allahabad, where, in the middle of January 2007, at 3 o'clock in the morning, in a freezing cold, I came to Mā's camp to join the devotees for their procession for the great bath. Despite having traveled thousands of miles from Canada with the intention of immersing myself in the icy waters of the Ganges, I was rejected by the swami in charge of the camp, because I was not wearing a sari, but rather was wearing pants. Some of Mā's devotees pleaded my case and I was eventually able to join Mā's *saṅgha* for the great bath.

If these stories are interesting to tell in retrospect, they were not however easy to accept at the time. As Arnaud Desjardins rightly pointed out concerning his personal experience when facing the orthodox brahmins of Mā's community in the 1960s, "It is an experience to be on the wrong side of the barrier."[87] Considering the difficulty of accessing Mā due to ritual purity and caste rules, Denise, Arnaud's wife at that time, suggested that they reincarnate themselves as brahmins in their next life![88] For the reasons stated, it was not possible then, as a foreigner and therefore a source of pollution, to talk to certain orthodox brahmins. My personal experience, like the experiences that are cited in this book by other Westerners, reveals an internal tension within Mā's community between devotees open to foreign influence, and others who consider the mere presence of Westerners to be dangerous. By the same token, some may perceive my work as a kind of "sacrilege." While relating my personal experience, I should nevertheless specify that my objective here is not to argue in favor of a removal of purity rules, which constitute the foundation of brahminism, but to show the implications of this exclusivity and to raise some of the concerns these rules bring today in a globalized world.

I

Aspects of the Postmortem Cult of the Guru

Organization of the Postmortem Cult

The postmortem cult in Hinduism is, in a certain sense, similar to a church, with its sacred spaces, its clergy, and its followers who search, through their pilgrimage, to bring themselves back into contact with the spiritual master. Through an investigation of the cult of Ānandamayī Mā, I investigate here the particular organization of the postmortem cult of the guru, not only in terms of its space but also in terms of the composition of its agents and its community.

The Sacred Spaces of the Cult

The cult of Ānandamayī Mā's practice takes place both in the devotee's house, as well as in the many ashrams of Mā's *saṅgha*. However, my study is limited to Mā's ashrams, not only because this is the cult's public space but also to engage in a more focused research. And, though in India there is the belief that on his or her death, the guru concentrates his or her power at the location of his or her tomb, I do not limit this study to Mā's Kankhal ashram, as this belief does not seem to be shared by all of Mā's devotees.

Mā Ānandamayī passed a large part of her life moving from sacred space to sacred space. So as to facilitate these movements, her followers decided to establish ashrams across India, particularly in Northern India. Although she did not necessarily want ashrams, Mā nonetheless selected their locations. Far from being insignificant, her choice of locations allows a vast network of sacred geography to become evident. Furthermore, this

FIGURE I.I Mā Ānandamayī:

"I am what I was and what I shall be; I am whatever you conceive, think or say. But it is a supreme fact that this body has not come into being to reap the fruits of past *karma*. Why don't you take it that this body is the material embodiment of all your thoughts and ideas. You all have wanted it and you have it now. So play with this doll for some time."

Source: Photograph courtesy of Shree Shree Anandamayee Sangha.

had some influence on the development of the cult, as the choice of location for a cult's space constitutes a determining factor in the cult's expansion. Ram Alexander, a Western disciple who long lived near Mā, describes these spaces as follows:

> To be in such a place with Ma was not only to receive Her blessing but to become initiated into the ancient power of the place itself which became profoundly activated and accessible through Her presence there. These ancient focuses of spiritual power are points on the energy grid that sustains the electro-magnetic field of Indian spiritual culture. Ma was particularly concerned with keeping this 'field' of sacred geography intact.[1]

This field of sacred geography is apparent in the locations of Mā's ashrams, which, although extremely diverse, form an undeniably sacred matrix. These "spheres of sacred jurisdiction" as Jackie Assayag likes to call these cult spaces where the saint reigns,[2] are often situated in strategic locations, often on the great pilgrimage sites, as is the case at Kankhal, next to Hardwar, or also Varanasi, the mythic city of Śiva, to name only a few. Some of Mā's ashrams are also located in ancient cult spaces, now forgotten by modern pilgrims. This is the case of a site not far from Vindhyachal, where, following a vision by Mā, archaeological digs brought to light an ancient space for worship.[3] Other cult spaces dedicated to Mā, often difficult to access, also reveal certain natural qualities that give a magical character to the place. Such is the case of the ashram at Bhimpura in Gujarat, which looks over the sacred Narmada River. This is also the case for the ashram at Dhaulchina, which offers a panoramic 180-degree view on the snow-covered summits of the Himalayas.

In interviews, devotees often speak of a different atmosphere at each ashram. Some feel a sense of gravity at the ashram in Kichenpur (Dehra Dun), space of Mā's *mahāsamādhi* (death of the saint, of the guru), while others evoke the lightness of the ashram at Vrindavan, where Mā, like Kṛṣṇa, performed numerous *līlās* or divine games. Others describe a pure atmosphere at the Himalayan ashram at Dhaulchina, comparable to a "type of crystal." The ashram at Bhimpura can produce a state of "bliss," according to one devotee, a type of sweetness stemming from its closeness to the Narmada: "You feel yourself anchored in an ocean of sweetness and of infinite love." Thus for devotees there is an atmosphere specific to each ashram, and whatever their sensibility or predisposition, the faithful can stay at the ashram that he or she prefers, as is the case of this early disciple, an Indian man, who feels a marked preference for the ashram at Bhimpura:

My favourite ashram is only Bhimpura. So many things are there. The vibrations of Bhimpura are special to me. *Ṛṣi* were gathering here. The Narmada shore is a place of *tapasya*. The Ganga and Hardwar, there are so many pilgrims coming and going. Here, in Bhimpura, you come, it is not easy. No vehicle. This place is for *tapasya*.

As Mā has more than twenty-six ashrams, it would be laborious to describe them all in detail. But a fundamental point is the importance of the Indian land to foreign disciples when it comes to their devotion to Mā. At the time of our interviews, some devotees spoke of their attachment to India, which for them could not be disassociated from Mā, as is the case for this American man, a long-time disciple of Mā's:

> The experience of India was as important as, every bit was impor-
> tant as the experience of Mā. They were not separated. And moving
> around in India with Mā, she initiated to all these powerful places.
> You really became one with this vibration. So, the hardest thing
> of all was losing India, because then I lost the context, the entire
> context. I could go back to the West and meditate all day long, but
> there is no context.... When I come back to India, all the lights go
> on. There is an energy structure here that just activates everything.

Both the cult spaces and the Indian land hold an important place in Mā's cult. The specific positioning of Mā's many ashrams within in a sacred geography participates in the development of her cult, permitting the cult to attract pilgrims still today.

The Agents of the Cult

To examine the postmortem cult is also to discuss those who lead it. It is thus necessary for this study to establish the role played by this plurality of actors that I call the "agents of the cult" or the officials charged with the maintenance of the cult and with the management of its sacred site. I refer here to the cult's space at Mā's tomb in Kankhal, which is the prin- cipal space of the postmortem cult of Mā.

At Kankhal, there is a diversity of religious officials who are engaged in Mā's cult on a regular basis, contrary to other less important spaces where the officials are only present sporadically (with the exception of cel- ebrations). At Mā's tomb, there are two categories of officials, the ritual specialists and the musicians. In his study on saint's cults among Indian Muslims, Marc Gaborieau demarcates a third category, that of mediums. Mediums are, however, absent from Mā's postmortem cult, as the pres- ence of swamis, who are considered a type of oracle through which Mā may speak, have perhaps been judged sufficient for communicating Mā's message.

Following the example of Jackie Assayag in her study on Indian saints in Islam, I address here the role of the cult's agents in stimulating and channeling the energy (*śakti*) emanating from the tomb of the saint, which is transferable not only through objects but also through individuals. The religious personnel become a type of "support" for this energy and as such, the "servant" of the saint, to use Assayag's terms.[4] As a result, the role of these religious actors in mobilizing *śakti* is of utmost importance to the upkeep of the space's sacredness.

The ritual specialists, who may be described as a sort of clergy, without referring to this word in all of its Christian dimensions, constitute the first category of officials present at the cult space dedicated to Mā. They are the *pūjāris*, the "technicians of the ritual" who are charged with the maintenance of the cult's space as well as the daily performance of rituals. The *pūjāris*, as specialized priests, are in many ways considered by devotees to be intermediaries between themselves and Mā, who is perceived as the supreme divinity. As they have a religious vocation, the *pūjāris* are brahmins and must have taken the vow of *brahmacārya* (celibacy and chastity), something not always required for *pūjāris* in the Hindu tradition. As opposed to the general Hindu practice, their function is thus not hereditary. As elsewhere in the Hindu tradition, there is a noticeable absence of women *pūjāris* within Mā's ashrams. Although a *brahmacārini* on occasion replaces the *pūjāri* in the *samādhi*, because of sickness or any other reason, such an event is not routine, especially in a patriarchal organization like the *saṅgha* of Mā Ānandamayī.

A regular body of three *pūjāris* assures ritual service year-round, every day, morning and night. One has the function of performing daily rituals of *yajña*, and two others are responsible for the *pūjā* at Mā's *samādhi*. These functions trade off every three months. As Mā's *pūjāri*, one must of course be Mā's disciple. And although it is not an explicit condition, it seems that the Bengali origins of the incumbent *pūjāri* also constitute a criterion in their recruitment by the Kankhal ashram's committee. The *pūjāris* at Mā's *samādhi* are everyday charged with a number of tasks attached to the habitual practice of the cult to the *mūrti* (statue), such as waking, washing, and feeding the *mūrti*. This caring for Mā, through her *mūrti,* is accompanied by ritual functions, such as the performance of the daily *ārati* (offering of light), a ritual which one finds in Hindu temples throughout India.

The work of these *pūjāris* is associated with that of other disciples of Mā, who could be called "servants" of Mā. They are charged with panoply of services such as cleaning Mā's temple, leaving flowers at the *samādhi*, and so on. They must also be brahmins so as to maintain the purity of the space according to brahmanical rules.

Finally, the priests, who perform only occasionally in Mā's ashrams and live outside of them, have functions each year in the context of certain celebrations such as the *Durgā Pūjā*. These priests, specialized in a specific type of ritual, do not act in the function of the priesthood except on the occasion of these celebrations.

Another type of religious actor involved in the postmortem cult of Mā is the musician. Music essentially plays an important role in the cult, as Joachim Wach specifies that it is a way to emphasize the impression given by religious rites.[5] The musicians at Mā's *samādhi* are not engaged in this function on a regular basis; they are often disciples in permanent residence at the ashram or devotees who came to the ashram for a determined period and who performed *kīrtana* as *sādhanā*. Chants are particularly common at the big annual celebrations of Mā's birth and *Gurupūrṇimā* (holiday in honor of the guru). Thus, musicians represent essential religious actors in the cult.

There exists one more category of religious agents, the mediums. Mediums are absent from Mā's cult, though they are found marginally in other postmortem cults,[6] often manifesting themselves in trances and in possession.

The Community of Devotees

The society of devotees, commonly called *bhaktas*, reflect considerable diversity within the *saṅgha* of Mā Ānandamayī. The followers come from diverse social classes, various castes, and even different religions. Still, the predominance of a certain type of devotee is nevertheless fairly apparent, as Mā's followers are for the most part Hindu, essentially coming from urban environments and belonging to the upper levels of society. In this community, it is not rare to meet rich families of industry or political personalities taking refuge at the feet of Mā. It was so during Mā's lifetime and remains the case today. It is also interesting to note that Mā Ānandamayī counted among her disciples many powerful political figures, such as Kamala Nehru and Indira Gandhi,[7] as well as scholars like the philosopher, Gopinath Kaviraj.[8] Ram Alexander, a disciple of Mā speaks of these rich and educated disciples in the following words: "Often these were highly educated people who had to face serious social opprobrium, particularly as it was unheard of to receive such guidance from an

FIGURE I.2 Mā Ānandamayī with Nehru (right) and Indira Gandhi (left) who became her disciple.

Source: Photograph courtesy of Shree Shree Anandamayee Sangha.

uneducated village woman."[9] It is also evident that the presence of higher class devotees, the wealthy and intellectual elites plays some role in the visibility of the cult.[10]

As Gaborieau notes in one of his studies on Muslim saints, the cult of the saint generally comes from the social group the saint is associated with.[11] Therefore, certain factors such as the caste or the region of origin of the saint can influence the composition of the community. Mā being born brahmin, it is not then surprising to observe a marked presence of the brahmin castes within her community. Mā also comes from Bengal, and accordingly, there is a considerable presence of Bengalis among her followers. Thus, the importance of Mā's community of devotees in Bengal, and notably in Calcutta, is not surprising.

Women also represent a large part of the community of devotees, and it seems, following my observation at celebrations such as the anniversary of Mā's birth, that their number is greater than that of male devotees. Far from considering Mā, the Supreme Goddess above all, as a source of inspiration or as a model, the presence of so many women within Mā's cult may be attributed to the fact that they could have access to Mā's body more easily than men.[12] In the main cult spaces dedicated to Mā, notably at her *samādhi*, there is a separation of women and men. Far from being specific to Mā's ashrams, this separation of men and women is present in the vast majority of spaces dedicated to Hindu cults in India.

The postmortem cult of Mā Ānandamayī is also characterized by a presence of foreigners, although their number is grossly inferior to the number of Indians. This presence of foreigners is associated with Swami Bhaskarānanda, but mainly with Swami Vijayānanda. This French monk, who passed away in April 2010, had not left India since his encounter with Mā in the 1950s. Many Westerners, especially French people, considered him to be a living presence of Mā. As Mā requested of him, he welcomed foreign devotees to Mā's tomb at Kankhal. The increased diffusion of books about Mā in English and French, and more recently in German, Italian, and Spanish, is another major factor contributing to the attraction of Westerners to Mā. For example, there are more than a dozen works on Mā in French today,[13] some of them available on the Internet on the website dedicated to Mā's organization. The biannual publication of reviews on Mā, in English (*Ananda Varta*)[14] and in French (*Jay Ma*), reviews that relate the events of Mā's life and news regarding the *sangha*, also contribute to the expansion of Mā's community in the West.

So as Weber and Gauchet might say, this attraction of Westerners toward divine beings, even to the extent that they consider an "invisible" guru such as Mā, may also be a response to the growing "disenchantment" of the Western world, to the increasing rationalization of modernity, which, as Lindholm argues, "pushes individuals towards immersion in a charismatic group."[15] This idea of extreme rationalization underpins much of the theories on new social movements.[16]

To understand Mā's cult since her death, it is important to distinguish between early devotees, that is to say devotees who knew Mā during her lifetime, and new devotees, or those who venerate Mā despite the fact that they never met her. Throughout the interviews and informal discussions with members of Mā's community, we see that the vast majority of new devotees essentially differentiate themselves from the early devotees by their belief in a past life spent with Mā,[17] as the comments of this new disciple demonstrate:

I think that I had a past life with Mā Anandamayī, between 1936 and 1961. I had flashes, reminiscences, some snippets, not complete scenes, but some snippets. Swami Vijayānanda confirmed this for

FIGURE 1.3 Swami Vijayānanda: "In the case of a great sage like Mā, who left a residual presence, one may enter into contact with this presence. And this contact can become a considerable aid to our spiritual pursuit. The guru transmits power and he can do this even after leaving his physical form."

Source: Picture taken by French photographer Caroline Abitbol.

me. It's very, very intimate. I was normally in a place not far from the Himalaya where I was responsible for a temple. I was in the priesthood. That's all I can say. After, it's too intimate. Mā was there and she guided me, she gave me information. It's all I can say, it's very, very intimate. It's of the experiential order, one cannot speak of it.

In another case, a young Indian woman associates her present attraction to Mā with a life spent with Mā:

Sometimes, I feel sad. I tell Mā during my prayers, 'why did you make me born so late? I could be born at least three four years earlier. I could have seen you, at least once in my life time. But I feel that in my previous birth, I must have seen her. I must have done some good deeds, so this is why I have come over here and I have been able to have contact with her.

If some new devotees regret the fact that they did not know Mā, they nevertheless seem to find a sort of consolation and comfort in their belief in a past life with Mā, as this English woman specifies:

> I was alive most of the time when she was around in her body. If she wanted me to see her, she could have drawn me to her. Couldn't she? She didn't. I was born in 1950. I was over 30 when she left her body. Easily, I could have seen her. It was not supposed to be. I do feel that there is something that links those who have been around. Or maybe everybody who had some connection with Mā already, who had not seen her in her body this time, there must be some connection that goes further back than this life time. I think we must have had at least one life time before with her. We must have. Otherwise, this wouldn't be happening.

Another new disciple, a French woman, also shows her acceptance of the fact that she never knew Mā:

> I believe that it was perfect as it was. I am sure of it. This is how it should be for me. It's perfect. I realize what I am. I do not speak of her in the past tense. There are thousands of people who never saw her and who will never see her. It's like that, it's like that.

New devotees seem to find in this belief in a past life with Mā a sort of comfort that helps them to accept the fact that they never met her in their present life.

There is also another distinction between the early and new devotees, that of a more marked attraction for the impersonal. As Dr. Jacques Vigne reveals: "Personal relationship, that would be saying too much. For me, I did not meet her in her body; it's a very profound relationship, I have the tendency to say an impersonal one. That does not impede it from being very strong."[18] Although the attraction of new devotees for Mā essentially stems from having seen photos of her, and so, still belongs to the realm of materiality, new devotees nevertheless seem to manifest a stronger attraction for the unquantifiable formless aspect (*nirguṇi*) of Mā, in comparison to early devotees.

Functions and Manifestations of the Postmortem Cult

Here, I examine first the concept of pilgrimage in relation to Mā's post-humous cult, notably pilgrimage to her tomb. From the perspective of sacred exchange, this type of cult does not differ from a temple dedicated to a divinity, in that it makes of the tomb a type of sanctuary. The central concepts of *tīrtha* (place of pilgrimage), sacred transactions, merits, and *darśana* are outlined here, but also those of *communitas* and vows (*vratas*). Second, I concentrate on the rituality of the postmortem cult, in demonstrating the diverse functions of the rituals specific to Mā's cult. In another section entitled "Celebrations and Retreats," I define the role of the large assemblies of followers within Mā's ashrams, at the anniversary of Mā's birth, the most important celebration of the year, and also at *Gurupūrṇimā* and the *Samyam Saptah* retreats. I also discuss the participation of Mā's *saṅgha* in the *Kumbhamelā*. Finally, the cult of images and of statues (*mūrtis*) is studied in the context of posthumous devotion to Mā, and I examine the different functions of these two aspects of the cult.

Pilgrimage and Sacred Exchanges

Pilgrimage constitutes a way for Mā's pilgrims to accumulate merit and to purify themselves from their "sins."[19] A recompense (*phala*), whether material or spiritual, is generally either consciously or unconsciously expected by the pilgrims who come to engage in private prayer at the guru's tomb; this recompense may take the form of a change in karma, of protection, of fertility, or even of a spiritual realization.

The pilgrimage can often take either a social or an individual form, thus distinguishing two types of pilgrimage: a pilgrimage performed individually at any time of year and a collective pilgrimage on the occasion of certain communal events. As Chambert-Loir and Guillot specify, while the individual pilgrimage represents a more conscious and reflective journey, the collective pilgrimage conversely tends to assimilate the personal volition of the pilgrim into that of the community,[20] thus resulting less in a resolution of a personal question than in a celebration of the guru within an assembly of the community. Every year, the spaces of Mā's cult, and especially her tomb at Kankhal, are the destination of collective pilgrimages on the occasion of annual events, such as Mā's birthday. Similarly, there is another type of collective pilgrimage observed at Mā's tomb, the pilgrimage of Indians who travel by bus to the ashram at Kankhal, and who remain there generally for thirty minutes, quickly heading off to the next destination in their pilgrimage. The growth of this type of group pilgrimage in recent years is strongly associated with the modernization of India and the development of transportation in the countryside. Distinct from the community of Mā's devotees, these pilgrims are generally of modest origin, with a limited education, and generally are not interested specifically in Mā.

This place of pilgrimage (*tīrtha*), Mā's tomb, represents by virtue of its role as a crossing and turning point, a place of transition between the world of humans and the world of gods, here being the world of Mā.[21] It may also refer to the *Vaitarani*, the fetid river that runs between the world of the living and the world of the death, ruled by the God of death, Yama. It may also signify a passage from the world of *saṃsāra*, that of suffering, to the world of the eternally One. This pilgrimage, which may be related to a true initiation, corresponds to a transformation of death into life, accomplished through a sacred exchange.

The effectiveness of the pilgrimage essentially lies in these sacred exchanges between the pilgrim and the guru. A sort of "contractual relation," to use Chaput's expression[22] is then established between Mā and the devotee. The pilgrim, by exchanging a gift from himself or herself, receives the benediction of Mā.[23] These exchanges can also be of a material order. Offerings (fruits, rice, flowers, silver, etc.) can be presented to Mā, who, in return, distributes them through the intermediary of religious agents as a blessed support, called *prasāda*. The *prasāda*, which McKim Mariott calls biomoral earnings,[24] is said to be imbued with the beneficial aura of Mā. As Werbner specifies, it is nevertheless important to not interpret this type of sacred exchange as a sort of "commerce," which would remove any disinterested dimension from the pilgrimage. Although it is true that pilgrims travel in search of merit, the reality of their personal experience is much more complex than that of a simple transaction.[25]

Likewise pilgrimage cannot be discussed without mentioning the idea of *darśana*, which, in *bhakti*, means "seeing and being seen by the deity." Far from being a passive action, the *darśana* corresponds to an "exchange of sight" between the devotee and the guru. Here the pilgrim not only sees the guru but is also seen by him or her so as to reach the power of this superior being.[26] This concept of *darśana* generally implies the idea of some sort of gain to be obtained in the experience of this divine presence. The *darśana* of the guru has not only the merit of bringing good fortune and well-being to the pilgrim but also of leading him to a personal transformation. In the case of the *darśana* of the Divine Mother, here being Mā Ānandamayī as she is considered by her devotees to be an incarnation of the goddess, it is referred to as "*śakta darśana*." Mā's devotees then are moved by what Tulasi Srivinas would call a "proxemic desire," that is to say the need of a visual closeness to Mā.[27]

Through its liminal character, the pilgrimage marks a true rupture with daily life and the past, leading to not only a spiritual renewal for the pilgrim but also a renewal of the community. Pilgrims experience then a feeling of unity and camaraderie that only this experience of *communitas* can engender, as the limits between themselves and the group disappear. In this state of *communitas*, "the other" becomes "a brother," as Turner expresses it,[28] and ceases to play his normal social role. If this spirit of *communitas* is especially present during these large assemblies in honor of Mā, for example, on her birthday, it nonetheless can be checked by the strict brahmanical orthodoxy within Mā's ashrams, notably for Westerners who can often feel excluded by virtue of their status as outcasts or *mleccha* (foreigners).

Pilgrimage can also become an occasion for the pilgrim to make a vow, called a "*vrata*" in the Hindu tradition. This vow corresponds to a personal engagement of the pilgrim with the guru to fulfill a particular desire. The practice of writing the pilgrim's request on a slip of paper and of attaching it to the gates surrounding the tomb, typical of cult spaces of Muslim saints, does not exist, as far as I know, in the Hindu tradition. Some postmortem cults to Hindu saints however may have adopted this practice due to their syncretic nature, caught between the Hindu and the Muslim traditions.

In reference to the *vrata*, the devotee can go so far as to become the servant of a guru (*atima*) to thank him or her for having fulfilled his vow. Bhardwaj also notes the ties between requests of a material nature, more spiritual requests, and the veneration of the goddess *Devī*.[29] It is said that the veneration of the goddess should be more material and less spiritual than for male deities, as, according to *śakta* theology, the material world represents the manifestation of the goddess. However, although material requests are said to have a greater chance of being granted in venerating *Devī*, here represented by Mā, for her followers her cult is nonetheless very spiritual.[30]

Pilgrimage, which Brown calls a "therapy of distance,"[31] can be interior as well. The body may be compared to a *tīrtha*, and the journey to the place of pilgrimage can be accomplished within the pilgrim, who should adopt the attitude or the emotion appropriate toward the guru.

Rituality of the Postmortem Cult

Rituals constitute an essential aspect of the guru's postmortem cult. They must be, though, acknowledged or legitimate in order to be effective and valid.[32] Rituals constitute a path of access to the divine, a way to be associated with superior powers, making the cult's space a space of mediation between the profane and the divine. They create and control the religious experience, acting as a way of "harnessing," of "domestication," and of "administration" of the sacred[33] and contribute to the creation of a direct link between its participants.[34] Finally, rituals call to mind (anamnesis) this past that gives a sense of the present.[35] They constitute the very basis of collective memory.[36]

In relation to the ritual activity in the postmortem cult, the concepts of activity and of inactivity[37] are often present. These concepts, both found in the Sufi and Hindu traditions, refer to the posthumous action of the sage toward devotees, particularly at the tomb. If the absence of offerings and of rituals dedicated to the sage would make him or her "only a potential" sage, according to Jamous, and would render the tomb "inactive," with no presence of power or of the sacred, the ritual activity conversely is said to return to the sage the ability to act among devotees, to confer upon them certain powers, from which comes Jamous's expressions of "redoing" and "undoing" the saint. The sage then must be sufficiently honored, so that he or she may continue to release grace unto the faithfuls and to assure their protection. In the same manner, it would then not be "recommended" by the Hindu tradition to demonstrate an excessive indifference toward the sage.

With regard to the ritual activity performed daily in Mā's ashrams, one of the key moments consists in the rite of illumination (*ārati*), which takes place twice a day, at morning and at night, in the presence of lay devotees and of ascetics. Fuller evokes the importance of this ritual that for him constitutes the climax of the cult.[38] Although the focus here is on the cult within Mā's ashrams, it nevertheless seems important to mention the presence of a daily ritual activity in the houses of lay disciples. The devotee usually lights a stick of incense and a candle before Mā's image, and performs offerings, such as fruits and flowers, to Mā. A meditation or a prayer can also accompany this daily ritual activity.

In addition, there is not strictly speaking a day of the week dedicated to Mā when ritual activity would gain greater importance. This is, however, the case for the majority of gods and goddesses venerated in Hindu temples, as well as for some gurus like Nadar, whose *samādhi* is visited every Friday, a day said to be auspicious to venerate the guru,[39] as well as in Sufism, where the saint is generally honored every Thursday.[40]

If Indians are much inclined to perform daily rituals both in Mā's ashrams and in their homes, this is not necessarily the case for Westerners who, according to some informal discussions with them, attach much less importance to the ritual aspect of the cult. As to whether Westerners are missing out on something, Swami Vijayānanda has the following to say:

> The true *pūjā* is a mental attitude. The ritual serves to awaken this attitude of love and of veneration. Westerners do not need to use the same ritual as Hindus; but when one begins to meditate, it is good to establish contact with the master (here being Mā) for whom he (or She) transmits to you the necessary spiritual energy. And for that, a certain type of *pūjā* may be useful: to recite several mantras, to light a stick of incense, to do *pranām*, etc.[41]

Swami Vijayānanda adds this on the subject of rituality:

> The people of this world are like fish out of water. They need these rituals and these ceremonies, as the fish on the market shelf needs a glass of water from time to time in order to survive. But for those who already live in God, rites and rituals are not only superfluous, but they can be an obstacle to spiritual evolution, a sort of strong straightjacket which the spiritual seeker would need to remove.[42]

Westerners then would seem less inclined than Indians toward rituals and celebrations, returning us to the question of secularization in the West. In this context, there is a cultural detachment among Westerners who generally have not been in contact with Hindu culture from an early age, and who demonstrate much less sensibility for the ritualistic Hindu accoutrements.

Celebrating the Guru

The celebration, this great ritual through which the sacred is experienced, becomes a privileged moment for Mā's entire community to gather together and to refresh their memory of Mā's presence. As Raimon Panikkar specifies, the celebration comes to mark the communal character of joy, something that would seem to be essential for a great being called Mā Ānandamayī, whose name means "Mother Full of Joy."[43]

If one may always pray to Mā, there are nevertheless certain moments of the year during which it is especially beneficial to pray. These are the great celebrations such as the anniversary of Mā's birth, *Gurupūrṇimā*, and *Durgā Pūjā*, three occasions being the only times during the year (along with the *Samyam Saptah* retreat at Kankhal) during which every devotee, regardless of their caste or religious status, can touch Mā's tomb. These celebrations are accompanied by other annual celebrations, such as *Mahāśivarātri*, *Holi*, and *Rakṣabandhan*.[44] The following is a description of four gatherings: the anniversary of Mā's birth, *Gurupūrṇimā*, the retreats (*Samyam Saptah*), and the participation of Mā's *saṅgha* in the *Kumbhamelā*.

Anniversary of Mā's Birth

The anniversary of Mā's birth in the month of May is the most important celebration in honor of Mā and brings together a large number of her devotees. Astrological calculations are completed in order to determine the exact moment of Mā's birth according to the lunar calendar. As this moment is fixed each year, a series of celebrations and of rituals takes place the preceding week of her birthday. Mā's birthday, marked when she was alive by Mā's going into *samādhi*, unfolds throughout the night and is characterized by successive rituals, moments of silence and chants. It is not uncommon to hear resounding in the *samādhi* the famous Bengali cry, the "ulu."[45] An impressive number of flower garlands are placed on Mā's tomb, garlands that will be redistributed to the devotees at the end of the night, when each of them may come to prostrate themselves directly before and touch Mā's tomb. For this celebration, the *samādhi* is decorated by garlands of lights, which gives to Mā's birthday the allure of a Christmas night. Televisions are placed outside to simulcast the event for those who were not able to find a place inside the *samādhi* temple. The culminating point of Mā's birthday comes in the early morning when, in a surge of devotion, her devotees dash toward the interior of the *samādhi* in order to penetrate the sacred space, "the saint of saints," the *sanctum sanctorum*, usually reserved for monks, for some of Mā's brahmanical disciples and for "VIPs," that is to say principally the biggest donors and some political and religious personalities. A long line of devotees tries to form in the crush of people. Each devotee brings with him or her an offering for Mā, generally flowers. Alternately, starting with the oldest, swamis come to circle around the tomb in a rite called *pradakṣina*, and then perform a *pranām* (prostration) to Mā. Next come the *brahmacārins* and *brahmacārinis*, that is to say those who have performed the vow of celibacy or *brahmacārya*, the VIPs, and finally the simple lay devotees. This succession of devotees demonstrates a type of religious hierarchy that persists to this day.

Although the anniversary of Mā's birth constitutes an important event for Mā's community, the anniversary of her death (*mahāsamādhi*) seems to be of much less importance. It is interesting to note that the Hindu tradition does not generally celebrate the anniversary of a guru's death; and if there are some exceptions, they are fairly rare. Among these exceptions may be noted the celebrations of the anniversary of the death of the saint Ekanath (*punya-tithi*), who did not leave mortal remains behind and who is venerated each year in the person of his descendent,[46] and the *mahāsamādhi* anniversaries of Swami Muktananda and Bhagavan Nityananda (Siddha Yoga). The near absence of celebration of gurus' deaths stands in stark contrast to the Sufi tradition, which conversely holds large celebrations for the anniversaries of the death of the saint, also called *urs*. The *urs* is literally viewed as the mystical marriage of the saint's soul to Allah, the soul of a saint being essentially perceived as a woman in Muslim theosophy, and Allah as her beloved.[47] And contrary to the Hindu tradition, forgetting to celebrate a saint on the day of his death constitutes one of the greatest offenses that can be committed against the saint in the Sufi tradition.[48] If the anniversary of Mā's death is not celebrated among her disciples and often remains a rather painful day for some of them, nonetheless her disciples perform a special thirty-minute meditation on the day of her death, August 27.

Gurupūrṇimā

Gurupūrṇimā is the other major celebration of Mā's community, although it is less important than the anniversary of her birth. *Gurupūrṇimā*, which takes place during the full moon in the month of July in India, celebrates the guru throughout India. In Mā's time, she was the subject of a *Gurupūjā*, which can be seen in Arnaud Desjardins's film *Ashram*, in which the lives of several great spiritual beings in India, including Mā Ānandamayī, are documented.[49] Despite Mā's departure, devotees continue to celebrate the *Gurupūrṇimā* in her honor even today.

Kumbhamelā

Mā's *saṅgha* is also present in the *Kumbhamelā* and *Ardhakumbhamelā* at Hardwar and Allahabad.[50] These immense religious gatherings represent not only an occasion for Mā's community to celebrate Mā in an exceptional religious setting but also to continue to insure Mā and her cult an important place within the main Hindu religious organizations. During my visit to the *Ardhakumbhamelā* at Allahabad in January 2007, I was able to regularly visit Mā's *saṅgha*'s camp and to observe the cult in its functioning during such an occasion. Half a dozen girls from Mā's school at Varanasi traveled there to participate in the event, performing daily *bhajana* at the camp. My participation in this *Kumbhamelā* at Allahabad also provided me the occasion to follow the procession of Mā's *saṅgha* within different religious orders or *akhāḍas*, during the days of the great bath (*śahisnāna*). It is interesting to remark the incorporation of Mā's *saṅgha* into the ascetic order of the *nirmālaakhāḍa* during the *Ardhakumbhamelā* of January 2007. The order of the procession of Mā's *saṅgha*, as well as the incorporation into the ascetic order (*akhāḍa*), seems to vary with each *Kumbhamelā*. Another interesting anecdote to relate concerns the participation of Mā's *saṅgha* in the *Kumbhamelā* at Hardwar in 1998, where the *Nāga Bābās*,[51] naked *sādhus*, furious that the cart of another, much less that of a woman, Mā's, had passed in front of theirs during the procession of the great bath, were overcome with rage and overturned Mā's cart pursuing her devotees. This contrasts starkly with times when Mā was alive and was honored by riding on an elephant in front of everyone during *Kumbhamelā* procession.

Samyam Saptah

The postmortem cult of Mā also includes the collective, weeklong retreats which take place every year, not only in India but also in Europe and America. I had the opportunity to participate in these retreats several times and they seem to form an important element of the cult's sustainability. These retreats, called *Samyam Saptahs*, were instituted during Mā's time and today continue to gather her devotees together from across

FIGURE 1.4 Young girls from Mā Ānandamayī's school (*Kaṇyapīṭha*) sing daily at Mā's camp during the *Ardhakumbhamelā* (Allahabad, 2007).

Source: Photograph by Orianne Aymard.

India and the West. "It's the planet of Mā," says one devotee discussing the *Samyam Saptah*. The principle retreat takes place at the ashram at Kankhal in November and the other in January at the ashram of Bhimpura in Gujarat. These weeks of collective asceticism, which united thousands when Mā participated in them, still gather between two and three hundred people every year. Having only participated in the *Samyam Saptah* in India at the ashram in Bhimpura, I cannot make comparisons to the retreat at Kankhal, but it seems that, according to interviews and informal discussions, the retreat at Kankhal draws much more orthodox devotees than the retreat at Bhimpura. This may be explained by the marked preference for Bhimpura among Mā's Western followers. The *Samyam Saptah* retreat mostly consists of devotional chants, daily recitations of the *Bhagavadgītā*, readings of Mā's words as well as silent meditations. During this retreat, each devotee is directed to follow a strict diet, including a single daily meal of rice, lentils and vegetables, without spices. All stimulants like coffee or tea are prohibited and only water is allowed for drinking. A glass of hot milk is finally permitted every evening. For some rare devotees, a water fast is followed during the entire week.

Replicas of these retreats also take place in Europe and America, but due to the majority presence of Westerners attending, the rules concerning purity, such as the exclusion of menstruating women or the rules concerning pollution tied to the caste system are not observed. I had the opportunity to participate in two of these retreats near Paris and each of them brought together around thirty people.

Worshipping Images and Statues

The cult of images constitutes one of the essential manifestations of worship in the Hindu tradition,[52] including the postmortem cult of gurus. By the term images, I include photos, a very important element in Mā's cult. Here then I describe this tradition of the cult of images in Hinduism, then show the importance of this practice in Mā's ashrams. I also address the cult of statues (*mūrtis*) in terms of veneration of Mā Ānandamayī.

All images used in the cult need to be consecrated by a rite of initiation called *prāṇapratiṣṭhā* or the "establishment of the breath." This introduces divine power, *śakti*, and transforms the image into the incarnation of the divinity, here the guru.[53] This is also how the statues in Mā's ashrams were consecrated. So as to conserve the presence of *śakti* in the image, these rituals need to be performed daily,[54] for an unattended image is inappropriate for the cult. Mā is thus invited to enter into the image each time by a ritual called the *avahana*.[55] There also exist certain extremely rare exceptions, where the image does not require the rite of initiation in order to be considered sacred. These are self-manifested images or *svayamvyakta*, such as a certain self-manifested stone called *shaligrama shila,* symbol of Viṣṇu, or the *jyoti liṅgam* (pillar of light), Śiva's symbol. To the best of my knowledge, there are no such types of images found in Mā's ashrams.

The role of images hinges above all on their function regarding the *memoria* of the guru, permitting the reactivation of evidence of a presence to use the expression of Chenet regarding the role of the image in Hinduism.[56] Images also represent a source of support for concentration and facilitate meditation on the guru.[57] A number of Mā's disciples use a photo of Mā to help them concentrate, as this disciple describes: "When I am having a bit of trouble concentrating, I meditate on the photo, and by doing so, she takes me with her." This is also the case of this early Indian

disciple, a woman, who, discussing photos of Mā, affirms the importance
of form in supporting the concentration:

> I am attached to her form. I loved to see her body. Mā's form is very
> beautiful. It's easier to concentrate for us who are much below. If
> you can realize the *Advaita* (non duality), it's ok, but for most of us,
> we can't. We need an image, we need a focus, a form, we need a
> point, and what can be more beautiful than a mother, really?

Thus, the image of a god is a way to hold on to him or her solidly, to guar-
antee his or her presence.

Another point to address concerning the cult of images is whether
the divine presence of the guru is in the image itself. According to Diana
Eck, the image of the divinity does not simply constitute a meditative
support or even a sort of reminder for the devotee but also represents
a true incarnation of the divine.[58] Clémentin-Ojha also refers to this
Hindu belief, which holds that the cult's image has a life of its own.[59]
To a disciple who asked Sarada Devi if Ramakrishna continued to live
through these photos, she responded "Of course he does. The body and
the shadow are the same. And what is this picture but a shadow....If
you pray to him constantly before his picture, then he manifests himself through that picture. The place where the picture is kept becomes
a shrine."[60] This belief is found in many Indian traditions, such as that
among the Radhasoamis who also consider the image of the guru to be
a true manifestation of his physical presence.[61] As opposed to ordinary
images, photos of the guru are thus said to be images endowed with life
and capable of transmitting power through its gaze despite the guru's
death. In the case of photographs of Mā, Mā is said to have "breathed
force" into these images. For Mā's devotees, there is no doubt that
images of Mā are instilled with her presence, as the following commentary by a new disciple, an Indian man, reveals: "Sometimes, I have the
impression that the pictures of Mā are becoming real. Yesterday night,
for example, during the *kīrtana*, I was looking at the big picture of Mā
under the banyan tree and I felt that Mā is alive and she is looking at
us." Another disciple, a French woman, who is a recent devotee of Mā's,
described her experience with photographs of Mā to us in the following
way: "It is truly her presence. I no longer see the photo as flat. I see the
photo in three dimensions. She is there across from me. There are only
one or two photos that I particularly like, with this tenderness, this love,

this support, this protection." Similar testimonies abound among Mā's devotees:

> Picture is no picture, it is Mā.
> Picture of Mā is a living presence.
> By seeing her photograph, I come to know what Mā wants from me.
> I always have an altar, even if I am travelling. I put the pictures of Mā. It's just material but they radiate some kind of presence, undoubtedly.

One Indian man, an early devotee, perceives changing expressions in Mā's face in her photographs, according to the attitude that he himself must adopt:

> I feel that whenever I have a genuine problem, she has ways of solving it without being here. There is a particular picture that I use. There are only two or three pictures of Mā when she makes an eye contact with you. She talks to me. If there is nothing to talk about, then, she goes to sleep [laughs]. If there is a genuine problem for which I am not able to find an answer, then, she talks to me. The expression is always changing. Sometimes, she is very angry with me. I know I have done something wrong [laughs]. I don't know if it is my imagination or what. I have shared that with Swami Bhaskarānanda. It's an illusion? There is something wrong in my head? Maybe, this is my imagination. He said no, no. Whenever I come back to Swamiji, he gives me the impression that yes, believe it, it's not an illusion. The way I look at it, it's giving me the right message. And that's more important than how it is happening. Right message and I follow that and I have a good result. What else do I want? The rest is really theoretical, how it came, why it came.

The comments of this disciple in a sense correspond to what Arnaud Desjardins used to say regarding the variations of Mā's expressions according to the inner disposition of the devotee: "Mataji has very correctly been compared to a crystal that, completely pure and transparent, reflects everything that passes around her. I have even wondered if different people do not see her at the same moment with ten different appearances—different according to their respective interiors."[62] Thus, Mā's images can similarly

FIGURE 1.5 Arnaud Desjardins: "Mataji has very correctly been compared to a crystal that, completely pure and transparent, reflects everything that passes around her. I have even wondered if different people do not see her at the same moment with ten different appearances—different according to their respective interiors."

Source: Picture belonging to the collection of the photographer Sadanand; now in the possession of Neeta Mehta, also called Swami Nityananda.

be compared to a crystal that reflects our own state, from which comes the importance of the gaze brought onto the sacred image, as Schmitt describes here: "One does not look upon the sacred without impunity, whether it takes the form of an image or of a relic."[63]

Photos of Mā then hold an essential place in her posthumous cult, whether among early or new followers. Carried by devotees or situated in their home, the pictures seem to reactivate the presence of Mā. Mazzarella has called this dialectical effect "close distance."[64] More so even than Mā's words or eyewitness accounts of her, photographs of Mā are an essential way to mobilize new devotees as this new follower, a French woman, specifies:

> In the beginning, I was touched more by photos of Mā than by her words. The image of Mā really touched me. I completely entered into

her gaze and I had shivers in my body, a sort of loss of the concept of time between Mā's gaze and myself, it was of that nature, I was really in the image, in her gaze, in that which she freed I plunged completely. And little by little, I started to become interested in Mā, to read her books, and I started to want to go to her *samādhi.*

And although devotees no longer confine Mā to a physical form, they nevertheless keep a photo of Mā at their side, as was the case with Swami Vijayānanda: "I no longer see her as a form, I see her as an omnipresence. Although I do have a photo of her with which I do my *pūjā.*"

Still, the use of images in the postmortem cult does not appear to suit everyone. Some of Mā's devotees are little inclined to adopt this type of practice, as can be noted in the following testimony by this French woman, a new devotee:

Mā is closer to the ultimate than anything else I could have seen or felt. I should not say "seen," "felt," because if I see her, I find her ordinary. I even amuse myself by looking at her face close up and finding that, at heart, she had a very ordinary face, contrary to what people usually say, that her charm must operate by an attitude and not by the beauty of her face. Her facial features are too large, her face is too big. There is a lack of delicacy in her face. It's the delicacy of energy, it's not corporal delicacy. I would even say that all of these images turn me off. But from another side, it's nevertheless extremely difficult to adore the ultimate without a form. For a human being this is very difficult. To make it easier, you have to go into this world of light. Once that you are in this world of light, it's comparatively easier. But, without the image, I believe that one cannot uphold the postmortem cult. This is clear if we consider our Western world, with Jesus Christ and the Virgin Mary, we need images. It's images that maintain a cult, not writing. When I see the type of images that they placed for us in this hall, I ask myself where am I? But I shouldn't relate this to myself, because I am in India where every image of a guru is sacred. I don't think that Indians can understand. They do not know what it is to adore abstractly. The only people who adore God abstractly, for better or for worse, is Islam. Islam is truly God without form.... I meditate a lot in front of photos of Mā, and of Amma, but I do not look at them. Sometimes, I even forget that they are there. I think I put them there because of some superstition on my part, and that, like many other people, I have a need for my *gri gri*.[65] Here, for example, I am wearing my two medals, of Mā and of Amma. So, I don't know what that means but that's the way it is.

This devotee seems in some ways to agree with the thought advanced by the *Yogavasiṣṭa* which forbids the cult of images. According to this Hindu text, the inner veneration of the divine constitutes true veneration and only simple people require the support of a divine image.[66] The pervasive presence of the divine within the devotee in reality permits him or her to follow a more conventional type of adoration, to which the cult of the image belongs.

If some devotees have absolutely no inclination toward the cult of images, others also speak of less and less frequently using photos of Mā as they advanced in their *sādhanā*. This is notably the case of this man, a new disciple who affirmed in an interview that he is less and less likely to use photos of Mā in his religious practice:

They come to life less and less. They no longer want to say anything. Just a reminder, an old memory. What we live in the moment, it's more present, very fresh. Everything that is form, image, that seems a little denatured. I don't really like the statue of Mā in the *samādhi*, it doesn't touch me. I have respect because that recalls her, reminds us of her. It's like a reminder of a name. There was an evolution, first it was a form, a photo, the texts. There are different reasons. Either we may be bored before the photo because it's not alive, or because we have a level of presence that is stronger, which doesn't need the support of a photo. There are many possibilities. But still, I always have a small photo to remind me of her presence, it's like an exterior protection, a reminder, in case of a small failing, of a lack of consciousness. But I don't always walk around with it. It's not a fetish. It's a protection at the house, but it's not on my person all the time.

Even devotees less disposed to use photos of Mā as a type of support for their devotion consider that her images offer a form of protection, as shown in the two preceding witness accounts.

The guru may also be venerated through the cult of statues, a cult which is related in many ways to the cult of images. Like the image, the statue of the guru (*mūrti*) also functions as a reminder and as support for meditation, and in so doing, the *mūrti* is often perceived as the living being in the eyes of the devotee, who sees the guru as residing in it. In

FIGURE 1.6 *Mūrti* (statue) of Mā Ānandamayī in the ashram at Kheora in Bangladesh, her birthplace.

Source: Photograph by Orianne Aymard.

fact, for many devotees, the *mūrti* represents the very manifestation of the guru, as this anecdote regarding one of the *pūjāris*, also a new devotee, at the ashram at Kankhal demonstrates:

> One day, I was joking [with] one didi (sister). She said you should give to Mā, everyday, one glass of water and flowers before you go to sleep. All these things you should do. One hundred eight times you should also chant one mantra. I said, "Come on, it is only a stone." I have been giving water for three years, she is not drinking. When I came back, I saw that there was almost no water. The mosquito net had gone. I thought a theft has come. All the doors were closed. I said, "I am very sorry Mā." I felt at that time a strong presence. I repeated, "I am very sorry, it was only a joke." Then, I heard someone walking in the *samādhi*. I called the guard.

And so, many of Mā's devotees believe that the *mūrti* represents the guru, making the *mūrti* a body of presence. Throughout the Hindu tradition this practice of venerating the *mūrti* as if it were the guru can be observed, and it is notable in Mā's postmortem cult.

In Mā's temple at Kankhal, also called *Ānanda Jyotipīṭha*, there is one sole statue of white marble representing Mā and it seems that the absence of statues of gods and saints framing the *mūrti* of Mā confers on her the status of supreme divinity. There are other *mūrtis* within the ashram, but they are situated exterior to the temple and are not the objects of such attention. There is, for example, a *mūrti* of Shankaracharya in the great hall adjacent to Mā's temple, as well as a *mūrti* of Mā's mother, Didimā, in a building outside the principle interior section of the ashram, in the same place as her tomb.

Although Didimā was considered by some to be a guru during Mā's time, as she held the responsibility of conferring initiations, today few come to prostrate themselves before her *mūrti* at Kankhal, except for a few devotees like the following woman:

> I do not know her at all, I don't really know who she is, I find it marvelous that she is the mother of such a being and the manner in which Mā treated her throughout her life. I just did a *pranām* to the grandmother. It's the Mother of my 'spiritual God Mother' I come to say hello when I am here. It's the least I can do.

The fact that Didimā sparks only a limited interest among the members of Mā's community represents a paradox for some. Regarding the reason for this near indifference toward Didimā, a new devotee, an Indian man, had the following to say:

> That's the paradox. She is the one who has given birth to God. She is the one who has given *dīkṣā* to everybody. This is human nature. We are attracted towards God, towards light, but we do not see what is behind that thing. This source of light comes from somebody else. So, Mā used to tell 'go to do *pranām* to Didimā first, then, come to me.'

This lack of attention paid to Mā's mother could even stem from a belief held by some devotees that Didimā was not the biological mother of Mā,[67] as this Indian man, an early devotee, seems to imply:

> I am not sure whether Mā came out from Didimā's womb, there is no evidence of that. But Didimā has been identified as Mā's mother.

FIGURE I.7 Mā Ānandamayī and her mother Didimā, who took vows of *saṃnyāsa* (renunciation).

Source: Picture belonging to the collection of the photographer Sadanand; now in the possession of Neeta Mehta, also called Swami Nityānanda.

There is one swamiji who told me about an absence of navel on Mā. He told me not to discuss it very much. Since I have not seen myself, I cannot say, but this was told to me by a very sincere devotee of Mā. He said that Mā had shown it to him.

Despite then the presence of a *mūrti* of Didimā in the Kankhal ashram, as well as in other ashrams dedicated to Mā in India, Didimā's cult is completely secondary to Mā's. The posthumous cult to Mā is also associated with the cult of her husband, Bholanāth (who died on May 7, 1938), of whom there is also a *mūrti* at the ashram in Kankhal and at the ashram in Calcutta. The statue at Kankhal was installed there only in 2006 in the same courtyard as the *mūrti* of Didimā. As in the case of Didimā's, or even to a greater extent, his cult is of a minor importance compared to Mā's.

Similarly to pictures and *mūrtis*, there exists the possibility of worshiping a doll that represents the deity or the guru. Although the use of dolls does not pertain to Mā's cult, it has developed among other cults, such as in the cult of Mātā Amṛtānandamayī (Amma). The "Amma doll" represents a kind of protection for devotees and helps them to connect with the guru wherever they are, ensuring her presence even at a physical distance.

The cult of images and of *mūrtis* appears then as an essential element in Mā's cult, although a small number of Western devotees feel somewhat averse toward this type of devotional practice. The idea of a presence associated with these sacred images and statues seems then particularly central to describing this aspect of the postmortem cult.

The Cult of Relics in Hinduism

Some Aspects of the Cult of Relics in the Hindu Tradition

I turn now to a central aspect of the postmortem cult of the guru in Hinduism, the "cult of relics." Although the cult of relics is very common in many religious traditions like Catholicism and Buddhism, it is less important in the Hindu tradition. Its role is nevertheless central to Mā's cult, and it thus seems important to describe it. I shall first present the Hindu cult of relics in several ways, addressing its origin and its place in Indian geography, but also in considering the related practices of burial. Here I explore the cult of relics in its feminine dimension and endeavor to show the place of the sacred in the cult of relics, calling on the ideas of presence, power, and death.

Relics and their Origin

The Hindu Relics in the Religious Landscape

As Patrick Geary specifies, the cult of relics constitutes a common method of expression in numerous traditions.[1] Buddhism, for example, the classic religion of relics according to Gerardus Van der Leeuw,[2] places a fair amount of emphasis on the veneration of relics, as manifested by the cult of Buddha (i.e., procession of the Buddha's tooth, veneration of his footprints). Within the Christian tradition, the cult of relics is also especially important, as the veneration in France of the body of Bernadette of Soubirous at Nevers, who died in 1879, attests to. Another example is the relics of James, son of Zebedee at the Cathedral of Santiago de Compostela in Galicia, Spain. Peter Brown's work on later antiquity and André

FIGURE 2.1 Mā Ānandamayī's *samādhi* (tomb) in Kankhal, near Hardwar.
Source: Picture taken by French photographer Caroline Abitbol.

Vauchez's work on the Late Middle Ages have made major contributions to the field of the cult of saints in Christianity.[3] Although Islam, with the exception of the Sufi tradition, is little inclined toward the veneration of relics, paradoxically it also manifests a fairly important cult of relics, as shown by the veneration of the tomb of the prophet at Medina.[4] And far from being limited to religious traditions, the veneration of relics appears in society in general, as the veneration of Lenin's body at the mausoleum at the Red Square testifies to. And so, because the cult of relics is common in numerous traditions, it is perhaps surprising that it is less common in the Hindu tradition. Catherine Servan-Schreiber explains the attraction Hindus have to the *dargah*, the location of the Muslim saint's tomb, in the following way: "The fascination that the *dargah* holds for Hindus is more linked to the fascination for the space of a saint. It implies a relationship to death, to the body, to the relics, fundamentally absent from Hinduism."[5] It is thus interesting to consider the reason for the relatively limited adoption of a cult of relics in the Hindu tradition.

Before addressing this question, it is necessary to precisely define the term "relics." Nicole Hermann-Mascard, a legal historian who was the pioneer in studies on relics in France and whose thesis *Les Reliques des saints: Formations coutumières d'un droit* (Paris, 1975) is still the authority on the subject, distinguishes three types of relics: "corporal relics," "non-corporal relics," and "representative relics."[6] Corporal relics, often called "real relics,"[7] refer to the corporal remains of the saint and are the definitive relic. In Mā's case, her body in Kankhal represents the "real relic." Non-corporal relics include objects used daily by the saint, like things shown at the museum dedicated to Mā at Kankhal (e.g., a sari worn by Mā). Finally, relics said to be "representative" are made up of objects that had contact with the tomb of the saint or with his or her bones and which are thus permeated with his or her sanctity. These are, for example, jewels or gem stones that devotees place on the tomb of Mā.

These three categories, which are also present in the Buddhist tradition, specifically in the Theravada tradition in the respective forms of *dagaba* (*stūpa*), the *Bodhi* tree, and the image of the Buddha,[8] are also to be found in the Hindu tradition. This reminds us of the distinction made by Tulasi Srivinas regarding Sathya Sai Baba's sacred objects, as she looks at their meanings and patterns of circulation in the Sathya Sai movement. Srivinas distinguishes between what she calls *ephemera* and *sacra* in terms of closeness to the guru, emphasizing the value of proximity to Sai's subjects and objects. While *ephemera* refers to secondary types of relics (i.e., the representative relics), *sacra* constitutes the real relics, the most valuable ones, like the objects considered as a sacred gift, such as jewels and *lingams* coming out from Sai Baba's hands and mouth.[9] It remains to be seen today how the sacred objects will be construed by devotees after the recent death of Sathya Sai Baba.

Two factors may be considered to explain the relatively limited adoption of the cult of relics in Hinduism. The first one may lie in the inclination that Hindus have for living gurus. The second one may lie in the brahminical beliefs that hold that a dead body is a source of pollution. As far as the second factor is concerned, various scholars give the following explanation. For Jean Przylusky, the body of the deceased is seen as an impure and dangerous object that must be removed: "Nothing [in India] prepared people's minds for the celebration of a cult of relics. The corpse was [generally considered to be] an impure, dangerous object, to be kept away from human habitations."[10] For Charles Malamoud, Hindus have a pressing need to get rid of the dead body as soon as possible: "funerary ceremonies...seem to have no other purpose than to give an abundant, minute, passionate response to this question that the collective asks itself when it is in the presence of a dead body: how do we get rid of it?"[11] Monier

Monier-Williams also speaks of a certain rejection of the cult of relics in relation to impurity and death:

> Adoration of relics constitutes an important point of difference between Buddhism and Brāhmanism; for Brāhmanism and its off-spring Hindūism are wholly opposed to the practice of preserving the ashes, bones, hair, or teeth of deceased persons, however much such individuals may have been revered during life. . . . Articles used by great religious teachers—as, for example, robes, wooden shoes and seats—are sometimes preserved and venerated after their death. All articles of this kind, however, must, of course, be removed from the body before actual decease; for it is well known that, in the minds of Hindūs, ideas of impurity are especially connected with death, and contamination is supposed to result from the contact with the corpses of even a man's dearest relatives. . . . Hence in the present day a corpse is burnt, and its ashes are generally scattered on the surface of sacred rivers or of the sea.[12]

While the first factor, the inclination of Hindus for the living guru, may be a possible reason to explain the relatively limited adoption of the cult of relics, the second factor, the body as source of pollution, however, should not be taken into account. The bodies of realized beings such as Mā are in fact considered by Hindus as pure and sacred bodies.

Origin of Relics

The origin of the cult of relics in the Hindu religion seems uncertain. For some, like Bharati, the cult of relics in the Buddhist tradition constitutes the first instance of a cult of relics in India and is not the sign of an earlier cult of Hindu origin:

> The desire to keep and perhaps display the Buddha's relics cannot be explained from any known Hindu precedence—nothing of the sort is mentioned in any pre-Buddhist literature. The building of memorial stupas over them, following the distribution of the relics, cannot be traced to anything older—in fact, the Buddhist stupas and caityas are the oldest instances of relic worship in India.[13]

For Agehananda Bharati, the cult of relics in the Hindu tradition did not appear until after the arrival of Buddhism (in the fifth century B.C.E.). On the other hand, it seems likely that there may have been a Hindu cult of relics preceding the appearance of Buddhism. According to Johannes Bronkhorst, the cult of relics in Hinduism actually traces its origin to the movement of the *śramaṇa*, a movement that Buddhism, Jainism, and other religious currents stem from.[14] He gives the following explanation of the origin of the practice of burial of deceased *saṃnyāsin*s (renunciants):

> It seems justifiable to believe that the practice of burying the *saṃnyāsin* ascetics continues an old custom whose origin is located in the *śramaṇa* movement, a tradition that does not find impurity associated with the dead body that characterizes Brahmanism, and in which the veneration of the tomb of a saint is customary. Thus considered, the treatment reserved for the *saṃnyāsin* in modern India is an expression of the same tradition that we find in ancient Buddhism and Jainism.[15]

Thus, the veneration of corporal relics in Hinduism most likely had its origin in the *śramaṇa* movement, probably appearing before the arrival of Buddhism.

If the origin of the cult of relics in the Hindu tradition is uncertain, there is nevertheless no doubt that the cult developed with the Muslim invasion, as R. L. Mishra notes: "Many foreign scholars and art critics have consistently opined that the practice of building of sepulchral or commemorative monuments in India coincided with the advent of the Muslims in this country. It was, according to them, a result of inspiration provided by the Muslim tombs."[16] Thus, the practice of burial in the Hindu tradition is said to have developed alongside Islam in India, which explains the sometimes syncretic character of the cult of the tomb,[17] such as the tomb of the hero-saint Rajput Ramdev, which attracts thousands of pilgrims, both Hindu and Muslim, each year.[18] Other examples are the tombs of the nineteenth-century saint Shirdi Sai Baba[19] and of the recently deceased Sathya Sai Baba,[20] who, due to their ambiguous position straddling both Hinduism and Islam, are venerated both by Muslims and by Hindus and could be considered the most popular deceased saints in India today.

If the Hindu saint is not canonized after his or her lifetime but is declared a saint by the *vox populi*, "the voice of the people," the relic is similarly the fruit of popular consensus, making of Hindu sainthood not an "official" sanctity but a "popular" one, as Jean-Claude Schmitt terms it.[21] Because Hinduism is not institutionalized, as shown by the absence of a superior decision-making body that determines an individual's spiritual value, the relic cannot be recognized officially as authentic. Considering the absence of canonical texts codifying the rites of such a cult, Hinduism thus has a fair amount of freedom, a true system of free choice. The cult of relics in the Hindu tradition occurs then in spontaneous popular devotion, not monitored as in Catholicism. In this spirit of religious expression, some Westerners have even been elevated to the level of saints among Hindus and venerated as such after their death, despite being considered technically impure by Hindu orthodoxy. L. S. S. O'Malley mentions many surprising cases regarding this subject.[22] He cites the example of Colonel William Wallace who died in 1809 at the age of 47, and who has since been venerated at his tomb in Sirur not far from Pune. Considered a sage and a *sat puruṣa* (true being), he is venerated by the group of Hindus at Sirur, with the exception of the brahmins, and receives offerings on a regular basis. An American missionary tried to put a stop to these practices, but he died suddenly of cholera, which only served to reinforce the belief in the posthumous powers of Col. Wallace.

Geography of Relics

The very choice of location for the relics of a holy person, and notably the body, is a significant one and inserts itself generally into India's sacred geography, a geography said to be "real," as Mircea Eliade says, distinguishing it from profane, diffuse, and undefined geography.[23] The sacred thus becomes localizable, *Hic locus est*, "this is the place."[24] The tombs of spiritual masters are usually located in spaces marked by their mythic character, and/or in places of great and sometimes spectacular beauty, thus contributing to the master's prestige. It is not rare to venerate a sage at his or her tomb located at the foot of a sacred mountain, as is the case with Ramana Maharshi, whose tomb is found at the base of the sacred mountain of Arunachala, Śiva's mountain. This is also the case with the Marathi saint Nivrittinath, whose *samādhi* is at the foot of the sacred *Brahmagiri* mountain, where there are regularly chanters who come to interpret the mystic chants (*abhaṅga*) of his little brother Jnaneshwar.

We often observe that there is water near the tombs, which, by its symbolic character of regeneration, recalls both death and rebirth. It is certainly no accident that Mā's tomb is located only a few meters from the edge of the Ganges. There is a presence of trees, and notably of banyan trees, which are often associated with tombs of great spiritual beings. It is said that the spirit of the sage inhabits certain species of trees, making them the object of devotion.[25] This explains the reason for the devotees of Sri Aurobindo and of Mother touching their foreheads, in a sign of reverence, to the banyan which is located by their *samādhi*s. There is also the case of Ramakrishna who had the habit of meditating under an immense *pañcabati* (a sacred fig tree or *ficus Indica religiosa*), which is today the object of devotion for his devotees and which constitutes a privileged site for yogis.

Saligrama K. Ramachandra Rao emphasizes the importance of the tree in the Indian tradition and affirms that it was always associated with Indian temples:

> The Upanishads speak of the 'inverted tree', *asvattha*, with roots hidden above and branches spreading below (*Katha*, 2, 3, 1). The tree is an ancient analogue of life here and beyond. We find references to it in the *Rigveda* itself, and we find it illustrated in the Indus Valley seals. The folk cults are filled with reverential involvements of trees. Trees have been claimed as totems, trees have been worshipped as divinities, and trees have played an important role in our economy. The two trends in the growth of the tree, the normal upward and the spiritual downward, emphasize the principle of complementarity in human life. The Indian temple has not only been associated with trees, but it is in fact a representation of the life-tree. It pictures the principle of complementarity. The sanctum is a model of the normal tree with roots below and branches above; and the spiral tower of the sanctum symbolizes the inverted tree, with roots above and the spreading branches below.[26]

Mā's *samādhi* is located in the exact same place where there had previously been a banyan tree that fell naturally a few months before her *mahāsamādhi* (literally great *samādhi* or the death of the saint). Designating the tree's location, Mā had always let it be understood (even years before her death) that her body would one day be found at that spot: "One day, this body will rest here. It will not speak, but it will see absolutely everything." Mā paid a lot of attention to trees and compared them even to gurus: "Let trees be your guru. They give their fruits and their shade."[27] She also said: "Go, sit under this tree. The tree signifies a saint, a truly realized Being that can lead you to God."[28] Although there is no longer a tree at Mā's tomb, some disciples can still remember the presence of the banyan tree. Thus, the tree is strongly associated with great spiritual beings, to the point of even awakening the sage in his tomb, as a legend of the Marathi saint Jnaneshwar demonstrates. He appeared in the dreams of saint Eknath, asking him to remove the root of a tree that had wrapped itself around his neck in his tomb.[29]

We also may note the mythic character of the place where Mā's tomb is located. The fact that her tomb is found in Kankhal, near Hardwar, is not due to the simple fact that the Kankhal ashram is larger and more recently built than the Kishenpur ashram at Dehra Dun, the place where Mā left her body. It is certain that the placement of Mā's tomb at Kankhal is due in no small part to the sacred nature of the space, as it is located a few meters from the mythic site of *Dakṣinesvāra*, where *Satī* is said to have thrown herself in the fire before the refusal of her father to accept her love for Śiva. Eliade also gives the following description of Kankhal and *Dakṣinesvāra*:

> Kankhal is located on the other side of Hardwar, two miles from the ghat. You arrive on a road bordered by large, wealthy white houses and by gardens full of cypress trees. The route follows for a while the banks of a channel with green and rapid water. At all hours of the day, you meet from both directions groups of travellers and of pilgrims who walk without haste, not thinking of the time spent travelling, their gaze attentive, greeting everyone they meet on their path.
>
> The temple of Daksheshvara [*sic*], famous throughout India, its old, humid walls surrounded by giant poplars and acacias. I enter after having deposed my shoes before the door into the courtyard; the shadow of oaks, the calm. The Ganges runs in front of the temple, and this sacred, supernatural silence is no longer broke by the rumble of these waves of cries of monkeys that leap among the trees. A few old devotees take care of the small altars—they are numerous and ancient—next to the temple of *Siva*. Ruins, columns of burned brick, laurel and virgin vine, creeping white flowers, squirrels. Pilgrims come to bathe in the Ganges, anointing their forehead with the sacred golden dust.[30]

Thus, Mā's *samādhi* is located next to the mythic site of *Dakṣinesvāra*. However, for Mā's devotees, the true location where *Satī* left her mortal shell would be at the very place where Mā's tomb is now located, as the

FIGURE 2.2 Temple where Mā Ānandamayī's *samādhi* (tomb) is located.
Source: Photograph taken by an English devotee of Mā, Christopher Pegler.

following Indian old devotee says: "The *samādhi* is a very important place because *Satī Devī* left her body in that place. To me, that is the original place. That place is very auspicious." Some devotees go so far as to affirm that the exact location of the *Satī* would in reality be at the level of the tomb of Mā's mother, Didimā.

The proximity of Hardwar, one of the most famous cities for pilgrimage in India, also reinforces the mythic and sacred location of Mā's tomb. Eliade speaks of Hardwar as the archetypal location for Hindu pilgrimage: "All of those who demonstrate some interest in religiosity and have a certain respect for these moral 'athletes' of asceticism and solitude speak of Hardwar; that is to say that all of India talks about it. Hardwar is the location for salvation for orphans of fate and those thirsty for true freedom."[31]

Mā's tomb is inserted then within a geography already considered to be sacred, not only due to its proximity to the sacred Ganges River, but to the mythic sites of Hardwar and of *Dakṣinesvāra* at Kankhal as well. In its location, the tomb thus contributes to the development of Mā's cult.

Burial Practices and Sanctity

In traditional Hindu society, death is often perceived as a source of impurity, as it is the synonym of pollution. As the dead body taints the atmosphere, there is a pressing desire among Hindus to dispose of the body as soon as possible through cremation.[32] Despite the idea that pollution is inherent to the dead body, there are nevertheless several situations in which the body is considered sacred. This is the case with the bodies of a sacred person, or renunciant (*saṃnyāsin*). Contrary to traditional custom in Hinduism, the body of the liberated being, the enlightened one, is buried and not cremated, counter to the brahminical attitude regarding death. The body of the deceased saint, designated by the term *ucchiṣṭa*[33] to indicate physical remains, is far from being considered a polluting agent, as it is viewed as sacred. The tomb of the realized being becomes an imposing place due the fact that it houses a "body delivered into a state of permanent meditation"[34] and in which energy continues to circulate.[35]

The Indian tradition of burying renunciants seems to be a fairly old one.[36] It is described in two ancient texts, the *Baudhayana-pitṛmedha Sūtra* and the *Vaikhanasasmārtasūtra* (V, 8), as well as in more recent texts such as *Smṛtyarthaśastra* (written in the year 1200), which Pandurang Vaman Kane examines in his work *History of Dharmaśastra*.[37]

We should specify that this practice of burying renunciants also applies to two other cases, that of children dead before the age of 2 and those who suffered a cruel and unusual death. Children are considered to be like renunciants, liminal figures due to their position outside of the caste system. As they performed no real actions before their death, their karmic baggage is also considered neutral, at least as to what was accumulated in that lifetime. In the same way, individuals who suffered horrible deaths are not cremated after their death; these people died violently, some accidentally, others drowned or were bitten by a snake, etc. (cf. *Vaikhanasasmārtasūtra* V, 11).[38] In addition to renunciants, young children, and victims of horrible deaths, there are other cases in which the deceased is buried instead of cremated. For example, the *Vīraśaivas* or *Liṅgāyat*s (bearer of *liṅgam*) practice burial among their initiated *Liṅgāyat* devotees, whose status then has nothing to do with caste, social background, and life stages (*āśrama*). Also the members of the Tiruvavatuturai order (Tamil Nadu) are considered on their death (*civaparipuranam*, or death) to have attained the "fullness of Śiva."[39]

Although the burial practice does not apply to *satī mātā*s, these women who burn themselves alive in the funeral pyre of their deceased husband, and to *vīra*s, heroes sacrificed on the field of battle, it is however important here to mention them. By virtue of the violence of their death, these individuals are generally deified and steles are dedicated to them, which is unusual considering the little presence of funerary art within Hindu culture.[40] Due to their heroic sacrifice, *vīra*s and *satī*s are considered powerful beings, often endowed with powers of healing or protection, and, to a certain extent, are viewed as renunciants or saints, as they become the object of a cult at a funerary monument.[41] It is interesting to observe that, although these heroes are deified and their memory is preserved by a stone tomb, for many, these sorts of violent deaths would nevertheless hardly be considered auspicious, as horrible deaths are perceived as more polluting than natural deaths.[42]

To return to the subject of renunciants, the practice of interring their bodies can be justified by the symbolic self-cremation that they perform on entering into a state of renunciation (*sannyāsa*). Therefore, they cannot be cremated a second time after their death.[43] This ritual cremation could be at the origin of the burial of saints.[44] Charles Malamoud has the following to say on this subject:

> The complex ceremony which marks one's entry into 'renunciation' consists of allowing one's sacrificial fires to extinguish after having incinerated one's sacrificial utensils, as an ultimate fuel source, in a final oblation. One's fire are not abolished for all this: they are rather internalized, inhaled; they are made to 'mount back' into oneself (*samāropaṇa*), such as the renouncer's own person thenceforth becomes at once the seat of, and the raw material for, a burning up, a permanent oblation, offered upon that internal flame that is the Veda.[90] We can see that the renouncer settles down at the *dīkṣā* stage of sacrifice: his non-sacrifice is an endless *dīkṣā*. For the *dīkṣita* proper, the internal sacrificial cooking process is separate from the act of cooking. As for the renunciant, who is often designated as a *tapasvin*, as 'one who heats himself up', he eschews cooking, since by definition, he has in a sense done away with his external fires. Constantly performing the essential fire, the cooking of the self, he renders useless and impossible the cooking of any substitute.
>
> Furthermore, because he is cooked from the inside while still alive, the *saṃnyāsin* had no need of being cooked after his death: he

is therefore not burned, not buried.[91] The funerary arrangements for 'men of the world' are different from those reserved for 'renouncers'. They have given their lives a different orientation; therefore, their postmortem fates carry them in different directions. But, more than this and most especially, they are not made of the same oblatory stuff: ordinary men, like animal victims, are first put to death and then offered into the flames that cook them and carry them up to the world of the gods. As for the renunciants, they begin by cooking themselves. But by internalizing their fires, they have also abolished the possibility of being borne upwards to a divinity located outside of themselves. By establishing themselves as offerings from the outset, and by adhering to this role down to the very end, they have transformed their own persons, their *ātmans* identified with the universal Self, into their divinity: they are *ātma-yājins*. To 'renounce', therefore, is to raise one's *tapas* to that temperature at which a fusion occurs between the divinity, sacrificier and victim—and this is both the climax and final death of a sacrifice.[45]

Thus, the renunciant's body, this temple of God, cannot be exposed to this burning by the sacrificial funerary fire that constitutes cremation, and his body can no longer be the object of oblation through fire. The cremation of the bodies of renunciants is also marked by the absence of friends and family mourning them. All post funerary rites or *śraddhas* are absent, and the cult of the Manes, or the cult of ancestors, is for this reason not required.[46]

After this discussion on the burial of renunciants, it is important to describe its process. It calls on numerous rules that take account of astrological and mathematical information. The following is how the entombment of renunciants' bodies is carried out:

We dig a grave, generally on the banks of a river; you place the body in the sitting position of meditation said to be *samādhi*. We fill the body with salt so that the body will be supported, fixed in this posture by the mass of salt surrounding him, rising up to his chin; only the head rises above the salt; we break the skull by hitting it with a coconut or a large shell: the soul reaches the world of Brahman more surely, as popular opinion holds, if it leaves through an opening made at the highest extremity of the body. Above the grave, around their head, we erect a burial mound, also called a *samādhi*. This tomb is the true location of the cult, it is a sanctuary, a place for pilgrimage, a place for those who feel spiritually linked to the deceased (I am not speaking of blood relations) to come to commemorate him with offerings, prayers, absolutions, and to leave these things at the site.[47]

We should specify that the body of the renunciant is placed in a lotus position in the *samādhi* facing the south, as was the case with Mā's body. This custom of breaking the skull is not limited to *saṃnyāsins*, but is also practiced by the families of non-renunciants before their relatives' cremation.[48]

Thus, this practice of interment was applied to both Mā's body as well as her mother's. The other *saṃnyāsins* and *saṃnyāsinis* in Mā's *sangha* were immersed in the Ganges, a practice known as *jhal-samādhi*, as is often the custom for *saṃnyāsins*.[49] This was the case with the Austrian disciple Atmananda, who, although a foreigner, was given this honor due to her status.

If the bodies of sages are generally buried, it should also be noted that they are sometimes cremated if they were married, as was the case with Gandhi, who is today venerated at his memorial at Delhi,[50] or with Lahiri Mahasaya, whose ashes are located at his ashram at Kankhal. Other examples include the couples of Ramakrishna and Sarada Devi, and Ramdas and the Mother Krishnabai. This is not always the case, as some married gurus are interred rather than cremated on their death. Mā Ānandamayī is, of course, one such example, for, although she was married to Bholanāth, her body was buried. This is explained by Mā's affirmation that her marriage was never consummated physically, as the renunciation associated to sanctity generally precludes the absence of sexual desire in the Hindu tradition.

I should also address another element associated with the burial of realized beings, which, in the West, is called burial *ad sanctos*. Some devotees wishing to benefit from a sage's protection after his or her death may express a desire to be interred next to his or her tomb. This type of practice that is often encountered among Muslims,[51] Christians,[52] and sometimes Buddhists[53] does not occur in Hinduism, however, for as we stated earlier, only sages, children, and those who suffered a cruel and unusual death (and occasionally kings) may be interred. Thus, is it normal to observe the absence of tombs of devotees surrounding Mā's tomb.

Incorruptibility and Odor of Sanctity

Another aspect of the cult of relics is a belief in incorruptibility of the body of the sage. The non-decomposition of the saint's body or at least the belief therein may be an important factor in the development of the cult after his or her death. Far from being considered a malediction, as was the case with vampirism in Central Europe during the seventeenth century, manifestations of an incorruptible body contribute to the recognition of the person's sanctity,[54] and is thus perceived by many as a major characteristic of sanctity. This sign of incorruptibility that defies the laws of nature actually reflects a state of sanctity already present before death. As Sofia Gajano says in her study on relics, the body of the saint, this "physical reality in which is written the spiritual path" can only remain "holy" after death.[55] It is then natural that the powers of the saint should be conserved beyond death, and in his or her body.

If this phenomenon of incorruptibility is often encountered in the Christian tradition, as with the case of Saint Francis Xavier's body in Goa, whose toe was reportedly bitten by a follower in surge of devotion years after his death,[56] it is also found in Hinduism. According to Hindu belief, the body of the sage does not undergo *rigor mortis* as an ordinary man's body does, but retains a "state of freshness" in the tomb, also not undergoing putrefaction and decomposition for thousands of years. The body of a deceased sage continues to be inhabited by his or her soul that travels in the three worlds (*loka*s), the sky, the earth, and the lower world.[57] This idea is often accompanied by the belief that a devotee's intense prayer may reanimate the body of the guru. Some of Aurobindo's followers, seeing the incorruptibility of their master's body, thought he was coming back to life.[58] The testimony of the Mother of Pondicherry also illustrates this belief in the postmortem life of the physical body of the saint:

> This body must be left in peace…they should not be in a hurry to put it into the hole…because even after the doctors have declared it "dead" it will be conscious—the cells are conscious—and it will know it, it will feel it, and this will again add one more misery to all those it has had.[59]

Thus the tradition of *corpus incorruptum*, the body remaining intact after death, is present in the Hindu tradition. The body of Shirdi Sai Baba, one of the most famous examples, showed such signs after his death, as well as the famous yogi Yogananda's body. There is also the case of Swami Ramatirtha whose body was found intact a week after his death from drowning in the Ganges.[60] The phenomenon of incorruptibility is not said to be present with all great spiritual beings, only some who have a specific reason for making use of it, such as Yogananda who wanted to demonstrate the value of yoga in the West. This corporal non-decomposition is sometimes said to be accompanied by other extraordinary manifestations, such as emanations of light coming from the saint's body. This is a common belief in the Hindu tradition, particularly in the *Siddha* tradition. It is often expected by disciples, as was the case in the death of Aurobindo, described by Alexandra David-Neel:

> Many devotees expected to contemplate miracles around the funeral bed. That didn't happen. Some followers declared that they had seen luminous emanations from their master's body. No trace of decomposition appeared for four and a half days (exactly eleven hours and thirty-six minutes, according to ashram officials). The 'Mother' interpreted this fact in declaring that Sri Aurobindo's body had been impregnated with such a concentration of supernatural light that it had stalled his decomposition.[61]

As Mā's body was conserved in ice for her last physical *darśana*, her followers were not able to establish what kind of state her body would have been in without refrigeration. Devotees are thus free to believe in the incorruptibility of her body if they wish. Interviews however reveal some indifference on the part of devotees regarding this question, and whether her body decomposed or not after her death does not seem to hold much importance. The absence of signs of the incorruptibility of her body would not question her divinity, and if they had discovered a *corpus incorruptum* on reopening her tomb, as it is practiced in the Catholic tradition when there is an elevation or a transfer in the course of the canonization process, this would constitute only a supplementary sign of her power. For the majority of her followers, the question of the incorruptibility of Mā's body is thus a relatively insignificant one, only pertaining to "material" matters: "I have no opinion on that. For me, this is material. Whether her body has turned into flowers, or something else, it is only a question of inquisitiveness which I don't have. I am concerned with Mā only." In invoking scientific reasons, some followers imply that it is possible that

Mā's body did not decompose due to the fact that 40 kilograms of rock salt were placed in her tomb, suggesting the absence of infiltration with water. Thus, if signs of incorruptibility contribute to the construction of divinity, it does not seem to be a determining element in the cult's expansion after the death of the sage.

Another sign of sanctity is related to the smell of the body after death, that is, the famous "odor of sanctity," the "sweet smell" which is often mentioned as present during the life of accomplished spiritual beings. As to the incorruptibility of their body, this phenomenon of the odor of sanctity is associated mainly with the Christian tradition. However, it is not rare to hear it said in India, and notably among Hindus, that there is an odor of sanctity emanating from a saint's body, an "inversion of the funerary to the vernal," as Debray describes it.[62] This odor, which as Van Der Leeuw specifies is not completely metaphorical,[63] is said to be a sort of pleasant perfume originating from the saint's body at death and contributes to the mysterious conservation of the body an additional sense of the sacred. It reflects, according to Catherine Grémion, a certain monism demonstrating the union of the soul and the body.[64] This odor of sanctity at death is sometimes said to be associated with a state of purity present in the body of the sage before his or her death. Buddha's body, according to some Buddhist texts, did not need to be washed for his funeral.[65] This physical purity preceding the death of the liberated one also is manifested in the absence of excretions and unpleasant smells.[66]

In the case of Mā Ānandamayī, there are no accounts testifying to the phenomenon of the odor of sanctity on her death, although many of her followers have remarked on the divine smell Mā emanated during her lifetime. Thus, the existence of a pleasant smell after death becomes a supplementary corroboration of divinity but does not seem to be absolutely necessary to recognizing the sanctity of sages, as Mā's case demonstrates.

Relics and the Feminine

As Ānandamayī Mā was a woman, it seems necessary to address the existing relationship between relics and the feminine, especially the reasons why the cult of relics is even less common for female gurus in the Hindu tradition.

Relics and Women

Mā Ānandamayī's tomb constitutes an exception in the Hindu universe of guruship, as it is extremely rare to find tombs of female gurus in India. This inequality is all the more surprising considering the greater participation of women in the cult compared to men.

First of all, it is difficult for a Hindu woman to follow a spiritual path, and thus to be recognized as a saint, as women traditionally marry and are dependent upon their husbands following the laws of *Manu* and the ideals of the *pativrata*, that is to say the ideal of the perfect woman. In fact, the Hindu tradition considers the renunciation of the world to not be the destiny of women.[67] The ascetic way, often symbolized by the body's nudity, which is forbidden to women by societal norms, thus constitutes a masculine path in Hinduism, and female renunciants are to a certain point considered dangerous as they are free from men.[68] Regarding this matter, do the *saṃnyāsins* not say that the woman is the way to hell (*narak kā dvāra*)? Thus, this lack of female gurus' tombs can be explained in part by how difficult it is for a woman to follow the path of the renunciant.

This inequality also stems from the lack of societal recognition for female gurus, as women are perceived as *śūdras*, the fourth and most inferior of the Hindu castes, and are thus not able to access sacred writings.[69] Although some women were in the past perceived as true saints, their role as a spiritual master or soteriological agent (guru) however was never really recognized. This is the case with the saint Mirabai and the saint Andal, both of whom continue to be venerated in Rajasthan and Villiputtur, respectively,[70] in Southern India, despite possessing no tomb. For if these women represent models of devotion, their capacity to teach and to transmit was never truly recognized. For this reason it has been historically rare for a female Hindu saint to be seen as a guru[71] and to be venerated as such during or after her lifetime. The *Dharmaśastra* specifically holds that the role of the guru is principally destined for men. The role of the female guru was seen as a marginal one and was far from being recognized by traditional Hinduism; the absence of a female form of the word "guru" also reflects this state of affairs.[72] In orthodox circles, it was even thought until recently that a woman could not become enlightened and could not thus lead individuals on the path to liberation.[73] A book by Bhaiji, a close disciple of Mā's, mentions this in relation to a story in which Bhaiji's brother-in-law affirmed that a woman like Mā could not lead a being to spiritual enlightenment.[74] In an informal conversation, Swami

FIGURE 2.3 *Samādhi* (tomb) of Mā Ānandamayī, Kankhal. Swami Vijayānanda: "Make a vow at the *samādhi*, it will be fulfilled."

Source: Picture taken by French photographer Caroline Abitbol.

Vijayānanda also evoked the statements of a brahmin at Varanasi who had suggested that he follow a male guru as opposed to Mā Ānandamayī, as a woman could not perform the role of guru.

Thus, this lack of recognition for female renunciants as gurus is reflected in the near absence of sects founded by women[75] and is closely associated with the rarity of women's tombs today. In this context, Mā Ānandamayī, during her lifetime, constituted one of the rare exceptions. Although she was never affirmed as a guru, she nevertheless performed that role for many disciples, for they saw in her a being capable of guiding them on the path to realization. The fact that Mā Ānandamayī was at the basis of a religious movement, along with the establishment of nearly thirty ashrams across India, without a doubt contributed to the construction of a *samādhi* in her honor.

Although it has been extremely rare to encounter female saints venerated on the site of their own tombs, such a practice, however, might develop in the near future considering the growing acceptance of female gurus (referring more specifically to Amma or Gurumayi).[76] Mā, in some sense, opened the door to affirming the religious leadership of women within a strongly patriarchal society.

Feminine Configuration of Relics

If the internment of female gurus is uncommon in the Hindu tradition, there are nevertheless some rare cases of female gurus interred on their death. With the exception of Mā Ānandamayī, these women are almost always venerated in association with a male guru. As a result, the sacred space is not the location of the woman's tomb but of two tombs, that of the woman and the man with whom she is associated. If this association often reveals the woman's subordination to the man, sainted though she may be, there may also be a complementary relationship between them, *Śiva* and *Śakti*. The *samādhi* of Aurobindo and the Mother constitutes an interesting example of this, in the sense that the placement of the two bodies, hers on top of his, consciously calls to mind tantric representations of *Śakti* placed upon *Śiva*. This demonstrates the complementarity of the feminine *prakṛti*, active and dynamic, and the masculine *puruṣa*, which is passive and unacting.[77] Ramdas and Krishnabai are also venerated in their ashram in Kerala, the *Anandashram*, on the same principle, although in different tombs, or cenotaphs as it were, in which their ashes were preserved. The case of Ramakrishna and Sarada Devi, whose ashes were also conserved under their respective statues in Belur Math at the seat of the Ramakrishna Mission, differs slightly, as the cult of the sainted couple is more centered on Ramakrishna than on his wife Sarada Devi. This of course reveals two facets to her role, the "woman who follows," that is, the traditional Hindu woman, and the "complementary woman," demonstrating that *Śiva* cannot be separated from *Śakti*. Finally, it is interesting to look at the case of Ramana Maharshi and his mother, recognized as a saint since her death. If she does not hold a central role in the cult, she nevertheless plays an important one as she is a figure of the Divine Mother, and as such, her tomb is located next to her son's.[78] This brings us back to the considerable role the Divine Mother plays for those who wish to attain supreme liberation, as seen in the devotion to the Mother by Shankaracharya, this great philosopher and religious reformer of the eighth century. Though a *saṃnyāsin*, someone who had died to his old life, he is said to have defied the norm to light his mother's funeral pyre.

Because of the absence of an association with the masculine, Mā's tomb represents an exception in the relics' landscape. Her *samādhi* is characterized by its independence and, in this sense, can be considered a *śakti pīṭha*, a powerful site where a relic of the goddess lies and where it is venerated in all its splendor.[79] This brings us back to the vision of the goddess present in the *Devī-mahātmya*, that is to say, that of an autonomous, independent goddess with no partner.[80] The Hindu tradition generally recognizes the independent, supreme goddess, or the Great Goddess, that is to say she who was not fashioned in relation to a male consort, to be more powerful but also more violent and more dangerous than the goddess associated with a masculine partner, the so-called "small goddess," possibly due to the absence of erotic associations and the subsequent retention of her sexual energy.[81] In this context, Fuller speaks of the "hot" goddesses to designate these independent and celibate goddesses whose power is not channeled by a sexual relationship,[82] and whose *prakṛti* is thus not checked. As Marglin specifies, if the power of the woman (*śakti*), which is neutral at its base, is not channeled by a sexual relationship, it oscillates between a destructive and beneficial force.[83] In this respect, Mā could be seen to represent a powerful but also dangerous figure, in that she disturbs the profane world with respect to its sacred dissolution. Thus, the examples show that through the configurations of female relics, different visions of the feminine can be seen. Relics of Mā Ānandamayī, in their autonomous presentation at her tomb, reveal a divine woman completely assuming her powers.

Despite her status as a married woman and the historical scarcity of *postmortem* cults associated with female Hindu religious figures, Mā Ānandamayī is certainly an exceptional figure. Within a male-dominated funerary tradition, Mā represents then the beginning of independent female spiritual leadership in the Hindu world, and her tomb a symbol of the affirmation of the feminine. The cult of her relics offers a new possibility within the Hindu universe of guruship, opening up a path for veneration of future women gurus after their death.

Presence and Relics

By virtue of the presence and the power conferred upon them, but also because of the reflection on death that they encourage, relics constitute key agents in accessing the sacred. This study consists then in approaching the sacred at Mā's *samādhi*, not only through its traits of presence (*sannidhi*) and of power (*śakti*) but also through its association with death.

Relics as Central Points

As Jacob Kinnard affirmed, in addressing relics, the language of "presence" must be employed.[84] Muslims hold saints to be continually present at their tombs,[85] as the Christian tradition does at their sepulcher. Brown calls this the *praesentia* of the saint, going so far as to consider the relic to be the saint himself or herself, for as Thomas Head emphasizes regarding medieval Christianity: "The relics of the saint in the shrine are the saint."[86] The Theravada Buddhist tradition also affirms the presence of the Buddha in his relics, as is indicated by the comments of the monk Mohinda, the son of the emperor Ashoka, who affirms that to view the relics of the Buddha is equivalent to beholding the Buddha himself.[87] Bareau confirms this: "The participation of the *stūpa* in the sacred character of relics and of the Buddha or the saint tends to personalize the monument...since before our era then the *stūpa* has been more than a symbol of the Buddha, it is the Buddha himself."[88] And if others contend that the relic is not the Buddha and is only a substitute, it is nevertheless totally permeated with the qualities of the Buddha, possessing the ability to act as the Buddha did during his lifetime.[89]

We similarly find this idea of presence inherent in relics in the Hindu tradition, where it is said that the holy person leaves his or her presence, also called *sannidhi*, or at least some part of it at his or her tomb.[90] Before dying, Sai Baba de Shirdi is said to have stated the following concerning his posthumous presence at his tomb: "I shall be active and vigorous even from the tomb" or even that "my mortal remains will speak from the tomb."[91] The Hindu tradition also holds that the presence of the sage is strong at his or her tomb, from which the name *samādhi* (*camati* in Tamil) to designate the tomb comes, as the sage continues to meditate there in a state of profound beatitude. Some episodes in Mā Ānandamayī's life reflect this belief in a posthumous presence of the holy being at his or her tomb, as this event related in writings on Mā demonstrates:

> Mā's husband and several friends met her, when she was praying near the grave of a Fakir according to the tenets of the Koran. Occasionally similar situations were repeated. And Mā was completely fluent in the complexity of the Muslim prayer, although she

said, "she knew" nothing about this, when asked. She also said then that she communicated with the spirits of the deceased Muslim sages and saints, as she was often visited by beings no longer alive among us.[92]

This belief in the presence (*sannidhi*) of the sage at his or her tomb is very strong within the cult in relation to Mā's *samādhi*. Atmananda affirmed this: "You know, you can't even say that she left her body. There where it lies, at Kankhal, you feel the radiation of her Presence."[93] For the large majority of her followers, Mā's presence at her tomb is beyond doubt and, for this reason, many consider her *samādhi* to be a special place, a place where Mā's energy is felt with greater force than elsewhere: "*Samādhi*, that is the concentrated Mā there, as a shrine. Naturally, it is an important place. When we go there, we feel her presence stronger.... If you sit in the *samādhi*, or around the *samādhi*, you get very easily cut off from the rest of the world. It is very obvious." Some also evoke the existence of a "living energy" at the *samādhi*, as this old male devotee:

> I do feel the *samādhi* really has a vivid energy. It's close to Mā as possible you get. Even now, maybe more than ever now, I feel greatly benefited by being by the *samādhi*. I don't like it here that much actually. For myself, for example, I prefer to live in Varanasi. But still, I have to admit that this unique energy here is important for me. It doesn't mean that I am going to stay here all the time. But it is definitely a special place for me.

Others also perceive Mā's presence at her *samādhi* as a sentiment of well-being, like the sensation of being returned to yourself: "The energy of the *samādhi* helps me, I feel like I am at home. I feel really well, I feel the presence of Mā." People also mention positive vibrations to evoke this feeling of presence at Mā's tomb: "You get positive vibes at *samādhi*, you can concentrate in a better manner, it's a cool, calm place. Moreover, you feel Mā's aura is there, because Mā's remains are there. So naturally, it is one of the most sacred places for us." As testimonies on this subject are numerous, only a few others will be cited:

> As soon as I go into the *samādhi*, I feel the atmosphere is so charged. Nothing is needed. It is like one to one with Mā when I sit there.

It is very special. It is the only special place...Where Mā's body is and where so many *pūjā* are taking place everyday, it has to be a very special place.

For me, Mā's presence is very strong there. There is something very special.

We note that this quality of presence, this energy that devotees mention at Mā's *samādhi* seems to differ according to the *samādhi*, as the account of this new follower, a Western woman, testifies to; she compares the energy at each tomb's location to the smell of perfume:

The *samādhi* of Swami Muktananda, it's a completely different energy than the *samādhi* of Mā. It's not the same quality. It's like perfumes, there are different perfumes. It's not in the form of perfume but it's an intensity, a quality of energy that is different. At Ganeshpuri, there is also the *samādhi* of Nityananda, and there is again a totally different energy. At Shivananda's, it's different. At Alandi, it's teenage. Aurobindo, it's again something else. Ramana Maharshi, it's also a different quality. But the "divine" presence, as we say, to put it into words, it is truly very concentrated.

It is also interesting to look to the expression of the "residual presence" used by Swami Vijayānanda regarding the *samādhi*: "In the case of a great sage like Mā, who left a residual presence, one may enter into contact with this presence. And this contact can become a considerable aid to our spiritual pursuit. The guru transmits power and he can do this even after leaving his physical form."[94] This residual presence may be like a form of a trace, a memory, as this close disciple of Swami Vijayānanda explains:

With the word residual, you touch on something that is seen also with the memory, but a memory that lies with physical elements, elements that have existed, and it's there where I distinguish it from the 'virtual', it's concrete. You address to a physical presence. For me, it's very important that Mā existed. It's not the Divine Mother in the absolute, the fact that there was a passage to earth, that there was a body, that she was born into a body and that now there is the *samādhi*, it's very very different. There is a presence on the earth.... We don't speak like that of the Divine Mother in space.

The fact that Mā took form, that she came into a physical body,
I think that it's very important.

Thus, the tomb of the sage, this sacred enclave where time is abolished, represents a "real and living point" to many, defined by Eliade as
the very origin of creation, as the source of "life's energy."[95] Only in the
hierophanic space of the divine tomb is time overcome and transcended,
thereby allowing access to a radically different reality, a true and permanent reality. The tomb of the sage symbolizes in this sense a point of rupture of levels, a center access to which serves as a true initiation. Devotees
often speak of Mā's *samādhi* as a "central point," as this old disciple, a
Western man, affirms: "It is somehow a kind of consolation sitting in this
place, at the *samādhi*. I do feel Mā's presence very strong. It's a kind of
a central point where her power radiates from. It is definitely a special
place." Another old follower, an Indian man, also evokes the role of reori-
entation associated with the *samādhi*:

> It's a very powerful place. No question about it. Mā has given me
> there a new direction in life. Sometimes, you lose track. That's why
> this place becomes very important to me. I relate that place to the
> change of direction in my life. The inner pursuit is so complex.
> You don't know whether you are going in the right direction or not.
> Sometimes you think that everything is fine, but actually everything
> is not fine. That's the time when she guides you. I had very peace-
> ful, very good experiences in this place. That's why I keep going
> back and I look forward to any excuse to go back there. I would find
> any excuse to go there. The presence of Mā is very strong there. It's
> really a special place.

As such a center, the *samādhi* responds to disciples' questions, as the following testimony demonstrates: "Time passed, I came back with all sorts
of questions, serious or futile, I have never returned from the *samādhi-
mandir* without a response."[96]

The *samādhi* constitutes then, in the eyes of devotees, a true point of
convergence, a space of spiritual affluence. By its liminal character, Mā's
tomb thus represents a point of junction between the earth and the heav-
ens, an intermediary between two distinct symbolic orders, between the
world of the living and the invisible world,[97] and as a *tīrtha,* assures the
passage from the profane world, that of illusion, to the sacred world, that

of reality. In the same way that the *stūpa* allows us to escape from the sam-saric wheel, the relic of the Hindu sage opens to us the door of entry to this sacred reality, to this "other."

Although for devotees, prayers, chants, and *pūjās* performed at the *samādhi* serve to amplify Mā's vibrations, today it seems that for some the *samādhi* has lost some of this energy. This French man implies that this is due to a less intense spiritual call:

> That's changed with time. As far as I'm concerned, it's no longer the same presence that I feel at the *samādhi*. At the very beginning, four years ago, I felt a much stronger presence. And today, almost nothing. It changes, but there is also a progression....It's not an insignificant center. It's a spiritual center. But one feels less of a presence, as if maybe there are fewer devotees. The cult is perhaps qualitatively less important. You feel less divine energy than before. I think that it's not subjective, it's more objective because I'm used to feeling through experience. I think that it's due to the environment; I don't think it's me. You can ask other people too. There is still an emanation from her remains, from her relics but they carry less grace than before. It's as if people weren't calling [her]. The relics do not need to emanate grace for nothing, for absolutely nothing. That may explain it. So you have to call her, you have to invoke her. The request of the people is not necessarily there. When I often speak to devotees, they tell me, me, enlightenment, it will be for future lifetimes. There is no urgency. There is not this call, this urgency, as if it was the last life. This isn't there, there isn't such a call, so I don't see why there would be a reactivation of the relics.

This recalls in a certain sense the comments of Jamous who also evokes the idea of inactivity of the tomb when there is an absence of rituals and of offerings to the saint. Without an intense call among devotees, the rel-ics are essentially inactive, ceasing to emanate or to radiate their "grace."

Although some devotees today feel less of a presence at Mā's tomb or *samādhi*, there is still a large portion of followers who consider Mā's *samādhi* to be the principal location of this presence. The corporal relic of Mā forms then the central point of the postmortem cult for a significant number of devotees. This vision of Mā's tomb as a place of her presence is opposed to the view of other devotees who hold that her presence is not confined to a particular location. As this view conforms to a more *Advaitic* conception of presence and relics, I will now address in detail the *Advaitic* model with regard to these topics.

Presence and Relics in the Non-dual Vision

A certain number of devotees refute the affirmation that holds that Mā's presence is felt more strongly at her *samādhi* than elsewhere, for from a Vedantic, non-dualistic perspective, Mā is everywhere and is not limited to a particular place as this swami firmly declares:

> People, out of their spiritual impulse, out of love for their mother, feel the strong presence of Mā in and around *samādhi*. I don't believe it. If you feel the presence of Mā, you feel the presence in full, anywhere. It is not "Mā's stronger presence." It is your strong interaction with the place. It is your interaction. It is from your side. There is nothing wrong in it, nothing bad in it. But be sure that wherever Mā is, she is there in full but, because of our limitations, we cannot feel her presence in full. So, we need some specific place. If you are convinced about the universality of Mā, she must be present anywhere, anytime, and in her fullness.

The assertion that holds Mā's presence not to be limited to her tomb is repeated in many testimonies, as in the following by this Indian man, an early disciple of Mā's:

> I know that Mā is here and everywhere. Mā is a worldly Mā. Why, you people, came over here, from so far away? Mā is everywhere. The world is Mā. Her body is a flying bird. Two, three times, I came back to Mā's *samādhi* but I don't feel that I have to go there especially. Mā is everywhere, in any place. Why should I go there?

For this other early male disciple of Mā's, a Westerner who is also a devotee of the Mother Krishnabai, the vision of the divine must be enlarged and not simply reduced to a tomb:

> I like it there [the *samādhi*] but I don't feel that it is so special. I have a little box in my room, in England, with a little bit of the ashes of Krishnabai. I consider it as a *samādhi*....Of course, it's a very nice atmosphere in Kankhal. We should have respect for things that are

truly sacred. But we shouldn't particularize too much. If we say that the sacred is only there and nowhere else, then it becomes very difficult to widen our vision, which they want us to do, they want us to widen our vision.

Like many great spiritual beings, Mā had always affirmed that she was not "this body." The cult of her *samādhi*, in that sense, would be like a regression from the *Advaitic* or non-dual teaching that she supported. In this regard, she also affirmed her refusal to be confined to a particular place:

> "I never leave you. Why do you want to push me away? I am always with you." And someone asks, "Mā, you live then in our heart?" And Mataji responded, "In your heart? Why do you want to confine me to a special place? I am in the blood of your blood, the bones of your bones. It's the truth. You can believe me. I never lie."[98]

For Swami Bhaskarānanda, who was perceived by many as being one with Mā, "Mā is not there, She is inside and outside." He did not consider her *samādhi* to be particularly important as, for him, the force with which an individual feels Mā's presence depends on his own spiritual aspiration and not on a particular place: "It depends upon your intensity and aspiration, your own faith." Others agree with this view, as the following testimony from an Indian woman, an early disciple, shows:

> I wouldn't say Mā's presence is more in the *samādhi*. It is your own expression. If Mā is within you all the time, you will see Mā anywhere. If I am walking on the road, and if I am thinking of Mā very strongly, I feel Mā on the road, walking right next to me. It is a projection of your own self. It's a projection of your own thoughts. It's a projection of your own feeling. It is your projection of your own belief, that Mā is this or that. If Mā is within you all the time, you will see Mā anywhere. My feeling is that Mā is with me all the time. I will love you also because you are also a part of Mā. Mā is everywhere. That's why love and compassion for everybody just draws. Everything belongs to Mā.

But although certain devotees refuse to confine Mā's presence to her *samādhi* or to another place, the *samādhi* seems to represent for them a particular place where Mā's presence is objectively easier to feel: "She is everywhere but we feel her presence there, at her *samādhi*." Mā's *samādhi* represents a place where her presence is easily perceived compared to other places, as Swami Kedarnath affirms: "I feel her presence everywhere. To me, Mā is everything. There is no particular place attached to her. Everywhere I get her vibrations, because everything is Mā. But, it is true; some places have got special vibrations. The *samādhi* is one of these places. You feel strong vibrations there." Although the presence felt at the *samādhi* does not equal the presence that is felt within, the following French disciple, a recent devotee, also recognizes the importance of this place:

> It's a recentering. Instead of going on vacation at *Club Med*, I prefer to come to the *samādhi*. It relaxes me. I feel more in harmony. And then, that's all. It's not extraordinary.... But it's nevertheless important. You can't banalize the *samādhi*, and neither can you place it under a highway. History, it counts. Even if you have to leave history to become enlightened. But it counts, it's a way to recenter yourself, it's a memory. It's like a book, a photo. It's charged, but it's not this extraordinary presence that you feel on the inside, when you do a *sādhanā*.

While affirming that Mā is everywhere, another new Western disciple, a woman, evokes her "concentrated" presence at the *samādhi*: "Mā's presence is everywhere, she is not only here. Here, it's concentrated if I can put it that way. It's a bit like your mother. You go to see your mom, you go to see her on vacation and then after, you will continue on with your life. When you're a certain age, you're not hanging around your mother all the time anymore."

There seems to be a wide range of perspectives on the presence's significance at the *samādhi*. If for many devotees, there is no doubt that Mā's presence is felt more intensely at her *samādhi*, for others, her presence is not at all associated with a specific place, although they admit that the *samādhi* is a special place. In addition, notable differences do not seem to exist between men and women or between Westerners and Indians regarding the question of Mā's presence at her *samādhi*. And, as to the differences between old and new devotees, it is difficult to make a comparison due to the limited number of new devotees interviewed compared to early devotees; on the whole though there does not seem to be a large divergence in their views.

Regarding the presence attached to relics, one can ask oneself, as Copeman and Ikegame remark and as do Urban and McDermott within the Tantric context, whether the recent developments in media technologies can contribute to extend this presence and so, contribute to gurus' expansive agency.[99] As new ritual spaces with virtual temples and online *pūjās* are developed, one can wonder if, in the same manner, this sense of presence could be communicated while virtually attending the rituals at the *samādhi* of Mā.

To conclude, the *samādhi* seems to have an influence on the cult, in the sense that it represents a central point for the devotee, not only because of the presence associated with it but also because of the power that is attributed to it.

Relics as Centers of Power

The relic in the Hindu tradition can be considered a truly living entity, in the same way as in the Buddhist, Christian, or Muslim traditions, which also confers upon it the power of the deceased saint. The relic of the Hindu sage is a "center of power," power which is designated in Hinduism by the word *śakti*[100] and which also corresponds to the *baraka* of Muslims[101] or to the *virtus* of Christians. The tomb of the enlightened one, this place of *augustum*, of magnificence, thus becomes the guarantee of sacred power. While the previous section discussed the relics' power in relation to the feminine aspect of the divinity and in terms of "presence," the following section considers the appropriation of this power.

Relics and Appropriation of the Sacred

If this power is said to be attached to all the places where the sage lived and to all the objects associated with him or her, it is especially associated with his or her tomb. An early disciple of Mā's, a Western woman, evokes this power, this "*śakti*" associated with Mā's tomb:

> I feel that there are some special vibrations at the *samādhi*. Being in the *samādhi* really helps you to focus on Mā. I feel great love when I am around that place for a long time. It is said that the body of an enlightened person is purely sadhvic. I cannot really explain. If people pray a lot, have a lot of faith at a specific place

where they direct all their feelings and thoughts, this also adds
to the sanctity of the place. But I think also that, somehow, it has
Mā's *śakti*.

This power (*śakti*) associated with Mā's *samādhi* is also felt by a large number of devotees, as is the case with this other follower, an Indian man, new
devotee of Mā's: "The blessing of Mother is all time playing here. I don't
know why I came here. I just feel that some power is playing here. What is
the reason, what is the cause? I don't know. The only thing I know is that
Mother is living here."

In the same way that the body of a Christian martyr has been capable
of "making a worker fall down dead in a room of the catacombs,"[102] the
body of the Hindu sage, through the singular presence of the sacred, can
rattle a devotee to the core. Swami Muktananda speaks to this effect in discussing the power associated with the saint's tomb as one strong enough
to violently shake their body: "Now when I visit a temple, *samādhi* or *dargah*, I become acutely aware of the *śakti* present there, to the extent that
my body shakes very violently."[103] In the same way, Jacques Vigne talks
about a "shock" that can be felt by some who come to Mā Ānandamayī's
samādhi.[104] Thus, this power seems to be inseparable from the holy tomb.
The body of the sage, far from being perceived as a polluting or dangerous element that must be disposed of as soon as possible, thus becomes
an object of veneration, making the tomb into the cornerstone of the cult.
Regarding transformations such as this one, Caillois speaks of a "horror"
that transforms into "confidence."[105] The comments of the Indianist Paul
Mus also take on greater significance in this context: "the tomb becomes
much less the dwelling of death and more a sort of artificial body substi-
tuted for the mortal shell, a funerary 'cosmic man,' where the magical
entity will be that which will prolong the deceased."[106]

By the veneration of the sage at his or her tomb, the faithful hopes to
benefit from his or her power; devotion and rituals play then a key role in
the mobilization and the absorption of this energy emanating from the
tomb. As a result, contact with the tomb becomes an essential element in
this quest for the appropriation of the sage's *śakti*, a power that Assayag
specifies as an "extraordinary warehouse of charisma."[107] By this contact,
followers look to assimilate the qualities of death, or to absorb the mystic power of which the body is the seat. The sage's head seems to be of
great importance for some devotees as it concentrates the power of death.
But although followers can sometimes prostrate themselves at the tomb,

touch it and even embrace it, as is the case with Sri Aurobindo's and the Mother's tombs, this is not always the case.

Mā Ānandamayī's tomb is not accessible to devotees except on certain occasions (her birthday, *Gurupūrṇimā*, *Samyam Saptah*, and *Durgā Pūjā*), revealing a management of the sacred by a body of religious specialists (*pūjāris* and priests). In this context, Bourdieu would speak of the "management's monopolization of the goods of salvation" by these ritual specialists.[108] The existence of certain auspicious periods for the veneration of the sage and his or her relics is also noted; the power exuding from the tomb would be more active at certain times of day, its intensity attaining a maximum during *ārati*. Thus the peaks of the sage's powers vary according to the hours of the day.

In this quest for the appropriation of relics' power, some followers go so far as to leave an object on the holy tomb, so that the object will be permeated with the subtle vibrations of the relic. Douglas, like Frazer,[109] also speaks of "contagion" in evoking this "power of success," this auspicious power that is transmitted to objects along with the pollution:

> Another characteristic of success power is that it is often contagious. It is transmitted materially. Anything which has been in contact with *Baraka* may get *Baraka*. Luck was also transmitted partly in heirlooms and treasures. If these changed hands, Luck changed hands too. In this respect these powers are like pollution, which transmits danger by contact.[110]

Some of Mā's followers often ask for authorization to leave one of their objects, like a jewel, on Mā's tomb for it to be permeated with the relics' energy. It is interesting, in this context, to observe that Hindus have adopted certain practices associated with the tombs of Sufi saints, like covering oneself with pieces of cloths left beforehand on the saint's tomb, so as to capture the mystic power of the dead.[111] If these practices are not necessarily visible at the tombs of Hindu saints, they nevertheless seem to be adopted by Hindus who frequent *dargah*, these cult spaces where one comes to venerate the Muslim saint at his tomb.[112]

If the follower appropriates sacred power at the holy tomb, he or she can also appropriate it through objects that belonged to the sage. Mills speaks of the flow of the sage's "idiosyncratic presence" through his or her objects, transforming them into anthropomorphic extensions. These extensions of the physical presence of the sage permit a sort of physical

survival of the sage and thus serve as "solid material" in the construction of divinity, as Mills says.[113] Devotees of the saint Ekanath of the Sant
tradition make up for the absence of a tomb by coming to touch a pillar
at the saint's house, the same pillar upon which Ekanath had the habit
of leaning on to write.[114] This idea of an "anthropomorphic extension"
returns us to the comments made by Stanley Tambiah who, in his study
on Buddhist saints in Thailand, speaks of a process not discussed by Max
Weber, through which this sacred power of the sage's charisma is concentrated and accumulated in objects, these non-corporal relics. Far from
being eliminated, the routinization of the deceased sage's charisma continues through the materialization of his or her charisma, notably through
rituals and the distribution of the charismatic power.[115] If objects permeated with the sage's charisma can bring certain benefits to the devotee, it
is nevertheless recognized that these benefits are generally much more
important on contact with the corporal relic of the sage. The power radiating from whatever object belonging to the sage would not then equal the
power of the corporal relic. This is even more true for the cenotaph, the
funerary monument absent a body where the sacred being is honored in
the case of his or her place of burial being unknown or if his or her tomb
is too far away to be visited by his or her followers.[116] Although the cenotaph can act as a gravestone, it is nevertheless considered to be much less
powerful than the true tomb containing the body of the sage.

    Thus relics, as vehicles for the "spiritual influence" of the great sage, in
this case Mā, constitute true objects of power for believers. Taking on the
role of a theurgical aid through which the beneficial and protective forces
of the sage are carried, they are the object of a real veneration, through
which the follower looks in vain to benefit from these forces, in order to
appropriate them. Mā's relics represent then, in the eyes of her devotees,
a center of power altogether apart.

Multiplication of Relics as a Source of Conflicts

Related to this search to appropriate the sacred is the dissemination of
relics and the conflicts that sometimes surround this dissemination. In
certain traditions, notably in the Christian tradition, the corporal relic can
be divided and redivided indefinitely, so as to assure what Brown calls
an effect of "inversed magnitude," a preservation of the integrality of the
power associated with the sage's body in the smallest of his relics.[117] For as
Caillois says regarding the division of relics, the sacred is "indivisible" and

"always whole."[118] By this process of reducing the relics, the grace of the enlightened being can thus be exercised through a multitude of fragments as powerful as the intact relic, contributing to the creation of new centers of sacredness and thus to the expansion of the cult. Brown also sees in this practice of multiplication and dissemination of relics a way to overcome death: "What better way to remove the fact of death than to dislocate a part of death outside of its original context, the tomb that is already too saturated?"[119] Bernard Faure sees in the relic two opposing yet complementary aspects: the relic as a fixed presence, *in situ*, as for the tomb of the sage, and which thus defines a sacred space of pilgrimage, and the relic as a "circulating token of salvation," that is to say as a sort of circulating good of liberation, which distributes the sacred through its pilgrimages.[120]

If this practice of dividing relics and of disseminating them takes place in some religious traditions, this seems to be very rare in the Hindu tradition. There are, however, some existing cases where fragments of corporal relics are venerated in diverse locations. Within the religious movement of the Radhasoamis of Soamibagh, for example, fingernails of the former master are exposed for devotional ends.[121] The case of Aurobindo can also be cited; similarly to the veneration of his body at Pondicherry, his nails and hair are used as relics in different ashrams in India. Regarding the figure of this study, Mā Ānandamayī's teeth have been conserved by some monks, but they are not the object of a collective cult of relics. This dissemination of relics can also take place in the case of great sages who have been cremated. Some of Ramakrishna's ashes are found in several of his ashrams across India, along with Vivekananda and Sarada Devi's ashes. If this multiplication of relics is uncommon in Hinduism, it is thus not entirely absent from it either.

Associated with this multiplication of relics and search for the appropriation of the sacred, the relic of the saint, this "powerful mobilizing force for pilgrims," as Kaplan calls it,[122] can become a source of conflicts and the object of intense competition. The appropriation of the relic confers power and a certain prestige on the individual, the community, or the institution. The question of possessing Ramakrishna's ashes has provoked conflicts between young monks and family members, conflicts that ended in the theft of the sacred ashes by a young disciple.[123] However, the theft of relics does not seem to be a common phenomenon in Hinduism, as compared to the Muslim, Christian, and Theravada Buddhist traditions. It is also interesting to note that the theft of relics is not considered to be reprehensible or condemnable, as relics cannot be stolen without the approval of the saint. Thus, if the cult of relics is less practiced in the Hindu tradition as compared to other religious traditions, the theft or even the purchase of relics is all the more so, as are the official or secret translations like the *pia furta* in Christianity.[124]

Miracles and Danger of Relics

We cannot discuss the power of relics without addressing miracles. The tomb is often associated with the manifestation of miracles and followers generally believe in the sage's supernatural intervention particularly at his or her tomb. "Miracle" means a positive extraordinary act, beyond the natural course of things, that the believer attributes to a divine intervention and to which he gives a spiritual provenance. The miracle as such cannot be recognized except by the believer and the essential idea is that it is a "sign." Referring to an "anthropology of credibility," Babb argues that miracles are central to create and maintain the relationship between the devotee and the guru.[125]

This belief in the supernatural intervention of the sage is found among Mā's followers, as is demonstrated by this affirmation of Swami Vijayānanda during one of his daily *satsaṅgas* before Mā's *samādhi*: "Make a vow at the *samādhi*, it will be fulfilled." This dovetails with the belief that holds that the closer you are to the tomb, the greater the force of the call. Among the miracles attributed to the relics is that of healing, though this is attributed specifically to certain beings more than to others. Assayag distinguishes between two types of sainted beings, the "literates," generally little inclined in their lifetime to openly use their thaumaturgic power, preferring anonymity to crowds, and the "rustics," who do not hesitate to display their powers to every comer.[126]

Within the context of miracles, relics can also appear mysteriously (*swayambhu*). When Mā died, a cushion bearing an image of her is said to have magically appeared in the house of one of her followers in Chandigarh. This cushion, today surrounded with garlands of flowers, constitutes an object of veneration and is the gathering place for Mā's devotees. Although similar mysterious appearances of objects in Mā's community have not been heard of, this phenomenon seems to happen for other guru's devotees, such as Sathya Sai Baba's, who witnessed, at least during his lifetime, the appearance of objects, especially in times of difficulties.[127] In the same way, relics can sometimes disappear for mysterious reasons. While there is no written or oral tradition one can reference in these matters, Theravada Buddhism recognizes this and affirms that Buddha's relics are supposed to disappear by disintegration at the end of a period of five thousand years, so as to make room for the future Buddha.[128]

If the sacred tomb represents a fascinating and attractive place, notably because of the miracles that take place there, it also embodies danger. Because of its sacred nature, one cannot approach the tomb of a great sage without running some risks, for if this sacred power is accompanied by *fascinans*, it can also manifest its terrifying aspect of *tremendum*. To question this sacred power is to place yourself in a perilous position and to openly expose yourself to danger. One does not frequent with impunity the sanctuary of a saint, the sacred place par excellence, without exercising some caution. For one who would like to appropriate some of this sacred power, there is a certain level of purity that is required—from whence come rites of purification. The profane must then pass by a purification process, so as to protect oneself from the effects inherent to a force so difficult to control, a force that can even result in death.[129] Thus, if the sacred at the sage's tomb leads the faithful to immortality, it can also lead him or her to death, as Caillois expresses in saying that the sacred is that which one does not approach without dying.[130]

Because of its dangerous energy, the sacred at the sage's tomb is the object of a series of prohibitions designed to protect devotees. Being compelled to keep a distance from this dangerous and unpredictable power through a number of ritual prohibitions, the follower is thus informed of the dangerous effects associated with the contagion of this power. The restriction of direct access to Mā's tomb permits the demarcation of a boundary to this sacred power and allows the religious experience to become a domestic one. Mā's tomb, this sacred space rendered taboo by a system of restrictions established by the religious authorities, is not accessible, except by a periodic lifting of these restrictions, that is to say on certain holidays dedicated to Mā. Thus, the tomb proceeds from a paradoxical dialectic, which simultaneously reveals its accessibility and inaccessibility. As Jean-Claude Schmitt says regarding the rituals of veiling and unveiling relics in the Christian tradition, "the sacred escapes from our gazes to make itself more desired, so that the clerics cover their treasures, so to better remind us of their monopoly over the management of the sacred."[131] The longer these periods of inaccessibility are, the more effective the sage's action will appear to be.

But, if one has to protect against the undesirable effects of sacred objects, one also has to protect the latter against too frequent contact with the profane.

This is because this contact could lead in the long term to a change in the nature of these objects' sacred power. This is doubtlessly one of the reasons why access to Mā's tomb is usually forbidden. As well as warning followers against the dangers inherent to the power of the place, the lack of access to her tomb aims to maintain the purity of the space, to avoid any pollution of the sacred by the profane. This is especially the case with menstruating women, who are considered impure, and who are forbidden access not only from Mā's *samādhi* but also from the temple in which her tomb is located.

By virtue of the intensity of the force (*śakti*) attributed to them, relics thus constitute a true source of power. In this sense, they represent a privileged way to access the sacred, and so, contribute to the development of the postmortem cult, notably Mā Ānandamayī's cult. This connection between relics and the sacred is reinforced by the reflection on death engendered by the cult of relics.

Relics and Death

Although the connection between relics and death seems to be quite obvious, it is however important to explore this link. The next section will examine the direct link between "female relics" and death, and consider the assimilation of Mā to Kālī.

Relics as Symbols of Death and of Immortality

The relics of the sage represent to many a support for reflection on death, in the sense that they recall the impermanence of the body and the transitory nature of existence. To meditate on the relic thus calls one to meditate on the evanescent character of the body, to realize the ephemeral, and the "[domestication] of death". As Bernard Faure expresses it: "Relics also constitute, in the symbolic, a way to 'tame' death in creating a form of familiarity with some eminent deceased people and in contributing to the development of a cult...of saints."[132] In this sense, relics form a precious tool for those who want to awaken their consciousness to the transitory character of life. This can be seen in tantric Hindu practices with regard to the sites for cremation,[133] but also in Buddhist practices like *maraṇasati* that designate a form of meditation based on contemplation of a dead body.[134] Likewise, the Zen tradition advises one to "meditate on the bottom of his casket," and St. Antoine, the founder of Christian monasticism, lived in a tomb in

Egypt. Meditating on a tomb can also represent a tool for liberation in itself. Mā's *samādhi* is proven then to be a meditative support to cultivate this sense of impermanence, so as to integrate death into consciousness. Far from demonstrating a depressive attitude on the part of disciples who cannot say goodbye to the incarnation of Mā, the cult of the *samādhi,* on the contrary, leads the disciple to accept death's reality and thus his or her own death.

If relics of the sage symbolize death, they also paradoxically affirm the eternality of life. In assuring the continuity of life in death, relics are guarantees of the immortality of the soul. For Singh, the tomb reflects the belief in an after-life, becoming the "symbol of the material expression of spiritual beliefs."[135] For Schmitt, corporal relics also represent indications of life after death: "Relics are on earth like hard parcels of eternity."[136] In the same way, Weinberger speaks of "the fleetingness of terrestrial life finding in the funerary inscription a taste of eternity."[137] Edgar Morin relates the preservation of the deceased's body to a continuation of his or her life, and, in this context, affirms that the non-abandonment of the dead implies their survival.[138] Thus, the tomb of the sage becomes a place to encounter eternity, a space where time has no hold, an assurance of a future life after death. The tomb then openly contests death. Assayag takes up this challenge of death in her study on the burial practices of the *Liṅgāyat* where she speaks of the deceased's body in his tomb as the symbol of a conquest over death: "His emblematic corporal position provides the living with a model of the meditative Absolute. The dead person repudiates death."[139] In becoming a symbol of deliverance from death, the imagery of relics strives, in every way it can, to proclaim the elimination of death.

This elimination of death attached to relics is also reinforced by the function of relics as an aid in preserving the sage's memory, as implies the name *"memoriae,"* which was attributed to relics in the Christian tradition. Meslin speaks of relics as "material supports of a collective religious memory"[140] and Trainor confers on them the role of "technology of remembrance."[141] In so preserving the memory of holy beings, the cult of relics strongly contrasts with the common practice of cremation that, on the contrary, looks to retain nothing of death as Maurice Bloch and Jonathan Parry note:

> In Hinduism nothing of the individual is preserved which could provide a focal symbol of group continuity. The physical remains

of the deceased are obliterated as completely as possible: first the corpse is cremated and then the ashes are immersed in the Ganges and are seen as finally flowing into the ocean. The ultimate objective seems to be as complete a dissolution of the body as possible.[142]

Accordingly in India, cremation tends to remove all physical trace of time spent on earth,[143] while the saint's relics, and especially his or her tomb, looks to preserve the memory of the renunciant. As Malamoud states, the saint's tomb should not then be confused with *smasana*, these lugubrious spheres of cremation fated to be forgotten, nor with these strange tumuli mentioned in the Vedic texts (*Satapathabrāhmana*):[144]

> The mortuary of the *samnyāsin* remains then as different as possible from the *smasana*, from these sinister crematorium fields, haunted with vampires and disgusting spirits, where one reduces to ashes, in what is nevertheless a sacrifice by fire, the body of ordinary men; different also from these mysterious tombs, which the Vedic texts tell us were sometimes lifted around funerary urns, but which also tell us that they are designed more for oblivion than for remembrance, and which are never mentioned in the perspectives related to the cult of the dead.[145]

It is also interesting to note the paradox attached to the sage's relic and to his or her memory. The relic comes to perpetuate the memory of a being that is presented as totally lacking an ego, of a being without any desire for recognition or glory before or after his or her death. Malamoud specifies that this paradox is particular to brahminical India since, in other ages, funerary monuments were erected for lay individuals, like kings.[146] And so, not at all making the deceased a "dead person without a face" and of removing all memory of him or her, relics, on the contrary, allow the preservation of his or her memory and the subsequent maintenance of an intimate relationship between the living and departed sages. Mother Meera, a female guru who today lives in Germany, holds that the tomb of a sage constitutes an important aspect of the preservation of memory: "the existence of a tomb gives a stronger impression of the dead's presence than a small urn of ashes. This memory then will live on in hearts and minds."[147] The tomb represents, then, an essential element in the preservation of the deceased sage's memory, and as such leads the devotee to surpass his own death, for, as Hervieu-Léger writes, to believe that a man survives in the memory of those who loved him represents a way to embody the desire that every man has to surpass his or her own physical death and to cope with the deaths of those who surround him or her.[148]

By virtue of their paradoxical nature, relics, then, remind us of both the transitory and eternal nature of existence. Regarding this matter, Goody speaks of relics as "pure symbols of impurity, ongoing representations of impermanence, signs of mortality enduring after death, embodiments of bodilessness."[149] This paradoxical aspect of relics returns us to the testimony of one of Mā's disciples, a French woman and a new devotee, regarding the apparently contradictory character of the dual reality of the transitory and the eternal:

> What's really interesting in Mā's case is that it references the two realities discussed in the *Vedānta* that are not contradictory. You have to learn to live both in a transitory reality and a reality that is permanent. Vijayānanda always uses this metaphor, it's like water, there is the bottom of the ocean, this permanent reality and there are the waves, which are transitory. The fact of knowing that Mā had a body, that gives us this concept of the incarnated divine, of the transitory and the permanent. We, as humans, this helps us even more in our path. We have this to realize, to be both in the transitory reality and the permanent reality.

This dialectic of contraries associated with Mā and her relics makes us perceive the true nature of the real in a totally different way, as it is situated well beyond opposites in which contraries coexist. As a result, meditation on Mā's relics leads us to transcend contradictions in order to access the true nature of the Real, the Ultimate Real. This necessity of abolishing the polarity of the human condition in order to realize its true character is found in the *Bhagavadgītā*, where Kṛṣṇa reveals to Arjuna that to know God, it is necessary to surpass these dualities: "It's in renouncing all virtues that you will find me," for as Daniélou specifies, virtue in reality is only the opposite of vice: "One is as far removed as the other from the transcendent reality. Neither one nor the other can lead us to God."[150] By virtue of their dialectical and paradoxical nature then relics represent a true aid in the path to enlightenment.

Relics, Death and Feminine Sanctity

The reflection on death engendered by the cult of relics is reinforced by the identification of Mā with the goddess Kālī, the goddess of death par excellence, as her iconography shows very clearly. While Kālī's right arms promise freedom from fear, the two left ones bestow death, with one holding a sword and the bottom one a decapitated head. Mā Ānandamayī, sometimes referred to as the "Human Kālī" in Bengal, represents the incarnation of Kālī in the eyes of some of her devotees, and, in this sense, symbolizes the inevitable reality of death.[151] Regarding this matter, one of Mā's long-time disciples, a Westerner, evokes that which being beside Mā signified for him:

> You could never stay with Mā. You could come and see Mā for two weeks out of the year, have a deep experience and go home. That's one thing. But if you stay with Mā, all the time, you could never do it unless you were beyond death. That was the price to pay. She would take you to death again and again, one way or the other. And that was the beauty of living with Mā. You live beyond death. What is death? Who cares about death? You live on the other side of death. That was the thing of being with her physical body. You were not in this world. Never for a second in those years was I in this world. I was in some other *loka* [world] and that *loka* had much more reality than what people called this world. What extraordinary grace allowed this to happen? But then, that *loka* is hard to maintain without Mā there.

As such, to be in Mā's presence led to accepting the reality of death but also to surpassing it, for if Kālī symbolizes death, she also represents the victory over it.[152]

Even today, despite Mā's departure, some devotees learn to reconcile themselves with death through their devotion to Mā as an incarnation of Kālī. To meditate on Mā through her relics helps in becoming conscious and accepting death in all of its dimensions, suffering (*duḥkha*) and destruction, for one does not conquer death in ignoring it. In a sense, this leads us to Pierre Feuga's comments on the acceptance of death in order to better undo it: "The fundamental intuition is that you cannot vanquish death if you do not constantly integrate it into life. To push it towards an 'after' or an 'over there' only serves to multiply its force. It is here and now, at the end of each breath, at the end of every desire, in each night's sleep."[153]

Like Ramprasad then, the great Bengali poet and fervent devotee of Kālī, Mā's disciple must demonstrate a complete abandon (*prapatti*) to Mā, so as to die to oneself to be reborn and thus to triumph over death. And if Mā represents an incarnation of the goddess Kālī to some, she can similarly be identified with *mṛtyu*, the feminine form of death created by *Brahma*,[154] reinforcing this reflection on death initiated by the cult of relics.

In the context of feminine sanctity, this meditation on death inherent to the cult of relics is also supported by the idea of a return to the maternal womb, into the uterus of the Mother, *regressus ad uterum*, a return that symbolizes death in the profane universe and rebirth in the sacred sphere.[155] This symbolic regression to the embryonic state, in which time is abolished, is related to the devotee's death to the profane condition but also to his mystic regeneration.[156] This recalls Otto Rank's comments that conceive of death as a metaphor for the return to the maternal matrix.[157] The aspiration towards the return to the mother, the security of the maternal breast, then, is not different from that of death.

If the cult of relics inevitably implies a form of meditation on life and death, it can also be reinforced by the idea of a return to the mother, to the primordial unity. Mā's relics reveal themselves then to be directly connected to the idea of fording and of passage, in assuming the role of one who passes not only between birth and death, but also between the world of humans and the world of God, for as Ysé Tardan-Masquelier notes, "the sacred passes through the feminine that is the necessary mediator of its presence in the world of men."[158]

This idea of an inter-uterine return associated with the personified aspect of the feminine principle, here being Mā, is also accentuated by the analogy between the womb and the tomb. The tomb symbolizes the womb, as Filippi explains here:

The womb is considered as the tomb of the preceding state. Analogously, the tomb ritually used for deceased children is considered a womb in which the dead person is collocated as an embryo in view of a successive rebirth. The burial of a corpse is really a *regressus ad uterum*, an idea widely attested to even among the ancient Western civilizations.[159]

To meditate on the sage's tomb can then be related to a symbolic return into the Mother's womb. In the same context, David Wulff speaks of the tomb as an impersonal symbol of the Mother archetype under its "negative" aspect:

> The mother archetype is commonly personified, especially as the mother goddess or the Great Mother. She may also appear, however, in a variety of impersonal forms, including city or country, earth, the woods, a tree, the moon, or the cow, on the positive side, and a witch, dragon, the grave, or deep water, on the negative.[160]

Consequently, along with the *sanctum sanctorum* of the temple, the saint of saints, the inner enclosure of Mā's temple where her tomb is located can be designated under the Sanskrit name of *garbha-grha*, which means the motherly chamber.[161] Access to Mā's tomb, to the *garbha-grha* symbolizes the idea of death and rebirth, *kālakirtimukha*, in the sense that the devotee dies in the exterior world to be reborn to himself.

By virtue of their direct relationship with death, relics (and notably the relics of female gurus) come to represent aids in accessing the sacred. In serving as a support to a reflection on death and immortality, relics in this sense constitute true tools of meditation on the nature of the Real. The sacred cannot then be disassociated from relics, as the direct link that relics maintain with the concepts of presence, power, and death reveals. Because of their nature, relics are placed then as turning points for reaching toward this other reality, the sacred.

While ideas of the sacred and miracles, of power and danger, of agency and presence attached to the cult of relics are found across various religious traditions, Hinduism, however, brings new elements, in addition to the practice of burial, the rituals, and so on. Considering the distinctive stance of Hinduism vis-à-vis death and pollution, the Hindu cult of relics essentially shows the ability of a religious tradition to overthrow its established norms for achieving its spiritual aims. The ideas of impurity, of the cadaver as a contaminant, disappear in favor of an embodied religion rooted in the tantric concepts of flesh, as in Tantra the body is seen as a vehicle to liberation. There is then a reversal of *bhakti* to *śaktism*,[162] something no less surprising in the case of Mā Ānandamayī as she comes from Bengal, the land of *śaktism*. Here, pure and impure, sacred and profane are ultimately identified, in what Eliade refers as a *coincidencia oppositorum* to attain the experience of spiritual liberation.

This strength to overthrow *dharma*, to transmute the impure into pure, brings us to the centrality of the master (*guru*) in Hinduism, whose dead body is venerated despite rules of purity related to death. The *guru* is well beyond concepts, beyond opposites, and must look after his disciple both in life and death. The relics are, in this respect, a support, a reminder of the eternal bond between the *guru* and his or her disciple, celebrating the victory of the master over death.

This tantric perspective obviously brings us to the importance of the sacred feminine. Through the veneration of Mā Ānandamayī and female religious figures who are associated with male gurus (Sarada Devi, The Mother, Krishnabai), the Divine Feminine or *Śakti* is honored in all its splendor and relics of female spiritual figures become a site of worship dedicated to the goddess, a kind of *śakti pīṭha*. As such, the Hindu cult of relics brings to other religious traditions a new perspective on the feminine and the sacred, including its terrifying and "deadly" aspect. As the cult of relics of female gurus situates itself at its inception, new developments in the future should be considered with the proliferation of women gurus in India and elsewhere in the world.

3

Death of the Guru

The Departure of the Guru

I turn now to an exploration of the guru's death so as to better understand the development of the postmortem cult in its entirety. The guru's
death, generally perceived as a "departure" and not a definitive end, can be
regarded from two different angles: death from the guru's perspective and
death from the disciples' point of view. In Mā's case, I refer here especially
to the account of the Austrian disciple, Atmananda, but also to the work
of Professor Bithika Mukerji, another close disciple and Mā's principal
biographer. Finally, I also turn to the subject of the posthumous future of
the guru on more subtle levels.

What is Death for the Guru?

It is important to examine the meaning of death for the guru so as to
better grasp all of the aspects related to his or her death, such as the
behavioral aspect (funeral rites, formal grief, etc.), the affective aspect
(the emotional shock of devotees) and the cognitive aspect (meaning of
the guru's death among their devotees). I will thus turn to Mā's view of
death, for this view impacts the disciple's attitude when the guru does
depart as well as the devotee's will to "sustain" the cult of the guru after
his or her death.

   Like other great beings, Mā always affirmed the death of death: "There
is only one real life, namely, the one that is dedicated to the search of
God; only one real death, which is the death of death. After that there is
no more birth and no more death."[1] For Mā, there is in fact no death in
and of itself, for as she says, "appearance, continuity and disappearance

FIGURE 3.1 Mā Ānandamayī: "You may want to banish this body from your mind. But this body won't leave you for a single day—it does not and never will leave your thought. Whoever has once been drawn to love this body will never succeed in wiping out its impression even despite hundreds of attempts. This body rests and shall remain in [her] memory for all times."

Source: Picture belonging to the collection of photographer Sadanand; now in the possession of Neeta Mehta, also called Swami Nityānanda.

occur simultaneously in one place."[2] Thus does she emphasize the vanity of mourning the departure of a person.[3] "To be distressed by the death of someone close to you, to regret the loss of human joys that they brought us is bad both for the person who is dead as well as the person who is alive."[4] This reminds us of the words of saint Ramdas, who also affirms the illusion of death and the insignificance of mourning: "To lament the death of someone close is pure ignorance,"[5] or the discourse of Ramana Maharshi: "They say that I am dying but I am not going away. Where could I go? I am here."[6] Mā's way of perceiving death can also be seen in many different events of her life, where, on the announcement of someone's loss, even someone close, she would demonstrate no sorrow. She thus demonstrated no sign of sadness, no change in her *bhāva* (state of being) on Bholanāth's death, who was both her husband and her first disciple.

Following the announcement of hundreds of deaths at the *Kumbhamelā* of 1954, which Mā attended, she similarly showed an attitude of detachment at the news, declaring the absence of death and of duality and repeating that all of this only represented a manifestation of *līlā*, or divine game. Other incidents also reveal Mā's attitude towards death, as is the case of this woman who came to Mā's side following the sudden death of her daughter:

> "My husband died. I could handle that, for I had my only daughter. An amazing and talented child. At 12 years old she died. And that I couldn't understand..." Ma spoke to her at length and concluded in telling her: "I am your child." The same woman reappeared months later, serene. She confided to us: "When Ma told me: I am your child, her voice was that of my daughter... my emotion was indescribable. Since then, my heart began to heal."[7]

In the same way, Mā said this:

> Every sorrow stems from the fact that one holds oneself to be apart from God. With Him all pain disappears. Your thoughts should turn towards Him. Remind yourself that your daughter is now with Him. The more you think about God, the more you will be close to her. If you need to shed tears, let them be destined to Him.

Mā would often cry at the news of someone's death, not, as she said, for the loss of the person, but to relieve him or her who suffered from this loss, as this episode reveals:

> One day a lady who had lost her son fell at Her feet wailing bitterly. Mother began to weep and shed tears so profusely with the bereaved mother, held close in Her embrace, that the latter came to forget all her woes; on the other hand she showed so much concern at Mother's weeping that she exclaimed, "Mother, be comforted, I shall not weep over my son's death anymore."[8]

And so, Mā did not generally demonstrate any regret or grief following the death of an individual, and, if she did on rare occasions, it was to discourage the grieving person from their sorrow, as for her, dying was simply changing clothes. Mā's view of death returns us to the central position of *Advaita*, of non-duality:

> On the level where there is only one Self, there is no question of birth and death. Who is born? Who dies? All is one Self. The same mind that identifies itself with the body can be turned towards the Eternal and then the pain the body experiences will be a matter of indifference. Since the body is bound to get hurt at times, there must be suffering as long as one is identified with it. This world oscillates endlessly between happiness and sorrow; there can be no security, no stability here. These are to be found in God alone. How can there be both, the world and the One? On the way there seem to be two, God and the world, but when the goal has been reached, there is only One.[9]

These words, spoken by Mā on the existence of the Self and the true absence of death resonate with the *Bhagavadgītā* (II, 19–20), which also affirms the indestructibility of the One, of the Self, which is eternal: "He is never born, nor does he die at any time, nor having (once) come to be will he again cease to be. He is unborn, eternal, permanent and primeval. He is not slain when the body is slain."[10] In the same spirit, a stanza of the *Kaṭha Upaniṣad* (2, 18) also affirms this: "The intelligent Self is neither born nor does It die. It did not originate from anything, nor did anything originate from It. It is birthless, eternal, undecaying, and ancient." Mā's discourse on the true absence of death reflects thus Hindu sacred writings but also the thought of other Hindu masters, like Swami Vivekananda: "There is no change whatsoever in the soul—Infinite, Absolute, Eternal, Knowledge, Bliss, and Existence. Neither can there be birth or death for the soul. Dying, and being born, reincarnation, and going to heaven, cannot be for the soul. These are different appearances, different mirages, different dreams."[11]

During many pilgrimages throughout India, in this *Advaitic* spirit Mā affirmed her continual presence to devotees who bewailed her departure:

> Why do you say I am going away? I am your little child and am always with you. Remember this, that I am always with you. I am not asking you to hold your breath, to sit up straight, to purify yourselves. Just as you are, I am with you. A child stays with his parents, whatever they may be like.[12]

And to those who wished to leave her presence for one reason or another, she also said, "You may want to banish this body from your mind. But this body won't leave you for a single day—it does not and never will leave your thought. Whoever has once been drawn to love this body will never succeed in wiping out its impression even despite hundreds of attempts. This body rest and shall remain in [her] memory for all times."[13] This reminds us of the case of Atmananda, a Western disciple who, on numerous occasions, wanted to leave Mā due to the difficulty of living as an untouchable in Mā's ashrams, but who then remembered some of Mā's words: "You are mine wherever you go" and "Where will you go? There is no place where I am not."[14] These statements thus reveal Mā's thought regarding her omnipresence beyond time and space, beyond death (*mṛtyu*) and birth (*jāti*). Mā declared throughout her life that she was always there, "like the atma, I will always be with you," thus showing that her body is in itself as illusory as death: "Here, there is no question of a body. You see a body, but there is no body."[15] Mā's discourse is thus marked by a profound kinship with the sacred texts of the Hindu tradition, as this *Upaniṣad* reveals: "He goes from death to death, who sees difference, as it were, in It. It should be realised in one form only, (for) It is unknowable and eternal. The Self is taintless, beyond the (subtle) ether, birthless, infinite and constant."[16]

For the guru, then, death is nothing but a simple passage, that of the river Vaitarni, also called the "Styx of the Hindus" by Herbert,[17] and thus implies no fundamental change, as Coomaraswamy specifies:

> Death in *samādhi* changes nothing essential. Of their condition thereafter little more can be said than that they are. They are certainly not annihilated, for not only is the annihilation of anything real a metaphysical impossibility, but it is explicit that "Never have I not been, or hast thou not been, or ever shall not be" [*Bhagavadgītā*, II, 12].[18]

This view of death is reflected in the designation of death in the Hindu tradition. Hindus say that the deceased "left his body" (*sharīr chorā*) or "abandoned his body," so as to emphasize that the death of the body does not at all mean death itself, the physical shell representing nothing more than an old dress that is taken off, not be confused with the eternal and indestructible Self.[19] Regarding this matter, Ramana Maharshi also said: "The body is like a banana-leaf on which all kinds of delicious food have been served. After we have eaten the food from it do we take the leaf and preserve it? Do we not throw it away now that it has served its purpose?"[20]

FIGURE 3.2 Room at the ashram of Kishenpur (Dehra Dun, north of Delhi), where Mā left her body on August 27, 1982.

Source: Picture taken by French photographer Caroline Abitbol.

Thus, the guru's death is considered to be a "departure" and not a definitive death. In this respect, there are a certain number of terms and of expressions to evoke this departure. Hinduism generally designates the death of a great sage with the term *mahāsamādhi*,[21] or great *samādhi*, the *samādhi*, or state of total illumination, representing in Eliade a sort of inner ecstasy, when the realized being completes a "withdrawal from time" and joins this "eternal present," this *"nunc stans."*[22] The death of a great spiritual being is also termed *dehānta*, "the end of the body," to differentiate from the term *mṛtyu*, which represents a more global term that points to the belief that even subtle bodies disappear. We should state as well that in certain cases, the sage has reached the "attainment of *mukti*," that is to say liberation. In Mā Ānandamayī's case, it would nevertheless be inadequate to use the latter expression in discussing her death, if one takes into account her followers' belief that she was born liberated, having thus nothing to obtain and nothing to attain. Similarly, one can sometimes call the death of the sage as *brahmalina*, which means the disappearance of the sainted being into Brahman, or *antardhana*, that is to say invisibility, for as the Hindu tradition holds, realized beings have followed an alchemical process (*rasayāna*) on their path toward supreme liberation and can dissolve directly into the ether (*ākāṣa*) after their death. This tradition of the body's dissolution, well known in the Tibetan tradition (body of light), is also found among many great sages of the Hindu tradition. It's notably the case with Kabir or Dattatreya, but also with more contemporary saints like Swami Rama. Again, in speaking of death, one speaks of absorption. Ramana Maharshi also employed this term in speaking of his mother's departure after he had led her to the final liberation:

> When someone said that Mother had passed away, Bhagavan corrected, "No, she did not pass away, she was absorbed"; "There is no pollution. Let us now eat." There was no need for any purificatory rites as Mother has not died but has become universal. The unique power and filial love of Bhagavan alone made Mother's liberation possible.[23]

There are also many vernacular terms to designate the death of an enlightened being. Among them, one often finds the expressions of *liṅgaikya*, which means "union with the *liṅgam*," as well as the expression *śivaikya* "absorption in Śiva,"[24] as with the *Vīraśaivas*. It is important to note that this view of death as a departure and not as an end is found among Mā's Indian devotees as well as her Western followers. If we sometimes used the word "tomb" in the course of an interview, the devotees would consistently return to the use of the term "*samādhi*" to emphasize the absence of death in the case of Mā. Upon mentioning the subject of this study, a French follower also suggested that the expression of postmortem cult should be replaced by a totally new and innovative expression, a "*postcorpus* cult!"

Decline of the Guru's Body

Toward the end of the year 1981, Mā's health began to deteriorate and she ate nothing but an extremely reduced liquid diet. The worsening of her state of health finally resulted in her death on August 27, 1982, a Friday, like Jesus', some remarked. Mā left her body in her small room in her ashram at Kishenpur, near Dehra Dun, around eight o'clock at night, repeating the mantra of Śiva in its inverse form, *Śivāya Namah*. A funeral procession from

Dehra Dun to Kankhal took place and Mā's body was placed in the *samādhi* of the Kankhal ashram on the 29th of the same month, after many disciples, including the Prime Minister Indira Gandhi, had taken the last *darśana* of Mā. Atmananda describes the last weeks preceding Mā's departure:

> Mâ was not well and barely spoke. She was always lying down, as she couldn't sit up. There was always someone around her. We often massaged her because she was growing cold. But she took no medication. The doctor who cared for her practiced Ayurvedic medicine. He could come to Mâ's quarters day and night, I think and, from then on, Mataji no longer vomited. But her respiration became more and more difficult. It was very painful![25]

Despite her weak state of health, Mā nevertheless continued to give daily *darśana* to the residents of the ashram as well as a weekly *darśana* to those outside the ashram:

> For us, during the last weeks, the *darshan* took place once a day. But for the people outside, it wasn't more than once a week. Mâ had decided that it would be Sunday, at six o'clock, and for only a half an hour. Many people came. They practiced *pranam* and thus could see her a little. It was very good. Mâ didn't disappear brutally. No! She got us used to this idea, little by little.[26]

In fact it seems that, for her followers, Mā had wished to accustom them gradually to her departure, as Atmananda implies:

> When we went to see her during the *darshan*, she was often turned to the other side and we could only see her back. As she wasn't eating and was weakening, a side had become...how should I say...Well, she couldn't hold herself up on this side. We could only rarely see her face. But I think that she wanted that for us, to accustom ourselves to not seeing her anymore.[27]

Thus, this slow death was desired by Mā, as the devotees interviewed on the subject also think: "She let herself die. It took time. She was sick for a longtime, as if she wanted people to get used to it, to see that she was losing her light." Atmananda describes her progressive retreat from this light, from this radiance: "She laughed! She was full of joy. But at the end, no longer. It was over. She was always radiant. So radiant. She radiated. Always. Always. But the last weeks, there was no longer this radiance."[28]

Despite the decline in Mā's radiance, it seems that for some of her devotees, her presence was more and more strongly felt as her departure approached, as Atmananda affirms:

> You know, when I sat before her room, I noticed and felt that, the more her body weakened, the more her presence became strong, more and more strong. I was standing above her and I felt this immense presence. I didn't want to look at her anymore because her face wasn't like it was before. But her Presence was so strong, so strong.[29]

These comments reflect the assertions of the *Skandapurāṇa*, which hold that the liberated being, on the hour of death, transmits to disciples a part of his beneficial energy (*punya*).[30] Regarding this transmission of energy from Mā at her death, some of Mā's devotees believe that she had transferred her energy to her closest disciples, as the testimony of this follower demonstrates: "I think Mā has transferred lots of energy in Swami Bhaskarānanda. Asking Swamiji is like asking Mā. If Mā wants to tell me something, she will tell through Swamiji."

This reminds us of the belief that holds that Ramakrishna had transmitted, just before leaving his body, his *śakti* to his disciple Narendra, who would later be known under the name Swami Vivekananda:

> Towards the very end, only two weeks before he died, Ramakrishna called Narendra to his side and in an ecstatic state transmitted his mystical energies into him. Afterwards, Narendra claims, his body was so charged that, when he asked another disciple to touch it, the disciple received a palpable shock (*Śriśrirāmakrṣnakathāmṛta* 3.274.20).[31]

There is thus this belief, among some of Mā's followers, that she had passed some of her energy to her closest disciples.

Mā's death, far from being a sudden and rapid event, was on the contrary slow and progressive. If we refer to the theory of three phases (preliminary, liminary, postliminary) of which Van Gennep speaks in this work on the concept of the rite of passage,[32] the period preceding

FIGURE 3.3 Swami Bhaskarānanda, early disciple of Mā Ānandamayī, was for many years the secretary general of her organization. He passed away in April 2010.

Source: Photograph by Orianne Aymard.

Mā's death corresponds to Van Gennep's initial phase, the preliminary period in which the dying person is separated from the living. According to Mā's disciples, this phase was intentionally prolonged by Mā so as to better prepare her followers for her departure. Similarly, Mā's death itself can be linked to Van Gennep's liminary phase and corresponds to the dying saint's entry into death. This marginal phase is accompanied by a reinforcement of the *communitas* ties among the community's members, with a great solidarity and brotherhood being felt among them.

Although there is no real mention of miraculous events surrounding Mā's death, either in her followers' comments or in writings on Mā, some followers share anecdotes that reveal that there was a mysterious aura around Mā's death. Among these anecdotes, one follower speaks of a shooting star that was glimpsed above Mount Arunachala at the time of Mā's death.[33] In this mysterious atmosphere, some cite the example of the health crisis of Mother Krishnabai, which was said to have been directly related to Mā's departure, as this Western man, a long-time devotee of Mā, explained:

> Swami Ramdas's grandson said to us a story. Mother Krishnabai was very sick the night when Mā passed away, in '82. Then, she said something: "One half of my strength has left this world. Tomorrow, you will come to know." The next day, they could read in the newspapers the departure of Mā Ānandamayī....They are trying to teach us that we shouldn't individualize views of the divine into a specific shape or form.

Among her followers, there are thus a number of beliefs surrounding Mā's death. These beliefs attribute the slowness of her death to Mā herself, as in preparing her followers, she had voluntarily slowed her departure; they also evoke the transmission of Mā's energy to her close disciples. These beliefs do not however seem to result in miraculous signs around Mā's departure.

Reception of the Guru's Death

Mā's death was received in different ways by her devotees, ranging from a serene acceptance to despair. The general tendency however was for devotees to experience great sadness. For many, Mā's departure was inconceivable and the announcement of her death was seen as a tragedy, a true shock, as this Indian male devotee tells:

> On the 16th of August, I met her. Mā was very sick. I asked Mā, "please recover from this." I thought that she would recover because she said "accha" [good]. I thought that she was giving me the word that she wouldn't go. So, I couldn't think that Mā could pass away. And when I learnt the news of her departure from the paper, I couldn't believe it. So, I cried, I cried and cried, like a child. I never cried like that for anybody else.

It seems that very few of her disciples were ready to face her departure, as the following comments show:

> We were not prepared for that.
> I don't think anyone thought it was possible.
> We never contemplated this issue.

The attitude of disciples toward Mā's departure thus seems to correspond completely to the description Edgar Morin gives of reception of death:

> It's more the forever-new stupor that provokes the consciousness of the ineluctability of death. Everyone could state like Goethe that the death of someone close is always "incredible and paradoxical," "an impossibility that suddenly is changed in reality" (Eckermann); and this appears like an accident, a punishment, an error, an unreality...
>
> Naturally blind then to death, man is ceaselessly forced to relearn it. The trauma of death is precisely the eruption of real death, the consciousness of death, at the heart of this blindness.[34]

In this context, we are reminded of the attitude of the Mother of Pondicherry's disciples who, in the years following the death of Sri Aurobindo, did not think that she was also going to leave her body; or also of the behavior of Ramakrishna's disciples toward their master's death, behavior that resembles in many ways that of Mā's disciples shortly before she died:

> All he could do was pronounce that Ramakrishna's cancer was in fact incurable (JV[4], 144).[35] From his perspective, there was no hope. But the disciples continued to hope anyway, some of them going so far as to believe that the Master was actually feigning his illness for some hidden purpose. He would surely recover, they claimed, when that purpose was fulfilled. A suffering god was more than they could take. Denial seemed the best way out.[36]

Swami Vijayānanda, like others, preferred to deny Mā's death until its arrival:

> When I saw Mā for the last time, at Dehra Dun, she was lying down, very sick. You couldn't go into her room. Me, she called me. I entered into her room. I sat next to her. I looked at her. From a medical point of view, you could see that she was almost done. But, as I had known her for a long time, I knew that, sometimes, when she was sick, she seemed to be dying. And then, she would get up and walk away! We thought that she was going to do the same thing. When I left, I stayed a long time at the door, looking at her. Maybe a half hour or less, I don't know. You don't feel the time pass in these

things. She looked at me very intensely. In her look, she mentally transmitted, "Don't worry, everything is fine." That was the message that she sent to me. Me, I understood, everything was fine for her. When I returned to Kankhal, I said to people, don't worry, Mā will be there for the *Durgā pūjā*. And then, later, I learned that she was dead. Later, I interpreted, "For you, everything will be fine."

If many devotees did not envision the possibility of Mā's departure, others on the contrary had no illusions regarding her imminent death during the last weeks of her life, as Atmananda specifies:

> The last day, it was a very big celebration: Radha-ashtami, the day of Radha's birth. Do you know Radha? She was Krishna's wife. We had asked for advice from the appropriate people. Some astrologists had said that this day was very fatal. And one of them, known to be particularly skilled, had told us that if Mā could live beyond this day, she could remain on earth for several more years. But we realized that Mataji's state was only getting worse. It was then the 26th of August, 1982....We knew that she would not stay on earth. Personally, I believe that I was under no illusions. She had become so weak the last days, that those who cared for her had to work in pairs to turn her over. So it was so painful for me to see her like that. There was no longer this extraordinary radiance that had been there before.[37]

Followers went so far as to dream of Mā definitively leaving her body shortly before her *mahāsamādhi*. This is notably the case of this swami who sensed Mā's immediate departure with a revelatory dream:

> Two days before *mahāsamādhi*, I had a dream that Mā had left her body. Suddenly, I said "no, no Mā, you cannot go." I became emotional. Suddenly, Mā rose from her bed and came to me. I said, "Mā, you are leaving?" She said, "No, no, I am not leaving." I told her: "Who will answer my questions? Even if someone answers my questions, I will not believe. What will happen?" And she said, "Remember one thing. If a question comes in mind, it means that ego has come. It is only ego who raises the question." When I woke up, I lost my voice. I couldn't speak anymore. *Mauna* came naturally. After two days, I got the message that Mā has left her body. I had the last *darśana* in Kankhal.

And so, if some devotees did not expect Mā's *mahāsamādhi*, others "sensed" Mā's approaching departure.

Following Mā's departure, the whole of her community was plunged into complete pain. Although Mā had always affirmed that death must die and she had insisted her not having a body would never be an obstacle between herself and her devotees, her disciples had great trouble accepting her departure and experienced it as an incommensurable loss, as the following testimonies show:

> Losing Mā was losing everything.
> I openly cried in front of everybody. I thought I lost something.
> There is no word to express what I felt.
> We were all very upset. We took it for granted that she would always be there. You know, we didn't realize how valuable it was to have her around.
> It was a great shock for me, my family and all of my friends who were close to Mā. I was not accepting this.
> All the close devotees of Mā, all the ashram people, for the first few years were completely lost, though Mā had trained us definitely to find her within.

One of Mā's *brahmacārin*s, sent by her to Mount Kailash during the same period, even tried to end his life in learning of the news:

> When I learned of it, it was the greatest shock of my life. It was when I returned from the pilgrimage from Mount Kailash, we had just crossed the Chinese border and had entered into Indian territory, a soldier who escorted pilgrims told us the news. At the beginning, I couldn't believe it. The soldier said that it had been announced on the National Indian Radio the evening of August 27, 1982. It seemed to me that the sky had fallen on my head. My mind was paralyzed, in a state of shock. One thing that I remember, it's that I wanted to kill myself by jumping from a cliff in the mountains. One of the older monks of our ashram coming up behind me saw me and saved me from suicide.[38]

Shortly after, this same *brahmacārin* who wanted to put an end to his time on earth was designated *pūjāri* of the *samādhi*. During an interview conducted with him, now a swami, he described the difficulty of his position:

> Naturally, we were used to do *pūjā* when Mā was in her physical form.
> Mā was in front of you at that time when you did *pūjā*. And after that,
> you have just the *samādhi*, a platform. And you have to think that Mā is
> here, in the platform. So, it was very painful for me. Gradually, we had
> to think, at least, I cannot see Mā but Mā is there, her body is physically
> there, inside the stone. Then, gradually, it came up. I was feeling bad
> actually, but in any case, we had to do that and I had to do that.

This feeling of loss felt by Mā's community returns us, several decades earlier, to the departure of Sarada Devi, also perceived by her disciples as the Divine Mother:

> Her *mahāsamādhi* has cast a deep gloom over the hearts of all devo-
> tees, and has created a void which will never be filled, until perhaps
> it pleases the Divine Mother to incarnate Herself once more. To all
> those who personally knew her, the loss is terrible, and their only
> consolation is in the thought that such personages are born once in
> an age through the Divine Will, that they play their part, and that
> when the play is over they are once more gathered to the Primal
> Source whence they came. And we know that wherever else such
> souls may be, the devotees' heart is their best throne, and we are to
> seek there for the Presence of the Holy Mother.[39]

Mā's departure thus led to profound disturbance within her community, and particularly for those who were in regular physical contact with
her. As she had become the object of intense "sociality" for them, Mā's
departure provoked a sort of social crisis.[40] For most devotees, her death
even paralleled a parental loss. One of the disciples interviewed said to
us that "Mā was like an extended family." This recalls the comments of
André Rousseau, who states that death is initially the death of someone
that occupies a place in relationships of kinship.[41]

Although difficult to accept, Mā's death was nevertheless perceived by
some as a sort of liberation for her, as this Western man tells:

> I felt that there was such a deterioration of the situation in the ash-
> ram. I felt that no one was doing what Mā wanted them to do. This

kind of dark energy had descended on the ashram, with Mā's illness. Mā was withdrawing. A lot of weird things were going on in the ashram. People were freaking out. They were worrying about what was going to happen to them when Mā is no longer. There were a lot of power struggles, who is going to control which ashram. There were a lot of petty stupid things going on. I thought it was so bad, but in a way, I thought that maybe, it's better for Mā to leave, that she has to do with this impossible situation. I don't know if you can say it's better for Mā to leave. It's a kind of release in a way. I was aware that everything was falling apart around her. That was how I saw it. I think other people saw it that way too. You could feel this energy, this sort of dark energy that was sort of closing everything down, including Mā. Many many things I could say, which I won't say about all that.

The state of Mā's health seriously deteriorating, disciples also saw in her departure a way to abbreviate her physical suffering, although others affirm that she did not suffer. This view of Mā's death as a liberation has much in common with what devotees of Mother Krishnabai say about her departure. Because Mother Krishnabai was believed by some of her devotees to have been the object of black magic, as some of her disciples say, the announcement of her death was perceived by them as a way to free her from the load burdening her.

It also seems that Mā's departure was easier to endure for foreigners, as this German woman disciple says:

I was in Basel, the Swiss town, at that time, together with my husband. I got this message on the phone. This was very peculiar. It didn't feel real, but I think that for Western devotees who had not been in such close physical contact, it was different anyhow. We had to accept more distance compared to Indian devotees. So, we were trained in a way [laughs] to focus more on the inner quality. So, this inner quality was not lost. And the funny thing was, it was as if she didn't give so much time to mourn or to be sad. She gave us so much spiritual work, in terms of making new books about her, making *satsaṅgas*. We couldn't be too sad because she gave us so much work which was centred on her. The work came from inward and outward, by itself. We couldn't be sad. She was quite alive after that because we did this intense work for her.

Another Western disciple also told us of his reaction to the announcement of Mā's death: "It didn't seem to have much effect on me; I was being weaned off of personal contact. And also I was in England. So, that was not too bad."

Some Westerners also evoke the rules of purity and the language barrier as an aid in detaching themselves from Mā's physical form; "The lack of comprehension of Hindi and of Bengali, the distance and the rules of separation imposed by Mā's entourage were factors that helped me not to attach myself to her body."[42] In addition to the language barrier, the brahminical rules and the distance between India and the West, the Vedantic orientation (meaning non-dualism) of Western devotees certainly also contributed to a greater detachment on the part of Western devotees regarding Mā's departure. Western devotees are generally much more inclined, in their relationship with Mā, to a type of Vedantic relationship, that is to say less personal and less emotional than in *bhakti*. While being profound, this Vedantic relationship is accompanied by a less personal attachment toward the form of the master. This could also explain why Mā's death was easier to accept for her foreign devotees. It thus seems that there were different attitudes among Westerners and Indians toward Mā's death. This contrast of attitudes between Indian and Western devotees is also noted in the comments of a foreign woman interviewed at Kankhal:

> I was amazed when I heard that some swamis got depressed, even Atmananda was wondering, "Didn't they understand the nature of Mā that they keep so much to the physical body?" No, it was not like this.... Here (in India), people, they grow up in such a devotional, religious atmosphere; it is in your blood. In the West, you have sometimes so many adverse circumstances that you had to develop a real strength to keep up this devotion. At the same time, it's grace. If you have succeeded to keep up this bound even in these material circumstances, there is this strength that cannot be lost so easily.

Thus, the difference in reaction to Mā's death between Westerners and Indians was principally due to several factors. Because of these different factors, it was less difficult for Westerners to accept Mā's departure.

Regarding new devotees, Mā's departure was nowhere near as impactful as it was to the followers who knew her, as this Western woman says: "It doesn't mean as much as I am sure it means to all of the people who were with her." Having always known Mā in a "disincarnated" form, new followers do not feel a lack, a nostalgia toward her physical presence, even if some of them confess that they would have liked to meet her, as this French woman says:

> I cannot say that I miss her physical presence, as I didn't know her in her physical body. My relationship with her was always of this nature, that is to say, with her *samādhi* or in her ashrams. I haven't had a relationship with her; I am not like some people. Me, I don't have such a relationship as I didn't know her.... On the other hand, I essentially think that it was a great opportunity to meet her in her body, I would have liked it, and I think that only could have helped my practice.

Other new disciples also affirm that they are content not to have known Mā during this period, as they would have had a hard time dealing with her physical suffering and her later departure. An early disciple of Mā's, a Western man, admits that devotees who never met Mā during her lifetime are almost fortunate to have avoided the pain of her departure:

> Not only me but most of the people around here were really depressed for the first four or five years. Everybody there was depressed. So, undoubtedly, on that level, new devotees are almost lucky. In my case, I went to the very highest level and just fell off the cliff all together. And then, I had to climb, back up again.

Thus, the period following Mā's death can be compared to Van Gennep's postliminal period, which consists of a period of reincorporating the deceased person into his or her new status.[43] What must be done is to accept the new state of the saint, as Hertz describes:

> We cannot bring ourselves to consider the deceased as dead straight away: he is too much part of our substance, we have to put too much of ourselves into him, and participation in the same social life create ties which are not to be severed in one day. The "factual evidence" is assailed by a contrary flood of memories and images, of desires and hopes. The evidence imposes itself gradually and it is not until the end of this prolonged conflict that we give in and believe in the separation as something real.[44]

Although it is now more than thirty years after Mā's departure, some devotees still feel this loss like a painful event, as the following excerpts from an Indian male disciple, an early devotee of Mā's, emphasize:

> I don't want to think of this event. I always avoid this. We do not like that. Mā is always alive for me, all the time. For *bhakta*, her departure is not a good experience. Yes, we lost a great personality...I am not saying that the body is not important. It is very important for us, very important. Even yesterday, I didn't want to watch the movie of Mā.

It nevertheless seems that Mā's devotees are finally no longer going through the grieving process and have integrated Mā into her new status as deceased, as demonstrated by the comments of this swami, who during a retreat evoked his reconciliation with Mā's departure:

> That took me a long time, but now, I feel that I love Mā in the same way as I did when she was in her physical form. If I claim to love Mā I should love her words too. She said: 'Remember, wherever you may be, at every instant, this body is constantly watching you; but you don't want to see me, should I be there?' This statement of Mā brought me great consolation and I was penetrated with the conviction that Mā was always with me.[45]

This conviction is shared by the group of devotees who today affirm the absence of death in Mā:

> To me, there is no death of Mā, there is no end.
> Mā never left us.
> She was never lost to us.
> I don't feel that she had gone from this world. She is everywhere. Mā is here and there. She is watching everything, every aspect of our life. Mā is always there. Even when I leave this world, Mā will be with me. And definitely, she will be with me in another birth.

To conclude, there appears a clear distinction between Mā's view of death, a vision tinged with detachment, or even a certain indifference, and the manner in which her devotees reacted to her death. The grief and the despair present in the devotee's reaction starkly contrasts with Mā's position regarding death, a position that one could summarize in the simple affirmation that death must die. The despondency and great sadness of her followers seem in reality to be clearly tied to the almost symbiotic relationship they had with Mā, perceived above all as their mother. Despite Mā's non-dual teaching of the true absence of death and of the unity of all things, the large majority of followers experienced Mā's death as a true rupture, an irreparable loss, or even as an abandonment. As we have seen, it nevertheless seems that her death was more easily accepted by Westerners, as compared to Indians. As a whole, the new devotees seem to be untouched by an evocation of Mā's death, thus revealing a major distinction between them and early devotees, and notably Indians.

Toward a Return of the Guru?

Here we examine the beliefs attached to the postmortem identity of the guru, in this case Mā Ānandamayī. For the majority of disciples, Mā is perceived to be totally merged with everything, as this swami states: "After Her death, She has become all pervading" or again as this devotee emphasizes on the subject of saints: "They are really enlightened people, and after leaving their body, their aura is there. The believer has to feel it, has to believe it. Mā is there in our mind, in your heart." Others speak of "omnipresence" to describe Mā's posthumous identity, but also of the "ocean of existence," of "*satcitānanda*." Swami Vijayānanda, for his part, evokes an identification of Mā with the divine: "Now that Mā left her physical body, She is completely identified with the divine power,"[46] and also speaks of an "omnipresent consciousness" to describe Mā's state since her departure: "I am in contact with Mā as an omnipresent and formless Consciousness, but not as possessing a subtle body."[47]

If Mā is totally identifiable with the One, some nevertheless accept the vestige of a subtle embodiment of hers. A new male disciple from France speaks of his own experience regarding this topic:

> From a dual point of view, from a samsaric point of view, I think that it's over, there is nothing left, there is no more future. From an ethereal point of view, or from what we call the body of Glory, it is evident that the person who sent me the *śaktipāta*, it was something of a formal nature. There was a presence. I think that there is a

divine body, a body of light that was individualized. I think that the word body of light is the most appropriate.

Mā would also speak of the existence of this subtle body after death:

The ethereal body also perishes. All the same supermen (mahāpuruśa) quite often assume special forms. This is due to their inherent disposition. Yet, some even after assuming a particular form can remain immersed in Supreme Being. Again, the simultaneous existence in a formlessness is also possible.[48]

Many female gurus interviewed by June McDaniel affirm that they maintain a relationship with their deceased guru who lives on in a subtle body.[49] This returns us to the revelations of the Holy Mother Sarada Devi, who affirms that her husband, Ramakrishna, had announced to her, in a posthumous apparition, that he would continue to live on in a subtle body for three centuries: "When the Master passed away, I also wanted to go. He appeared before me and said: 'No, you must remain here. There are many things to be done.' He said that he would live for three hundred years in a subtle body, in the hearts of devotees."[50] If Mā is today identifiable with the Everything, with the formless, some of her devotees hold that she can also assume a certain form, such as a subtle body.

It is also interesting to consider the question of Mā's return to earth. Three approaches are possible here. Mā might return first as an individual soul (jīva) in a human body. In the Hindu tradition, there is the belief that the master's personal soul can reincarnate itself after his or her death in another body. Regarding this point, we could mention the case of Sathya Sai Baba, who affirmed that he was the reincarnation of the very popular Shirdi Sai Baba[51] and who announced his future incarnation in the body of a certain Prem Sai.[52] There is also the case of Meher Baba who is believed to have incarnated in different times.[53] Ramakrishna also predicted that he would be again incarnated in the body of a monk a hundred years after his death. If Mā, for her part, always affirmed that she had no past lives and that she would have no future ones, some nonetheless believe in the possibility of a new incarnation of her in future, as this Indian woman, an early devotee of Mā's states: "Mā has to come back. Whether she will come back in this form or not, that I am not sure, but she will come back. She as a 'she' or 'he,' whatever." Others, on the contrary, do not believe in a possible return of Mā on earth, whether it be in the body that they knew or in another body: "It's over. We don't want to backtrack. No, no, no, she will not return." "Personal Mā" can no longer return: "I feel that there were certain souls which were destined to come in contact with her. Now, it's finished."

Second, we can consider the possibility of Mā's return from an impersonal perspective, a return as avatar. Pierre Feuga, author of many books on the Hindu tradition, and notably on the Tantric tradition, sheds some light on this subject:

> If we sometimes affirm that some of these realized sages "return" or redescend onto earth in the form of an avatâra, by that we don't mean a return of the individual soul, as these sages, strictly speaking, no longer have that. It's much more an impersonal principle that is cyclically manifested, for a determined mission, each time that the spiritual consciousness of humanity is obscured.[54]

Thus, there is the possibility as a spiritual principle and not as a particular soul.[55] Some devotees evoke the possibility of a return of this spiritual principle that we here call "Mā," as this Western man, a new devotee of Mā's:

> I think that 'that' will not even be the same person, as in the way that we represent her. It's impossible. For me, it's impossible that she would return in the same form, but she could return in other forms. Yes, why not, the divine in the past was manifested in many forms, Kṛṣṇa, Jesus. She can return. It's the divine, it's not physically Mā. The Divine can be manifested when it wants.

Swami Vijayānanda, for his part, also affirmed that it is possible that the divine principle, which he defines as an "omnipresent mass of Consciousness–Bliss," could reincarnate itself in a body to reply to a call:

> Mā says that she came among us because that was a call that had attracted her to our plane. We suppose that a group of spiritually developed people who had an intense devotion for the feminine aspect of the Divine had launched this call; but in fact, where did she come from? It should be understood that these things cannot be conceived through the mental. However, schematically, we can say that there exists an omnipresent mass of Consciousness–Bliss that

has neither form nor place but which is the support and the base of everything that exists. Modern learned people approach it when they speak of the "unified field" which is at the base of all atoms, molecules, etc....Thus, what appeared to us in the physical form of Mā was in a way a sort of crystallization of this Omnipresent, crystallization allowing us to enter more easily into contact with the Supreme. The physical form was removed from our visual field, but the Supreme of which She was the crystallization is always the same. He (or She) will always respond to our call if we make it with sufficiently intense devotion. Of course, the majority of people cannot enter into contact with the Formless and need a visual support. For those who have been touched by the splendor of the divine apparition of Mā Ānandamayī (even if they have not personally met her), a photo, the reading of a book or a meditation before her *samādhi* (tomb) can produce the intensity necessary for the call to be effective.[56]

As another disciple, a new Indian female devotee, says, this call has to be intense enough for the spiritual principle to take form: "That depends on the present devotees, whether they are dedicated, whether they are devoted. If they call with that perfection, then, she can come over again. But that depends on us, on the next generation, on the devotees." The intensity of the devotee's call seems thus to constitute a determining factor in the descent of the divine principle on the earth, as this other commentary from an early Indian male devotee demonstrates:

The question, "Mā, why have you come?", the answer was that the collective prayers manifested themselves in this body, that's what she is. I believe that if you have a desire that is so strong, it will take a physical form. I am convinced but I have no basis. I cannot prove it. If you think very, very strongly about something, this takes form.

In addition, others think that this spiritual principle, formerly incarnated in the person of Mā is to be found today in Amma, the female guru that many perceive today as the Divine Mother, as Mā Ānandamayī was. A new Indian male devotee explains: "I think that Mā has already come back in a body. I read the biography of Ammachi and there are many similar things between Mā and Ammachi." Regarding the question of whether

Mā could return to earth, another male devotee, an early disciple from England, similarly responded: "Why, is she not already back? Have you met Ammachi? I think that she is not an ordinary person." Although this is clearly not possible (at least on the personal mode, i.e. the return of an individual soul) given that Amma was born in 1953, when Mā was 57 years old, we observe some noteworthy similarities in the personalities of these two female gurus, especially in relation to their perceived incarnation as Kālī and their authority independent of affiliation to a religious order.[57]

Finally, the question of Mā's potential return to earth can also be addressed using the principles of *Advaita Vedānta*. For some devotees, among whom the *Advaitic* conception takes precedence, one cannot speak of coming or of a return of Mā on earth since she has always been there, as the following two commentaries show: "Mā is there. There is no question of coming back on earth" or also: "Mā is with me. So, I don't think of Mā coming down in another body." These are similar to the comments of Mā who, regarding avatars, says this: "There is no coming and no going. All are Atma. There is no question of an Avatar descending into the world. He is always there, but takes shape for the 'bhakta'."[58]

On the same subject, Mā also made the following comments:

> In the realm of phenomena there is much differentiation, such as "above" and "below". But There—what is and what is not? Where ascent and descent can still be spoken of, what will you call such a state? Must you not admit that various directions have remained? If you speak of descent and ascent, it is implied that there must be a place to descend to; but whither can He descend? To Himself alone of course. Ascending and descending are one and the same thing, and He who ascends, is He who descends, and the acts of ascending and descending are also He. Although *you* speak of Divine Descent (*Avatāran), He* surely does not become divided. You see fire flare up here and there, but this does not affect its unity: fire as fire is eternal. This is how you should under-stand it. No simile is ever complete. He who descends, whence He descends, and whither—all are one. There is nothing whatsoever outside of THAT. A QUESTION: *If the Real remains what it is, what then do ascent and descent mean?* MATAJI: What you say represents a particular viewpoint of the world. Where the Ultimate, the Supreme is, the question you ask is impossible. On a certain plane, descent and ascent exist. It is you who say: "God descends".

On the other hand, there is no such thing as descent: where He is, there He remains, and all possibilities are contained in Him. To understand (A play upon words: *bhoja* means 'to understand', as well as 'burden'.) intellectually—which means to 'stand under', in other words, to be burdened by mental conceptions—prevents one from grasping the Truth.[59]

Thus, the question of "descent" or of "coming" at a certain level is not asked. The words of this new disciple, an English woman, dovetail nicely with Mā's comments:

I think it's a bit irrelevant. It doesn't matter. I mean whatever. She (Mā) could or she couldn't. There is that thing that whenever there is a need, then, an incarnation will come. But I just don't feel that she actually has gone anywhere. That's the problem. I think that she is still around. I don't know about her being manifested. I only know about her in an unmanifested state. As far as I feel, she is here all the time. So, the question doesn't seem important to me.

There are then three manners of envisioning Mā's return to earth, according to whether one perceives Mā from a personal or impersonal point of view, or if one places her on the plane of non-duality. These diverse opinions on the question nevertheless remain limited for some who perceive in this line of questioning nothing but an intellectual exercise: "It is very difficult to say. We have no basis of saying. Basically, it's only an intellectual exercise. It won't serve any purpose. It doesn't matter." And for some followers, it is not possible to respond to this question. One cannot make predictions about beings like Mā: "A spirit like Mā, or like Shivananda, we cannot predict anything about them."

If the diversity of beliefs tied to Mā's posthumous identity are revealing of the absence of a dogmatic authority in the Hindu tradition, above all it shows us that the question of a posthumous future for Mā does not seem to constitute an "issue" for the people currently in charge of her cult.

Death of the Guru to the Devotee

If Mā was that which her devotees say she was, that is to say an incarnation of the divinity on earth (avatar), a being that has exceeded death, a being bestowed with superhuman powers, capable of miraculous healing, why did she leave? Far from being specific to Mā, this question generally arises among disciples following the death of their spiritual master. Alexandra David-Neel notes this incomprehension stemming from the death of a Hindu master:

> Common traditions want the great yogis to be inaccessible to sick-ness. These eminent individuals leave our world at the moment they choose, without physical deterioration: they do not succumb to an involuntary problem. Now, Sri Aurobindo suffered from a renal problem that resulted in a fatal uremia attack. The famous yogi Ramakrishna is dead from cancer of the throat and another guru, that I will mention later, died from cancer in his arm. These are the facts that bother the convictions of some Indians (it would be more precise to say some Hindus, as Buddhists have never maintained the idea that spiritual perfection rendered the saint unsusceptible to physical ills). The Buddha died from sickness (probably dysen-tery) at the age of 81.[60]

This question tied to the death of the master has also been present in the mind of some of Mā's devotees, as this excerpt of an interview with a new male disciple from France reveals:

> At the beginning, I asked myself this question, which led to me doubting in my *sādhanā*. Why did she leave? If she's an avatar, why did she die like everyone else? In addition, she died at a time when there was much less spiritual presence outside, that's what Madou said, that it was somber, it was sad. She turned her head away to die.

And so, it seems important to examine the meaning of the guru's depar-ture in the eyes of her devotees, for, Mā's posthumous representation and her cult after her death depends in some ways on the interpretation of her death by her followers.

Powers of the Guru over Death

Before addressing the possible meanings of the guru's departure, it is nec-essary to describe the powers over death recognized in the guru, so as to better understand what motivated the guru to cast off his or her mortal coil. For, if the guru controls death, why did he or she leave?

Gurus are generally recognized as possessing certain supernatural powers (*siddhis*) over life and death. One of their most notable powers is to predict their own death.[61] Shirdi Sai Baba is said to have predicted his death and to have even envisioned the site of his future tomb. Other great sages, feeling their death approaching, have also decided to initiate their postmortem cult. This is notably the case of Jnanananda of Tirukovilur, the guru of Father Henri le Saux, who, on his last birthday, blessed his statue, around which today his followers gather. Concerning Mā Ānandamayī, certain signs led some disciples to believe that Mā already knew the hour and exact location of her death. Indicating a tree that used to occupy the place of her tomb, she had said to one of her disciples at Kankhal: "One day, this body will lie there."[62]

Gurus are also said to be able to choose the moment they leave their body, as may have been the case with Swami Vivekananda, who voluntarily left his body while meditating, or also with Sri Aurobindo whose death is described by the Mother: "He told me that the world was not ready (that He told me). He told me that He was leaving deliberately because it was 'necessary.' "[63] We could also cite the case of a lesser known sage, Tyagara, who apparently foresaw his last day on earth[64] or that of the young Marathi poet saint, Jnaneshwar, still venerated at his *samādhi* at Alandi, near Pune.[65] He is said to have decided the moment of his own death and to have sat in his tomb in the lotus position in leaving his body. It is interesting to note that some moments are more favorable than others for leaving the body.[66] Swami Purushatamananda, a hermit living next to Rishikesh, in the cave of Vasiṣṭa on the banks of the Ganges, left his body in 1961 on the day of *Mahāśivarātri*, the great day of Śiva, the archetypal God of death.[67] The saint Thevar, whose *samādhi* is found in Tamil Nadu, not far from Madurai, died on his birthday, a revealing sign for some of the sanctity of the figure.[68] And so, sages are often renowned for seeing and even controlling their own death.

Regarding Mā Ānandamayī, nothing in writing would indicate that Mā had deliberately decided on the hour of her own death. However, for devotees, it would not be surprising if Mā had herself decided the exact moment of her departure. Mā would have been able to prolong her life if she had wanted to, according to her disciples. One is reminded of the years 1939 and 1940, during which Mā had developed a generalized cancer and surely would have died, had she not healed herself in a single night.[69]

There are many situations in which Mā was extremely sick and, from a day to the next, she would recuperate instantaneously, leaving doctors in complete incomprehension:

> Her diseases discouraged all doctors. Their diagnoses were con-
> stantly questioned due to symptoms that from day to day were con-
> tradictory. She recovered her health in a dazzling way. Her pulse
> from one moment to another would accelerate and then be barely
> perceptible. Her temperature varied considerably. No doctor dared
> to prescribe her medicine (whether they were allopathic, homeo-
> pathic or ayurvedic). The rare times when it was tried, the sickness
> only became worse. She said: "Diseases are beings like you. I do not
> send you away when you come to me. Why would I make an excep-
> tion with them? This is also His game."[70]

Thus, according to her disciples, Mā had control over her own death. Some masters, and notably those in the *Siddha* tradition,[71] were also said to have the power of being immortal.[72] This explains the names given to some masters like Babaji, who is often called the eternal guru or the eternal Baba who appears at certain times, in particular during *Kumbhamelā*. One of Mā's disciples also confided in us that she had hoped to meet him at *Kumbhamelā* in the 1970s, and that she instead met Mā for the first time. Regarding physical immortality, Mā also affirmed this:

> One method is to increase the duration of one man's life by tak-
> ing a period from another's. Then there is also a method by which
> the prolongation of a man's span of life can be effected without
> deducting the period from someone else's life. Yogis who are able
> to use their powers in this way do exist; where the power to create
> is at the Yogi's command, it obviously is beyond natural laws. . . . In
> the supreme state everything is possible as well as impossible. To
> say "this or that has never happened" is merely to speak from the
> worldly point of view. If the body has to be retained in one and the
> same state, this too can be done and is being done.[73]

However, there is no mention among disciples of a physically immortal Mā who appears on certain occasions, although disciples testify to having had posthumous visions of Mā in flesh and blood.

If everything is possible in the supreme state, as Mā specifies, it is not unusual to hear of this return from death to life among great spiritual beings.[74] According to the yogi Yogananda, an enlightened master has the ability to return a body to life, that is to say, to reanimate his own corpse.[75] The most famous case concerns Shirdi Sai Baba whose body is said to have returned to life three days after his death in 1886, an event that incidentally initiated the spreading of the Shirdi mission.[76] We should specify that this phenomenon of the reanimation of a corpse is something common in the yogic circles in India. Ramatirtha is said to have met many monks in the Himalayas capable of plunging themselves in a state of apparent death over periods of six months.[77] And so, these phenomena of natural reanimation, to distinguish them from symbolic death, such as the voyage of shamans in the world of the dead, is also found in these charismatic personages called saints. Some *siddhas* are also known for their power to bring the dead back to life, like Siddha Hadi, from the Dom cast, those who cremate bodies, who is said to have brought life back to these corpses by touching their feet.[78] In Mā's case, there are testimonies of her having reanimated individual bodies considered to be dead. Mā herself never announced an eventual return of this type.

Thus the gurus are generally recognized, in the Hindu tradition, as beings who have control over death, and notably over their own death. For disciples, there is no doubt that Mā had complete mastery over death, as different situations in which she accomplished the impossible reveal; that is to say she vanquished physical death, as our previous examples have demonstrated. But if this belief in Mā's supernatural powers over death validates her charisma and reinforces her sanctity, Mā's death itself challenges these beliefs. It seems necessary then to turn to devotees' view of this death. How do followers justify the departure of an enlightened being who had control over death?

Natural Death and the Call to the Formless

Asked about the reasons for Mā's death, disciples give a number of explanations. The first and most common is in relation to Mā's desire to follow the natural course of things and to not call on her power (*siddhi*) to prolong her life on earth, as the following commentaries of different devotees emphasize:

> I felt that Mā just allowed the normal way of things to happen to her physical body.
> All the saints do not want to break the natural rules.

That would go against the spirit of all of nature. Nature is created by her.
Though Mā had control over her body, she had those powers, this is nature, each one has to go when time comes, and that, it happens naturally.

Despite her superhuman capacities, Mā's disciples hold that she did not wish to intervene in the natural process of death, as this Indian woman, an early devotee of Mā's, explains here:

She decided herself to go. She let her body become weak. You know, she got blind and they put glasses on her. She never paid attention to her body. Everybody had to look after it. She never did anything. She didn't need to do anything. She was beyond all that. She let her body grow old slowly. She didn't have to do that. She could be a young girl of sixteen, twenty, anytime. She could change her body. She could do anything, of course. They are God incarnated. They can come and go at will, do anything at will. But she let it be like a normal human being but she was not a normal human being. You know, they put glasses on her. Why would she need glasses? You see, things like that.

In the same context, another Indian female disciple, also an old devotee, adds:

She had a physical body. It had to go sometimes or the other. It is never permanent a physical body. On a physical plane, the maximum life span is 80/90. She fulfilled those rules. She said, ok, the body is 90, I am dropping it. It's as simple as that. It is not a question of old or young. She could have become younger but the limitations were 90 years. Saints don't do those things. They are not there for miracles. God doesn't do miracles. Miracles are done by these so called God men because they want fame, name and power. See, they get these *siddhis*. In *sādhanā*, you get all these powers. They show this, and show that. They want to attract more people. God doesn't need people. He never shows all these miracles to you. These people who have *siddhis*, they want to show you those things. Those things are very temporary things. They have to make lots of efforts to show you something which they call a miracle.

Thus, according to her disciples, Mā wanted to let nature take its course in not calling on her supernatural powers to escape from death. This perception of death is also found, in many ways, among Sri Aurobindo's disciples regarding their master's death:

> Then the "illness" took off at a gallop. He could have left his body, like Mother, by a simple act of will: draw the breath above and leave the garment behind. But He bore it right to the end, with all the suffering and even the medical tortures, "without resorting to miracles"—an honest work. "Why don't you use your force and cure yourself?" his secretary asked him. *No*, he replied in his tranquil, neutral, indisputable voice. They did not want to believe their ears, they were stunned. They repeated the question a second time: "But why?"— *Can't explain, you won't understand.* Mother later told us: *Each time I entered his room, I saw him pulling down the supramental light.*"[79]

Like Sri Aurobindo, Mā then accomplished this "honest work" by not resorting to miracles to prolong her life or to suppress the suffering of her body. Thus, for many devotees, Mā wished to leave according to the natural course of things, having simply no *kheyāla* or divine inspiration of healing, like Atmananda specifies:

> Many mahatmas, saints, sages came to see her. They said to her, 'Mā, you must rest. You aren't doing well. You have to get better'. But Mā invariably said 'Kheyâla nahim baï' (there is no Kheyâla). You know, Mataji often said that. In the end, she had decided to leave. She had Kheyâla.[80]

Regarding this topic, a Shankaracharya who had come to see Mā shortly before her death is said to have affirmed that even Mā Ānandamayī must endure the fruit of her karma. In response, Mā said: "In this body, there is no karma. That which you see here, it's 'the call of the formless.'" And so to explain Mā's departure, many devotees today still evoke the call of the non-manifested, the *avyakta*, and this absence of *kheyāla* to heal. This natural death also points to Mā's will to conform to tradition in dying before her younger brother. To avoid breaking traditional rules in dying after her young brother, twenty years her junior, she let herself die a few months before his death, as Mā's great-nephew explains:

> My grandfather got liver problems. He was not meant to live long. It cannot happen that my grandfather leaves before Mā, his sister,

because Mā was much older than him. There was a twenty year gap between Mā and my grandfather. It was like a mother/child relationship. He couldn't leave before Mā. That's again the tradition. So, Mā finally left her body eight months before him.

Thus, it appears that Mā's death was tied in a certain way to family destiny. Another event reinforces this hypothesis of a direct link between Mā's departure and the destiny of her biological family. At the moment of Mā's death, her young great-nephew, at that time seriously ill with typhoid and near death, was miraculously cured as he himself affirms:

During that period, I was very ill, I was suffering of typhoid. I was unconscious for 3 days. The doctor said that I won't survive. I was at the last stage. The same night Mā left her body and, around 8h45, I believe, I got consciousness back. My family believes that the last thing Mā did is to give me life. My parents believe this very strongly. The doctor couldn't believe what happened to me. Mā gave life to me.

If we cannot prove that Mā would have given her life for her great-nephew, it still appears that Mā's destiny is strictly tied to her blood family. And so, for some of her devotees, Mā's death occurred in a natural way, without a desire to counter nature's laws. This absence of *kheyāla* on Mā's part to continue her existence beyond its natural course would then correspond to Mā's will to observe tradition in dying before her younger brother, at the same time showing the existence of close familial ties between her and her close relatives.

Death of an Avatar

Some of Mā's disciples additionally frame her death as a departure that marks the end of her mission as avatar, that is to say the incarnation of divinity on earth, as this French woman, a new disciple, thinks:

I think that she came to accomplish something, a sort of mission, and notably to put the Vedic texts back into practice, as in India, we were coming out of colonialism, and so Hindus were not at all proud of their traditions or their practices. And that's a way to explain why she was born into a family of brahmins. It was then very important to put the Vedic texts, the texts of Shankaracharya, back into the public mind. Maybe, at the end, she was asked to do things that she had no desire to do and she did not come here for that. And so she left. She surely had less desire, I don't know how to say, to extend the system of ashrams and all that... She came to reestablish the *dharma*, as with all avatars.... I think, at any given moment, she had done what she came here to do, and she was very tired at the end, because, although she was an avatar, you neverthe-less live in a physical body. I think that she did what she had to do. She wanted to leave for a while, finally, that's what her disciples say, but she stayed for some who asked her to stay.

This reminds us of what Ramakrishna, on developing throat cancer, said shortly before dying: "I've gone through this suffering because I fear the abundant tears that you will shed when I leave you. But if you tell me 'Enough with suffering—let your body leave,' then I will withdraw."[81] In the same way, Mā is said to have stayed longer in her body for a few of her disciples who asked her to stay. And so like other avatars, Mā's dis-ciples say that she was destined to leave this terrestrial world, as this new Indian male disciple also expresses: "Even Lord Rāma, Lord Kṛṣṇa, they have come for certain periods. It is the same with Mother. But nothing was impossible for her. If she wanted, she could have lived longer. She must have thought that this is the right time to go." Her divine game, her *līlā* was over, as others say: "Her *līlā* was finished."

If Mā, as an avatar, had to leave at the end of her mission, some devo-tees nevertheless thought that she was going to live to be 125 years old like Kṛṣṇa. This was notably the belief of the doctor who came to see Mā on August 27, 1982, a few hours before she died. Regarding this matter, Atmananda relates this:

When this lady [the doctor] told me, after having seen Mâ, that she found her to be well, I was stupefied. "But that's not possible!" I said, "She seems to be doing so poorly!" "Not at all," she responded, "the Mother is doing well now." She told me this because she was totally persuaded that Mâ was going to live to 125 years old.... A lot of peo-ple shared this conviction. Sri Krishna had lived to 125 years, many of Mâ's followers wanted to believe that it would be the same for her. As for me, I continued to say to the doctor: "I think all the same that Mataji's health is such that it is difficult for me to believe that she's doing well."[82]

Ramakrishna apparently believed that he would disappear following the recognition of his divinity, of his status as an avatar:

> One of the most striking aspects of these final days was Ramakrishna's belief that he would disappear in death as soon as it became known that he was an incarnation of God. As soon as the secret of who he really was got out, the secret would have to be concealed again. Accordingly, many times he was heard to say, "When many people regard this a god and show faith and devotion, it will immediately disappear" (*Śriśrirāmakṛṣṇalīlāprasaṅga* 5.11.5).[83]

No one in Mā's community however seems to have held this belief. For some of her devotees, Mā's death could thus be considered as the final chapter of her mission as avatar. In this sense, the death of the avatar, of the Supreme Being, voluntarily comes to pass in order to awaken her disciple's consciousness to the true nature of existence. This sentiment of separation and of loss so characteristic of Hindu *Bhakti* could have been desired by Mā in a certain way, in order to reinforce the mystical call in the devotee, as this swami specifies:

> When she left, it just broke our heart. It was so horrible. But that was to awake our self and make us realise we long for Mā. We couldn't long for an abstract idea of God, even for our soul, because we were too dead inside. But then, we became attached to Mā. And when she left, we'll be longing for her. Mā was saying that's the very path. She would say the longing for God is itself the path for God. The aspiration for God is itself a path. That's the most important thing. If you have the aspiration, everything will open up. If you have the desire for God, it will be fulfilled. It was a divine longing. Mā was God. There is no question about it. We are longing for not a person. There was this being that we felt so close to who was God. It woke up divine longing. So, this crying, this misery was wonderful. It snapped people out from this world and out of their complaisance, out of their sleep, the sleep of death. Mā brought joy and she brought intentional sorrow to realise we are in foreign

land. We shouldn't get so comfortable, thinking that this is home, everything is fun. This is not. We'll be broken up by death, the death of our body, not the death of the soul.

Mā spoke of this type of separation as a road to accessing the Divine: "The meaning of separation, let it be dissolved by devotion, or burn it with knowledge.... So, you shall know your Self."[84] This returns us to the experience of Ramakrishna, who, after having lost his father, had seen his mystical aspirations reinforced by aspects of a depression.[85] As Clément and Kakar specify: "The mystical path is also then a way to diminish the agony of separation, to weaken the pain of loss, to reduce the sadness of grief."[86] And so, for some, like Atmananda, Mā's departure occurred in some ways in order to help them overcome their attachment to the world of appearances and to awaken them to their true nature which is the Self:

> Perfection clothes itself with a physical body like Anandamayee Ma's in order to seduce us mortals whose perceptions are based on the physical senses. It uses physical attraction to captivate the senses and lure them into the fire of truth. Once we have become irrevocably attached to Her, She disappears and becomes 'That'— our innermost Self—the ONE.[87]

Death of the Guru as Absence of Devotion

One of the other reasons given by disciples to justify Mā's death is the lack of devotees' obedience toward Mā, as obedience plays a central role in the master/disciple relationship. It seems that Mā repeated many times that people no longer needed her as they didn't perform that which she recommended they do, as this early and very close disciple of Mā's says: "People were not obeying Her." Mā's departure is justified by a number of devotees as Mā's response to the indifference of her disciples before the instructions she had given them, as this Indian male follower, a new devotee, explains:

> There was a period in Mā's life when she used to eat on one grain of rice. Since she is God, she could have delivered herself. But to be very frank with you, at that time, there were discrepancies going on in ashram. There were some elements in the ashram, who were

not listening to Mā's instructions. So, at one point of time, Mā felt that the time has come to leave her body to make them realise that enough is enough.

Others also evoke the failure of disciples as one of Mā's reasons for leaving this world: "Mā wished to leave this world. Mā on her own left her body. Mā was very upset. Mā had many disciples. She gave so much to them. But on the spiritual side, they failed. Mā told me so many times, 'there is not a single person eligible to be *sādhu.*'" This is close to the Mother of Pondicherry's comments concerning Sri Aurobindo's departure: "*The lack of the earth's receptivity and the behavior of Sri Aurobindo's disciples are largely responsible for what happened to his body.*" Satprem adds that "this was even more true of Mother's disciples. And She left."[88]

This reported lack of obedience among Mā's disciples can be linked to their lack of devotion and of purity. A number of disciples recall Mā's departure as due to this absence of fervor and of transparence among Mā's followers: "Maybe, we did mistakes in worshipping her, we were not enough devoted" or "maybe, we were not pure enough." For Mā, who was very sensitive to the vibrations of her environment, the absence of a pure and devotional spirit among her disciples would have contributed to her departure, as this *brahmacārini* explains:

Mā took this form and came down for us. And what did she say? "The body is there for you, play with it or throw it away. It's up to you how you want to treat this body." In her younger days, when the body was younger, people who came to Mā, came with a very pure *bhāva*, purity they had in their heart, devotion they had, sincerity they had. They were going to Mā because they loved Mā. They wanted to be with her. Those vibrations and that *bhāva* reflected on Mā. Mā was like a sponge. That sponge was absorbing whatever was thrown at her because the body was meant for us. We are the care takers of that body. We are taking care of that body with pure devotion and love. Towards the end of her life, people were sceptic. People came to criticize. People came with not a pure *bhāva*. Mā was still a sponge. So, the body was withdrawing. Mā never suffered... Mā say: "Do I say no to a disease that comes in my body? Do I say no to you people who enter the room? Why would I say no to people who are giving bad vibrations? Everybody is giving and this sponge is absorbing. I am not throwing anything. Whoever walks in with whatever problem, Mā has taken it, finished, that body has taken it."

Mā had essentially always affirmed that true nourishment lies in the attitude of the devotee, as Atmananda mentions here:

> Sometimes, Mataji told us, "I eat for you, because if I didn't, you wouldn't have *prasāda* and you would be very disappointed. It's why I eat a little. But my true food is your attitude. If you constantly think of God and lead a pure life, that is food!" She often told us that.[89]

As Mā had descended from a very sacred line through her ancestors, her body, for her disciples, could only be a totally pure body, as Atmananda also explains in the reconstruction of Mā's past:

> She was a unique and unparalleled incarnation of the Divinity.... Her ancestors, for many generations, had been very saintly, and lived like the rishis in a state of great purity. It seems that this was necessary to produce a body so extraordinary. By that, I want to say that, for this Divine Incarnation, the body can only arise from a line formed by numerous generations of pure and saintly beings. Her mother was a great saint. She never experienced, even from her childhood, the least feeling of anger. I feel that Mâ's relatives did not come to the world to undergo the consequences of their karma, but only to produce this particular body. Also, it seems that it was of an immaculate conception. Mâ said, 'My father was like a sannyâsin for some time before my birth.'[90] Mâ's body could not support gross vibrations. She always said, when in a state of *samâdhi* one noticed that her pulsations and her respiratory movements stopped: "If you want to keep this body, you must repeat the Name of God ceaselessly. It's your purity that nourishes me. This body has no need for ordinary food." That's why it was absolutely necessary for Mâ to be surrounded by people leading very strict lives. From whence came her segregation.[91]

To illustrate Mā's purity, her disciple Atmananda additionally refers to Sri Aurobindo. He would stay alone in his room for a number of years for this same reason, and only certain people had the right to come see him.

In the same spirit, Ramana Maharshi permanently inhabited the sacred location of the Tiruvanamalai (Arunachala) and no one was able to touch him. Atmananda also adds something interesting regarding Mā and her body: "I am convinced that her body could not have handled the materialist atmosphere of Europe or of America. She is everywhere, always, and you yourself feel her Presence. But Her Body had to be protected. Mā was also in good health at the time of '*Samyam Vratā*'[92] when three to five hundred people performed a *sâdhanâ*."[93] Thus, the lack of purity among Mā's disciples at the end of her life would explain, according to her followers, the reasons for her leaving.

This absence of purity touches upon Mā's disciples' comments regarding the excess of karma among devotees for Mā to eliminate. In the Hindu tradition, the guru is said to have the ability to burn away a part of his or her disciples' karma. In this context, diseases would constitute the "digestion phase" of this karma and death, a sign of the surplus of karma to eliminate, a surplus that would end in "engulfing" the master himself.[94] The case of Ramakrishna and his throat cancer speaks to this principle in explaining the master's death.[95] Similarly to other great beings, it is also said that Mā had this ability to neutralize the karma of her disciples.[96] Some interviews of Mā's disciples conducted by Lisa Hallstrom for her study on Mā's life in fact mention Mā's ability to eliminate the karma of her disciples.[97] Arnaud Desjardins gives the following explanation of this matter:

> In Christian language, Mā Ānandamayī was "born without sin". She came directly from within the Absolute. There is not a "soul" (*jiva*) that crossed the path of reincarnations, but a new soul, born immediately from God and which, always conscious that she and God were one, didn't need to wake up to her true nature. She neither knew the descending ladder of involution, nor the ascending ladder of evolution. She was born "virgin of all corruption", of all traces of ignorance and all limination. Hindus accept that, outside of individual karma, there exists also a karma of Humanity, Mā Ānandamayī was also free from that. It's this absence of all forms of karma which permitted her to take upon herself not the "sins of the world" but at least a large part of the sins of those who were close to her, of their karma. And that seems to be especially true during the nights when we celebrate the anniversary of her birth. That this perfect Consciousness accepted sharing our imperfections is a

thing I think of often when I observe Mā Ānandamayī. She opened
herself to influences she could have freed herself from and participates, for example, in our physical pains and in our maladies, so
that this will not always be the case.[98]

Mā essentially recognized the possibility of taking on the suffering of others, taking on their karma as the following comments from an unknown
disciple show:

> The sages can relieve the suffering of others. They can take onto
> themselves the suffering or even split them up among other people,
> so as to diminish the suffering of the unhappy. It is also possible for
> a sage, by their remarkable grace, to deliver someone from all suf-
> fering. The sage can bring the person to the Divine Life that is his
> true Self. But such cases are very rare. For suffering accomplishes
> the purification (But how, someone asks, to distribute suffering?
> That seems totally unjust). No, there is no bad in that. The sages
> redistribute these fragments of suffering among those who are
> happy to share them. (Why, someone asks, should I allow a sage to
> endure my suffering and to carry my cross?) Now this is well said.
> This is to speak like a disciple. It's better to handle your own suf-
> fering. But sometimes they can become too heavy for someone, so
> that all he desires is to know how to get rid of them. For me, this is
> done automatically. I've stated that this body becomes charged with
> the ills of others. Once, I went to see a sick person who suffered
> from dysentery. On returning, I was struck with the same illness.
> And that lasted twelve hours. Another time, this was the case with
> the fever of someone else. We thought that I was having an attack
> of malaria and they wanted to make me take medicine. I refused as
> I knew at what moment the fever would break, which it did.[99]

Mā's capacity to take on the suffering of others, and thus to destroy their
karma, is recognized among her disciples, so much so that her closest disciple, Didi, is said to have died wanting to relieve Mā from this adoption of
karma, as Atmananda says:

> Didi died at Varanasi. Mâ then said: "The suffering and sickness
> of Didi were not the consequences of a karma." So? What was the

meaning of all of this suffering? There is an explanation: Mâ often said that the suffering of men can be lessened if some accept shar- ing the weight. And Mâ would often take on a great part. We think that that's the reason Didi suffered so much. It's possible that to relieve and maybe save Mâ's physical life, she took onto herself a large part of this load.[100]

Atmananda again says this regarding Mā's ability to assume a portion of her disciple's karmic baggage:

Sometimes I feel that the Guru has to take some limitations on Himself in order to provide the circumstances that will eradicate the disciple's karma. It is we who make Her seem imperfect and then we doubt. But that one sentence She said: "*What I do, I do for myself*," cuts out all arguments. As long as we see the many, we can- not possibly judge Her who is the One.[101]

This is similar to the comments of Sarada Devi, who affirmed that she assumed a portion of her devotees' sins after she had awarded their ini- tiation: "The power of the teacher enters into the disciple, and the power of the disciple enters into the teacher. That is why, when I initiate and accept the sins of the disciples, I fall sick. It is extremely difficult to be a teacher."[102]

Thus, today, many disciples attribute Mā's departure to an "overdose" from the taking on of her devotees' karma, an overdose that is said to have finally led her to leave her body. An early and very close disciple of Mā's even goes so far as to compare Mā's death to Christ's, who died on the cross to save humanity, in this way returning us to the theology of the Redemption in Christianity. Thus, to some devotees, Mā's sickness and death are but evident signs of her extreme compassion.

For others however it is vain to search for reasons for Mā's departure. Conjecturing about the motivations that pushed Mā to leave her body is not considered worthy of a true disciple, a disciple who loves Mā, as this swami emphasizes:

This is not the question of a person who loves Mā. That shouldn't be. Why means doubt. If you put "why" in between you and your beloved, doubt comes. "Why" is the greatest hindrance to love.

There should not be "why". There is no "why" for Mā. There is
no "why" for Mā. Mā, it happened, that's all. Accept it. Mā is more
intelligent than I. She thought it better. I never asked why Mā sent
me away when she left her body. There is no why. She wanted it.
She wanted me to be away, I was away. There is no why, that's all.
There is no why in love. This question never happens to me, why
Mā did it. She is free. She enjoys absolute freedom. What she did, it
is for the better. So there is no why.

In addition, this questioning about Mā's departure originates in a false
path, as this French man, a new disciple, affirms:

> In fact, it was a misconception... in the beginning, there was a con-
> fusion between the spiritual Mā and the physical Mā. Thus, a dis-
> tinction needs to be made. For me, there is an eternal Mā, eternally
> present who can be represented by her body, her images, her teach-
> ings but who does not depend on this. These questions on Mā's
> departure, I asked them myself in the beginning. But after, these
> questions dissolved through making this distinction by experience.

Thus, different ways of conceiving of Mā's death can be witnessed
among her disciples: a natural death without any will on Mā's part to
call on her *siddhis* (power) to prolong her physical existence, a death tied
to the end of Mā's mission as avatar, a death provoked by the absence
of devotion among the devotees, and finally Mā's taking on an overdose
of karma. With the exception of rare individuals who refuse to question
Mā's death, or for whom it removes nothing of her eternal character,
among followers there is then a system of different beliefs that legitimize her death. This discursive machinery evolves in order to justify a
death that is at its foundation impossible and thus inconceivable, Mā
being for her followers an immortal being, located beyond death. From
the construction of this religious discourse emerges then a necessity on
the part of followers to give a meaning to a death that otherwise would
seem absurd.

It has been critical then to investigate the system of meaning constructed by Mā's devotees following her death, a death above all experienced mainly by many devotees, both as an irremediable loss and
as an unbearable separation. In this search for meaning thus appears

the need to legitimize Mā's death by the establishment of a discursive mechanism.

If Mā's death has not changed devotees' belief in her divinity, meaning that Mā is immortal, then, what is the impact of Mā's physical absence on her cult and what is exactly the devotees' experience of Mā's presence?

4

Presence of the Guru

Incarnation and Presence of the Guru

This chapter examines the importance of the guru's physical presence for his or her followers. What role does the incarnated presence of the guru play in his or her postmortem cult? To what extent is the guru's presence indispensable at the level of the master/disciple relationship? In this context I cite Mā's words on the importance of this incarnated presence, and then I examine the contrary arguments that support the nonessential character of the master's physicality. In this respect, the concept of inner guru becomes central.

The Living Guru, a Necessity?

The Hindu tradition, and notably the yogic tradition, generally recognizes the necessity of a living guru for the spiritual quest,[1] for as Charlotte Vaudeville specifies, "to be without a visible guru (*nirguru*) is not respectable in the Hindu tradition as a whole since it is nearly universally admitted that a man cannot achieve salvation without a proper initiation imparted by a human guru."[2] This insistence on the living guru's presence on the path of liberation principally values two things. As Bugault notes, an autodidact working by himself or herself, would risk becoming an "ego-didact."[3] Additionally, it would be extremely difficult for the spiritual seeker to surmount the fear associated with the loss of the ego in the final process to supreme liberation. The quest of the living guru represents then a central aspect of the Hindu tradition, as David Miller affirms:

The Hindu, in all ages, swears his allegiance to a living guru whom he has chosen, and at the death of that guru, he probably will turn

FIGURE 4.1 Mā Ānandamayī: "A state exists where the distinction between duality and non-duality has no place.... But where the Brahman is, the One-without-a-second, nothing else can possibly exist. You separate duality from non-duality because you are identified with the body."

Source: Picture belonging to the collection of the photographer Sadanand; now in the possession of Neeta Mehta, also called Swami Nityānanda.

to another one in order to fulfill the spiritual bond that he has lost. The quest for the living charismatic guru is an unending one that the Hindu usually undertakes alone.[4]

Thus, the presence of a living master should not be replaced by the sterile cult of statues and of relics. The Hindu tradition is generally suspicious of those who consider themselves disciples of a guru whom they've never met in the body. Meeting a guru in a dream, in meditation, or in photos could constitute the beginning of a relationship, but it is far from being considered complete, as Jacques Vigne notes on this subject: "You must be close to the guru for a period of time for work to be done: to polish an object, there must be contact between it and the sandpaper."[5] Similarly, Vigne adds this:

To follow a spiritual master does not consist, in my opinion, in joining an international organization and hanging a portrait of the leader on the wall. This would be to fall back into a pattern of classic religious functioning, where one centers his devotion on someone he has never seen but whom he tries to make present in his interior. A personal relationship with a spiritual master is almost indispensable, especially at the beginning.[6]

The sweet eyes of a statue or the smile of a photo should not then be substitutes for the force of a relationship with a living guru. Without a living guru, there would be no exchanges, no litmus tests, no confrontation with the guru, or proof of sacrifice. The human guru appears then central for any person who wants to progress on the path of spiritual liberation, as the *Muṇḍaka Upaniṣad* affirms: "Having well scrutinized the worlds build by rituals, a brāhmin should naturally grow indifferent to them; the not-made is never attained through made-up means; for the sake of attaining that (the not-made), let him go, fuel in hand, to a guru."[7] Mā was one of the rare exceptions to this rule, as the near majority of great spiritual masters in the Hindu tradition also themselves had a human guru. Regarding this subject, the saint Ramdas speaks of Ramana Maharshi, who, it is said, had attained liberation without the aid of a living guru: "They say that Râmana Maharshi must have had a guru in a past life. But Ramdas did not use this argument. Before Râmana left his house he had to have had contact with a great saint who lived not far from him. A simple contact must have had the spark spring forth that was within him and that made him progress towards the Realization."[8] Aurobindo is also said to have had the aid of a human guru in guiding him towards his first experience of *nirvāṇa*.

Although Mā never had a living guru, she nevertheless affirmed that the physical presence of a guru was necessary:

> By virtue of the *Guru's* power everything becomes possible; therefore seek a *Guru*. Meanwhile, since all names are His Name, all forms His Form, select one of them and keep it with you as your constant companion.... So long as you have not found a *Guru*, adhere to the name or form of Him that appeals to you most, and ceaselessly pray that He may reveal Himself to you as the *Sadguru*.[9]

The human guru seems particularly important for the spiritual seeker to help him focus on the interior, as Mā affirms: "The guru who is God or the incarnated Self, works on the interior....And so is he both on the exterior and the interior."[10] Swami Vijayānanda speaks, in this context, of an awakening of the inner guru with the help of the external guru and adds that the physical guru marks in some ways the change of direction from human love to a divine love.[11] The relationship of the disciple with the human guru would then be first of a personal sort, transforming progressively into a more impersonal relationship, more turned toward the Divine. This returns us to another of Swami Vijayānanda's commentaries concerning this personal and impersonal aspect of his relationship with Mā:

> Mā once told me, in private, "This body is an appearance, I am omnipresent," and so she is always there....There was a personal relationship, an affection. At first, it hurt me a lot that she left as there was no longer this personal relationship, of friendship, but from the point of view of a guru, that changed nothing. It's the personal relationship that changed...I think that she is always present. You know, from the moment that is omnipresent, she is in me. In the beginning, you need a physical form, but after, you identify with the omnipresent Divine. Mā's body is a crystallization, but I almost don't see Mā as a person now. I always, let it be understood, have a photo in my room that I speak with. In reality, I think she is omnipresent.

The presence of the spiritual master thus shows itself to be indispensable up to a certain point, for, as discussed below, this presence would not always be a necessity.

Toward a Disembodied Presence of the Guru

If the Hindu tradition generally affirms the necessity of a living guru, there are nevertheless some who assert that a human guru is not necessary. Concerning this, René Guénon speaks of the presence of a spiritual influence that would not necessarily require the presence of an individual to be transmitted.[12] The guru's role can then be played, in a certain way, by this disembodied influence, that is in reality the inner guru, this interiorized and non-materialized aspect of the exterior guru, who is not separated from the Self and who never dies.

This idea that the physical presence of the living guru is not essential is found in the discourse of some spiritual masters. Concerning this point, Jacques Vigne recounts an anecdote reflecting this thought:

> One day, visitors came to see his master [the master of Nani Mâ] and confided to him that they were very drawn to Ramana Maharshi, but that unfortunately, they couldn't take him as their guru because he was dead. Mastaram Baba burst out laughing and told them: "If you still believe that the guru is limited to the body! If you feel him, concentrate yourself completely on Ramana Maharshi, sit yourself before his photo, meditate day after day on his teaching and he will truly become your guru."[13]

This tendency to associate the guru with a physical body, with a person, is roundly rejected by Rivière, who condemns the attitude of Westerners who materialize everything and attach such a great importance to the physical body.[14]

If Mā advocated for the presence of a human guru on the spiritual path, she nevertheless did not exclude its absence, as she affirms here:

> There are seekers after Truth who are bent upon proceeding without a Guru because along their line of approach emphasis is laid on self-dependence and reliance on one's own effort. If one goes to the root of the matter it will be seen that in the case of a person who, prompted by intense aspiration, does sadhana relying on his own strength, the Supreme Being reveals Himself in a special way through the intensity of that self-exertion. This being so, is there any justification, from any point of view, for the raising of objections against such self-reliance? All that can be said or questioned in this respect lies within the confines of human thinking. Whereas there exists a state where everything is possible.
>
> Thus the line of approach that is through dependence on one's own strength and capacity is, like other approaches, but a functioning of the One Power. Without doubt the very power of the Guru can operate in a special way through this self-reliance, so that there will be no need for any outer teaching. While some aspirants may depend on outer teaching, why should not others be able to receive guidance from within without the aid of the spoken word? Why

should not this be possible since even the dense veil of human ignorance can be destroyed? In such cases the Guru's teaching has done its work from within.[15]

In addition, Mā considered it to be a sin to confine the guru to a human body, the guru being above all interior:

> Yes, *prema*, love for God, is a way. But what the world calls "love" is *moha* [delusion]. There is no true love between individuals. How can one get pure love from one who is not pure, who is limited by selfish egoicity and possessiveness? People come to me and say: "My love for such and such a person is real love, not worldly love." But they are deceiving themselves. *Moha* invariably is love for that which is mortal and therefore leads to death. If you can't get the object of your love, you want to kill it or die yourself. Whereas love for God, "prema" leads to the death of death, to Immortality. For this reason it is said that to regard the Guru as limited to a human body is a sin. The Guru has to be considered as God.
>
> I know a woman who wanted to commit suicide when her Guru died. I said to her: "Does a Guru die? Because he has left the body it does not mean that the Guru is dead. The Guru is everywhere and never leaves his disciple. If you want to take your life because he has passed away, it shows that you love him as a person, not as a Guru."[16]

This then explains the reason she did not like people to become too attached to her physical presence: "Only flies can follow this body everywhere it goes, but they do not receive illumination for all that."[17]

Although early devotees miss Mā's physical presence, it seems that today her physical presence is not indispensable in their *sādhanā*, as they do not feel the necessity to direct themselves to another master, another *sadguru*, as the following Indian woman, an early devotee of Mā's, affirms:

> Mā is my friend, philosopher, guide, everything. I am sitting on her lap. Why would I want anybody else? . . . I don't want to go to anyone. Mā is with me. Why should I go? When I have a pot of gold in my house, why should I run after bracelet, anything else? This is gold. This is *Bhagavan*. Don't you think that we are lucky? I think

FIGURE 4.2 Mā Ānandamayī: "Only flies can follow this body everywhere it goes, but they do not receive illumination for all that."

Source: Picture belonging to the collection of the photographer Sadanand; now in the possession of Neeta Mehta, also called Swami Nityānanda.

we are absolutely special and lucky to have met Mā. There is nothing else. What more do you want?

Another Indian woman, also an early disciple, also confirms that they do not feel the necessity, since Mā's departure, to turn toward another exterior master:

Once you have been to Mā, you don't need to go anywhere else. I don't have to go anywhere.... She is always there, she is always there. And now, you don't see anything else. Mā is everywhere, everywhere, I don't need to see anybody. She is everybody. She is

in anybody. Mā is the only thing I should think of. There is nothing
else in the world left.

Some evoke the role of memory, as does this swami who insists on the non-
necessity of meeting the master exteriorly in experiencing his presence:

> Does it matter whether you meet a person physically or not? It
> doesn't. Just think of your own life. I am giving you a silly example,
> don't mind. Most of the fans of the great heroes, they never had the
> chance to meet their heroes. Still, they feel a strong affinity. They
> can die for their heroes. If this is possible, why not with Mā? What
> do you need to establish a strong relation? And relation is not physi-
> cal. Relation is always mental. So, new devotees cannot say that they
> don't have memory of Mā, that they don't have interaction with Mā.
> Memory means, a simple definition, you interacted with an object
> of the world, it has its impressions in you, it remains always active
> and this is called memory. How can I say that I am still with Mā? Mā
> is not physically there. Now, their positions and my positions are
> same. I am missing Mā physically, but still I feel I am carrying Mā
> with me because I live with my memory, that's all. Memory never
> dies. It's the same, my position and their position.

This monk's comments are related to the idea that holds the memory to
constitute the basis of all approach to the true. And so, by the intermediary
of memory, Mā's physical absence would not constitute an obstacle to living in her presence, as this monk assures: "If I say that Mā is everywhere,
it is some theoretical thing but I am sure that Mā is within me, because
Mā's memories are in me and I am always carrying my memories. So long
as I live, Mā will be there."

New devotees would certainly have liked to have met Mā in her lifetime, but in general do not appear to accord an important place to her
physical presence, as this Western woman declares:

> I like being around saints. I like it very much. It feels good, I like
> the energy of Amma, for example, but it doesn't feel necessary
> because it's all happening inside anyway, that I have to more and
> more trust. I just have to trust that everything is leading me in
> the right way. It feels so much that everything is just happening

in the right way, what need do I have to look for anything? I don't feel that I have, since my whole experience has been that she [Mā] has come to me really when I needed it. Why would I start looking, for what, I don't know.

This Indian woman, a new disciple, affirms the same thing; she says she has never felt the desire or the necessity to speak to a living master, as for her, photos and statues of Mā are totally sufficient:

> I feel that she is here. Why should I go to some other place? I feel that she is above all. She is the one who has brought me in this world. She is the one who has given me this voice to sing. I feel that she is doing everything. Everything is predestined. But I never felt to visit any living saint. I am seeing her photograph, her statue, her idol. Why should I go somewhere else?

In the same line, some new disciples mention Mā's presence as an inner guru, declaring that they thus do not need a physically incarnated master, as this man from France says:

> I don't need that. I have Mā! There was a moment when I really needed a physical master for specific answers. I looked everywhere for a physical master. I went to see Amma, I went to see all of those people. Useless, it didn't help me at all. That brought me nothing. I saw Karunamayi, I helped her come to France. I saw Amma many times. It's Mā. It's this quality of grace that I found nowhere. Nowhere.... But I had many *upagurus* (secondary masters), but the master, the inner master, who is the *sadguru*, it's her. It's still her. I had Tibetan masters who led me to very fine states of consciousness. I am truly very grateful to them. They led me to states of consciousness that I hadn't suspected were possible. These are like *upagurus*, emanations from Mā, aids. Even if they knew to lead me to these states, I do not see the same quality of divinity, of grace that is Mā Ānandamayī, who is much more fulfilling. It's more holistic, it's a totality of spiritual functions, not only a state of consciousness. It's a totality. It's why I say that there is an extension, a surplus of the Mother's grace itself, for you feel that she is both specific and total.

Thus, the *sadguru*'s physical presence, which is nothing other than the inner master, does not reveal itself to be necessarily indispensable for the disciple, as he can always receive the concrete aid of living masters called secondary gurus or *upagurus*, complementing the action of the inner master. The testimony of this disciple then recalls in some ways that which the Hindu tradition says concerning *upaguru* and *sadguru*, for as Jean Herbert says, the Hindu tradition accepts the existence of secondary gurus who come to be associated with the work of the *sadguru*, the principal guru: "Beside the sadguru with whom the disciple forms these remarkably tight ties (*sadguru*), it is also possible, for the Hindu, to receive a complementary teaching from other people, who are then for him 'secondary' gurus (*upa-guru*)."[18] The inner guru, however, would have to be regularly reactivated, as this same disciple implies here:

> The inner guru, there are moments when it needs to be awoken and to be led to the surface of the person, of the presence, and that is done by Mā, either in invoking her, in looking at a photo of her, in entering her *samādhi*, in speaking with people who are in contact with her. This reactivates the inner guru who puts these functions back in place. To help my sick mother, I was not well, I was not centered, I needed to do something. Whereas normally, when I am well, it's there. Things do themselves, there's no need to make efforts. But as I am still far from being awoken, there are efforts to make. When I make efforts, that relaunches the presence, the inner guru. There is a flow that passes and that immediately arranges things, after working.

This awakening of the interior corresponds to what Jung calls the process of individuation that leads to the realization of the Self, of the *ātman*, which is neither individualizable nor incorporable. Vivekananda also speaks about "super-imposition" to define what recovers the Self, or also what prevents the inner guru from re-emerging. For Swami Vijayānanda, it is not a question of progression, but simply of pulling away the veil concealing the inner guru:

> The inner guru is the sadguru (or God) and there is no question of evolution but simply of progressively removing the impurities that deform the sadguru. The inner Guru guides you well in the spiritual life as in the material life.[19]

To be connected to Mā as an inner guru would be a return then to becoming conscious of the Self, of the Divine, as "God is above all and ultimately the *antaryāmin*, the inner master. He who resides in our own heart and who is none other than the very essence of our personality."[20]

And so, as shown throughout these interviews, the physical presence of the master, here being Mā, is not an absolute necessity for either early or new devotees. For a large portion of followers, Mā's physical absence is not an obstacle to the inner quest or to their relationship with Mā. Swami Kedarnath specifies that for him, Mā's physical absence does not represent a limitation, as Mā continues to perform her role as guru in innumerable forms:

> The knowledge of her real nature came to me with her first *darśana*. Though I was attracted to her body and wanted to see her again and again, still, I felt that Mā is not only this body. Mā is everything. So when she left her body, it made no difference, except that I couldn't ask her questions, get normal guidance. I didn't feel that she has left. The feeling was that she is still here, in every form. The relation was not broken. It is still there. Previously, I found her in a body, now, I find her in a big body. Everything is her manifestation. No questions are arousing whether she is here or not. Nothing like that. She is appearing in every form. She was in one form. Now, she is in innumerable forms.

Swami Bhaskarānanda also affirmed that Mā is not limited to a physical body and that she is always present: "She is not bound by the physical form of the body.... She is ever with me." These comments are probably close to Mā's own words, which maintain that the true guru would not "leave" the devotee, as the Guru is the Everything:

> There can be no question about it, no "taking" and no "leaving" as the Guru is the Self. If he is not, he may show you a path but he cannot take you right to your goal, to enlightenment, because he is not there himself. You may make someone your Guru and then leave him, but in this case I say you have never had a Guru. The true Guru cannot be left. He is the Guru by his nature and he naturally fulfills all that is lacking in the disciple. As the flower gives its fragrance naturally, so the Guru gives diksha—by sight or hearing or touch or teaching or mantra or even without any of these, just because he is

the Guru. The flower does not make an effort to give its fragrance, it does not say: "Come and smell me." It is there. Whoever comes near it will enjoy the scent. As ripe fruit falls from the tree and is picked up by man or eaten by the birds, so the Guru is all that is needed for those who are his own, whoever they may be.[21]

If some of Mā's devotees do not seem to be affected in their *sādhanā* by the physical absence of their spiritual master, many of them affirm the need to be in the company of living saints (*satsaṅga*), something also that Mā herself recommended. Retreats, celebrations, teachings, and others become then occasions for devotees to benefit from the presence of living saints. The coming of beings like these can be a sort of aid on the path that leads to liberation, as this new disciple, a French woman, affirms:

> I do not know who is liberated, enlightened but I sense that there are people who are much farther along than me on the path. To share something with these people, even to receive their teaching. It's like food. We need it. I am on the path, so anything that can help me, because alone, it's not possible.... To go see the family, to go see the older brothers of the family. It's my *spiritual big brother*. Me, I do not consider myself yet to be a spiritual adult [laughs]....I don't look for a physical guru, I mostly have what I need. It's the company.

Participating in these types of retreats, in other teachings not directly tied to Mā, for some devotees, does not seem to contradict their personal relationship with Mā, as the testimony of this Western woman, an early follower, demonstrates:

> Mā herself said that whatever brings you closer to God, you should use. So I always felt that Mā is the foundation and on that foundation, different rooms could be built. So I was always opened to other teachings when I felt that they were not contradicting Mā and that I could learn from them. In '99, for example, I met a Sufi teacher, Arina Treedy. She also had seen Mā three times. She said that she was completely without ego....Mā remained but certain aspects that I had to learn presented themselves in the form of teachings also....I always see Amma when she comes. But it's not always the same. Mā said, "Try to see your guru everywhere." So I concentrate on this. And so there is no contradiction. Mā for me is not

only this physical Mā, whom you can see on the photo, who lived from 1896 to 1982. I think that Maharishi Mahesh Yogi said that we are mistaken if we take the guru as a historical person or a form. The guru is actually a state of consciousness. We make this state of consciousness very small if we limit it to a certain age, to a certain country, or a certain form. So I focus on this divine consciousness.

The company of other sages, even outside of Mā's community, does not then seem to be an obstacle to the spiritual path of some devotees. If the company of saints (*satsaṅga*) is important for Mā's devotees, this nevertheless is reduced and limited by a number of them, who only swear by introspection in Mā, as this Indian man, an early devotee of Mā's does:

> The physical presence of the guru is very important. It is good if you can have it, but it is not absolutely necessary.... Mā always insisted on *satsaṅga*, the company of saints, but there are very few people who are helpful. So there is no need now. Everything is inside. There is nothing outside. Mā will give us everything.

All told, it seems that there is no absolute response concerning the necessity of having a human guru, as the following comments of Swami Vijayānanda reveal:

> If you really have intense faith, someone will appear to you in order to represent Mā, if a physical form is necessary. You know, the guru in reality is the supreme Divine. It's he who takes care of you. When you need a physical form, he sends it to you. There is only one sole guru, it's the supreme Divine. All other physical gurus, these are channels of the supreme Divine.

This is also what this early disciple, a Western woman, thinks:

> It's a difficult question. It cannot be generalized. I think, if you are very strong and very one pointed, you may not need a physical guru and if you have the deep faith that Mā will send you an answer in your life itself, maybe you don't need a guru. And if do you need, he or they will come. You will feel it. You won't feel it as opposed to Mā. I think it's not so much a matter of conscious choice, it's the inward focus or direction, what you want, and what you believe in.

Then, you do your steps, and you are opened, and life will give you what you need.

This question of the physical presence of a guru is thus complex and very relative, for, if the exterior rests on the interior, reciprocally, there is no interior without an exterior.

Although the Hindu tradition then generally affirms the necessity of a human guru on the path to liberation, it does not however seem to be always indispensable. Early devotees miss Mā's physical presence, but for them, it is not strictly speaking a necessity as the inner guru is at work. Beyond this discourse, there may be a desire on the part of early devotees to legitimize Mā's departure, to make of this death a favorable event, to give it meaning. And as one would expect, the position of new devotees regarding Mā's incarnated presence shows the nonessential character of the master's presence. For both types of devotees, however, the living presence of a secondary master (*upaguru*) and the company of sages (*satsaṅga*) seem to be of great importance to their *sādhanā*.

Disembodiment and Direct Access to the Absolute

The absence of Mā's body today seems to present a number of advantages in the eyes of devotees. One of them would first be a greater detachment from Mā's physical form, a detachment that renders interior contact with Mā and the Absolute easier, as this French woman, a new follower of Mā's, affirms:

> As I like abstraction, the fact that she is not humanly present disallows me from having a human relationship. I can enter into this relation with the absolute, precisely because she is not present.... Up until now, if I have an experience of God, it's not in seeing Mā, but knowing that she is the Divine Mother. But above all, I don't need to see her in a body for her to be the Divine Mother.... Me, I can only accept a conception of the ultimate ... I think that through this sort of disembodied cult, it is this desire to join an absolute.

It seems that the absence of Mā's body helps devotees to connect with their Inner Self, to concentrate themselves on the unmanifested aspect of the Divine, that is to say on the aspect of God not defined by qualities (*guṇa*), as this disciple also says: "It's easier to identify her with God, with the Divine, or to the Divine Mother, it's much easier, that, it's a clear advantage." This *nirguṇa bhakti*, that is to say, this devotion to God with-out qualities, seems then to suit a number of disciples, who see in this path of the formless a way to access Mā, the Divine, in this way joining the words of the *Muṇḍaka Upaniṣad*: "As flowing rivers, casting off their names and forms, disappear in the ocean, even so does the awakened one, freed from name and form, attain the effulgent *Puruṣa*, higher than the highest."[22] To know Mā during her lifetime would have essentially represented, for some, a diversion, as this English woman devotee states:

> I would probably just be following her around all the time and then she would need to push me away because I would not want to go. I have to work with where I am. It just seems right about how it is....At the beginning, of course, I did feel "oh I have not seen her in her body," but now, it doesn't mean anything really. I just think it might have been a distraction for me.

In this sense, many devotees today feel closer to Mā due to the very fact that they look more to her non-limited, unconfined aspect. Some go so far as affirming that it is now easier to communicate with Mā in the absence of the innumerable *brahmacārinis* (renunciants who had made a vow of celibacy) who surrounded Mā in her lifetime: "Mā has ways to communicate with me, much better than when she was alive. When she was alive, I couldn't get close to her. There were six circles of women around her. Being a man, I couldn't get close to her." The fact that many disciples feel closer to Mā since her departure returns us, in some ways, to what Milarepa, one of the greatest spiritual masters of Tibet from the eleventh and twelfth centuries had said in leaving the house of his master Marpa, to live alone in a cave: "Now, I can begin to finally be continually with my guru." Far from the physical pres-ence of his master and the agitations of life in a community, it was easier for Milarepa to focus on the presence of the master within himself. This is also what Nanima, a saint who lives on the banks of the Ganges, affirmed when she told us that she felt her guru to be much more present since his death, as she had ceased to limit her master to his physical body. There is an awak-ening of the inner guru in the devotee, an awakening that may have been facilitated by Mā's departure, as one of Mā's early disciples affirms:

> Over the years, I have come to experience Mā very differently. When I was with Mā, she was an external person to me, like I said, it was

wonderful, just divine. It was something totally unique. But still, she was something external to me in one sense, although I felt connected with her. But I found over the years, there is this saying that the guru grows inside of you through *dīkṣā*, and really this is true. I felt Mā being more and more awake inside of me, more present. Now I feel Mā as close as my own breath. Before, she was close, but it was always as an external object. Now, she is like in the self of my self. She grows in meditation. And now, I meditate a lot. This presence within you grows. Now, I feel that even in small matters, Mā is doing everything. I can't even give examples. Mā is just taking care of everything, to the minus details. The more I kind of give myself to her, the more she does it. It is not just a philosophical concept, it is really a reality. I think that all who were with Mā found it. We don't feel separated from Mā.

Although a number of devotees today claim to have easier and more direct contact with Mā since her departure, this opinion however is not shared by other devotees. Some, on the contrary, recognize that they have had more difficulty communicating with Mā since her *mahāsamādhi*. If it used to be possible to directly pose questions to Mā, today followers must make an inner effort in order to ask her anything: "Today, we have to focus on our heart to question Mā." Contact is more difficult, as Swami Vijayānanda specifies:

> When Mā was present in her physical body, she was not identified with this body but with the supreme Divine; now that this body is gone from our presence, the supreme Divine, that is to say the real Mā who is omnipresent, is always the same. But, from our point of view, contact is more difficult as you must be receptive and you must call out to her.[23]

Mā's departure is not then perceived by everyone as facilitating more direct access with Mā. In this context, some devotees speak to a less refined feeling in Mā's physical absence, recalling the comments of Frembgen concerning the postmortem cult of the Sufi saint Majzub Mama Ji Sarkar at his tomb. These comments confirm that knowing and experiencing the sage in his lifetime, feeling his personal magnetism, touching his body, exchanging visual and verbal contact with him, creates a quality of emotions and of presence difficult to feel in his physical absence.[24] Devotees, early or new, feel Mā's absence to a type of measurement of their *sādhanā*, as this disciple who never met Mā while she was alive expresses: "I think that it is a big disadvantage. I need to have a form.... I would have liked to meet her. It would have made a big difference."

Even though a number of devotees do not envisage Mā's postmortem cult as a way of more easily accessing her and the Absolute, on the whole, devotees perceive Mā's absence as a more direct way to knowledge.

The Postmortem Cult, Supporting Reflection on Death

The postmortem cult also represents a form of reflection on death, as meditating on the deceased master, can lead the devotee to awaken to the ephemeral consciousness of existence, and thus to anticipate his or her own death. In meditating on the guru's departure, the follower learns to die to the world, to die to ego. This turns meditation on the guru's death into an efficient instrument to attain supreme liberation. The postmortem cult of the guru constitutes then a form of victory over death, where "death conquers death" to use the words of the Bengali poet Ramprasad. This recalls the comments of Mā Ānandamayī, who affirmed that "death must die" and who insisted on the importance of preparing yourself for death: "So long as there is coming and going there will be birth and death. He who is jubilant at the birth of a child must be prepared for tears of grief at the time of death. While everything in life is uncertain, it is an undeniable truth that every man must die. To end this ceaseless coming and going there is only one expedient: the realization of the one Supreme Being."[25] Evoking a passage from the *Mahābharata*, she also has this to say:

> People asked Arjuna, the hero of the *Mahābharata*, what was the most extraordinary thing that he had ever encountered. He responded: "Everywhere man sees death but he thinks he will not die." If man was afraid of death at every instant, he could not continue to live. And yet, for people who meditate, every day is a way of dying. Death itself is a form of death and every day, in the oral traditions, masters explain that death represents the death of the greedy ego.[26]

To meditate on death also leads to rendering it inoffensive and incapable of inspiring fear,[27] as this new female disciple of Mā's affirms: "It helps me. My death has nothing to do with Mā's as I am far from being enlightened, from being at that stage. But it helps me to meditate on death, on time, and, of course, on the fear of death. It helps us to liberate ourselves from this fear of death."

This idea of meditation on death seems to be present among Mā's devotees, who conceive of the *postmortem* cult as an aid to reflection on death, as the following French man, a new devotee, emphasizes:

> This comes back to the Buddhist idea, that everything is impermanent, that death is imminent, that it can happen at any time, that everything is transitory. When you remember that the master was there and that he is no longer there now, that brings us back to our own death. If Mā, she left, then us, it's certain.

The postmortem cult then reinforces the meditation on death that is already present in the *guru/śiṣya* relationship during the lifetime of the master, as affirms Ram Alexander, an early disciple of Mā's who helped publish Atmananda's diary, now entitled *Death Must Die*:

> Aside from the great difficulty of finding a qualified Guru, very few are prepared to undergo the rigors such a relationship demands— the sine qua non of which is the journey beyond death, the death of the ego. From the point of view of the individual mind this is the same as physical death and the disciple must have complete faith in the Guru in order to successfully make this transition. This ego death entails abandoning all of one's beliefs and concepts that make up one's passionately held idea of who one is.[28]

This reminds us of the figure of St. Benoît who incited monks to constantly keep in mind the presence of death, *mortem cotidie ante oculos suspectam habere*, or of the Latin expression *memento mori*, "remind yourself that you are mortal." The permanent memory of death constitutes then a sort of preparation for the birth into a superior way of being, to the spiritual life, for if memory constitutes a tool of liberation, forgetting conversely signifies death.

In referring to religious traditions besides Hinduism, Mā also affirmed this regarding the death of death:

> He who yearns for God will find Him and for the man who found Him, death dies. You must turn your gaze towards the vision of

God that is the death of death and force yourself to maintain a mind continually absorbed with activities and practices that can prepare you for such a vision. Speaking of death, the Bible tells us: "Learn to die so that you can begin to live." And the Koran: "Die (learn to disengage your immortal mind from your mortal body) before the hour of your demise."[29]

And so, Mā's postmortem cult can offer a way to liberate oneself from these repeating deaths in the cycle of *saṃsāra* (*punarmṛtyu*), as a path toward immortality. To meditate on Mā's departure and thus on her omnipresence, as a result, comes to be a way of conquering death, similar to the profound meaning of the following words found in the *Bṛhad Araṇyaka Upaniṣad*.

> *From the Unreal lead us to the Real,*
> *From Darkness lead us unto Light,*
> *From Death lead us to Immortality.*
> *Reach us through and through ourself,*
> *And evermore protect us,*
> *O Thou Terrible, from ignorance,*
> *By Thy sweet compassionate face.*

The Postmortem Cult as an Intermediary Stage

The postmortem cult can also be envisioned as a sort of preparation or preamble to the cult to a living guru. A person who is used to following a cult to a guru of the past will have less difficulty in establishing a relationship with a living guru. This is notably the case with some followers of the Ramakrishna Mission of Kerala who, after having venerated the deceased guru Ramakrishna for many years, turned toward the living guru Māta Amṛtānandamayī (who today also lives in Kerala) and became her disciples. Ramdas additionally affirmed that it is possible to adopt a deceased master while waiting to find a living one:

He who really wants to have a guru can find one. Until then, he can fix his faith on a saint of the past, considering him to be his guru. If later, the seeker meets a master and wants to be initiated by him, he should consider him as the incarnation of the saint and let himself be guided by him. All gurus are one.[30]

Thus the postmortem cult to Mā Ānandamayī could also constitute a sort of initiation into the cult of the guru before turning toward a living master. This ease in passing from a ritualized cult to a cult dedicated to a living being additionally emphasizes the flexibility and vitality of Hinduism.

The postmortem cult can also serve as an intermediary, transitional step while waiting for a successor. For example, the followers of the religious movement of the Radhasoamis of Soamibagh continue, in the middle of this interregnum, to venerate their deceased master while waiting for the *dhara*, this subtle current, to manifest itself in a successor.[31] In the case where the transfer of devotion for the old guru to a new guru is not possible for the devotee, the postmortem cult can also be presented as an alternative.

Independence and Responsibility in the Postmortem Cult

Another positive aspect of the death of the guru is the greater sense of responsibility that it invites on the part of the devotee, as this French man, a new disciple of Mā's, declares:

> When the physical master is there and does not want to come see us, there are sometimes emotional breakdowns, there are emotions, there are psychological complications that there are not when he is not there. You are more responsible for yourself. You are in front of yourself, there is no one who is there, you must get along by yourself. It's like when you leave a child alone. He becomes an adult. In nature's Yoga, in life's Yoga, there are rites of passage. These are necessary, the passage from adolescence to adulthood, from adulthood to spiritual maturity, it is necessary. It's the law of nature, Yoga is nature. From one side, it's easier to be responsible for yourself when the master is not there. Because I saw many people who followed Mā in a bit of an addicted way, as psychological dependence and she had to respond. That becomes complicated. And then, there is dependence on the physical place. When a master is there, you are dependent on the place where he is. You need him, you call him, you have to come see him. When he is not there, there is more of a need for him. You are responsible to yourself.

But, if Mā's physical absence implies a greater independence and a certain responsibility, this can also lead the devotee to lose his or her way, particularly when exposed to the temptations in the West, as this German woman, an early devotee of Mā's, tells here:

> The fact that she is not in her body, in one way, it can make you more independent, strong, and free. On the other hand, I feel that she gives you quite a scope of experiments and experiments always have the risk that you can lose yourself [laughs]. And I feel that she is a permissive mother. She lets her children experiment quite a lot. I can only trust that she keeps us like a dog lined [laughs]. This is very easy in the West to get lost. You have such a vastness of information and spiritual paths. If you are clever, you can combine everything and justify everything. So, this can be quite an obstacle. And the freedom in personal life also. In the West, you are more concerned with your relationship, while in India, once you get married, that's it. In the West, you can experiment endlessly. You can change every half a year and you get so lost, and you have to work so much psychologically to remain intact [laughs]. I would be happy if Mā would be there in physical form, for a certain kind of protection. But on the other hand, as Eckhart Tolle said, if you have three times a separation in your relationships, he says that you advance more quickly than staying in an ashram. So I don't know if this is a new wisdom [laughs]. I have no idea. This may be the modern kind of initiation. I didn't get this confirmed. I only pray to Mā that she keeps an eye on me. I think she knows about the paths and the ways. I don't think that she is sitting personally on a cloud, in heaven, watching you. It's like a certain presence which you are related to and which is protecting you, I hope.

Thus, Mā's absence may involve the risk of losing your way on the path, and in particular among Westerners, as this powerful mirror that was Mā while she was alive is today more passive, as the following early male disciple says:

> I really like to do *sādhanā* and I know how to do that. And that *sādhanā* is based on nothing but the relationship with Mā and on finding Mā within, this whole energetic exchange between you and the guru, like that. But the thing with Mā's physical presence, as the physical presence of the saint is something extraordinary. And although you can theorize on how everything is one, that you can

find it within, the reality of the saint is unbelievable. There is this amazing generator of spiritual energy. To be in their presence is to be in a deep spiritual state effortlessly. You don't have to try. Say you make a big mistake in your *sādhanā*, you can just go and sit with Mā. Maybe Mā would pretend to be very angry at you. Maybe, she won't look at you for two weeks. And you wanna die because she won't look at you. She would make you feel horrible. I will never do that again. But then, everything would be ok again. Then, the energy structure would be totally back in place. But without that physical presence, you are on your own. If you make some mistakes, you may have to spend a few life times, well, maybe not a few life times.... You don't have that powerful mirror, this generator. In that sense, you definitely miss this presence.

These comments on the absence of a powerful mirror since Mā's death echo, in a sense, the words of Swami Vijayānanda, who, evoked Mā's less direct action since her death, "Before, when Mā was in her physical body, she could awaken someone tepid, someone who didn't have a strong desire,"[32] which is apparently no longer the case, as the devotee's desire must be much more intense for a real transformation to take place. Jacques Vigne, in the same way, speaks of a less radical transformation produced in the devotee since Mā's departure:

It is possible for an inner work to happen around this *samādhi*. The difference from the time when she was living in her body is that then, she could turn over complete unbelievers "like a crepe," people who were not at all interested in interiority, and awaken them to this world. Thanks to her *śakti*, to her energy, she could transform them from one day to the next. Now, it's more unusual. The transformation is made progressively, but there is undeniably a work of transmutation.[33]

If the postmortem cult thus presents a number of advantages and can sometimes serve as a transitional stage while waiting for a living guru, it also signifies, for the devotee, a greater difficulty in communicating with the guru and the risk of losing one's way on the path due to the absence of this "powerful mirror" that is Mā's incarnated form. Two tendencies emerge here, one being the tendency to experience the master's absence as an opportunity to find the guru inside, and the other being the tendency to affirm that inner progress is slower in the absence of the physical guru and that there is an elevated risk of the follower's falling from grace.

To conclude, it seems important to return again to the devotee's need to give a meaning to Mā's death by making it into a beneficial event. But although the absence of the incarnated master encourages old devotees in their quest for truth, it is questionable as to whether it can draw many new devotees, as they seem much less numerous than early devotees at this time. The success of postmortem cults may not match that of cults to living gurus, like Amma, who draws millions of followers around her. If the absence of the incarnated guru appears to be a positive factor for early devotees and a minority of new devotees, it may not rival the guru's physical presence.

Experiencing the Posthumous Presence of the Guru

This section exclusively addresses the experiential dimension of religion, which James would also qualify as "first hand religion," to distinguish it from "second hand" religion that designates the institutional side of religion. For James, true religion essentially resides in experience, in emotion, and, to some extent, in the body,[34] and not in institutions, discourse, and different formulations.[35] Whereas James seems to be strictly concerned with "religious sentiments" or "religious feelings" to the neglect of social and institutional factors, Carrette, though, argues that James's theory in *The Varieties* is actually too caught up in social and cognitive analysis.[36]

First of all, I should specify what I mean by experience. For the purpose of this study, I will adopt Panikkar's definition regarding the experience of God.[37] For Panikkar, experience has four dimensions:

(1) Experience in itself, that is to say, "immediate" experience;
(2) The memory of this moment, which allows us to speak of this experience. The memory should however not be confused with the immediate experience;
(3) The interpretation of this experience, which is directly tied to the lived experience, to memory, and to language;
(4) Its reception, its inscription into a given cultural world.

The experiential aspect of this study on Mā's devotees concerns then memory and the interpretation of their experience, an experience which is inscribed in the Hindu world as well as in the Western world.

Religious experience, which Rudolf Otto defines as nostalgia for the divine, arises from the otherness, from the *ganz andere*, the "wholly other," that is to say from that which comes from elsewhere, from that which is totally different. The experience of Mā is in fact radically different from anything one would experience in the ordinary, suggesting the appearance of an unexpected new reality. In a sense, this is similar to Arnaud Desjardins's comments regarding Mā: "What does the presence of a being so totally other among us mean?"[38] Since Mā's departure, it seems that her presence continues to manifest itself according to the character of this "totally other," that is beyond all comprehension, all understanding. Belonging to the domain of the totally other, the follower's religious experience is therefore difficult to describe. In addition, as it arises from the private sphere, it belongs to the domain of the intimate as the following disciple says: "to describe this spiritual state, that too, it's something very intimate, private. It's in the realm of grace, in the dimension of the *ānanda*. It encapsulates, it awakens. It's in the realm of *awareness*. It's in the realm of the experiential." It is then necessary to specify that a description of religious experience cannot, in its totality, translate the lived experience.

Despite the difficulty of translating the devotee's religious experience in its totality, I shall here try to describe it. What is this "presence" that devotees experience as a part of their posthumous devotion to Mā?

Presence of the Guru

The posthumous experience of the guru cannot be spoken of without calling on the fundamental idea of presence, which constitutes the basis of *darśana*.[39] According to Champion and Hervieu-Léger, presence may be defined as the "feeling of an omnipresence that is found everywhere at the same time, but which is neither interior nor exterior. This presence is experienced as being sacred or divine."[40] In this respect, William James speaks of a strong conviction induced by this feeling of presence, much stronger than that of a logical reasoning. He specifies that, for the person who experiences it, there is a true perception.[41] In the same vein, André Godin emphasizes that this is not a presence in which one simply believes but a presence that one experiences in the most mysterious way.[42] And so the experience of presence as hierophany constitutes the foundation of religious experience, through which the partitioning of the world of the sacred and of the profane takes place.[43] This "spirituality of presence,"[44] in

the words of Isambert, is found in the experience of many of Mā's devotees, who evoke their experience of Mā by employing the word "presence."
Although today, the majority of Mā's devotees refer to the word "presence"
to talk about their posthumous experience of Mā, this was also the case
during Mā's lifetime, as evident in the written testimonies of early disciples like Atmananda:

> What I perceive of Her is surely not She, but only a tiny glimpse of
> a fragment of Her. If I think of Her as a PRESENCE beyond that
> perceived by the senses it has certainly a greater reality than Her
> physical form and is not subject to Her physical nearness but rather
> to the capacity of my mind to remain in that PRESENCE, which
> I have experienced through Her again and again.[45]

The experience (*Erlebnis*) felt by the group of Mā's devotees is then interpreted as a *hic et nunc* presence of Mā, *Erlebnis* meaning here that the sacred
is able to be experienced. It nonetheless seems important to specify that this
sacred experience of presence may be located well beyond the ephemeral
and changing aspect of emotions, as affirms Vergote, who criticizes James
for not having sufficiently explored the experiences of the mystics: "The
mystics see the 'night of the feelings' as a crucial test enabling them to
purify their faith and only then to achieve that mystical experience of the
divine presence, beyond all the trembling of the emotions and the oscil-
lations of feeling."[46] Although religion resides in feelings for James, and
Hindu *bhakti* emphasizes emotion (i.e., longing in separation as shown in
the *Vaiṣṇava* experience), the mystic experience may in fact be separated
from the emotional, which it looks to eliminate. Emotions, by virtue of their
transient and ephemeral nature, would tend in some religious orientations
within Hinduism, to be eradicated and not cultivated, as advocated by texts,
for example, like the *Yoga Sūtra* (*Yoga Sūtra* 1.2-*citta-vritti-nirodha*).[47]
    Thus, the religious experience of Mā's devotees is manifested as an
immediate presence, a presence that many often qualify as non-dual.
Panikkar additionally says this on this topic:

> It's not the claimed "presence of God" as the *prae-essentia* of a Being
> before us, but a more interior, more personal experience, not as if
> we were moved by another, but conscious that the source of our
> actions and the ultimate subject of our being belongs to this infinite
> sea that we call God.[48]

FIGURE 4.3 Mā Ānandamayī in the Varanasi ashram.
Source: Picture taken by English photographer Richard Lannoy.

Mā's devotees recall this non-dual experience of Mā's presence, as the following early disciple, an Indian man, implies: "Mā is with me. I am not alone. I have her help. She is with me. I am doing nothing. She is acting through me. I don't know how all these things are flowing out. Mā is talking. It is not me." From this observation, certain questions arise: Who experiences what? And, thus, what is the place of the personal "I" in Mā's devotees' religious experience?

If the experience of Mā's presence is often portrayed as a non-dual experience, it can also appear in the form of duality, and even in a physical aspect, as the testimony of this disciple shows: "I feel sometimes that Mā is touching me. There is no physical form but I feel something. I feel that she is present." Another disciple, a French woman, a new devotee, speaks of Mā's caress on her cheek:

> There is something very very sweet with Mā. When I think of her, she manifests herself in a physical way very often, always the same thing, it's a sweet caress of the cheek. It's splendid. I know that it's her. The brush of a caress always on the left cheek. I don't know why but I know that it's Mā, without a shadow of a doubt.

Thus, religious experience can be manifested in a physical way. In this context, I will speak of "physicality of the experience of the sacred."[49]

In addition, if one speaks of Mā as a "presence," one can also define her as an absence, for, as Marcel Gauchet would say, the sacred is specifically the presence of absence.[50] On this matter Mā said: "Even in the situation "without God," there is only God. Everything is He. You are in this situation where God is presence experienced as absence. Contemplate that which is present even under the guise of absence."[51] For devotees, Mā can be defined as an absence too, as this new disciple says: "I see both in her a sort of absence that may be a presence because, for me, Mā is everywhere, she is there." Absence can thus be transformed into a concrete experience of God. Because Mā is perceived by some devotees as an incarnation of the goddess Kālī, as her Bengali epithet "Living Kālī" implies, she is also said to have the tendency to bless by her absence, for as Kinsley notes, Kālī constitutes the goddess par excellence who blesses only by her absence.[52] To meet Mā is then to meet her as "presence-absence," for, in the end, there can be no presence without absence, as there can be no form without a void. Mā reveals this in the following comments: "Form is in reality empty. To realize this brings liberation from form. The world is revealed to be empty, ready to disappear into the Great Void. The void is the very nature of manifestation; it is thus the form!"[53] If Mā is felt as absence/presence, she is also then felt as form/emptiness, recalling the statements of a French woman, a new devotee of Mā's:

> Mā is truly that which engenders the everything, it's the Divine Mother in all senses, that is to say that which both engenders everything and is everywhere, in the least blade of grass, and at the same time, that which could give birth to it. She can be inside and could give birth to it. It's above every thing, and also with its two forms, the manifestation and the non-manifested. It's very important to have these two ideas and to juxtapose these two ideas in permanence. Me, I found that magnificent, the form. I like beauty. I like harmony. And then, the human relationship, that's form as well. I obviously like eternity, if I didn't, I would not be on this path. For me, the Divine Mother, it's both, it's at the same time the manifestation, the *mahāmāyā* and it's also eternity, beyond that which you can imagine.

If Mā is also revealed in absence, some devotees do not hesitate however to test her presence, as the testimony of this Indian woman, a new disciple, shows: "Once, I tested her whether she is present or not. I told Mā: 'I want to see if you are present or not. The same *māla* [set of prayer beads] that you have on the picture, I want it on my neck.' Ten minutes later, the *pūjāri* came and gave me one *māla*. Sometimes, I am testing her to see if she is there. I am naughty also [laughs]." Here is also the testimony of another disciple, an Indian woman, an early devotee of Mā's, who tells of her first real experience of Mā after her death:

> Finally, I entered the *samādhi*. I sat over there and I started a conversation with Mā, within myself: "Today, I have a little bit of sense of what you are, a little bit, with my limitations. I am missing you so much because you are just not there. I need that physical body. Whom can I talk to? Today, I have come back as a child. If you have accepted me, pick up that lotus flower on your *samādhi* and give it to me. Show me that you heard me." I just said that. Then, I shut my eyes and I went into meditation. I don't know what was happening around. I was spaced out. One lady from the *samādhi* comes to me with the lotus. She drops the lotus in my *duppatā*. When the lotus dropped, I remember my entire conversation with Mā. Again, I started crying like a fountain. And I am gone. I don't know where. That experience, I don't want to name anything. I woke up two hours after. The *kīrtana* was over, everybody had left the *samādhi*. I looked at everything around me. I didn't know where I was. I had lost my identity completely. Only when I came back, I realized that I am here. And what happened to me in these two hours, I have no clue. This is my first experience after Mā left her body.

Thus, the experiences of Mā that devotees recount are first of all defined by a "presence," a presence that both can be felt on the dual plane but also on that of non-duality. This experience of Mā is additionally perceived by her devotees as an ecstatic one, as subsequent testimonies suggest.

An Ecstatic Experience

Religious experience is often presented as an experience of moving past something, as a union with something infinitely greater. William James defines the religious experience as the possibility of feeling the union with something greater than our personality and of finding in this union a profound tranquility. This experience of moving past human consciousness is in a way related to the "oceanic feeling" of Freud, which corresponds to a particular state of consciousness in which the mind, the consciousness, goes through a kind of fusion with the cosmos.[54] In this vein, Acquaviva notes that the religious experience always appears as a peak experience, completely filling up the individual consciousness.[55] Antoine Vergote also speaks of the religious experience as an expansion of the human being, as the sensation and the taste of the infinite.[56] This aspect of religious experience seems to also be found in many ways among Mā's devotees who perceive their experience of Mā as a union with everything, with the infinite: "Because Mā, to me, is everything, and this is not only a sarcastic belief, I have experienced Mā that way. Beyond Mā, there is nothing." The experience of the Divine appears then as this awareness that in ourselves we are without beginning and without end.[57]

As James affirms, this feeling of union with something that is beyond us is accompanied by a tranquility, by a feeling of assurance, of deliverance. Experience leads to the disappearance of all tension, of all anxiety and makes way for a feeling of profound peace, of complete harmony and joy. According to many testimonies, Mā's devotees seem to feel this state of grace in their experience of Mā. Some speak of a sweetness tied to Mā's presence: "Mā's presence, it's something very subtle, very evanescent and very sweet. Probably, I must need this sweetness since it's what I search for." Others define Mā's presence as "very subtle, transcendental, very tender as a flower" but also as "full of love, subtleness, tenderness, alertness, devotion, surrender." Some even go so far as to describe this state of grace associated with Mā's presence as a "surplus of *ānanda* (bliss)," as the testimony of this French man, a new devotee of Mā's, shows:

> In the beginning, it was something much stronger than a maternal relationship, than a romantic relationship with a woman. It was a relationship a bit on the order of grace, something good, sweet, like manna, something that fills you, and nourishes you. Maybe one feels that before birth, in a prenatal state. It's possible, I don't know. But it's what I felt, it's this type of goodness, of love that can bring you everything. This quality of love, there is no word to define it. It's something that is supernatural. It's not a free *ānanda* when one attains realization. There is a mixture, as if there was a special grace that detached itself from *ānanda*. It's a surplus of *ānanda*, a surplus of grace that is granted to you to progress, to advance, to defeat obstacles. It's a surplus of grace. So, when I see these things, when this happens to

me, there is an aura that comes, of sometimes hundreds of meters that is recognized by the environment. People who are around this aura, who are surrounded by this aura, feel happy, in a world of joy. It's not normal. It's a very special *ānanda*. It's a radiance. It's incredible. Even the people who have nothing to do with spirituality feel it. They feel good, happy, suddenly. I'm sitting in a Parisian café, with no religious emblem, and all of a sudden, there is this grace and you see that people are well, happy. When I sense Mā's presence, there is a radiance, this surplus of grace radiates around and leads to joy, to peace that makes itself known, which is experienced by other people present, whomever they are. It's incredible. It's a force.

The same disciple adds that with time, his "anandic" [blissful] experience of Mā has become more interior:

The first experiences were exterior, and as I progressed, they became interior. It's as if that passed into the interior. It's a very intimate domain, it's not so appropriate to speak of it, it's very secret. In the beginning, there was this surplus of grace. I insist on that. As if it were Mā Ānandamayī in the flesh before you, who radiated from you. But as you continue, she brings you this realization. Thus, the closer you come to the realization, the less there is this phenomenon of bringing this surplus of grace necessary to lead you. These phenomena diminish on the exterior and are amplified on the interior. You are no longer a small individual.... There is this presence.... What presence, by the way? It became a spiritual presence. It's no longer Mā. Before, there was this surplus of grace that people called Mā. But once this surplus of grace has done its work...a surplus of grace, it's something that comes from the *ānanda* if you like. An *ānanda*, it's like a sky, a free space. It's something that comes from the heart of the *ānanda*, from this anandic space. It's a secret, it's a heart, another quality of *ānanda*, another thing, very personal, which is detached, that brings you this surplus to help to lead you to a state but once that state was acquired, there is no need, that would be a useless loss. So, it returns in this center.... It's not finished. There are levels. And I am very happy.

The experience of the sacred is additionally an experience outside time, in this "now of eternity," *nunc aeternitati* to use an expression of the Christian mystics. Concerning mystic experience, Françoise Champion speaks of a feeling of atemporality: "[the mystic experience] is feeling-certainty of the fundamental unity of the Real, a feeling of atemporality."[58] Mā's presence is experienced among devotees as the feeling of being outside of all temporality. Only the immediate, *hic et nunc* presence of Mā exists. This resembles the experience that Christians can have of Jesus today:

> The experience is not a memory; the experience is that which comes to us and transforms us. This experience can certainly be founded on an updated memory, in which case there is a memory broadcast by previous generations.
>
> If the Christ was only a historic person, the experience of the Christian is reduced to living the memory of his life, sent through the memory that has been conserved of him. In this case, experts have the maximum authority and Christianity is reduced to being a religion of a Book. But the experience of Jesus for the Christian is the experience of Jesus resurrected, that is to say living, *hic et nunc*, yesterday, today and forever.... The act of faith actualizes this experience of the ineffable.[59]

As with Jesus, one can thus speak of the experience of Mā as a transhistoric experience. Due to its atemporal character, religious experience is placed then beyond the intelligible as it relates to eternity. This evasive aspect of religious experience that is atemporal and eternal is by definition permeated with a mysterious feeling or of *anyad-eva*, which constitutes the central religious sentiment.[60]

And so, experience of Mā can be seen as an ecstatic experience, where the follower is completely immersed in this feeling of *ānanda*, of supreme beatitude, where time has no hold. In addition, this experience is accompanied by a profound transformation in the disciple and generally occurs in an unexpected and synchronic way.

A Transformative, Unexpected and Synchronic Experience

Religious experience then represents in a certain way an experience of profound transformation, of rebirth, involving a life change. Mā's devotees experience in fact the presence of Mā as a profoundly transformative experience. This is notably the case with this Indian woman, an early disciple of Mā's, who, well after Mā's death, experienced great changes in herself, changes that she attributed to Mā:

> It was just not possible that I would change. She changed my whole life...I was a very different person before, I told you. The day she changed me and made me this, since that day, all my attitude towards materialistic things in life just faded away. Those values have gone for me. When those values go, automatically you realize that the body is also futile. You're dressing up the body all day, you're putting on make up....Those interests have suddenly gone, completely gone out of the window. Then, what is the body? Today, everybody tells me when I walk around, even in the ashram, you're so attractive, and you're so beautiful, look at the glow on your face....I say it has nothing to do with the body. It is all Mā. Because she is here. It reflects. Your thoughts, your mind, your attitude, everything reflect. Your face is a mirror. Whatever you see, it's all because of Mā. Because I am eating, breathing, sleeping, I do nothing but Mā. It will reflect.

The transformation undergone by this devotee, following her interior encounter with Mā, can be related, in a certain way, to a true conversion. Other followers, like this Indian man, an early disciple of Mā's, also speak of revelations that cause true transformations:

> On one or two occasions, there were some revelations. Revelations actually convince you more than anybody can do. We all have problems in our life. Revelations convince you somehow that these problems are very small things, that you must see the big picture. Of course, when you wake up, you are confronted with the problems again, but then, you think about it. So, they bring a transformation which is very difficult to bring out. They have the purposes to transform you, which is very difficult to do. You can read, listen to lectures, you can have experiences but still, you don't change. Mā has a way of changing you for the better.

Thus, devotees' experience of Mā are said to lead to true changes, making this experience a sacred one, a real one, bringing, as William James says, a new wave of life, a "rejuvenation." It is also accompanied by a detachment toward things of this world, as the following Western woman, a new devotee, says:

> I seek the realization, that is to see God and I feel that sometimes she helps me. That is manifested through a presence. For example, my last trip to Paris was very very different from everything that I had lived in Paris. Despite the pollution, despite the beings with low energy, wherever I was, whether these were chic neighborhoods, livelier, or working class, I always felt myself to be in an aura. As if all that, it didn't reach me anymore at all. I saw everything. That took a distance. Even, that didn't reach me. In the metro, it's not particularly a place to feel yourself surrounded by an aura.

Still in relation to Mā, an Indian man compares himself in this respect to a lotus flower growing out of the mud, which nothing can reach: "My situation is like a lotus flower. I am living in society, but nothing is touching me."

From these testimonies, it is clear that religious experience for Mā's devotees is synonymous with profound transformation. This seems to resonate with James's comments on the transformative role of experience. Quoting Vivekananda, he notes the following in a discussion on the Hindu tradition:

> The Vedantists say that one may stumble into superconsciousness sporadically, without the previous discipline, but it is then impure. Their test of its purity, like our test of religion's value, is empirical: its fruits must be good for life. When a man comes out of Samadhi, they assure us that he remains "enlightened, a sage, a prophet, a saint, his whole character changed, his life changed, illumined."[61]

Another trait of religious experience that is found among devotees is tied to its unexpected character, to amazement. In fact, according to Otto, astonishment exclusively arises from the numinous.[62] The religious experience that one lives (*Erlebnis*) is related then to the unexpected and would erupt in the subject's life instantaneously and immediately. Mā's devotees perceive their experience of Mā always as a sudden and surprising experience, as this Western woman, a new follower, explains:

> Spiritual teaching surprises us a lot all the time, and Mā's teaching in particular. In Mā's teaching, I feel like when you expect

something, she will surprise you, well the teaching will surprise you, not at all like you expected it, not at all like you foresaw it.

And so, the religious experience of Mā's followers is founded on the new and the immediate. This recalls the comments of Panikkar on the subject of experience of the Divine:

> One of the phenomenological traits of God is to be novel and, for us, always surprising. If I didn't fear being too paradoxical (without further explanations), I would say that the ability to be surprised and to admire is almost a condition for the experience of God— which will not be confined in either physical form or metaphysical form. The God of the past is a simple "construction" of the mind and is not the "living God."[63]

Panikkar's thought then seems to reflect the experience felt by Mā's devotees. Through their devotion to her, devotees experience Mā as novelty, as the unexpected.

The experience of Mā's presence can also be defined by its quality of "synchronicity," a concept articulated by Jung. Devotees often speak of synchronic events while talking about Mā, as the following French man, a new follower, affirms: "Nothing but synchronicity, everywhere. Whether it be a book that you open, whether it be a person that you meet, an ill that comes to us, a visible problem. A visible obstacle." In the same context, some devotees also recall the many coincidences related to their experience with Mā, as this swami:

> I feel that she, very directly, will make events happen that are for my benefits, to teach me things. Coincidences are sometimes too extreme. Sometimes, five different people will tell me in different ways the same thing. This is the point; this is the point, wake up! Even in difficulties too. Two weeks before my *saṃnyāsa*, I got so sick. There was no doctor. I nearly died, but I had this spiritual experience. Mā was so close. I could see Mā telling me "how much can you take?" It was a forced malaria. It was a totally spiritual experience. I felt Mā was so close. The *dīkṣā* was coming up. And I know my mind was so impure. She was trying to burn as much as possible so that I can receive more. At the same time, I was like in bliss and pain. When you are sick, there is no romance.

This devotee's testimony seems to echo the belief that the spiritual master sends maladies that he or she then heals. In addition, it seems that experience of Mā in the form of synchronic events was also present in Mā's lifetime, as this testimony of Arnaud Desjardins suggests: "Whatever the number of those who turn towards her at the same time, it seems that these conditions are always best for each. Everyone has the impression that, during the weeks that have just gone by, Mataji consecrated all her interest to them and organized all these events of life at the ashram around them and around that which would best teach them."[64] Despite Mā's departure then, the experience of her synchronistic presence seems to be accessible to this day.

The posthumous experience of Mā can thus be defined above all as a "presence," a presence also felt by the followers from the time when Mā was incarnated in a body. This presence is manifested both on a dual, and notably physical plane, but also on a non-dual plane, making of the devotee a channel for Mā, as it were. But, if the posthumous experience of Mā is characterized by a presence, it is also manifested by an absence, making the posthumous experience of Mā, then, a paradoxical one, in which contraries meet. The posthumous experience of Mā is again defined by its ecstatic character, in which the devotee feels a profound beatitude (*ānanda*) and where time does not exist, as well as by its regenerative, unexpected, and synchronic character.

According to different statements by early disciples, their experiences of Mā after her death do not seem to differ significantly from experiences of Mā while alive. Interviews with new devotees also do not show a major difference compared to early devotees with regard to the quality of their experiences. Although they did not know Mā in a body, they do experience her presence.

Dreams, Visions, Guidance

Dreams

In the Hindu tradition, the dream holds an important place and, as the "mirror of reality,"[65] it is believed that it sometimes delivers real messages.[66] Devotees generally consider dreaming of a saint, and especially of one's own master, to be a very significant thing. If these dreams are produced when the guru is alive, they also take place after his or her *mahāsamādhi*, reassuring the devotees of the omnipresence and the omnipotence of their master. On this matter, one speaks of a posthumous *darśana* of the guru in dreams. According to the tradition of the Radhasoamis, for example, every true disciple will receive the *darśana* of their guru upon the master's death.[67] In this context, the guru may also manifest him or herself in a dream after his or her death to request a posthumous cult.[68] If Weinberger speaks of the "psychology of ancestors" to recall the intervention of Manes in dreams to ask for a cult,[69] I may, in the same way, speak here of the "psychology of gurus." Within Mā's community, there are many anecdotes on this subject. For example, shortly after Mā's *mahāsamādhi*, one of the *brahmacārinis* at the ashram at Kankhal forgot to leave a glass of water for Mā in what used to be her room. The following night, she apparently dreamt that Mā asked her for a glass of water.

If, among devotees, dreams of saints are particularly frequent at his or her death, they also persist many years afterwards, even centuries afterwards. Shirdi Sai Baba, to cite one of the best known, is said to continue to manifest himself in dreams nearly a century after his death among his devotees, often to guide them.[70] In the same way, after her departure, Mā is said to continue to manifest herself among the majority of her devotees.[71] Early disciples note, however, a decrease in these dreams since her death. This is notably the case with Swami Vijayānanda who expressed this concerning dreams of Mā:

> When I was with Mā, I practically always dreamed of Mā. I don't think that there was a day when I didn't dream of Mā. Then, after she had left her body, it became less frequent. And now, I dream of her, but less often. There were very varied dreams. Some dreams were banal, and some dreams had great significance. Those, I still remember them, the others, I forgot them immediately.

Dreams of Mā are also present among new disciples. This is the case with this Western woman, for example, who had a dream of Mā twenty-five years before having heard of her:

> When I think back, I had a very very strong dream of Mā twenty-five years ago and I didn't know who it was. What happened was that I had a still-born baby and I was very very unhappy. When I look back in my diaries, about four days after I had the labour, I had this really really powerful dream in the night. I went to

this Indian lady, and she was sitting, and there she was, and she was just so kind and loving. And she told me I had to go through the labour again but I had to go through the labour with joyfulness this time. So, I laid down and I had all this pain again, and not only in the reality but also in the awakening reality, but this time, it felt fine. I had this experience and that changed the flavor of the morning, something was all right about this experience, something positive came out because of this vision. Years passed and I forgot about this dream. I just had another boy. All through the childhood, I had no other vision, no other spiritual experience or whatsoever. I was fifty in year 2000 when the spiritual thing started to happen again. Mā was just kind of letting that part of life just go on, having children, or whatever, and so, it was time to move into the next stage. And then I remembered again about this lady, and the minute I remembered it, I just knew it was Mā. It was obviously Mā.

If Mā, in the devotee's dream, can take on a form different from her usual one (saguṇa), such as the form of a deity, she can also be without form (nirguṇa), as this French man, a new disciple, who recounts one of his dreams suggests:

Mā and myself were at the entrance of a temple. Then, all of a sudden, Mā, who was with me, disappeared, then, she was no longer around me. There were people washing their feet, their hands, in these basins to prepare to enter into the temple. I entered into the temple. I looked around everywhere for Mā. I descended into a room in the basement. I was told Mā was there. I open a door and I find Mā's figure carpeting the walls. But where is she? Then, after, another room. Then nothing. Emptiness. That, it was one of the dreams I remember, but I've had so many of them.

Mā's devotees often perceive these dreams as a way for Mā to communicate a message to them, to guide them. This is the case with this Indian woman, an early disciple, who affirmed having received instructions directly from Mā in her dreams, when she found herself in a difficult and dangerous position: "Every time, every day, Mā would come in my dreams and would give me instructions. In dreams, at night, while I am

FIGURE 4.4 Mā Ānandamayī's blessing with her hand

Atmananda: "What I perceive of Her is surely not She, but only a tiny glimpse of a fragment of Her. If I think of Her as a PRESENCE beyond that perceived by the senses it has certainly a greater reality than Her physical form and is not subject to Her physical nearness but rather to the capacity of my mind to remain in that PRESENCE, which I have experienced through Her again and again."

Source: Picture belonging to the collection of the photographer Sadanand; now in the possession of Neeta Mehta, also called Swami Nityānanda.

sleeping. She would say, don't do this, don't do this. Every day, every day, she was coming. That's the time Mā saved me." This same disciple additionally speaks of the importance of these dreams that are not ordinary dreams:

The fact that Mā comes is a very big thing. She doesn't come that often to people. The fact that she comes is absolutely fantastical. After that, if she gives you a message, it's even better. In that particular aspect, when we say we saw Mā, we are actually jumping our consciousness to that level where Mā is. So, you are actually relating to her. Actually, it is not a dream. And, then, she is giving you instructions. It's so true for me. It couldn't be more true than this world that is existing. That is more of a reality than this is.

It is interesting to consider the origin of these dreams of Mā. Responses to this question are diverse. The following French woman, a new devotee of Mā's, offers different hypotheses:

> I do not think that it is my imagination. Let's say that there are many hypotheses. Either, it's Mā who comes to see me, or it's also a sort of memory that would be placed somewhere in the universe and which is awoken at that moment. A memory, she came to this earth, she left memories. All these places where she came have memories of her. Even if you're not there, you can receive a memory of some places, even of a stone, of an object. And even if I am in Paris, for example, I can very well have a memory that comes to me from Varanasi or from Kankhal. . . . There is also a third hypothesis, it's a collective unconscious, I think. And then, the fourth, it's the source of life. In the work of the *Advaita Vedānta*, you are connected to the Self, to what is beyond the me, to what is our source of life. And, in this source of life, does there not exist also a sort of well where some realized beings live, and particularly those who have chosen to? Does this source of life that would be a bit like our inner guru, would it not be connected to Mā?

And so, the origin of dreams, according to this disciple, could stem from these four elements cited above. Regarding the origin of dreams in memory, one of Mā's swamis adds this:

> The root of your dreams is the memory you are carrying within you, the impressions you are carrying within you. Dreams come from within, from the memory. We call this memory *saṃskāra* in our Indian spirituality. So, these are the manifestations of memories, of *saṃskāra*, that's why dreams come. You saw Mā in dreams. It doesn't mean that Mā came. Mā's *saṃskāra* was there within you, in your subconscious mind, in the depth of your mental layers of consciousness. It comes out as a dream. That's all. Mā never comes in dreams.

FIGURE 4.5 Swami Vijayānanda: "No, Ma Anandamayi was not a human person. She was not a human being! She was, that is without a doubt, an Incarnation of the Divinity."

Source: Picture belonging to the collection of the photographer Sadanand; now in the possession of Neeta Mehta, also called Swami Nityānanda.

If dreams have some importance for the majority of Mā's devotees, they are nevertheless not essential for their *sādhanā*, as this Indian man, a long-time devotee of Mā's, specifies: "When I have a dream of Mā, that makes me feel happy. But from the beginning, I am not depending on these things. My aim is to achieve Mā or God. The only important thing for me is to live always in the presence of Mā." In a way, this recalls Mā's words that affirmed the reality of dreams, thus showing that you must not be attached to them: "All sorts of things can be seen in dreams: those that depend on the mental but also those that were not thoughts but which happened in the past or which will happen in the future. In any case, everything that happens belongs to the realm of dreams."[72]

Visions

Visions also constitute another type of extraordinary reality experienced by devotees. It is not rare to hear of posthumous visions of the guru after his or her death, and there are many examples of them. For example, there is the case of Sarada Devi who is said to have seen her spouse, Ramakrishna, appear shortly after his death[73] or the case of Indira Devi, a classical dancer and poetess, who met the saint Mirabai numerous times in her visions.[74] Ma Jaya, the American guru, also had visions of different saints during her *sādhanā*, as did Neem Karoli Baba or Swami Nityananda,[75] and Chandra Swami received the *darśana* of different deceased masters, like Ramana Maharshi, of whom he had never heard before.[76] The best known cases of visions of deceased saints in India however are attributed to Shirdi Sai Baba, who seems to regularly manifest himself to many individuals.[77]

If apparitions of Mā seem to have been particularly present just after her departure, they still occur today, more than thirty years after her passing, to early and new devotees, but also to people who have never heard of Mā. During an interview, an Indian disciple, an early devotee of Mā's, related that his son, who was 7 years old at the time and had never heard of Mā before, with the exception of seeing a photo of her in his father's office, recalled the presence of a woman at his hospital bedside. The young boy described this woman like the woman he saw in the photo of Mā.

If, in these visions, Mā generally appears as she is known to have been, a woman with long black hair, it seems that she also appears in other forms. Some speak for example of visions of Mā in the form of a young girl. One of the ashram's *pūjāris* relates the sudden appearance and instantaneous disappearance in the *sādhu kutira* of a small girl asking him for *prasāda* that he had failed to give during the *pūjā* at Mā's *samādhi*. Others, like this French man, a new devotee of Mā's, also relate visions of Mā in a luminous form:

> I saw her not in a physical form but in a glorious form. Not physical. There was not the appearance with her hair. It was not like that. It's difficult to describe. There was something like a form, but a luminous one, not really visible. It was here but not in a physical aspect like we knew her, with the hair and all that, the head. It was nothing like that. But it was the quality. This form emanated the same quality. Also, I received a beam in the middle of my forehead. It was at my apartment in Paris during my *sādhanā*. I threw myself onto the

bed and I said "take me." Bam. Incredible, incredible. After, every day, it started again, it started again.

This is also the case of another disciple, a Western woman, who saw Mā in the form of a luminous silhouette: "Three years ago, I was in the middle of something really difficult. One day, I was sitting on my bed in my room and I felt her presence before me. It was really a silhouette of white light and without a shadow of a doubt, it was Mā. It was she who came to my rescue."

Some spaces are said to be more favorable to appearances of Mā, notably Mā's *samādhi*, a favored place for apparitions. The different *pūjāris* in charge of the *pūjā* at the *samādhi* seem have been witnesses of supernatural appearances. One of the *pūjāris* had a vision of Mā in person, sitting inside a mosquito net during a morning *pūjā* at the *samādhi*. Another *pūjāri* also speaks of having glimpsed a shadow in the *samādhi* very early in the morning, when it was closed and no one could have entered apart from himself. It also seems that the young boys of Mā's school at Kankhal (Vidyapeeth School) are predisposed to having visions of Mā, as a *brahmacārini* at the ashram in Kankhal states. Thus, it seems that visions of Mā appear especially at her *samādhi*, making this place a space particularly favorable for this type of contact with Mā.

For the majority of devotees, visions are true benedictions and many of them ardently wish Mā would manifest herself to them in this way, like the following Indian woman, a new devotee of Mā's: "I do feel her presence but I would like visions of her. I am sure she will bless me with that. Maybe, I am not ready right now. Maybe something is lacking in me." For some, visions are perceived as a true sign of spiritual progress, as the expression of a connection with the master as this Indian woman, an early devotee says: "Visions? No, I am not in that high stage. Some people are in such a stage that they can see Mā. I am in a very low stage." For Swami Vijayānanda, this pertains to a psychic disposition that some people possess: "There are people who are psychics, who have real visions. There are people like that, psychic people." If for some, visions are a sign of grace, others however do not find them important at all, as the following Indian man, an early devotee of Mā's says: "Vision? That is not very important. I don't know what you mean by visions. Visions are only your own *samskāra*, it comes from your own imagination. Since Mā is everywhere, if you wish, you can see everything as Mā only. It is out of your own desire that you are creating Mā."

Thus, for some devotees, Mā continues to manifest herself in the form of visions. This recalls what a devotee of Mā, Anil Ganguli, affirmed regarding Mā: "Mā lives on a double plane, one visible from the exterior and the other from the interior."[78]

Guidance

The guru's presence can also manifest itself as guidance. Some devotees of a guru speak of a subtle communication with the deceased guru, of an inner voice that guides them, that shows them the path to follow. In this regard, Aurobindo confirmed that it is possible for the dead to communicate with the living: "It is perfectly possible for the dead, or I should say the departed, as they are not dead, who are still in neighboring regions, to enter into communication with the living."[79] In this context, we can cite, for example, the case of Śrī Mā of Kāmakkhya, who is said to have been guided from within by the deceased saint Ramakrishna to leave for America[80] so as to share a spiritual teaching there.

According to interviews, it is clear that, since Mā's departure, her devotees strongly feel her presence in the form of guidance protecting them and supporting them in their spiritual path (sādhanā). Some recall a force watching over their life, like this Indian man, a new devotee of Mā's:

I feel all the time Mā's force surrounding me, if I do something wrong or something good. All the time, I feel this force. All the time, I feel somebody overseeing me, from the top, in everything. I am very conscious about that, all the time. Whatever I do, she is overseeing me. Not only me, my entire family. She is overseeing us.

This force comes to guide the devotee at the right time, as this French woman, a new disciple, affirms:

I know that I am in a good place. I sense that it's she who leads, that I've not let go of the thread, that I'm going in the right direction.... It's amazing, it's as if she pulls back and she advances when it's necessary. It's as if she lets you go as far as you can. You are there to perform sādhanā, to purify yourself. She accompanies you. But when there is truly a need for a helping hand, she shows herself, she is there... it's she who is over my entire spiritual path. It's she who surrounds everything, who's in charge [laughs].

For devotees, Mā takes care of them at all levels, as this Indian man, an early devotee, says:

> Mā is taking care of every possible need of a person. It's not only spiritual. The purpose of the guru is to protect your *sādhanā*. That's the only purpose of the guru. That means that whatever comes in the way of your *sādhanā*, she has to take care of it. Sometimes things happen in life that disturb your *sādhanā*. To that extent, they get involved in your material affairs... Mā puts you on the way. This kind of things happened to me many times.

In this respect, Mā is sometimes described by her devotees as a "solution personified," for the devotee's difficult situations end by resolving themselves in invoking her aid: "Mā is called sometimes 'the solution personified,' because she is the Ultimate." It seems then that Mā comes to help her devotees in crisis situations, as this Indian male follower, an early devotee, says: "Whenever I feel helpless, I do tend to fall back on Mā and ask her for proper solution and I feel that I find some way out to convert the situation, to overcome the situation, the frustration." Mā's guidance can additionally occur in all sorts of forms: "She can come in any body, including yours. Whenever I have an enquiry, she sends me a person to answer to my questions, to show me the path." In a similar way, Warrier notes that Amma's devotees see evidence of her protection in times of crisis, when the miraculous appears to prevent them from harm.[81] Regarding Amma, it is interesting to note that some of Mā's disciples, today close to the living guru Mā Amṛtānandamayī (Amma), consider Mā to have guided them toward Amma after her departure.

Many devotees consider themselves to be instruments of Mā, as channels of this force, as the following testimony from an Indian *brahmacārini* shows: "I never thought of writing a book on Mā. I never liked to study. I don't know how Mā made me do this.... You won't believe. Sometimes, the words were coming out for the translation. I opened the dictionary and it comes right. Mā dictated." Another *brahmacārini*, in charge of the *samādhi*'s maintenance, similarly adds: "Mā is making [me] do all this work." Devotees perceive themselves then to be instruments of Mā, to be her tools.

And so, devotees today feel the presence of Mā in the form of an inner force that guides them in their lives, testifying to a recognition of this phenomenon, as this Indian woman, a new devotee of Mā's, affirms: "I pray to her that whatever is good for me, you do that. Till date, whatever has happened to me, I feel that I have got more than enough. That's what I feel. I don't know what will happen in the future. I am happy with what I have got. I am oversatisfied. I feel that Mā is always there." Some even hope that Mā will continue to guide them in their future life: "I think she has taken my hand and that she is leading me on the spiritual path, in this birth, and also next birth."

On the basis of numerous interviews, I can confirm a continuity of experience of Mā since her death among new and old devotees. These experiences differ little from such experiences occurring while Mā was alive. The idea of "presence" represents the leading thread. Devotees consistently return to the guru's presence, a presence that they also define as an absence. This experience of presence is portrayed as an ecstatic experience, in which this feeling of beatitude, of *ānanda*, surrounds them and leads them beyond time. The religious experience of followers additionally allows a profound transformation in the disciple and because of its unexpected and synchronic character is characterized as astonishing. These experiences notably occur in dreams, visions, and can additionally manifest themselves as a sort of interior guidance. And if for some early followers, these experiences declined in intensity and are less frequent since Mā's death, this is not the case for all. Many followers on the contrary perceive Mā's physical absence as a sort of catalyst for their *sādhanā*, helping them make contact with their inner guru.

If there exists a continuity in Mā's cult from an experiential point of view, other factors however are to be considered in terms of the cult's sustainability. So as to complete this study, it now seems essential to examine the institutional aspect of Mā's postmortem cult.

Sustainability of the Postmortem Cult

Routinization and the Organization

Using Weber's theory, I address here the process of routinization, this passage from the extraordinary to the ordinary, by which charisma tries to resist its decline after the departure of the charismatic leader through structuring and institutionalization. I discuss the case of Mā and of her "official" organization, the Shree Shree Anandamayee Sangha, but I also consider a less orthodox lineage that continues to grow and spread Mā's teachings and legacy. What is the future of the guru's charisma, and particular Mā's charisma, after death? How does the organization manage the loss of charisma involved in the guru's disappearance, notably with problems of succession and management? The Weberian ideas of charismatic and bureaucratic domination, of *Sect* and of *Church*, and of religious administration are used in this study going forward. References to Bourdieu's writings on Weber, to Habermas on the concept of public sphere, as well as to Lindholm on charisma, are useful in this regard. I also present diverse opinions of Mā's followers and analyze them, so as to question my initial hypothesis regarding the central role of institution in the cult's perpetuation.

Charisma and Routinization

To many, the guru represents the archetypical charismatic figure. He or she is the very incarnation of "charisma" which, according to Weber, is "a certain quality of an individual personality by virtue of which he is considered extraordinary and treated as endowed with supernatural, superhuman, or at least specifically exceptional powers or qualities."[1] Mā

FIGURE 5.1 Mā Ānandamayī: "This entire universe is my house. I am in my own house even when seeming to be roaming from place to place."

Source: Picture belonging to the collection of the photographer Sadanand; now in the possession of Neeta Mehta, also called Swami Nityānanda.

Ānandamayī represents this type of charismatic figure defined by Weber. She was and remains for her devotees the incarnation of God on earth and so is the object of total devotion (bhakti). Mā's performance of miracles also comes to legitimize her domination over her devotees. As they consider these miracles to belong to the realm of the extraordinary, their dominated status is reinforced, as they accept being guided by Mā.

The charismatic authority of the religious leader, which occurs in the context of hiatus often revealing a period of crisis, is assured by the will of those who believe in him or her. This complete confidence in the person of the guru constitutes the very basis of charismatic legitimacy and is located in the act of "recognition."[2] Whether it is understood or not, Mā's speech in this context becomes an authoritative speech due to the legitimacy given to the leader. Specifically, Mā talks in a legitimate situation, that is to say, in Bourdieu's terms, before "legitimate receptors."[3] This also recalls Lindholm's conviction that whatever the charismatic leader says is right, because *"the leader says it,"*[4] and Gauchet's on Jesus' discourse, that there is what Jesus said, and there is what his discourse conveyed, which is far beyond its immediate content due to the position he occupies.[5] And so, in breaking the routine order so as to develop a more rational order, according to Weber, Mā Ānandamayī can be considered to have the authority of a prophet. Weber's theory then paradoxically makes of the charismatic figure a factor of rupture of established order but also of its reconstruction into a more efficient form.

Charisma, by its very nature, which arises from the exceptional and innovative, is limited however in that it cannot endure, as the exceptional cannot arise from the commonplace or routine, but rather from the ephemeral.[6] For Weber, charismatic authority, which takes its strength from the power of rupture, in fact only can be observed *statu nascendi,* at the time of its emergence, that is to say at the very moment of rupture. It is thereafter destined to lose some of its purity, as well as its quality of being extraordinary and uncommon, so as to transform itself to endure either through traditionalization, legalization (rationalization), or both at once.[7]

The routinization of charisma also refers to the terms "banalization" and "conventionalization." There is a transformation of the religious movement of *Sect* into *Church.* If, during Mā's time, her movement was closer to a *Sect,* which is defined by Weber as a voluntary association of believers more or less in breach of the social environment and in which there is a type of charismatic religious authority practiced,[8] it is today closer to a *Church,* that is to say an institutionalized community, accompanied by a rationalized and a specialized religious body, which is essentially characterized by the separation of charisma from the person and its reattachment to the institution.[9]

And so, according to Weber, all charisma that succeeds in enduring must undergo routinization.[10] Through routinization, there is necessarily a passage from the extraordinary to the ordinary, from the exceptional to the repetitive, or as Lindholm says, from the visionary to the bureaucrat, from the prophet to the priest.[11] This process is related in this sense to that which Bastide calls the passage of "experienced religion," "living religion" to "administered religion," "preserved religion,"[12] a contrast that one also finds among other authors who display a "religion with two gears" or with two "levels" as Henri Desroche terms it.[13] If Henri Bergson speaks of "dynamic religion" (open) and of "static religion" (closed),[14] William James, for his part, evokes "first hand religion," that is that of religious experience, "original" and "powerful,"[15] and a "second hand religion," which is no more than its derivative. This passage to institutional religion inevitably leads to a weakening of the original experience, as Françoise Champion and Danièle Hervieu-Léger state:

> Entering into the long term, groups witness the fraying of this par-ticular exaltation belonging to its foundational times; there are still the practical necessities of the daily, ordinary management: the always delicate question of regulating power within the community, the control over economic survival, the formalization of relations between sexes and generations, the determination of conditions for entering and leaving the group, etc.[16]

And so, religious movements have always expressed this tension between the original effervescence tied to the direct experience of this charismatic force belonging to the religious leader and the routine of the institution and of bureaucratic domination. In this way, Mā's movement does not seem to be an exception to the rule.

This euphemization of the original experience linked to the transfor-mation of Mā Ānandamayī's charismatic domination seems to have taken place within her *sangha*, as the following Western man, an early disciple, suggests: "Whenever this big institution rises up, the spirituality falls down. See, the *Self Realization Fellowship of Yogananda*. He was such a great master. But the institution became so rigid. All these rules. The *sangha* is the same way. It becomes so institutionalized. They think they own Mā."

Far from being unique, these sentiments regarding the decrease of spiritual principle tied to the leader's departure were repeated during many interviews with Mā's followers. And for many of them, this spiritual weakening is reflected in the flawed character of the organization. Many speak of a bureaucratic and institutionalized character of the movement, as does this Western man, an early devotee of Mā's: "They have a very heavy organizational arrangement. Anytime you want to do something, you have this board of directors and meetings. They are fighting among themselves, they disagree all the time. It is very heavily institutionalized. It binds you." Another Westerner, an early male devotee of Mā says:

> Mā is an unbelievable being, an extraordinary, beautiful spiritual being. But so far, after twenty-five years, the organization has been

a total failure. You can underline that, you can quote me, I want to stress that point. And every devotee who is honest will agree with me. What would be the future? Will she become very well known, inspiring thousands of people or will she be totally forgotten. Who knows? In her life time, she was very famous. It is not that they don't have money....Anything you try to do with the *saṅgha* is caught in huge bureaucracy. And maybe, that will change but not tomorrow [laughs].

Another Western female disciple adds:

Personally, I think that Mā came with a mission for her lifetime and after, it will wither away; it will diminish little by little. I think that it will wilt afterwards. All that we have of her; it's still her. Her teaching is magnificent, a true wonder. But at the level of *saṅgha* and of the organization, slowly, that will diminish. Unless someone wakes up and takes everything back, but really, I don't see that really happening. Maybe the young generation will take it all back up again, and reuse everything that happened with her, her teaching, her videos, her life, her ashrams, the testimonies of those who were with her, to revive it. Well, I don't know. Look, Ramana Maharshi, he left, he left. Of course, there is still his presence, his teaching. But that's nothing like a physical guru, because we have a human body, it's the first tool we have.

And so, according to diverse testimonies, Mā's departure is for her devotees a synonym for decline. The charismatic objectives that were prevalent in Mā's time seem to be progressively weakened and removed from charismatic sources in favor of the banal and of daily life. Trigano would speak of an "attenuation of charismatic goals" as well as of a "removal from charismatic sources":

In daily life, these charismatic goals can be weakened and removed from charismatic sources. Sometimes they stay there, buried. Thus, in all institutions are left (even without appearances thereof) the "last ends" in whose service they had been created and which continue to orient the action of the organization's members.[17]

In a sense, this returns us to the statements of Meher Baba regarding the disappearance of the religious leader. He refers here to the death of a prophet and of the decline of spirituality within the religious organization:

> The prophets lay down certain rules and regulations to help the masses lead better lives and to incline them towards God. Gradually these rules become the tenets of an organized religion, but the idealistic spirit and motive force which prevail during the founder's lifetime, disappear gradually after his death. That is why organizations cannot bring spiritual truth nearer and why true religion is always a personal concern. Religious organizations become like archaeological departments trying to resuscitate the past.[18]

Thus, this spiritual effervescence associated with the presence of someone charismatic like Mā Ānandamayī seems to decline after the *mahāsamādhi* of the religious leader, in favor of the legalist religion that governs daily life. The disappearance of the leader's charismatic presence is translated into different levels, notably into the level of the exercise of power.

Like all new religious organizations that look to manage the loss of charisma due to the departure of the charismatic authority,[19] Mā's organization is the object of internal conflicts and conceals within it intense competition. This reality confirms Mann's work on the spaces of cults, when he emphasizes that the quest of those benefitting from a cult can sometimes bring about ferocious competition: "The spiritual and material resources of the shrine create an arena where powerful local interests converge, which constantly conflict with each other. Benefits associated with the shrine thus generate intense competition over their control."[20] On the subject of these conflicts within religious institutions, Panikkar additionally recalls what the medieval age called *regnum dissimilitudinis*, that is to say the realm of dissimilarity (divine), of disharmony. Mā's organization is located then in this *regnum dissimilitudinis* by the numerous conflicts of which it is the object, including the problems of succession.

The question of succession is an important one, if not the essential one, which comes into play after the death of the charismatic leader, in this case Mā, as this succession, or lack thereof, can dictate the future of the charismatic movement. The absence of successor or the non-recognition thereof by followers can essentially lead to the movement's break-up in the long or short term. There generally exists in the Hindu tradition two types of succession: a biological one (*binduparamparā* or transmission through semen) that corresponds to transmission of hereditary charisma and a spiritual succession (*natparamparā* or transmission through sound). From this succession, numerous quarrels often result, something which the guru Govind Singh avoided in discontinuing the spiritual line of the Sikh tradition at the tenth guru and in affirming that only the sacred texts are the guru, thus making a canon the charismatic center of the Sikh community.[21]

In the way of other spiritual masters like Shirdi Sai Baba, Mā Ānandamayī never designated a successor. Many followers, however, considered Swami Bhaskarānanda as a sort of continuation of Mā. Swami Bhaskarānanda, who was charged with initiations and who was the secretary general of the *saṅgha*, was perceived by some followers as being "one" with Mā, as these different testimonies show:

> Whatever Swami Bhaskarānanda tells me to do, I follow his instructions. I feel that all is coming from her.
> I feel that he is a true form of Mother...I feel that it is Mā in his body.
> Mā is behind Swamiji always, that's it. So, Mā and Swamiji, for me, it's like one.
> Swami Bhaskarānanda is one with Mā.

The testimonies of devotees are numerous on this subject. For example, an Indian man, an early disciple, gives even more detail on Swami Bhaskarānanda and his identification with Mā:

> Swami Bhaskarānanda exhibits the same traits as Mā to me, many traits that I observed. I spent a lot of time with him. I was close from him physically. I traveled with him. There are lots of traits which are common. I really feel the presence of Mā in Swamiji. It happened that he started talking like Mā also. Mā's style of talking was that many times, she didn't use a lot of words. The sentences were not complete. It was not perfect grammar. Even, he talks like that. With him, I feel that he exactly knows. Lots of my questions got answered before I ask them. I got used to it so much that the last two, three years, I haven't asked him any spiritual questions, it's all about material things, where are you going, is the eating all right, etc., because all these subtle things got answered. The answers reveal themselves and doubts disappear. That's the best thing a guru can do, make you independent. For me, Mā and Swamiji, they are both the same to me. There is no difference.

Thus, Swami Bhaskarānanda was identified to a certain point with Mā, in the same way that the Mother was identified with Sri Aurobindo after his death, as Alexandra David-Neel observed:

> The prestige that the "Mother" had among the deceased instructor's disciples is very great. Some of them declared that the latter is always actively present at the ashram and that his Presence is totally identified with the "Mother's." Of this attitude you can conclude that disciples are disposed to give to the "Mother" the place of guru that was occupied by Sri Aurobindo.[22]

Swami Bhaskarānanda then played the role of successor for some, although he could not truly replace Mā's physical presence. But since his death in 2010, the number of conflicts regarding the *saṅgha*'s direction has increased. Some feel that his departure may lead to the disintegration of Mā's organization: "After Swami Bhaskarānanda, I don't think the organization will last many few years. I think it will break itself up. There will be so much fighting, it will fall apart." And so Mā's official *saṅgha* is threatened by a number of internal conflicts.

Related to Mā's departure, there is the problem of the internal distribution of power between lay people and monks, notably in the choice of the *saṅgha*'s president. To better understand the situation, it seems necessary to briefly describe the manner in which the directing body of the *saṅgha* is structured. The directive sphere of the *saṅgha* is formed by a governing body, which is made up of forty-two members of both sexes. Lay members (twenty-one) are elected by secret ballot by the assembly of the *saṅgha* and religious members (*brahmacārins* and monks living in the ashram) are named, and not elected, by the governing body.[23] Concerning religious questions, there is a *Sadhu* Committee, made up of nine members chosen by the organization's most important monks and *brahmacārins*. All decisions made by the *Sadhu* Committee must be approved by the Governing body, which is the only one to have executive power.

Although Mā always expressed the importance of the organization being run by a lay person, as she held that a monk should consecrate himself entirely to religious life, some swamis want Mā's organization to be managed entirely by monks, as this swami affirmed:

> Of course, if it is a spiritual organization, spiritual guidance to the people would be better given by the monks, this is normal. It is not

that the householders cannot lead the people towards spirituality, they can do that but this is very difficult for them, because they are in the part time spirituality. They have other duties, other responsibilities, other preoccupations, other commitments in their household. They cannot have their full time devotion. But we don't have any other things. We have full time devotion in pursuit of spirituality. So, in my opinion, they can guide better. But not 'the monks' should run the organization, the 'right monks' should be there. The right monks.

A certain tension between monks and laypeople exists then with regard to the *sangha*'s governance, revealing a competition between clerks and laypeople to control the goods of salvation. Recently, however, a monk, Swami Nirvānānanda, was designated as the president of the *sangha*.

If the disappearance of the charismatic person is thus expressed in conflicts and in power struggles, it also can result in a total lack of organization. Since Mā's death, the *sangha* is essentially found in an advanced state of dysfunction, as the following critiques from a long-time devotee of Mā reveal:

> The organization is quasi dysfunctional. In twenty-five years after her death, almost all the books are out of print in all the languages, Hindi, Bengali, and English. Very few books are available. If you try to order a book, you will never get it. They have no ability. There are just incredibly dysfunctional, so realistically dysfunctional....Mā was such an extraordinary being and her life is quite amazing. Only a very small amount has been translated....The ashram, the organization, has failed completely. We have to go to a nearly dark side of metaphysics to even speculate on what the hell is going on here....The organization is just extraordinary bureaucratic stagnation. They don't want to be bothered with anything.

If some speak of dysfunction, others evoke a feeling of complete self-indulgence and an absence of discipline since Mā's departure, as this German woman specifies:

> If you go here in the office, sometimes, nobody is there, or they don't speak English. You see, you could arrange things very differently. They could organize some guidance of the ashram and they

could tell you about Mā. They could transmit this fire. This idea doesn't come to them. Maybe, they have the feeling that they possess Mā, as a Bengali family.

Some suggest that the absence of efficiency in the management of the organization may be linked to individualism and pride developed since Mā's departure, as this Indian man declares: "Everybody is doing his own thing" or this Indian woman: "I feel that after Mā has left, the things over here have quite changed. Pride has come. Everybody is feeling superior. If you believe in Mā completely, injustice and pride should be removed." It appears then that there is serious disorganization within the *saṅgha* since Mā's departure. In this respect, an early disciple, an Indian woman, testifies to this absence of organization within the *saṅgha* today:

> The organization of Mā is very poor, very poor, compared to all other ashrams, other organizations in India. Lots should be changed. The accommodation, the food, the whole organization should be changed. They should pay more attention to all people who are coming. You know, I would like something well organized.

In regard to the loss of charisma linked to Mā's departure, there is a type of formalism in the cult itself, as, for example the following interview with a French male new disciple reveals:

> I find Mā's cult a little surly, a little too set in its ways, sometimes a bit sad. There is a sadness. It's cacophonic, there are bells in the morning that hide, that conceal, that deform the chants of devotees, of children singing. It's not very harmonious. The people who practice are not enlightened. It's sadder, more routine. It's far from Mā Ānandamayī. For me, that hinders me from seeing these rites. In silence, it's better…the cult will become rigid, automatic, routine, I think. As the masters who knew Mā will disappear, you will have less and less direct contact. The cult will become very routine, more and more religious and sectarian. There will certainly be business done under the table, or this may already be happening.

Far from being unique, the comments of this disciple are shared by other devotees who also state that they feel a moroseness and a certain disharmony in Mā's cult today.

Finally, this impoverishment of the original experience linked to the institutionalization of Mā's cult is accompanied by a rigidity and a lack of openness within the *saṅgha* itself. Followers admit the necessity to be open to the exterior and to accept changes, as this Indian woman, an early devotee, explains:

> Radically, everything has to be changed, radically, radically, it has to be changed. Better people should come in. Younger thinking people should be come in. You can't be so dogmatic about your view. You cannot be taking Mā's name and say things that are very convenient to you. Then, you are just doing monopoly, dictatorship. We don't want things like that. We want a nice thinking group, minded people who are there only to promote and further Mā's activities. Now, it is not the case. They are comfortable with their own position right now. They want positions in the office. That is not a way to run a *saṅgha*. You have to have that love for Mā and want to share it with people. Then you will attract more people to the *saṅgha*. And you will attract better people.... They have to be better minded with younger people, who want to have this radical change. But if you just stick to the old rate, ok, they are comfortable in their positions. They don't want any change.

This lack of openness toward "the other" and the tendency to cling to old ways of functioning is reflected particularly in the *saṅgha*'s position toward Westerners. This contrasts with Swami Kedarnath's position, a close disciple of Mā and the founder of a parallel organization dedicated to Mā (see below). In this regard, a new disciple, a Western woman, affirms:

> I think the *saṅgha* of Mā is dying. It's dying. I think the part of Indore and Omkareshwar that Swami Kedarnath runs is not dying, it's going the other way, but the rest of it is dying. Kedar Baba is freer, much less orthodox, and more opened to foreigners and to women, everything. *Saṅgha* is just killing itself because of its rigidity. But I think that Mā knew that, I don't think there is a problem about it. I am not interested.

This opinion seems to be shared by a large portion of devotees, as this excerpt from an interview with a French man, a new devotee, shows: "They are afraid of foreigners....They don't want to share. They are not happy the outside is coming here." Some disciples suggest that the ashram at Kankhal, which represents in many ways the heart of Mā's cult, could become a center of international teaching, as this new male devotee explains:

> That we better teach the *dharma*, international languages. That this be a more universal, lively center. That there should be schools of teaching, that there should be a school of teaching the Sanskrit languages to everyone, on the *Tantra*, on Hinduism, on the Vedas. That this would open, that it would change, that this would become lively, it's not lively, aside from her, that's all.

Others also speak of the importance of inviting people in from the outside, such as monks from other organizations, scholars, professors, and so on: "We should invite more people.... Scholars coming should be properly treated." Thus, in the opinion of a majority of devotees, there exists today a true lack of openness and evident rigidity within Mā's *sangha*.

This distortion of the original experience of Mā's influence that comes as a result of the rationalization of Mā's cult since her departure is expressed today in power issues (i.e., the question of succession, division between laypeople and monks). Thus does the death of the charismatic figure represent at once the true challenge of and to formalization. Swami Bhaskarānanda, who demonstrated certain traits belonging to Weber's charismatic figure, may have revived the *sangha* for a time by infusing it with new energy, as this early disciple, a Western man, says: "Swami Bhaskarānanda has succeeded in the last few years in inspiring a lot of people, after a long time of stagnation. He has created some new energy, since the last four, five years." However, it nevertheless seems that the future of the organization today is compromised by the departure of the monk.

Future of the Guru's Organization

For a large number of devotees, the future of Mā's organization appears very fragile and uncertain, as this early follower, an Indian woman, declares: "I don't know how it will be. Now, at the hand of the present people, the organization is not going well." Many followers see a cult in decline: "The cult, I see it in the middle of declining. I don't necessarily have reasons for saying that, but it's my view. I find that, more and more, it's coming apart at the seams." The future of Mā's cult and of her organization then seems to be threatened if these declarations are accepted as accurate. But, if some deplore this state of affairs, others do not seem to be strongly affected, showing even a certain disinterest toward the future of Mā's organization, as the following Indian male devotee clearly suggests: "I never bother about *saṅgha*. My interest is only in Mā," or as this monk's statements also reveal:

> There are two points. If you are a *sādhaka*, a spiritual aspirant, you must focus your attention to Mā, and Mā only. Organization has nothing to do. If you see from the social point of view, you need a change according to your suitability....As for me, whether I am within the organization, whether the organization is running well or running badly, it matters little for me as long as I consider myself as a *sādhaka*. I see my involvement in the organization as a kind of duty. This is reciprocation. They give me shelter. I put some efforts. The duty has been entrusted. So, I am carrying on with it. But I have no mission with the organization. My only mission is to be with Mā. This is the main thing. I was entrusted with some duty, so I am doing it. But this is not my goal. My goal is not to run the organization. My goal is to live my life with Mā, that's all.

And so, some laypeople and some monks demonstrate disinterest toward the organization, as only their relationship with Mā is important. It seems that this disinterest in the *saṅgha* is also much more present among Western followers, as this interview with a Western woman, a new devotee, reveals:

> I don't know anything about the organization. I understood that there were cabals but I'm not really in the know. And I am not in the know in that I'm not interested because I don't care. It's like every organization once it becomes terrestrial. There are quarrels. Me, I really have nothing to say. I don't know it.

A French woman, a new follower, also told us of her disinterest toward the *saṅgha*'s affairs:

> Me, I don't know if it shouldn't decline, I don't know anything. Maybe it has to decline. Me, I only know that I've got nothing to

do with it. That, it's clear and simple. It's not me, in France, for example, who will call people around. I sense that it's more my job to do *sādhanā* in order to advance. Mā, it's the Divine Mother, she knows what she's going to do. It's not me who will decide what has to be done for Mā's *saṅgha*. InshaMa!

As evident in these statements, this disinterest toward Mā's *saṅgha* is accompanied by some resignation with respect to the destiny of the organization, which, in the end, would only depend on Mā, as these other interviews reveal: "Organization, *saṅgha*, I am not much interested. I feel that whatever is happening, it is Mā's wish. Mā will decide," or also, "Quite frankly, I don't foresee anything for the organization. I have no desire. Everything will be arranged by Mā. Whatever she does, whatever happens, it is Mā's work, it is fine for me. I accept it blindly." According to these devotees, everything seems already predestined, "Everything is predestined, it may be or not be", all this being but one manifestation of the divine game, of its *līlā*: "Now, what I see, it's the game, it's the *līlā* of Kṛṣṇa."

A majority of devotees interviewed seem then to manifest some detachment with regard to the *saṅgha*'s future. This detachment could reflect Mā's attitude toward the *saṅgha*. Similarly to other great beings like Ramakrishna or Shirdi Sai Baba, Mā did not show the slightest interest in establishing and promoting an organization in her name. If an organization was created and if Mā finally decided to pay attention to it, it was precisely to avoid risks of corruption, as Swami Vijayānanda says:

> The *saṅgha*, in the beginning, she didn't want to deal with it, but when it became so big and important, there was a danger of corruption, the danger of people putting money in their pockets. So, she took care of it. We didn't do anything without asking her. When she said something, it was final. But from the monetary point of view, she didn't want to deal with it.

This goes against the idea that the avatar-guru is to set up an institution to fulfill his or her earthy mission.[24] The lack of interest of Mā vis-à-vis institutions shows, on the contrary, that the creation of an organization is not a prerequisite for the avatar's completion of his or her life objectives. Although both Amma and Sathya Sai Baba established their own institutions, this does not appear to be a necessary step toward a guru-avatar's legitimization.

And so, far from encouraging the creation of an organization, Mā on the contrary showed a certain disinterest, even reticence toward this initiative. The absence of directives given by Mā concerning the *saṅgha* after her departure and the fact that she gave some money to each of her monks so they could be independent from the organization for the rest of their lives,[25] additionally demonstrate Mā's disinterest in the *saṅgha*. Her attitude can in part explain the indifference of some of her devotees toward the organization today. And like Mā, who condemned advertisement and had "no such *kheyāla* [spontaneous impulse of the Divine Will] of publicity," as one of the devotees put it, followers today feel the same way, orienting themselves more toward non-action and putting the *saṅgha* in the hands of Mā: "Mā does her own propaganda wonderfully." These devotees' disinterest in the future of the *saṅgha* could also have a more esoteric explanation, as this interview with an early male disciple of Mā's, a Westerner, reveals:

> I was talking to a swami of the Ramakrishna Mission. He said that when an avatar comes to earth, they have a particular mission, they have a particular power with them but they also have a dormant power within them. When they leave their body, it slowly begins to unfold. Ramakrishna has been gone for more than one hundred years but only now, his power is beginning really to unfold. If you look now at the influence of Ramakrishna Mission, and if you see the life of Ramakrishna, he never left *Dakṣinesvāra*. Vivekananda was preparing the work. Mā has a *śakti* that has not unfolded yet. Mā's presence has to come. More people will come to Mā.

This lack of interest for Mā's *saṅgha* could then also be explained by this conviction that, once Mā's *śakti* or energy is deployed, her cult and her organization will be more active.

The Organization and its Outgrowths

If the large majority of religious movements, such as that of the Radhasoamis, end in division after the death of their founder, Mā's movement does not seem to be an exception to this rule, as is demonstrated by the creation of a new *sampradāya* (spiritual line) in the 1990s by Swami Kedarnath. Swami Kedarnath first had the *darśan* of Mā in Kankhal in 1976 and, with the permission of his previous guru, Swami Avadhutananda, from whom he got his *saṃnyāsa* lineage, he received *dikṣa* from her. After his initiation, he lived in Mā's ashram in Vrindavan but his first guru requested him to return to his ashram to look after its governance. Mā gave permission for him to return to his former guru's ashram but told him, in the presence of other swamis and close devotees, that spiritually he belonged only to her. This event led Swami Kedarnath in later years to not only supervise the running of Swamiji's ashrams (which he still supervises to this day), but to independently establish two ashrams in the name of Ānandamayī Mā and create a separate Trust, the Sri Sri Mata Anandamayi Peeth Trust, which included Swami Bhaskarānanda, the general secretary of the Shree Shree Anandamayee Sangha. These two ashrams are located in Madhya Pradesh, in the cities of Indore[26] and Omkareshwar, on the banks of the Narmada River. A school was also established in Omkareshwar, where more than five hundred children receive a K–12 education as well as a spiritual education focused on Mā's teachings.[27] A successor by the name of Swami Guruśarānanda has already been designated by Swami Kedarnath to assure the maintenance of this new *sampradāya*.

Swami Guruśarānanda came to Swami Kedarnath as a 10-year-old boy. Seeing his spiritual potential, Swami Kedarnath taught him Yoga and many subjects. He then asked his father to "give him" one of his sons, namely Sarvameet, who he renamed Gurumit, which means "friend of the Guru." He later named him Guruśarānanda, which means, "The Bliss of Taking Refuge in the Guru." Swami Guruśarānanda completed his studies and under Baba's guidance obtained a doctorate (Ph.D.) in the philosophy of the *Upaniṣads*. He serves today as principal of the ashram school in Omkareshwar and is responsible for the daily running of the Omkareshwar Ashram.

Swami Kedarnath's *sampradāya* is devoted to the spreading of Mā's message and each year organizes a camp (*śivira*) destined to make Mā and her teachings known, as one of the swamis of this *sampradāya* explained to us:

> Actually, we feel that the best way to spread Mā's teaching is what
> we call the *śivira* camp. It looks like the *Samyam Saptah* but it is
> exclusively concentrated on Mā. We read Mā's words. We do medi-
> tation upon the different things Mā said. We pass the all day trying
> to hold this concept that all is God. It is a really Mā-centered event.
> We did it for one day, another one for three days. We haven't done

FIGURE 5.2 Mā Ānandamayī: "People talk and marvel about those who renounce the world, but in actual fact it is you yourself who have renounced everything. What is this 'everything'? God! Leaving Him aside, everyone is literally practicing supreme renunciation."

Source: Picture belonging to the collection of the photographer Sadanand; now in the possession of Neeta Mehta, also called Swami Nityānanda.

it for a week yet. People come to this camp to learn about Mā. They hear Mā's words and they find a practical way to apply in daily life, because otherwise, it's useless. If we just read philosophy and it doesn't change you, there is no point. I think it is going to be a major thing in spreading Mā's words and teachings.

This *sampradāya*'s commitment to spreading Mā's message seems to manifest itself in its growing interest in the West, as demonstrated by the annual concert and workshop tours across Europe by two of the organization's swamis, Swami Guruśarānanda and Swami Mangalananda. These tours are designed to gather funds for financing a school at Omkareshwar as well as to spread Mā's teachings to the West.

If Mā's devotees within the Shree Shree Anandamayee Sangha respect Swami Kedarnath, especially for his philosophical writings,[28] there is nevertheless criticism of his *sampradāya*. Some of the administrative members

FIGURE 5.3 Swami Guruśarānanda (left) and Swami Mangalananda (right), with Swami Kedarnath (in the middle).

Source: Swami Mangalananda; picture taken by the swami.

of Mā's organization accuse Swami Kedarnath of using Mā's name for personal gain, and some even don't want to know anything about this *sampradāya*: "Who is separated from Mā, I have no reason to know them [and I add: "not from Mā, from Mā's organization"]. It's ok, whatever. To me, Mā and Mā's organization are the most important." These administrative members actually removed from the website the information related to Indore and Omkareshwar's ashrams. They tried to prevent Swami Kedarnath from publishing his six volumes on Mā's teaching under the pretext that the information belongs to the Shree Shree Anandamayee Sangha. With the support of Swami Bhaskarānanda, these books did eventually get published. From some actions taken against Swami Kedarnath's *sampradāya*, there appears to be a dispute that Bourdieu would call the monopoly of the exercise of religious power. At the level of high religious authorities, there thus exists some rivalry between this *Church* that represents Mā's official *saṅgha* and the *sampradāya* of Swami Kedarnath, which here resembles the *Sect*.

This split reminds us of Habermas's building on Weber in drawing a distinction between the "representational" and the "critical," as he refers, for example, to Europe prior the eighteenth century.[29] While Mā's "official" organization, dominated by its orthodox followers, can be seen as a representational community, a kind of feudal authority, which seeks to be the only one to represent Mā and to keep other parties away, Swami Kedarnath's *sampradāya*, similarly, can be referred to as the critical one, pertaining to a liberal model of the public sphere (*Öffentlichkeit*), that is to say, a culture characterized by dialogue and the breakdown of religious hegemony.

Other members of Mā's official *sangha* additionally demonstrate indifference toward this new *sampradāya*, as the following swami does:

> It is their way. They must have thought it right, that is why they did this *sampradāya*. But my Mā is a frameless Mā. I never think of putting Mā in a particular frame. Mother has no religion. Why place Mā in a particular *sampradāya*? Swami Kedarnath must have some points and these points are unknown to me.

Mā's devotees on the whole though show some enthusiasm for this *sampradāya*. A large number of the *sangha*'s devotees have in addition already visited the ashrams of Omkareshwar and Indore. This enthusiasm is essentially tied to the work carried out by Swami Kedarnath on Mā's philosophy, but above all, to this open spirit present within this new movement, which does not seem to accord a fundamental importance to brahminical rules of purity, notably toward foreigners. Swami Mangalananda, an American devotee of Mā who has lived in Omkareshwar since 2001, is the best example of this openness.

In the early 1970s, Swami Mangalananda went to India to meet with Mā. There, he received mantra initiation from Mā and traveled all over North India with her during the years 1973 and 1974. Returning to the United States, he moved into an ashram run by a devotee of Mā and also lived in a Christian Monastery for some time. In 2001, Swami Bhaskarānanda sent him to Omkareshwar to continue his *sādhanā* and to help start the school there. He received *saṃnyāsa dīkṣā* and has lived in Omkareshwar now for twelve years.

And so, as with every *Church* phenomenon, Mā's organization has experienced a rupture, appearing in the creation of Swami Kedarnath's *sampradāya*, which parallels in a way the history of Christianity, as Trigano observes:

> All prophetic sects that succeed tend in fact to become a church, a hierarchical institution of orthodoxy. This is what explains why all church phenomena ineluctably engender a new prophetic rupture and religious reform....And so on, until the end. In history you find the following sequence: Protestantism, to reconstitute itself again, makes on Catholicism Christianity's operation on Judaism. Without talking about the exponential fission of protestant churches one after the other, after the advent of Protestantism.[30]

This phenomenon of fission in churches seems then to have taken place within Mā's *saṅgha*, as the appearance of a new *sampradāya* reveals. For some, the future of Mā's cult lies in the development of this *sampradāya*, which offers much greater freedom, notably with respect to rules of brahminical orthodoxy.

Community, Ashrams, and Orthodoxy

What is the role of ashrams and the community in the perpetuation of the cult of the guru? To respond to this question, I base this study on the many interviews conducted throughout my research and on field work in ashrams. I also discuss the question of the pertinence of brahminical rules of orthodoxy within Mā's community and its vast network of ashrams, notably through works of the Western disciple Atmananda but also via interviews. I distinguish here between the views of Westerns and those of Indians.

Community and Continuity of the Cult

It seems that the continuity of the cult of the guru after death is directly linked to the maintenance of his or her community. As Parita Mukta specifies in her study on Mirabai, the community first of all represents a way to keep the saint's memory alive.[31] The community holds a primordial place in Mā's posthumous cult, in the sense that it permits a reactualization of Mā's presence through her memory. The great annual celebrations, which gather together the lay and monastic communities, in this way, represent a means to reinforce the community's ties and to perpetuate Mā's memory.

The community also plays an important role at the level of experience. Not only does the exchange of experiences within the community constitute a way to reinforce followers' faith and to enrich their own individual experiences, it also permits the validation of an experience. And so, the community represents a central element in the cult's sustainability, nourishing the follower's faith through exchanges with the members of the community. The community also leads the devotee to new experiences that would not be imaginable for the lone follower and confers on their religious experience a framework into which experiences can take on greater meaning. In this regard, James, according to Taylor, undervalues the role of religious community in giving birth to religious experience, as Taylor specifies here: "What James can't seem to accommodate is the phenomenon of collective religious life, which is not just the result of (individual) religious connections, but which in some sense constitutes or *is* that connection."[32]

Finally, the community facilitates the perpetuation of the cult of the religious leader after his or her death by its role in the maintenance of religious identity, which would prove to be difficult without a continuous interaction between believers. By his or her inclusion in this community, the devotee recognizes his or her role in the transmission of this religious identity and, by the same token, contributes to some continuity on the part of the cult. This may return us to the idea of "sacred community" recalled by Van der Leeuw regarding the religious veneration of the dead.[33]

Although the raison d'être of the community is the living guru, it still has a critical role to play after the death of the guru. It may be, however, that Mā did not particularly desire the continuation of the community after her death. Although Ramakrishna's sole instruction on his death in 1886 was for his devotees to remain together,[34] Mā, on the contrary, gave no directions but rather gave to each of her monks some money so as to allow them to live independently, showing the flexibility that Hindu monasticism offers.[35] Mā did not then especially insist on the survival of her community after her departure.

According to many interviews with Mā's devotees, opinions seem to be divided concerning the community. For some, there is no doubt that the community constitutes a source of spiritual support, notably permitting them to exchange experiences and to reinforce their faith in Mā. Devotees, which are sometimes called *gurubhais* (brothers in the guru) and *gurubahins* (sisters in the guru), generally gather together once or twice a month on the occasion of *satsaṅgas* to chant and to perform rituals and collective meditation, as well as on the occasion of the large annual celebrations like Mā's birthday or *Gurupūrṇimā*. An early disciple of Mā's, an Indian man, told us of the central place that Mā's community holds for him:

> It is important for me.... Mā is in everyone. Someone who is think-
> ing of Mā, who is talking about Mā, who is doing anything for Mā,
> this person, is very very important to me in my life. For me, doing
> something for devotees of Mā, this is doing something for Mā. It is
> a kind of service for Mā.

For new disciples, the community also plays an important role, facilitating contact with devotees who knew Mā, as this new follower, an Indian
woman, affirms:

> I just believe that it is very good to be in a group where people have
> similar interests, similar vibrations. That also helps, rather than
> being in a social group.... I get more from the devotees who met
> Mā because they have witnessed many things. Those devotees who
> have been with her for so many years, they have so many things
> with her. I like to be in this atmosphere and meet people, who have
> similar interest, and who have Mā as their guru.

In addition, some speak of positive vibrations arising from contact with
Mā's devotees: "You are getting positive vibes from that." And others also
evoke the structural role that the community plays in their *sādhanā*: "Until
I really realize That, it provides some kind of structure, I suppose, some
containment for what is happening, some external kind of something, a
frame, something like that."

If many followers recognize the largely beneficial role of the community in the continuation of the cult, others nevertheless hold a more
reserved opinion on its role. They notably speak of the risk of becoming
removed from Mā's teaching through the contacts between members of
the community, as this French woman, a new devotee, affirms: "Yes, I like
to talk about Mā, but this really has to be in Mā's way. Because, afterwards,
there's a sort of projection of images on the person. Yes, in fact, it supports
devotion, but you have to be careful." Another follower, also a Western
female, early devotee, confided in us:

> I enjoy being in the company of devotees who have been around
> Mā, in whom I can feel close connection. The danger of coming

afterwards, after Mā's *mahāsamādhi*, is that, sometimes people are
more bound to a certain swami than to Mā, or they construct a little
bit their own Mā as she was. There is a difference between these
old devotees and new devotees. But new devotees can also be open
and very innocent. And, sometimes, I don't have the inclination
to be with certain devotees of Mā at all. Sometimes, I prefer to be
with devotees of other gurus. This cannot be generalized. Really, it
depends also on the person's attitude, on the individual seeker. This
is not so dependent on Mā.

While granting the beneficial role of the community, some devotees thus
give importance to remaining strictly with Mā's teaching and being wary of
creating a new Mā. And if other followers generally recognize the essential
place of the community in their spiritual path, they nevertheless deplore
the lack of vitality, the inability to evolve within Mā's community since her
departure, as this French woman, a new devotee explains:

The cave, it's not for me. The *saṅgha* plays a big role. For me, it's a
circle. I do nothing but take, there are exchanges, and moments of
sādhanā that you share and which, in my opinion, propel me forward and which correspond to what I need for my *sādhanā*. . . . For
me, there isn't much to do at Kankhal. I get bored a bit because
here, there is no *saṅgha*. Me, I like to be with people, to study
together, to chant together. Here, it's specifically for Indians. And
then, Westerners, well people with whom communication is easier
as we have the same way of thinking, here, there isn't that, except
when you come to the international center, you can always meet
people like you. But that doesn't work, you stay two, three, five days,
and that's all. I've lived in an ashram for a long time and I like the
ashram life. Here, you don't even have the right to enter the ashram.[36] You can't be there. That's all. When Mā was around, it must
have been different. Those who had the courage to hold on, there
was Mā.

Finally, there are those for whom the community does not assume, at
least now, particular importance in their eyes, as is the case with this follower: "to participate in the *saṅgha*, in meetings, discussions, yes, but not
all the time, because there are many things I prefer to do alone. For the
moment, I don't need that. I am fine alone." Others speak of the declining

importance the community holds in their lives, like this English woman, a new devotee:

> I go to *satsaṅga*, but I feel as time is going on, it is becoming less important and I am feeling like I am happier doing my own practice and carrying on my own. I find [it] a little bit alarming though because I am much much less interested in leading a social life, so I am losing touch with a lot of people, because they are all busy doing their own things. I am not finding that very attractive anymore, I am just finding myself wanting meditating as much as I can. I meditate now five hours per day.

And so, opinions on the community's importance are diverse among devotees. If some perceive the community to be an aid to their *sādhanā*, others see it more as an obstacle, revealing some tension between the individual and the community.

The Ashrams of the Guru's *Saṅgha*

As Alexandra David-Neel specifies, the death of the master is generally associated with the disappearance of his or her ashrams: "A list of ashrams may be extended indefinitely. There are hundreds in India, small and large whose existence, often ephemeral, ends with the death of their founder."[37] In the same way, Ma Indira Devi affirmed in her letters that there could not really be ashrams after the death of the master:

> An Indian Guru is not just the Head of the Institution or Monastery, he *is* the institution. In the former case one goes to a certain Monastery or takes to an order and then loves the Head of the place, but in the latter, ones goes to the Guru and resides in the Ashram because of him. There can be no Ashram, properly speaking, after the passing of the Guru. The disciples may stay on in the Ashram building for the sake of convenience, but that is all.[38]

If one believes these different statements, the departure of the guru would be accompanied, then, by the disappearance of his or her ashrams. And yet, if some, like Swami Vijayānanda thought that Mā's ashrams were going to disappear as soon as she left, this does not seem to be the case: "In the beginning, I thought that everything was going to rapidly disintegrate.

But not at all in fact. There is still a lot of activity, of movement."[39] Thus, despite Mā's departure, the ashrams of her *saṅgha* are still around, and so, it seems important to examine the role of these ashrams today and the necessity of keeping them up. Before addressing these points, a brief return to the past, notably Mā's attitude toward the question of ashrams, seems however to be necessary.

Mā never wanted ashrams and said as much: "This body does not found ashrams. There, where there is no tension, there is an ashram."[40] Mā also affirmed this regarding ashrams: "This entire universe is my house. I am in my own house even when seeming to be roaming from place to place."[41] This cannot but remind us also of Mā's comments to Arnaud Desjardins, the French writer and film director, when he was preparing to leave India and return to France:

> Mā Ānandamayī often declared and repeated to me when I had twice told her goodbye on returning to Paris: that she is never far, the entire world is her ashram…she repeated this many times, with an unspeakable love: "No boundaries, no boundaries, Paris Ashram, Paris Ashram, Ek: One, Ek: One."[42]

And so Mā never desired ashrams, as for her, the world is her ashram. Considering the insistence of her disciples, she eventually ceded to their wishes and ashrams were constructed across India. In this context, it is interesting to note that the day after the first ashram's inauguration, the Ramna ashram at Dhaka in 1929, Mā left for Dehra Dun in the Himalayas, to the great disappointment of her devotees at Dhaka. And later, when other ashrams for Mā were established in India, Mā began to decline to visit the ashram, preferring to stay elsewhere. It seems then that Mā never attributed great importance to the *saṅgha*'s ashrams.

On Mā's death, the *saṅgha* counted in total twenty-six ashrams. With the creation of such a network of ashrams, Mā then represents an exception to the history of India, as this was the greatest number of ashrams at that time constructed for a woman.[43] Although today, it is common for female gurus to found their own movement and have their own ashrams, as is the case with Amma and Gurumayi, this institutionalization of the cult of a female guru was inconceivable before Mā's time.

More than thirty years after Mā's departure, these ashrams still exist. And, if Mā never really desired their construction, followers nevertheless seem to attribute great importance to the preservation of these sacred spaces. In

addition to facilitating the gathering of devotees, and bringing material com-
modities to its residents, Mā's ashrams are said to be favored places for con-
tacting her, due to the subtle vibrations that she is said to have left during her
many stays, as this close disciple of Mā's, an Indian woman, explains here:

> If you visit any ashram, you will find something special. When Mā
> was in her body, I didn't realise how special these places are. It didn't
> come into my mind. Mā was the attraction. But now, when I visit
> those ashrams, I feel so strongly these high spiritual vibrations.
> People should visit the ashrams of Mā. No doubt that a person who
> visits a place leaves some vibrations. It is the same with Mā. In the
> case of Mā's ashrams, all spots are special. If you go there and sit
> for some time, meditate there, you will feel the vibrations. For that
> reason, those ashrams should be maintained.

Some even speak of a special presence associated with these places in
which Mā stayed: "The places where Mā has been, yes, there is a special
presence," and, in this context, others recall a memory of the place: "she
came to this earth, she left memories. All these places where she was have
memories of her." And so, it would be important to conserve these ashrams
due to the subtle presence that Mā is said to have left during her stays.

At a more symbolic level, ashrams are also important to the preservation of Mā's cult, as an early disciple of Mā's, an Indian man, affirms
regarding Mā's first ashram at Dhaka: "Siddheshwari, to me, it is a
very important place for the future, one of the very few places that will
unite the world." Finally, if the old adage that the ashram represents the
guru's physical body holds, then Mā's ashrams should be maintained, as
Ramakrishna's disciples also affirm regarding their *math* (monastic institution): "This Math represents the physical body of Shri Ramakrishna. He
is always present in this institution. The injunction of the whole Math is
the injunction of Shri Ramakrishna. One who worships it, worships him
as well. And one who disregards it, disregards our Lord."[44]

It seems then for devotees that it is necessary to conserve Mā's ashrams,
so as to assure the continuity of her cult. However, despite this desire, only
some ashrams are active today. Many ashrams are almost uninhabited, as
this early disciple of Mā's, a Western man, affirms:

> So many of the *saṅgha* ashrams now just go down. Maybe two or
> three people living and nothing happens. This ashram, in Bhimpura,

is very busy, very alive, very active. In Vindhyachal, no one there. Even in Varanasi, there are just two or three people in a huge ashram. I have been many times to Bhimpura ashram. There is always some kind of events happening here. This is a very active, a very good ashram, but so many of the *saṅgha*'s ashrams are so empty.

This neglect of the large majority of the *saṅgha*'s ashrams may be associated with a sort of resignation, as these comments from an Indian woman, a new follower, suggest: "I tell Mā, 'It is your duty to protect these ashrams. You have brought us over here.' So, this depends on Mā. Everything depends on Mā."

Although devotees seem to care about Mā's ashrams, only a few of these ashrams are really lively today. Only the ashram at Bhimpura (where Swami Bhaskarānanda used to live), the ashram at Kankhal, and the ashram at Calcutta (where the majority of Mā's community is found) still seem to be relatively active, at least during celebrations in honor of Mā.

Orthodoxy and Sustainability of the Cult

An essential question must be asked regarding the perpetuation of Mā's cult after her death, that is, the relevance of maintaining rules of purity in Mā's ashrams. These traditional rules of purity, called *Jhuṭā* or that which is dirty and inappropriate, have for thousands of years been observed by the brahminical orthodoxy, serving as a kind of propaedeutic, of preparation to mystical life.[45] This orthodoxy, contested by Sufism and Buddhism, as well as by Tantric Hinduism, was adopted by Mā following a meeting she had with the pandit Gopinath Kaviraj. While Mā, at the beginning, did not follow the purity rules, there was an increasing pressure on her to do so. Finally, one day, she said, "Whoever is coming today will decide." That day pandit Gopinath Kaviraj came right after her statement and told Mā that rules of caste should be maintained in the Kālī Yuga to form a barrier against immorality. Although Mā opted for these rules, Swami Vijayānanda maintained that Mā was not attached to a particular system, as she always said, *Jo Ho Jay,* "Whatever has to happen, will happen." For him, Mā would definitely have adapted herself if she had been born in the West.[46]

In relation to caste rules, devotees also mention Mā's desire to allow everyone to come together and to stay in her ashrams. The non-observance of these rules of purity would have then constituted a major obstacle for orthodox brahmins and would have prevented them from coming to Mā.[47] Despite the establishment of these rules, it is nevertheless interesting to notice that Mā did not really respect these rules of purity, revealing a certain lack of concern for such customs. Atmananda reports what Mā told her regarding these rules as, "What are these rules to me? I have eaten the leavings of a dog."[48] Although Mā approved these rules, she never really adopted them and even allowed herself to openly transgress them. In this context, transgression appears to be a way of affirming Mā's authority as spiritual leader, as Mā was the only person with the power to authorize the observation of these brahminical rules within her community. Defying rules of pollution regarding the untouchable status of foreigners, as well as the impurity associated with menstruation, she invited a menstruating Westerner to sit next to her. Jean-Claude Marol tells us of this anecdote in one of his books on Mā:

> A charming French older woman confided in me how when she was younger, she visited Mā, but didn't dare to approach her, as she was menstruating at the time. She didn't hide this fact from the Brahmins in Mā's entourage. As they considered her to be impure, they asked her to come back another day! However, Mā Ānandamayī, sensing the ruckus in the room, asked the young woman to come sit at her side; she cleared her a large place on her immaculate couch.[49]

Atmananda also testifies to Mā's attitudes towards brahminical purity:

> She told me there are different rules in every ashram and that neither through eating alone or with others does one get God realization. She told me to throw away all disturbing thoughts that come into my mind. She does not seem very interested in those rules, but seems to want people to observe them so that those who choose to be orthodox may also feel free to come to Her.[50]

Melita Maschmann, a German writer who lived near Mā for some time, testifies to her non-observance of these rules of purity:

> Obviously she herself is not endangered by my vibrations, like the āśramites, because she allowed me to put my chain I wore for years around her neck, and she often touches me. This may be the

reason why I do not have this feeling of 'ambiguity' in relation to her. She also respects the rules concerning the food, not because she is afraid of becoming impure, but out of consideration for her orthodox followers.[51]

Thus, if Mā, in consideration to her orthodox devotees, followed these rules of purity, she is said to have never really embraced them and was never upset by their non-observance, as the previous testimonies show.[52] In reality, for Mā, "purity is an attitude of the mind."[53] She also said: "Actually purity means truth, that which *is*. Whatever helps you to come nearer to that Reality, towards the realization of Truth, may be called pure and whatever retards that is impure."[54]

Because of these rules of purity, many Westerners speak of the difficulty during Mā's time of truly integrating into these ashrams. Arnaud Desjardins, who stayed many times near Mā, talks about this traditional Hindu society governed by this spirit of segregation towards foreigners, or "outsiders." Adding to this segregated environment the language barrier, he writes:

> It's not at all easy for a foreigner to stay in an ashram where Mā Ānandamayī is. He has no place in traditional Hindu society that surrounds him and numerous barriers are raised, making access to her room often difficult. Finally, knowing probably neither Hindi nor Bengali beyond how to say milk, water, rice and sleep, he is condemned to never understand a word of the questions posed to Mā Ānandamayī, nor the answers she gives, nor what is chanted, what is read, the commentaries given to what was read. What the devil then are we going to do in this hell and why did I return three times to her side, twice 18 months apart and for stays of several weeks each time?[55]

According to this testimony, it seems that Mā's presence largely compensated for the inconveniences linked with the untouchable status of the foreigner. Atmananda, who lived for decades in Mā's ashrams, also speaks of her ability to handle her status as a pariah thanks to Mā's presence:

> It's thanks to her that we could handle it. As to what concerned me, there was also the conviction, in light of other experiences

I had had near other sages, like Krishnamurti and even Ramana
Maharshi, that there was no one in the world comparable to Mâ
Ânandamayî. If there had been someone comparable, I would
have left the ashram right away. But there wasn't. So, I couldn't
leave Mâ.[56]

Atmananda seems to have been greatly affected by these purity rules in
the ashrams, as can be perceived in her posthumously published journal
entitled *Death Must Die*:

Today I heard that the three ashram *brahmacharini*s (nuns) could
not eat yesterday because I was sitting in the same room and the
Brahmanical rules prohibit them from eating under the same roof
with non Hindus. I again got violently upset and decided that I cannot remain in such a place. I must stay by myself and think this out.
My faith is gone. If I cannot understand these inhuman rules, then
how can I trust Her entirely?[57] . . .
      Yesterday there was a series of incidents that made me feel
very bitter about those rules. All the accumulated insults came to a
head and I burst out with everything to Didi and cried. Then I ran
away and sat under a tree. Meanwhile Mother was searching for
me and called me to Her as soon as I came back. In the morning
She had already asked me to follow Her to Almora after some days;
but meanwhile I had decided to go away, as I felt so bad about the
so-called 'Hindu Dharma'.[58]

Atmananda even speaks of the cruelty of Hindu *dharma*:

I know now how cruel this so-called Hindu *dharma* has become
due to complete abuse of its ancient principles. No doubt this is
responsible for much of India's bad *karma*. Yesterday there was
a problem over the 'rules' that upset me very much and I was
imprudent enough to tell one of the *sadhus* here that obviously
only Brahmins were made by God, and all others by the devil.
He evidently did not like it. Later I told Girinda that I could now
see why the British Raj could endure so long here and that it
was well deserved. He did not like this at all. So I am, as always,
standing in my own way and creating difficulties. I must not talk
to other.[59]

FIGURE 5.4 Mā Ānandamayī at Patal Devi temple (Almora). In 1937 her pilgrimage to Mount Kailash began from this place.

Source: Photograph courtesy of Shree Shree Anandamayee Sangha.

Conscious of the difficulty of Westerners in accepting these rules, Mā is said to have taken advantage of this situation to "work" on them, as Atmananda testifies to:

> Made a big scene with Mother because of the 'rules', but Her verdict was: "As long you have desires you will have suffering. If you go some-where else you will have other difficulties. You can't get peace as long as there is desire. Bear these things laughingly like Haridas who fol-lowed Sri Chaitanya in spite of all the difficulties, refusing to have any special privileges for himself. But Chaitanya took him to his heart and embraced him. If you contemplate God, the desires will go."[60]

Far from considering her Western devotees as victims of untouchability, Mā seemed to consider these brahminical rules to be a way to diminish their egos.

The brahminical rules in most of Mā's traditional ashrams (I do not include Indore and Omkareshwar ashrams, which do not abide by the orthodox rules) still seem to weigh on the majority of Westerners today, who must eat separately from Indians and be housed outside the ashram. It is not permitted for Westerners to eat with Indians and it is necessary to have an individual cup, so that Hindus, and especially brahmins, can avoid any polluting contact. This reminds us of another of Atmananda's remarks fifty years earlier: "How can I make her ashram my home when people have to bathe if they wash my cup? Today this trend of thought continued. In my mind I wrote Her a letter saying these things. All this makes me conscious that I am European and cannot and do not want to be a Hindu."[61] Interviews with foreign devotees of Mā also speak of the mistrust of some Indians toward foreigners, as this Western woman, a new devotee, states regarding the *Samyam Saptah* of Kankhal:

At Kankhal, we are bogeymen, we are bogeymen! There are some Indians who hate Westerners. The majority, they are charming. There are rules, they let you know gently. But there are a handful of Indians who hate Westerners; there are times when they insult you.... When there is the *Samyam Saptah* at Kankhal, it's all of Northern India who comes, it's not Kankhal. There are all of those from Delhi, from Gujarat who come here. Thus, it's really the *sangha* in general. They are really strictly orthodox.

The orthodox sensibility seems then to be truly disturbed by the presence of Westerners. But, to assure the continuity of the cult, this orthodoxy, for some, no longer has its place, as this new devotee, a Western man, states:

There must be many more points of contact between foreigners and Hindus. There is a barrier between foreigners and Hindus. With respect to Mā, there must be a universal, exemplary teaching, in practice as well, that is shown. As she was universal, she talked about Jesus, the Buddha as well as Kṛṣṇa, for her teaching to also pertain to foreigners. To open up a bit, to accept speaking with a foreigner, so that he is not regarded with a critical eye from the moment he arrives in the *samādhi*, that people not grimace.

A larger sense of openness toward foreigners, and thus a laxity or even a suppression of brahminical rules of purity within Mā's ashrams appears then to be necessary, according to this disciple, to assure the cult's future. This opinion seems to be shared by other Western disciples, as this German woman, an early disciple, for whom the attitude of Indians toward Westerners has detrimental consequences:

> The big mistake was that they were so very afraid of Western influ-ence that they didn't allow us to be helpful for their aims. If you com-pare to Ramana Maharshi ashram, Shivananda ashram, or Amma's ashram, everything is so lively, the *samādhi*, the ashram....Here, it is getting so few people. It is a pity I think. There are old forces which want to keep the new and with it, also the good ways. It's get-ting older and older. There are less and less people here. I think that Westerners will have to take over at one point. They are trying to keep the Westerners outside. In Mā's time, when she was alive, you had to overcome certain obstacles to be near her. People around her were not always very supportive. I didn't mind. I thought it is their problems. So there were never so many Westerners around. These orthodox, brahminical forces were quite strong. Some swamis, they have become so opened now, I think. Swami Nirgunānanda, for example, he drunk from a normal cup in my home, he didn't have his own cup. I think that they are seeing the necessity of things to be changed, to be more opened, even in term of materials. It could be so well organized if they would invite the Westerners to come with opened arms. You can live here, come, we show you how to do *pūjā*, come, we show you how to play *kīrtana*. There would be so many people who would be interested. They would even be willing to learn and observe certain rules of purity, or whatever. But, in a way, you feel that they treat you as if you come from a different star and you don't understand anything.

The discriminatory attitude of orthodox Hindus toward Westerners in Mā's ashrams is heavily criticized by other Westerns, who vigorously con-demn the Bengali orthodox brahmins' supremacy, as shown, for example, by the comment of this Western man, an early disciple:

> I think the approach of the *saṅgha* is really wrong. These rules are actually driving people away from Mā. See, Mā kept the ortho-dox rules during her life and people asked her about it. She said

that's because many orthodox brahmins wouldn't be able to come. In comparison, there are very few foreigners, and unfortunately, they have to suffer but more people are benefiting, because more people have access. But things have changed now. They are holding onto these theoretical rules which have no place anymore, all these orthodox rules. Many of Mā's ashrams are run by these east Bengalis brahmins who are orthodox at the point of being superstitious. In Gujarat, they say that they have broken up the Bengali slavery. Here (Bhimpura ashram), they don't have all these rules. Well, they try to keep the rules as much as they can, they keep the rules of the *saṅgha*, but they don't have the attitude, the bad attitude towards foreigners. They are much more open here. Like in Varanasi, these places around, they are run almost exclusively by Bengalis. This attitude has no place in the future, in spreading Mā's name.

Thus, for a large number of Westerners, these brahminical rules no longer have a place within Mā's organization and can only hinder the development of Mā's cult. However, a small number of Westerners admit the necessity of retaining the brahminical rules so as to remain as close as possible to Mā's directions, as the following testimony from a French woman, a new devotee, shows:

> I don't know if they should change the rules. Me, I think that what is most important is to stay close to what Mā wanted, to her way of doing *pūjā*s, the rituals, to what she wanted to teach and the instructions she wanted to give. And, in fact, these principle directions are to stay as close as possible to the *dharma*. To preserve a memory, yes, but not any memory, not in any way you like. There can be changes, and as long as these changes do not bring Mā's thought into play, why not. I think that you have to respect the tradition that Mā established. I think that, at a given moment, there are some things that she held to, and which seemed a bit strange to us, like the brahminical rules. Maybe it's necessary to spread the *dharma*, maybe [laughs], I don't know. But, in any case, there was definitely a reason. And, for that matter, why would she have been born in a brahminical environment? It's not she that chose to respect brahminical rules. She herself ate fish. In Bengal, everyone eats fish. Her husband Bholanāth was a heavy smoker. One day, she asked herself, is it necessary? She had a day of *kheyāla*, an inspiration.

The first to come will give us rules and it's a *pandit* that came. If you accept Mā, I think that you must be confident in many things, even if you don't understand everything.

Finally, there are some Westerners who are relatively indifferent to these rules, for whom these rules do not present real obstacles. Jacques Vigne speaks of his experience regarding this matter:

> For some Westerners, these rules have constituted a gigantic obsta-cle. I must say that for the eighteen years that I have been associ-ated with Mā's ashrams, in part with the main ashram at Kankhal, in Hardwar, these rules have not at all posed problems for me. It takes a few weeks to get used to, but in fact many of them are com-mon to monastic disciplines that you may find among Christians or Buddhists.[62]

These rules, far from being bothersome, may thus for some devotees con-stitute a form of discipline belonging to some monastic religious tradi-tions. A new English disciple also recalls her indifference toward these rules, which do not seem to unreasonably affect her spiritual path:

> I don't feel a foreigner to myself, and that's what counts. They may see me as a foreigner, but that doesn't bother me because I know that I need to have some access to the places at the moment, like here, in Bhimpura, and whatever. They can get on with doing their own things. It really doesn't bother me what they do. I don't mind to be a foreigner because I don't want to be part of their culture. I am not an Indian.

Demonstrating disinterest for all these rules, this disciple then declares that she does not feel herself to be a foreigner in this segregated envi-ronment. For others, these rules may even represent a positive element in their *sādhanā*. This status as foreigners, as "outcasts," leads them to a kind of inner renunciation necessary for an authentic spiritual path. The experience of being a Westerner in Mā's ashrams can in this sense be tied to what the Fathers of the Desert called the *xeniteia*, that is to say, the life abroad. This practice of isolation in a foreign land was recommended for liberation from the conditionings of society. Thus, through this sort of imposed *xeniteia*, Mā's Western devotees would learn to perceive Mā's cult from another angle, to take advantage of this singular pleasure of being a foreigner. Far from being a hindrance to Mā's cult, this sort of exclusion imposed on foreigners in her ashrams may, on the contrary, become a positive thing, in the sense that it privileges the "inner cult," as some Western devotees affirm.

In addition, it is interesting to enquire into the attitude of Indians toward these rules of purity. Some Indians demonstrate absolute disapproval of this orthodoxy that affects not only Westerners but also monks who wish to travel to the West, as the following comment from this early disciple, an Indian man, shows:

> The traditional organization has something against foreigners and our *sādhus* going to foreign countries, both ways. Now, they want to restrict that. I am against this. My argument is that if a *sādhu* cannot go to other country than India, then, what about Kailash? They cannot go to China? Mā was born in Bangladesh, a foreign country. Can't we go to see Mā's birth place? And Mā was born in Bangladesh and it was a part of Pakistan before. We are far from *sanātana dharma*. It's a Muslim country. And today, they would not happily welcome anybody who comes from a Muslim country. Mā was Pakistani actually, not Indian. The other argument that I give is that Mā always referred to the scripture. Lord Rāma went outside the country. We give a lot of examples. Look, Mā always welcomed all foreigners. Look at Swami Vijayānanda. Look at Atmananda. Look at Ram Alexander. Mā gave him a room in the ashram of Kankhal. He stayed seven years there. This is manmade. Mā respected the sentiments of everybody, including foreigners. But Mā didn't want to hurt the sentiments of the brahmins and she didn't want to hurt the sentiments of foreigners either. It's not one at the expense of the others. For Mā, there was no difference. Everybody is equal to Mā. The situation is unfortunate. Organizations go up and down. It's going through a very low phase right now [laughs].

In relation to traveling overseas for orthodox brahmin gurus, there are now, as Copeman and Ikegame remark, various ways for them to extend their presence on a global scale as media technologies have become more available to reach devotees.[63]

Other Indian devotees, despite their desire to see these rules disappear, also think that they are destined to last due to a strong presence of orthodox brahmins in Mā's ashrams, as this Indian woman, an early disciple, explains:

> These rules are going to be there. Nothing is going to change that. There are old thinking people already existing. Mā never used to change somebody's thinking. If you were born in a particular *saṃskāra*, or a particular family, she never tried to change that. Within your parameters, you live and think. If somebody says I cannot eat with foreigners, ok, we have to respect his view. Mā used to say that she is respecting that. I am not asking you to change. As far as the foreigners are concerned, for Mā, everybody is her child. This is exactly what Swami Nirgunānanda and Swami Bhaskarānanda are saying. They don't have any problem in sitting and eating with you. They are beyond that. They are beyond those limitations, whereas these people come from a very limited thinking. That is how it is going in the ashram. They are orthodox in their thinking. They have not advanced spiritually in that way. The moment you advance spiritually, you realize that this, itself, is a limitation on your path. It is putting a limitation and you are not growing.

Other Indians, while not really according importance to these rules of purity themselves, nonetheless speak of the necessity of preserving tradition, as this Indian man, an early devotee: "Rules should not change. Mā's tradition shouldn't change. Whoever has the *saṃskāra* will understand and accept these rules."

Some Indians demonstrate detachment or even a sort of fatalism regarding this question of orthodox rules, leaving all responsibility in Mā's hands, as this Indian man, an early disciple of Mā's:

> If I want to invite foreigners to go to ashrams, I may not do well because they may lose interest tomorrow. But if Mā wants the foreigners to come, there will be no foreigner, we'll be all one. Maybe, that day is coming. Why don't we wait for that day? If I invite you and don't treat you well, the way it should be, you will lose interest. But if Mā is inviting you one day, we'll all dance together in the name of Mā. And that day will definitely come. So if men create organizations, there is difficulty. But if Mā creates, it is flow

less. The word "foreigner" will not be there. Then, everybody will embrace each other, and dance and dance. There won't be any foreigner. Why hurry? It is going to come.

Finally, there are Indians who categorically refuse the least change in the rules present in Mā's ashrams and who are completely convinced of their validity. Being myself a foreign woman and thus a polluting agent, it was obviously not possible for me to discuss this with these types of devotees.

Thus, these interviews present diverse opinions concerning the future of brahminical rules installed in the ashrams of Mā's *sangha*.[64] On the whole, it appears that a greater flexibility with regard to these purity rules may be necessary for the large majority of devotees interviewed, Indians as well as foreigners, so as to assure the continuity of Mā's cult.[65] As the superior authorities of Mā's *sangha* are disinclined to make these changes today, it seems however that brahminical rules are destined to last and that Westerners will for the time immediately to come be forced to take on the role of pollutant, a role described perfectly here by Douglas:

A polluting person is always in the wrong. He has developed some wrong condition or simply crossed some line which should not have been crossed and this displacement unleashes danger for some-one. Bringing pollution, unlike sorcery and witchcraft, is a capacity which men share with animals, for pollution is not always set off by humans. Pollution can be committed intentionally, but intention is irrelevant to its effect—it is more likely to happen inadvertently.[66]

The rigidity of brahminical orthodoxy within Mā's ashrams in the long term, however, might place Mā's cult in peril, for as James specifies, when a religion becomes an orthodoxy, it loses forever its interiority. But as fate would have it, despite this strong discrimination toward Westerners, it nevertheless seems today that some Indians envisage the future of Mā's cult to be in the West, as Swami Kedarnath suggests: "I feel that Mā's work will start from foreign lands, from there it will start. That's why more foreign people are coming and getting more interested." This, in a sense, recalls the comments of Atmananda some decades earlier: "I am persuaded that it's the West, much more than India, that will spread Mâ Anandamayī's teaching. It's a universal teaching that can suit everyone."[67]

There exist then some tensions within Mā's community regarding the preservation of brahminical rules. Mā's *sangha* is split between two directions. On the one hand, many want to enlarge her movement, notably to an international audience, which necessarily would require both letting go of these rules and a rupture with the tradition of the group's founder. On the other hand, others desire a preservation of brahminical orthodoxy, which is ineluctably associated with exclusion and which hampers the cult's expansion. Mā's *saṅgha* is located then in the middle of this dilemma between "authenticity" and "dirtying," between "atrophy" and "expansion."

Hagiography and Perpetuation of the Cult

As hagiography represents an essential way of perpetuating the guru's cult after his or her death, it seems important to cast some light on this subject. Lee Novetzke's work on the saint Namdev, in this regard, is particularly interesting, as it examines how Namdev's life and literary production have been assimilated into the way religious communities in India remember the saint.

I shall first of all attempt to demonstrate the role of hagiography as a sort of amplification of devotion, then I will concentrate on the question of death in hagiography, the true challenge of hagiography.

Hagiography, a Form of Devotion

If, as Wilson affirms, the cult influences literature, the inverse is also true. Literature, and especially hagiography, can influence the posthumous future of sainted beings by making it enter into the "collective memory and space of the cult," as Albert specifies.[68] The literary heritage at the death of great sages, and notably the hagiographic heritage is then of utmost importance.[69] I must then define here hagiography and its functions, and show the role that this type of literature plays in the perpetuation of Mā's cult after her death.

For the great majority of academics, the term "hagiography," which designates writings related to saints, has a strong Christian connotation and should be exclusively applied to Christian saints, the term of "sacred biography" being preferred for other religious traditions.[70] Since hagiography presents the same objectives, structure, and literary processes as sacred biography, I will nevertheless use the term "hagiography." Hagiography, far from looking to present a historic picture of the saint, actually arises from religious discourse. In fact, according to Reynolds and Capps, hagiography does not aim to give a portrait resembling its subject[71] so much as to eulogize the saint. Thus as Stewart states, it would be inappropriate to question the historic accuracy of such a document, as this would deny the very nature of this type of document, which above all is based on religious belief.[72] Although hagiography sometimes presents historic aspects of the saint's life, there is often a discrepancy between the historic reality and the portrait given by the hagiography.[73] And if for some Hindus, history, synonymous with *māyā* (illusion),[74] has no tangible existence, this is even truer in the eyes of hagiographers. As Bader notes, the first objective of hagiography then is not to relate historic aspects of a religious subject so much as to establish the figure in the sphere of the sacred (*hagios*), which for hagiography constitutes the "truth."[75]

And so, hagiography, whether it presents the saint from a historic angle or not, above all aims to glorify the saint and to promote his or her cult. Far from playing the role of a historian or a biographer, the hagiographer looks to essentially attract new devotees by stimulating their devotion toward the saint. In addition, hagiography is for Tulpule a manifestation of *bhakti* and represents, according to the hagiographer Mahipati, a way to find the company of saints or *satsaṅga*.[76] Wilson also speaks of hagiography as a form of prayer, while Rinehart speaks of it as a way to remember the saint.[77] By the same token, Mallison refers to hagiography as a "contagion of the good" when it involves memorizing stories of the saint.[78] Hagiography can often relate examples of piety, of perfection, furnishing the readers with models for their own behavior.[79] Thus the term hagiography should only be applied to writings aimed at inspiring devotion toward the saint. In glorifying the saint, hagiography, in this sense, constitutes the key instrument of promotion.[80]

In the Hindu tradition, one of the most efficient ways to glorify the saint and to encourage devotion to them notably consists in describing them as the incarnation of a divinity, as an avatar, who came to earth to accomplish a specific mission so as to reestablish *dharma*.[81] The saint Shankaracharya is, for example, represented by the majority of hagiographers as the avatar of Śiva. The case of Shankaracharya, the archetypical promoter of *Advaita Vedānta*, is however paradoxical as little place is accorded to devotion in his hagiographies, although the stated goal of hagiography is to awaken devotion to the saint. Regarding this matter, Jonathan Bader speaks of austere devotion to express this paradox.[82]

In the numerous writings concerning Mā Ānandamayī, she is portrayed as an avatar, an incarnation of the divine, as Miller and Young also observe in their study on Mā's hagiography.[83] The purity of Mā's ancestral line, being brahmin and including numerous pandits and *satīs*, the divine conception of Mā, announced to her mother *Mokṣada Sundari* by the appearance of gods and goddesses in her dreams, as well as the extraordinary nature of her painless birth are only a few of a series of signs indicating Mā's divine nature from birth.[84] An exceptionally gifted student,[85] already in possession of some *siddhis*, hagiographers emphasize that Mā had a divine character since childhood. Hagiographers also do not hesitate to emphasize the sage's natural beauty so as to confirm her belonging to the world of the gods.

Another aspect of the avatar's pattern in the hagiographic tradition is the conviction that the events of his or her life are simply reflections of a divine play (*līlā*). The avatar is portrayed by his or her hagiographers as a simple social individual, but whose real nature far exceeds reality. The avatar's enlightenment belongs to the divine sphere of the game, to the *līlā*, and, for hagiographers, has nothing in common with a true interior transformation, but has everything to do with the will of the avatar to reveal his or her true identity to the beings who surround them.[86] Mā Ānandamayī is such an avatar figure, "disguised" during the early stages of her life. During her childhood she was taken for a simpleton because of her frequent states of absorption, then perceived by her husband and his circle as a woman under the influence of evil spirits; her true divine nature was only noticed by an exorcist who, not at all seeing a possessed woman, saw in her the Divine Mother, *Devī*. This was later confirmed by Mā who responded to the question of "who is she?" with "*Purṇabrahmanarayanan*" (God in all his fullness). The *sādhanā* that Mā practiced for many years is described in this context as being a part of God's game, of God's *līlā*.

Hagiography's emphasis on the extraordinary also constitutes another way of glorifying the guru. If the tomb of Sai Baba of Shirdi is today one of the most popular *tīrthas* (places of pilgrimage) in all of India, this is principally due to publications revealing him as a performer of miracles. The presence of miracles is an important element in hagiography as it contributes to confirming the guru's sanctity. The place of miracles in hagiographies of a holy being increase as years pass.[87] As in writings on Mā Ānandamayī, however, miracles are important. Miracles from Mā's time are described therein, as well as miracles that occurred after her *mahāsamādhi*, showing then the omnipresence of the guru that goes beyond death. These miracles could constitute not only miraculous healings but also reanimation of deceased bodies, accidents avoided, and so on.

In exalting the figure of Mā Ānandamayī, hagiographers represent then instruments of charismatic renewal and permit readers to have new experiences. Hagiography therefore constitutes a way to compensate for the loss of charisma caused by Mā's departure.

Death as a Challenge to Hagiography

Here, I must examine the guru's death in hagiographic narratives and show the role thereof in sustaining the cult. The future representation of the guru and, thus, the future of the cult will in fact largely depend upon the way that his or her death is treated in the hagiographies. As Rinehart specifies, the guru's death constitutes quite rightly a true challenge for hagiographers, in the sense that it greatly influences the manner in which the devotee perceives the master.[88]

If it is sometimes difficult to determine the date of a guru's death, as he or she is essentially perceived as being beyond time, beyond this cycle of earth and rebirth (saṃsāra), this does not seem to be necessarily the case with all gurus. In Mā Ānandamayī's case, her date of death, August 27, 1982, is mentioned in the majority of writings on her life. The atemporal character of Mā, however, is constantly stressed throughout her hagiographies, for, as Arnaud Desjardins said, to insert her into the narrow frame of the twentieth century would limit her. In fact, Mā was clearly beyond time or the limits of history.[89]

It is common to observe disparities in the narratives relating a guru's death. For example, in different writings about the Bengali saint Chaitanya, there are essentially different versions of his death, ranging from an infection of his feet to a sudden disappearance in a temple either in Jagannath or in Gopinath, or even a disappearance into the sea.[90] This is also the case with Mirabai, whose hagiographic narratives and oral traditions relate different types of deaths,[91] or even that of a lesser known saint, the *Siddha* Ratannath, of whom frescos at the monastery of Caughera in Nepal recall both his death by evaporation and the burial of his body in a *samādhi* at Bhatinda.[92] This divergence in writings relating to the saint's death in reality reveals the hagiographer's desire to emphasize a precise point, to send a message. All hagiographic narrative tends to serve a particular purpose. In the case of Mirabai, for example, one of the versions of her death finds Mirabai melting into the image of Kṛṣṇa. There is clearly a negation of the *bhakti* ideal of remaining in eternal relation with the divine and a desire on the part of the author to emphasize the *Advaitic* concept of non-duality. Regarding Mā Ānandamayī, narratives on her death seem, on the contrary, homogeneous, as they do not present notable contradictions. There are then no controversies regarding writings on her death, as there are in Chaitanya's case, where some texts, and notably the text relating his death as due to an infection of the feet, are considered heretical by the most orthodox of his followers.[93]

In addition, it is important to examine the place of the miraculous within hagiographies relating to a sage's death, as it is often accompanied by miraculous events. Lalla was said to dematerialize into fire, Shankaracharya to have fused with Śiva's *liṅgam*, and Kabir's body to have been transformed into a garland of flowers following quarrels between his Hindu and Muslim disciples concerning the funerary rites of their master. In the same way, Tukaram is said to have suddenly vanished before his disciples when he was in the middle of a state of mystical ecstasy,[94] and Janabai to have died at the same moment as her master Namdev.[95] The miraculous or semi-miraculous is also said to take the form of sudden changes in weather patterns, signs of the body's incorruptibility, and so on. If, in the case of Mā Ānandamayī, no sign of a miraculous death seems to be mentioned in writings dedicated to her, her hagiographers nonetheless imply, by virtue of their insistence on the miracles performed throughout her life, that Mā would have been able to maintain her life on earth longer if she had so desired.

Similarly to Bengali *Vaiṣṇava* orthodoxy's position on Chaitanya's death, it is unsuitable to mention death when speaking of Mā. How could God die?[96] A close reading of the writings relating Mā's death reveals that there is only mention of her "departure," of the "death of her body," of "*mahāsamādhi*," of the "end of her *līlā* on earth," and so on. To speak of Mā's "death" would amount to negating her true nature as eternal reality. It is thus important for the hagiographer to emphasize the lack of death of a guru, as for example the writings of this disciple for the 100th anniversary of Mā's birthday show: "Mā's *mahāsamādhi* is a phenomenon of the physical world. Mā is eternal. She exists as a brilliant flame within us. We need the perception to see Her. Her fragrant presence is always with us."[97] Thus, for the hagiographer, there is a desire to stress the absence of real death for Mā, who is eternal and beyond death.

This hagiographic tendency to emphasize the absence of true death for Mā is also reflected in the hagiographer's insistence on Mā's continued presence beyond death. In this respect, people mention the living presence or even the magic presence which is manifested in guidance, in protection, or in visions and dreams, as this excerpt essentially shows:

> Since Mā's passing from this world, devotees continue to have experiences of Her unfailing protection and guidance. Her living Presence has been seen many times by devotees in visions and dreams. Many people who weren't able to meet Mā in Her physical body still feel the warmth and attraction of Her magical Presence when they turn to Her in prayer. The transcriptions of Mā's words and teachings are eternally relevant and enlivening. Mā has told us, "It cannot be that anybody, anywhere is not My very own. I am with you at all times." JAYA MĀ.[98]

Hagiographers also go so far as to note the deliberate usage of the present tense in their writings, so as to underline Mā's continued presence, as is the case here in another extract from a book called *Ma Anandamayee: Embodiment of India's Spiritual and Cultural Heritage*, edited for the centennial of Mā's birthday: "To conclude, Mā Anandamayee is Herself A Source of Indian culture and spirituality. I deliberately use the present tense, for, She despite having left Her physical body, is still present, in subtlety. Only we need to be receptive, have faith and positive attitude."[99] This passage is additionally given in bold typeface, thus revealing the emphasis the hagiographer places on this precise point. Some hagiographers also note the absence of death for Mā by giving their books revealing titles, as is the case with two volumes entitled "I am ever with you."[100] The hagiographer constantly looks then to display the real lack of death for Mā in his writings on her.

Mā's immortal presence is also emphasized hagiographically by the numerous references to the attraction of new devotees: "They and many more new devotees who did not see Mā earlier are coming now to the *Samādhi Mandir* in Kankhal, Hardwar. The new comers are drawn to Mā just by seeing Her picture or by seeing Her in a dream or vision and in some cases by reading and hearing about Her from others."[101] Mā's physical absence, far from being presented by hagiographers as an obstacle, can even be described as a way to become closer to Mā: "There are beings who are close, so close that sometimes it takes decades to understand them. Sometimes, even you have to wait until you can no longer meet them to understand this proximity."[102]

Thus, throughout the vast majority of writings on Mā, there is a permanent weight given by the hagiographers to the absence of real death for Mā, which also contributes to reinforcing Mā's cult. The use of the avatar motif and the insistence on the master's continued presence after his or her death represent then two important tools in the sustainability of the cult through hagiography.

Initiation and Continuity of the Cult

The last part of this study looks to the initiation process as a way of perpetuating the cult. First, I turn toward initiation in its formal form, showing its function, and the manner in which it unfolds in the Shree Shree Anandamayee Sangha. In this context, the question of hereditary transmission is also addressed, notably using an interview conducted with one of Mā's family members. Second, I examine the formal initiation of the cult. The central concept of *śaktipāta*, or transmission of *śakti*, constitutes the support of my discussion.

Formal Initiation and Hereditary Transmission

One of the important aspects of the cult's sustainability is initiation, or *dīkṣā*. Initiation, that which the *Brāhmaṇa* refer to as a point of access to the sacred,[103] can be defined as the communication of an energy, of a vibration, of an influx to the initiated, or as the transmission of a spiritual influence that is said to be necessary with regards to the work of spiritual purification. This process of purification refers to the dissolution of the ego, which Mircea Eliade also terms a mystic death. Initiation generally involves the transmission and support of a mantra, whose function is to convey spiritual force (*śakti*), and is said to require belonging to a traditional organization, so as to permit a continuous transmission of the spiritual influence over the course of generations. Yvan Amar speaks on this subject of the "precious store" of spiritual tradition.[104] The role of the initiator, in this context, is not without importance to the efficiency of the initiation, as it should be performed by an individual possessing certain qualities specific to a spiritual master.

So as to address the question of continuity of initiation after Mā's departure, it is first of all necessary to return to a discussion of the initiation process during her lifetime.[105] As Mā never received a formal initiation, and never introduced herself as a guru, although she played that role in many respects, she almost never then gave a formal initiation as such. If it happened that Mā gave a mantra to a person, she nevertheless affirmed to the initiated persons that she was not their guru. She also said that "certain mantras have indeed emanated from these lips and others have accepted them. Therefore in one way or another the mantra has indeed been bestowed."[106] Swami Nirgunānanda speaks of this paradox:

> Of course, I was initiated but Mâ is not my guru. The first mantra that I got was from Mâ and not from a guru. My mantras of initiation are different from the mantra I received from Mâ. While giving me the mantra, she said: "This is not your initiation and this body is not your guru." She also added, "This body never asks anyone to take the dikshâ and never refuses when someone asks it of her." As for me, I needed a mantra and I got it before the formal initiation.
> [When then have you taken the dikshâ?]
> Mâ asked me to take it.
> [Did Mâ then not contradict herself?]
> In appearance, you could have that impression. In fact, I was also shocked when Mâ asked me to take the dikshâ. But afterwards, my doubts were cleared. One day, she called me and said: "Your initiation is set for tomorrow morning before dawn." I was totally shocked to hear her say that. I thought I would never have dikshâ. That made me suffer to think that Mâ had contradicted herself. I was overcome with emotion and started crying. She asked me the cause of this pitiful state. I told her, "Mâ, as you said that the dikshâ is given only to him who asks for it, it happens that I, I am totally satisfied with my mantra. I received it from your lips and I've never wanted a dikshâ from you. That shatters me to see that you are going against what you told me in the past." She said: "Do you really know what is hidden in the depths of your spirit?" Mâ explained to me then that I wanted this initiation at the bottom of my heart but that I had not realized it.[107]

For initiations, it was then common that Mā's mother, Didimā, herself conferred initiation on the follower in Mā's presence. A disciple confided to us that, following her initiation by Didimā, Mā herself affirmed that Didimā was her guru. After Didimā's death, the role of initiator was given to some swamis of the Shree Shree Anandamayee Sangha, including Swami Bhaskarānanda. And since Mā's *mahāsamādhi*, only some swamis chosen by the *sangha*'s committee are in charge of initiation, Swami Bhaskarānanda being the head initiator until his recent death.[108] Considered as a guru by many of Mā's devotees, Swami Bhaskarānanda affirmed this regarding *dīkṣā*: "We don't think that we are masters, we are Mā's instruments." Similarly to other religious orders, such as Ramakrishna's, swamis of the *sangha* are to specify, during each initiation, that the initiation is completed in the guru's name, Mā's name here.

The formal initiation is accompanied by rituals and the person to be initiated is to choose an *iṣṭa* (elected divinity) through which to venerate Mā. A new name is generally given to the devotee by the swami responsible for the initiation. In Mā's time, she could give a name directly to the initiated person, but she would also ask the people, or the initiated himself, what name he should have.

For many devotees, the power of the initiation does not seem to be affected by Mā's departure, as the subtle connection (*śukṣuma*) still continues to be established for the believer without Mā's physical presence (*sthūla*).[109] Whether the initiation was conferred before or after Mā's departure, its influence tends to remain the same, as the following early devotee, an Indian sir, who received initiation after Mā's death shows:

> After *dīkṣā*, my life changed completely. Lots of changes took place, in my attitude, in my thinking. Few years later I realized that it was the only thing missing in my life but I didn't know. If I knew, I would have asked. Sometimes, things are missing but you don't know what is missing. After few years, after this, I felt very peaceful, very powerful. All good things were happening inside. This was the only thing which was missing. From then on, it has been a very beautiful journey.

Thus, despite Mā's departure, spiritual influence continues to be transmitted, through the intermediary of a religious body composed by swamis chosen by the *sangha*.

Regarding formal initiation, there is also an initiation of a biological kind, that is to say a hereditary transmission of spiritual principle by members of Mā's family. From Didimā, the first guru of Mā's spiritual line, the spiritual flow is said to have been transmitted to Didimā's son, that is to say to Mā's younger brother who is said to have transmitted it in kind to his first son, Mā's nephew. Although he is not really in charge of formal initiations today, Mā's nephew's ability to transmit śaktipāta is recognized, as Mā herself confirmed. There is then a hereditary propagation of spiritual flow within Mā's family, a flow said to have been transmitted from a woman, Didimā, to a man, Mā's nephew. During an interview with Mā's great-nephew, he fleshed out the details of this hereditary transmission:

> In Hindu tradition, that is always [the] guru's family who gives dīkṣā traditionally. My grand-grand mother was the guru. Mā is never the guru. It is Didimā who is the guru. Swami Bhaskarānanda is a disciple of my grand-grand mother. This principle of delivering dīkṣā runs in the family. My grand-grand mother gave dīkṣā. My grand father gave dīkṣā, to few people. Mā gave him the chakra. Mā gave him the instrument. My father also gives dīkṣā to very selected people. He is very selective. There must be a special connection, a special bond between the guru and the disciple. You cannot give dīkṣā to anybody.... The guru is always a mediator. My father gives dīkṣā. He has the instrument. It runs in the family.

There is then a biological line through which this dīkṣā is transmitted from generation to generation. The perpetuation of the cult is today then assured, not only by a specific religious body but also by a type of biological line originating in Mā's mother, Didimā. It is nevertheless important to specify that this biological transmission is extremely minor compared to the transmission completed by the religious body, which carries out the vast majority of formal initiations. If the initiating system is today dominated by Mā's monks, it is however possible for members of Mā's family to play in the future a more important role in this transmission. The appearance of a charismatic figure within Mā's family could reverse the management of this good of salvation that initiation represents.

Informal Initiation

There also is an informal type of dīkṣā, which, although not formally recognized, plays a role among devotees. This informal initiation differs from formal initiation, in that it is not accompanied with a ceremony and does not necessitate the physical presence (sthūla) of the guru. For Swami Vijayānanda, this informal initiation, which is always interior, is the real initiation, that is to say the real transmission of power, the *śaktidāna*: "The *śaktidāna*, the transmission of power, which is in fact the real initiation, can be given in many ways, for example through contact, *sparśadīkṣā*, through a look, *dṛṣṭidīkṣā* and even at a distance."[110] These explanations regarding the initiation recall the comments of Alexandra David-Neel who affirmed that, the more important the initiation, the less they are surrounded with liturgic pomp.[111]

In this context, some devotees affirm that they have received an interior initiation from Mā, and notably in a dream.[112] If Mā affirmed the possibility of this type of experience and if this was not uncommon during her own time, as interviews with early devotees as well as their written testimony reveal, this type of initiation today continues to occur despite Mā's death. The devotee who has experienced it can sometimes receive a confirmation of his mantra from one of the swamis, often a swami in charge of initiation.[113] This inner initiation, that is to say the true transmission or *śaktipāta*, can also take place through looking at a photo, for, if gurus have the ability while alive to transmit *śakti* through their gaze, this type of transmission continues after their *mahānirvāṇa*,[114] through the intermediary of their photos, which are considered to be filled with life and power.

And so, far from being carried out only in formal initiation, the continuity of Mā's cult may also be maintained through informal initiations, which despite their marginal character, contribute to reinforcing the disciple's faith in the guru. We can also, in this context, ask about the relevance of the formal initiation that, for Atmananda, is in reality nothing more than a way of compensating for the lack of confidence in Mā's presence:

> You know, it's us that lack confidence. This is why we need to be comforted by different things like *dīkṣā* (initiation) and other ceremonies. But Mâ is there. If we have confidence in her, if we avoid involving ourselves too much in other things, for the mind then would be scattered, if we can concentrate ourselves on Her presence, be really conscious of it, then we will not need anything else anymore. We must have confidence in her word.[115]

This would explain the reason that some of Mā's devotees do not necessarily feel the need to receive a formal initiation, as the following Indian early male devotee confirms: "To become a *bhakta*, a devotee to somebody, it is not necessary to take *dīkṣā*." In addition to formal initiation, the continuity of Mā's cult seems to be assured through informal initiation, which for some has as much, if not more, importance that a simple formal initiation.

Initiation then constitutes a central way of maintaining the guru's cult after his or her death, not only in its formal dimension, where the follower receives officially a mantra, but also in its informal dimension. This aspect of the cult thus constitutes an essential tool for the postmortem cult of the guru, along with rituals, relics, or hagiography.

Conclusion

CALLING ON CONCEPTS of religious experiences and institutionalization, this study explores a little examined aspect of the Hindu tradition, the cult of gurus after their death (*mahāsamādhi*), particularly the cult of relics. Regarding the question of the impact of the master's death on his or her cult, a central question in this study, I have offered several perspectives as a part of my research on the postmortem cult of the Bengali religious figure Mā Ānandamayī (1896–1982). Because of the richness of data collected, this study may provide a platform for further research, especially with respect to the religious experience of the faithful, a complex and multifaceted phenomenon, as well as to the Westernization of the worship of Hindu gurus.

Considered to be the last of the great representatives of the Hindu Renaissance initiated by Ramakrishna, Mā Ānandamayī, called the "Human Kālī" in Bengal, is seen as an emblematic figure of female religious leadership. As a self-initiated spiritual master who dictated the terms of her own sanctity through her self-initiation, Mā Ānandamayī was a prominent charismatic figure within a society where only rarely would a woman receive the authority to be a spiritual guide. Through the magnitude of her religious movement and her vast network of ashrams—an unprecedented phenomenon for a woman in India—as well as through the establishment of reforms aimed at promoting women's religious equality, Mā Ānandamayī marks a major transformation in the landscape of Hindu guruship. As an exceptional being, Mā Ānandamayī is today the object of a cult at her tomb, a cult generally reserved for male gurus, and in a few cases to some women venerated in relation to a male guru. Within a male-dominated cult of relics, Mā represents then a powerful figure.

In answer to the question of the impact of the guru's death on his or her cult, it is possible, in Mā's case, to discern some diminution in her cult since her death, most notably in the decline in the number of

FIGURE C.1 Mā Ānandamayī: "Why do you say I am going away? I am your little child and am always with you. Remember this, that I am always with you."

Source: Picture belonging to the collection of the photographer Sadanand; now in the possession of Neeta Mehta, also called Swami Nityānanda.

Mā's devotees. There is no doubt that the number of devotees is well inferior to that at Mā's time, as can be seen in the weak presence of new devotees compared to early ones. This trend of Mā's cult to decline after her death may come first of all from the Hindus' preference for a living guru.

A Competition between Living and Dead Gurus

Through numerous interviews made with the devotees of Mā, I have observed a continuation of experiences of Mā's presence since her *mahāsamādhi*, both among former devotees who have "walked" with Mā in her lifetime and among new devotees. Although photos, books, and videos of Mā play an important role in the emergence of these experiences, the relics, though not essential for the vast majority of devotees, also have

FIGURE C.2 Tomb (*samādhi*) of Swami Vijayānanda in Père Lachaise Cemetery in Paris, qualified by the ambassador of France in India (2010) as "a miraculous tomb." One day, in Benares, Mā asked Swami Vijayānanda, "Vijayānanda, what do you want to do with your body?" He said: "Mā, it does not matter for me. This body may be burnt or put into *Jhal-samādhi* [immersed in the Ganges River]. She jumped up and replied with great force: "No Vijayānanda. This body has done so many *tapasya* [ascetic practices], it is a sacred body. It should be neither burned nor put into *Jhal-Samādhi*!"

Source: Picture taken by French devotee Béatrice Abitbol.

an important role in the continuity of experiences. They lead the faithful to overcome their fear of death and discover their ultimate nature.

On a par with experiences of Mā during her lifetime, the experiences after her death are characterized by the same feeling of presence, on both

dual and non-dual planes, as well as a sensation of ecstasy, close to the oceanic feeling mentioned by Freud, through which the follower is touched
in his or her inner being by a profound beatitude (*ānanda*) and loses all
concept of time. The regenerating experience of receiving dreams, guidance, or visions of Mā also coincides with the experiences of Mā's devotees
in her own time. In this respect, Mā's followers sometimes mention the
central role of the inner guru, which becomes a substitute for the physical presence of the master, recalling Mā's statements that never ceased to
affirm this: "Detach yourself from the physical appearance of the master.
The guru is in you."[1]

Despite the persistence of experiences and the benefits brought to the
practicing devotee (*sādhaka*) by the postmortem cult, such as a greater
interiorization, an easier contact with the inner guru, a more direct access
to the non-manifested (*nirguṇi*), a greater independence, or even a deeper
reflection on death, one cannot but recognize that there is not at this time
a sufficient renewal of devotees to maintain Mā's cult as said before the
time of her death over a quarter of a century ago. As we have said, one of
the reasons may lie in the tendency within Hinduism to privilege direct
contact with the guru more than contact with an invisible being never
met in person. The incarnated presence of the guru permits in fact an
easier communication with the follower and a lesser risk of straying from
the path.

The postmortem cult is engaged in a sort of competition specific to
the logic of market economics, in which living and deceased gurus compete for devotees. In the context of the pluralism of gurus, dead and alive,
Bourdieu would speak of the "market economy of salvation goods" to
describe this rivalry associated with the cult of gurus. In the "market-like
conditions of modern life,"[2] to use Habermas's words, religion, indeed, is
subject of intense competition. Thus Mā Ānandamayī's cult is the object
of great competition with deceased gurus, but above all with living gurus.
Among the first are the special figures of Shirdi Sai Baba, whose success
is mainly related to his ties to both the Hindu and Muslim traditions,
Ramana Maharshi, who has his *samādhi* in Southern India, Ramakrishna
whose relics are at Belur Math (Calcutta), and recently, Sathya Sai Baba,
who now has his *samādhi* in Puttaparthi.[3] Among the living gurus, there
is no doubt that the international popularity of Amṛtānandamayī Mā
far exceeds that of Mā Ānandamayī at this time. Known as Amma and
regarded as an incarnation of the Divine Mother as was Mā Ānandamayī,
she brings together millions of followers worldwide. Gurumayi, who

currently lives in the United States, is after Amma the most popular living female guru today. Although Mā was the best known female guru in India while she was alive, her popularity today must compete with the presence of living gurus like Amma or Gurumayi. The postmortem cult of the guru is then found to be party to customer satisfaction or a "market of supply and demand," a demand which manifestly favors a living presence of a guru. The faithful, in fact, may find the cult of the living guru more attractive than the postmortem one, as it is more immediate and filled with more power and excitement.

As a reflection of this competition between living and dead gurus, a "migration" of devotees of the deceased guru such as Mā to a living one is possible. If, in Mā's case, a move among her devotees to a living guru may have taken place since her *mahāsamādhi*, this move is now even more likely with the departure of Mā's key monks. These include Swami Bhaskarānanda, who was in charge of initiations, Swami Vijayānanda, who was considered as a guru for many Westerners, and Swami Śivānanda, surprisingly all deceased during the same month, in April 2010, a few days apart.[4] The disappearance of these important monks, regarded as the living presence of Mā, may indeed accelerate the decline of Mā's cult. This may discourage the advent of new devotees and encourage the migration of old and new devotees to living figures such as Amma. Perhaps in preparation for his own departure and to provide some guidance and support to his disciples in the future, Swami Vijayānanda advised some devotees to see Amma, whom he also considered to be an incarnation of the Divine Mother, like Mā.

The living presence of the guru, however, is not the only factor in the continuation of the cult. The institution also plays a key role.

The Institution, a Marketing Agency

The decline of the postmortem cult of a guru is also directly tied to the decline of the religious institution responsible for this cult. Following the inevitable routinization of the guru's cult after his or her death, the passage from the numinous order to the administrative order of affairs, from the extraordinary to the routine or the ordinary, the religious institution sees its role grow considerably, holding a prime place in the continuation of the cult. The role that the religious institution, this "marketing agency," plays in the cult can however be altered when the gap between the institution's activities and the spiritual principles at its foundation becomes too wide, leading then to a decline of the cult.

The diminishment of Mā's cult after her death seems to be significantly associated with the decline of its religious institution, the Shree Shree Anandamayee Sangha, originally founded to promote and safeguard Mā's teaching. As in the case of many other organizations founded by charismatic leaders, such as the Siddha Yoga organization or the Hare Krishna movement,[5] this decline can mainly be seen through conflicts of power, such as observed in the designation of a successor to direct the *saṅgha* or in the distribution of power between lay people and monks. As Timothy Miller observed from various studies on postcharismatic movements,[6] these conflicts, however painful and destructive they may be, constitute a normal process for the great majority of organizations and do not necessarily lead to a fatal conclusion, although some movements do die. These power struggles and this dogmatizing, though "normal," may persuade some to agree with James's undervaluing of institutions, as he explains here:

> A survey of history shows us, as a rule, religious geniuses attract disciples, and produce groups of sympathizers. When these groups get strong enough to organize themselves, they become ecclesiastical institutions with corporate ambitions of their own. The spirit of politics and the lust of dogmatic rule are then apt to enter and to contaminate the originally innocent thing.[7]

Within the cult of Ānandamayī Mā, in addition to these struggles, we also observe a total lack of management (i.e., delay in publications, translations), a disinterest on the part of the community (i.e., neglect of ashrams), a cult rigidity (i.e., excessive formalism), and finally, an increased distancing from "the other," as evidenced by the strict maintenance of brahminic rules imposed upon Westerners, who may feel ostracized by the community vis-à-vis meals, lodging, and rituals.

No doubt that the institution's current dysfunction is mainly due to the presence of an older generation of brahmin Bengali Hindus, who for various reasons seem to have difficulty accepting this routinization, this setting up of a routine structure. This has put them in a position of mourning the loss of their situation of origin, when Mā was present. Resistant to change, they do not seem to see the need to undertake the necessary actions to ensure the continuity of the cult (better management of ashrams, publications, translations, loosening of the orthodoxy). There is thus a tension between, on the one hand, the older Indian devotees who continue to live in the past, when the role of the institution and of the organization was secondary compared to the charismatic presence of Mā, and, on the other hand, the new and Western devotees, who realize the importance of effective actions at the institutional levels.

Mā's cult is therefore currently undergoing this routinization process, which will be completed only after the disappearance of the older genera-tion of Indian devotees. Two options, then, present themselves. First, the cult could continue to fade with the deterioration of its institution and Mā's movement could remain a declining movement, which perhaps would not be contrary to Mā's will, as she desired neither organization nor ashram and she certainly never adopted a marketing attitude. As she left no successor or instructions at her departure, except for dispensing money to her monks so that they could choose to live independently of the institution or not, could this decline be a normal thing and perhaps even desirable? Didn't Mā actually encourage the decrease of this organization, as one of her devotees pointed out to me?

The second option would necessitate an appropriation of the organiza-tion by the new generation with the arrival of a charismatic figure that can breathe new life into this organization and to the cult as a whole, as Swami Bhaskarānanda, one of Mā's closest disciples, had done for a while. In the absence of such a person, the future of Mā's organization seems very unclear, as many devotees suggest. For others, the future of the cult may even be assured by another organization, the Sri Sri Mata Anandamayi Peeth Trust, founded in the 1990s by a close follower of Mā's, Swami Kedarnath, which already has two ashrams (Indore and Omkareshwar) open to Westerners.

Swami Kedarnath, whose successor, Swami Guruśarānanda, has already been designated, and his new *sampradāya* could stand as a guar-antee that a charismatic renewal will insure the survival of Mā's cult. It would then compete with the official *saṅgha* for what Bourdieu calls the "monopoly of management of the goods of salvation."[8] This dynamic orga-nization publishes new books on Mā, runs a school where 500 children get to know Mā's life and teachings, is establishing new liturgies,[9] and is currently building a retreat center dedicated to Mā in Dharamsala. The non-observance of orthodox brahminical rules also represents one of the traits of charismatic renewal within this *sampradāya*, leading to a greater openness and a wide propagation of Mā's teaching to the lower castes and to the West. This can be seen, for example, in the travel to the West that the two main swamis, the American Swami Mangalananda and Swami Gurusarananda, accomplish each year to spread Mā's teachings and raise funds for Mā's school in Omkareshwar.

A Difficult Transition

The issue of the death of the guru, and the necessary loss of charisma associated with it, represents a real issue for modern Hinduism. It is interesting to consider the figure of Sathya Sai Baba, the guru and avatar known for his many miracles, who presented himself throughout his life as a reincarnation of Shirdi Sai Baba, absorbing in some ways the charisma of the earlier saint. He died on April 24, 2011, at the age of 84 years, after a cardiac arrest, and left behind not only tens of millions of devotees across the world but also astronomical sums of money and a colossal amount of property evaluated at between $9 and $30 billion. His holdings include ashrams, educational institutions, hospitals, schools, and universities. After a ceremony attended by 500,000 people, including the highest dignitaries of India, the body of Sathya Sai Baba, was buried in a white marble tomb, in his main ashram in Puttaparthi. With no designated successor, as with Mā's cult, we may wonder about the future of his cult. The brahminical orthodoxy, very powerful in Mā's ashrams, is not present within the organization of Sai Baba and is therefore unlikely to hinder the development of the cult. Other factors however can affect the newly postmortem cult. Given the huge sums of money and the great number of properties to manage, what will be the risk of corruption and power struggles? How will the organization of Sathya Sai Baba, the Sri Sathya Sai Central Trust, manage the cult?

As the religious leader died recently, it is still too early to tell. Today's evidence suggests however a difficult transition, as shown for example by the disappearance of sums of money, and this questions the ability of members of the organization to manage the cult and its organization in all its dimensions, including the financial ones. It remains to be seen if Sathya Sai Baba will reincarnate in eight years after his death like he predicted in the person of a certain Prem Sai, who, maybe, would come and regain control of the organization. Similar to Shirdi Sai Baba, Prem Sai Baba stands for the continuation of Sathya Sai Baba or, in Weberian terms, for an institutionalization of his charisma, inserting himself within a chain of remembering typical of the religious traditions in South Asia.

As in the case of other gurus, the departure of the religious leader initiates a difficult transition at different levels, and demonstrates the importance and complexity of transmission, which affects both India and the West. In the case of Muktananda or Shree Rajneesh,[10] the transmission was easier though as these gurus were open to the West.

Toward a Westernization of the Cult

When it comes to the potential for the Westernization of Mā's cult, it seems relevant to return to the brahminical rules within the Shree Shree Anandamayee Sangha, Mā's "official" organization. These rules, which were described as inhuman by Atmananda, an Austrian woman and close disciple of Mā, may have been originally a way to reinvigorate the Hindu tradition, the *sanātana dharma*. However, today, in a globalized world, with the economic and social transformations that India is experiencing, the presence of these rules constitutes a major obstacle to the expansion of Mā's movement. This attachment to brahminical rules of purity by a small number of devotees within the Shree Shree Anandamayee Sangha reflects, for a large number of Indian and Western devotees, something that keeps potential devotees away.

Obviously, Mā's movement has been unable to keep up with the ever-changing realities of modern India. Incapable of reconciling with the requirements of Indian modernity, the movement has been in decline since Mā's departure. This differs with other devotional movements, such as the movement of the living guru Mā Amṛtānandamayī (Amma), which has integrated the new imperatives of Indian society.[11] Although Amma is a living guru, and therefore is more likely to attract devotees, her institution's relative openness and freedom of expression plays an essential role in the success of her movement.

In spite of the orthodoxy in Mā's ashrams, we observe however an expansion of Mā's cult in the West, with the very recent emergence of a new cult revolving around the French monk Swami Vijayānanda, one of Mā's closest disciples. Coming to India in the early 1950s, at the age of 36 to find a guru, the French doctor met Mā in Benares on February 1951. Following this meeting, he never left India and lived in the ashrams of Mā until his death, April 5, 2010. Despite Mā's words that Swami Vijayānanda's body should not be cremated but interred, orthodox brahmins refused however to welcome his tomb in Kankhal as he is a foreigner and therefore impure.[12] Swami Vijayānanda's body was repatriated to France a few days after his death,[13] then placed in a tomb in Père Lachaise cemetery. Parallel to the veneration of Mā, or through it, Swami Vijayānanda is now the subject of veneration, acting as a sort of bridge between East and West.

This East–West connection reminds us somehow of the "Pondicherry tandem," Sri Aurobindo and the Mother, whom Aurobindo had recognized as his Tantric *śakti*, his feminine force on earth. While roles are reversed here, with Vijayānanda as the Mother (both French) and Mā as Aurobindo, the East–West dialectic is also present.

Another example of Mā's cult becoming increasingly international can be seen in the growth of the more inclusive movement of Swami Kedarnath, simply called Kedar Baba by his devotees. Kedar Baba annually sends his two ambassadors, Swami Guruśarānanda and Swami Mangalananda, to Europe and America to sing Mā's praises and offer teachings on all aspects of Mā's *sādhanā* (spiritual discipline) and on its place within *sanātana dharma* (the eternal law, the Hindu tradition). The Indian religious phenomenon of Mā's cult then has branched out into the West through the growing number of devotees in Europe and America who meditate daily before a picture of Mā or at Père Lachaise where they gather to chant her name. Globalization is also religious!

Clearly, this East–West connection highlights some dissension between the Indian orthodoxy and the Western orthopraxy, between purity and liberalization, and between exclusivity and inclusivity.

Conclusion

Based on the particular case of Ānandamayī Mā, it is important to conclude this study by enumerating the factors or the conditions required for a cult to survive and be revitalized after the death of the guru. Despite a renewal of experience by followers who continue to perceive Mā as an incarnation of the divinity and to feel her presence despite her death, the postmortem cult of Mā appears to be fragile and uncertain. While the decline of her cult may lie in the inclination of Hindus for a living presence of the guru, the dominant reason seems to be directly connected with the institution and its willingness or not to change and share outside of family and caste.

The cult of Mā may then continue decreasing or even disappear with the decline of its religious institution, for, if the memory and the relics of a guru who just passed away are held tightly by an exclusive Hindu community, his or her memory may not endure or survive.

A parallel though contrasting example is the postmortem cult of the movement of the Hindu guru Neem Karoli Baba, also called Maharaji by his followers, where we can see clearly the conditions underlying the success of his cult. Neem Karoli Baba, a popular charismatic figure whom his devotees believed was an incarnation of Hanumān, died in India in 1973, only a few years before Mā. Although he was a man, which certainly helped him to be recognized during his lifetime as a guru in the Indian society, his cult after his death, contrary to Mā's cult, continued to grow, especially in America.

The success of Neem Karoli Baba's cult, in fact, may be directly linked to the openness of its institution, to its inclusivity. As Mā, Maharaji never came to the West but foreigners were openly welcomed in his ashram and not subject to segregation due to purity rules. The famous Harvard professor, Richard Alpert, later called Ram Dass, is one of the best examples. Coming to India in the late 1960s to meet with Maharaji, he greatly contributed to spreading the teachings of Maharaji in America, authoring very influential books such as *Be Here Now*. We can also refer to the famous kirtan singers, Krishna Das, author of *Chants of a Lifetime*, and Jai Uttal, who made Neem Karoli Baba famous in the West.

The establishment and preservation of an institution that is open to change, open to "the other," appear then as the single most important condition for the continuation of the cult of the guru after his or her death. This calls into question James's idea that the institution is secondary to religious experience. Religious experience without institution, indeed, is tantamount to remaining within the transient, the ephemeral sphere. The appearance of a charismatic leader/teacher, such as Vivekananda for Ramakrishna's movement[14] or Ram Dass for Neem Karoli Baba's, who breathes enthusiasm into the community and introduces changes necessary for the sustaining of the cult, is presented as the most likely alternative to a continuation of the guru's cult after his or her death. A religious movement that stagnates and lacks dynamism is destined to disappear.

Finally, while the guru's cult after his or her death goes through various institutional stages and is subject to a number of changes, for

FIGURE C.3 Mā Ānandamayī: "I see the world as a garden. Men, animals, crea-
tures, plants, all have their appointed places. Each in its particularity enhances the
richness of the whole. All of you in your variety add to the wealth of the garden
and I enjoy multiplicity. I merely walk from one corner of the garden to the other."

Source: Picture belonging to the collection of the photographer Sadanand; now in the possession of Neeta Mehta, also called Swami Nityānanda.

better or for worse, this study highlights a major change in this significant aspect of Hinduism. This is the appearance of a new mode of
veneration, that of the cult of a female guru at her tomb, which has been
initiated by the cult of Mā Ānandamayī, in so doing it reveals a turning point within Hinduism. In the context of globalization of religion
and the growing interest in Hindu holy figures in the West, especially
women gurus such as Amma, who travels around the world, Gurumayi
in the United States, or Mother Meera in Germany, the emergence of
such a cult is not without consequences. If in the future there is a development of this type of cult among women gurus at their tomb, it could
well take place in the West. This study has, therefore, a global dimension and helps us to understand better how these key figures of Hindu
spirituality are redefining the religious.

FIGURE C.4 The author with Swami Vijayānanda (beginning of January 2010)

Notes

INTRODUCTION

1. Mircea Eliade, *L'Inde* (Paris: Editions de l'Herne, 1988), 155.
2. Gopinath Kaviraj, "Mother," in *Selected Writings of M. M. Gopinath Kaviraj*, edited by Gopinath Kaviraj (Varanasi: M. M. Gopinath Kaviraj Centenary Celebrations Committee, 1990), 190.
3. One can refer for instance to the film documentary *Ashrams* of Arnaud Desjardins on the guru *pūjā* performed on Mā. Arnaud Desjardins, *Ashrams*, France, Alizé Diffusion, 2006, Dvd 35 + 20 mn.
4. Marie-Thérèse Charpentier, *Indian Female Gurus in Contemporary Hinduism: A Study of Central Aspects and Expressions of Their Religious Leadership* (Åbo: Åbo Akademi University Press, 2010).
5. James Frazer, *The Golden Bough: A Study in Magic and Religion* (New York: Touchstone Press, 1995), 9; Mary Douglas, *Purity and Danger: An Analysis of Concepts of Pollution and Taboo* (London: Routledge & Kegan Paul, 1966), 112.
6. Tulasi Srinivas, *Winged Faith: Rethinking Globalisation and Religious Pluralism through the Sathya Sai Movement* (New York: Columbia University Press, 2010), 314–315; "Articles of Faith: Material Piety, Devotional Aesthetics and the Construction of a Moral Economy in the Transnational Sathya Sai Movement," *Visual Anthropology* 25 (July 2012): 292–293.
7. Atmananda, *Death Must Die: A Western Woman's Life-Long Spiritual Quest in India with Sri Anandamayee Ma*, edited by Ram Alexander (Delhi: Indica Books, 2000); Bithika Mukerji, *Life and Teaching of Sri Ma Anandamayi (A Bird on the Wing)* (Delhi: Sri Satguru Publications, 1998) and *My Days with Sri Ma Anandamayi* (Varanasi: Indica Books, 2002).
8. William James, *The Varieties of Religious Experience* (New York: Signet Classic, 2003).

9. Rudolf Otto, *Le Sacré: L'Élément non rationnel dans l'idée du divin et sa relation avec le rationnel* (Paris: Payot, 2001), 56–57.

10. As Lindholm notes, much has been done on charisma in the Western context and fieldwork on charismatic movements in various cultural contexts is needed. Referring to the 11th of September, he emphasizes the utility of these studies, which do not have an academic purpose only. See Charles Lindholm, "Culture, Charisma, and Consciousness: The Case of the Rajneeshee," *Ethos* 30, no. 4 (2002): 373.

11. Max Weber, *Sociologie des religions* (Paris: Gallimard, 1996).

12. Jürgen Habermas, *The Structural Transformation of the Public Sphere* (Cambridge, MA: MIT Press, 1991).

13. Karen Pechilis, "The Female Guru: Guru, Gender, and the Path of Personal Experience," in *The Guru in South Asia: New Interdisciplinary Perspectives*, edited by Jacob Copeman and Aya Ikegame (London: Routledge, 2012), 122.

14. Bhaiji, *Mother as Revealed to Me* (Kankhal: Shree Shree Anandamayee Sangha, 2004), 6.

15. Gopinath Kaviraj, "Mother Anandamayi," in *Mother as Seen by Her Devotees*, edited by Gopinath Kaviraj (Varanasi: Shree Shree Anandamayee Sangha, 1967), 169.

16. Pechilis, "The Female Guru," 114; Maya Warrier, *Hindu Selves in a Modern World: Guru Faith in the Mata Amritanandamayi Mission* (London: Routledge Curzon, 2005), 4.

17. C. F. Keyes, "Charisma: From Social Life to Sacred Biography," in *Charisma and Sacred Biography*, edited by M. A. Williams (Chico, CA: Scholars Press, 1982), 2.

18. This differs largely with the attitude of most gurus, like Sathya Sai Baba, who used to demonstrate openly his magical powers to devotees and perform miracles, referring to them as his "visiting cards," his "calling cards," or also as "love transactions." Mā Ānandamayī's miracles were said to be more subtle, less exhibited in public. See Tulasi Srivinas, *Winged Faith: Rethinking Globalisation and Religious Pluralism through the Sathya Sai Movement* (New York: Columbia University Press, 2010), 187 and 286.

19. Arnaud Desjardins, *Ashrams* (Paris: Albin Michel, 1982), 190.

20. Ibid., 74.

21. Ibid., 91.

22. This message of condolence was left by Indira Gandhi at the ashram in Kankhal.

23. As Cornille notes, avatars are generally male. Mā Ānandamayī is an exception to the rule. See Catherine Cornille, "Mother Meera, Avatar," in *The Graceful Guru: Hindu Female Gurus in India and the United States*, edited by Karen Pechilis (New York: Oxford University Press, 2004), 134.

24. Richard Lannoy, *Anandamayi: Her Life and Wisdom* (Rockport, MA: Element Books Ltd, 1996).

25. Atmananda, *Death Must Die: A Western Woman's Life-Long Spiritual Quest in India with Sri Anandamayee Ma*, edited by Ram Alexander (Delhi: Indica, 2000), 405. *Saṃsāra* means the action of passing (from one state to another), transmigration, the cycle of lives and deaths, and finally the world this entails.

26. *Words of Sri Anandamayi Ma*, translated by Atmananda (Kankhal: Shree Shree Anandamayee Sangha, 2001), 158; see also Jean-Claude Marol, *La Saturée de joie Anandamayi* (Paris: Dervy, 2001), 77.

27. *Words of Sri Anandamayi Ma*, 145.

28. Atmananda, *Death Must Die*, 440.

29. Ibid., 41.

30. R. Chattopadhyaya, "Sri Anandamayee Ma: Mother of Eternal Bliss," in *Gurus, Godmen and Good People*, edited by Khushwant Singh (Bombay: Orient Longman, 1975), 19. On the monist tradition of *Advaita*, see Louis Gardet and Olivier Lacombe, *L'Expérience du soi* (Paris: Desclée de Brouwer, 1981).

31. Marol, *La Saturée de joie Anandamayi*, 178.

32. Atmananda, *Death Must Die*, 478.

33. Tulasi Srivinas, "Relics of Faith: Fleshly Desires, Ascetic Disciplines and Devotional Affect in the Transnational Sathya Sai Movement," in *Handbook of Body Studies*, edited by Bryan S. Turner (London: Routledge, 2012).

34. *Words of Sri Anandamayi Ma*, 61.

35. *Words of Sri Anandamayi Ma*, 123.

36. Desjardins, *Ashrams*, 200.

37. *Words of Sri Anandamayi Ma*, 132.

38. The term "adualism" was suggested by Raimon Panikkar in a letter he wrote to Jacques Vigne. See Jacques Vigne, *La Mystique du silence* (Paris: Albin Michel, 2003), 86.

39. Desjardins, *Ashrams*, 80. See also the very end of the interview "Arnaud Desjardins talks about his experiences with Ma Anandamayi," while he speaks of the silence as the best way to talk about Mā, http://www.youtube.com/watch?v=eMFoqInjohk.

40. See Joel D. Mlecko, "The Guru in Hindu Tradition," *Numen* 29, no. 1 (July 1982): 33–61.

41. Karen Pechilis, "Gurumayi, the Play of Sakti and Guru," in Pechilis, ed., *The Graceful Guru*, 222; see also "The Female Guru," 114 and 123.

42. André Couture, "La Geste krishnaïte et les études hagiographiques modernes," in *Constructions hagiographiques dans le monde indien: Entre mythe et histoire*, edited by Françoise Mallison (Paris: Librairie Honoré Champion, 2001), 16.

43. Guy Bugault, "La Relation maître disciple en Inde," in *Maître et disciples dans les traditions religieuses*, edited by Michel Meslin (Paris: Cerf, 1990), 25.

44. Lisa L. Hallstrom, "Anandamayi Ma, the Bliss-Filled Divine Mother," in Pechilis, ed., *The Graceful Guru*, 88; Lisa L. Hallstrom, *Mother of Bliss: Ānandamayī Mā* (New York: Oxford University Press, 1999), 128.

45. Lawrence A. Babb, *Redemptive Encounters* (Berkeley and Los Angeles: University of California Press, 1986), 147; Srivinas, *Winged Faith*, 66.

46. Jacob Copeman and Aya Ikegame, "The Multifarious Guru: An Introduction," in Copeman and Ikegame, eds., *The Guru in South Asia*.

47. John Stratton Hawley, "Morality beyond Morality in the Lives of Three Hindu Saints," in *Saints and Virtues*, edited by John Stratton Hawley (Berkeley and Los Angeles: University of California Press, 1988).

48. André Padoux, "Le Sage hindou: Renonçant ou surhomme?" in *Les Sagesses du monde*, edited by Gilbert Gadoffre (Paris: Editions Universitaires, 1991), 113–114.

49. Katherine Young and Lily Miller, "Sacred Biography and the Restructuring of Society: A Study of Anandamayi Ma, Lady-Saint of Modern Hinduism," in *Boeings and Bullock-Carts*, Vol. 2, edited by Dhirendra K. Vajpeyi (Delhi: Chanakya Publications, 1990), 133.

50. Bharati Dhingra, *Visages de Ma Anandamayi* (Paris: Cerf, 1981), 22–23.

51. Rachel F. McDermott, "Epilogue: The Western Kālī," in *Devī: Goddesses of India*, edited by John Stratton Hawley and Donna M. Wulff (Berkeley and Los Angeles: University of California Press, 1996), 285; Sarah Caldwell, "Margins at the Center: Tracing Kālī through Time, Space, and Culture," *Encountering Kālī: In the Margins, at the Center, in the West*, edited by Rachel Fell McDermott and Jeffrey J. Kripal (Berkeley and Los Angeles: University of California Press, 2003), 249; Jeffrey J. Kripal and Rachel F. McDermott, "Introducing Kālī Studies," in *Encountering Kālī*, 4; Jeffrey J. Kripal, "Why the Tāntrika Is a Hero: Kālī in the Psychoanalytic Tradition," in *Encountering Kālī*, 215. As Rachel McDermott argues, however, the perception of Kālī in Bengal has been through a sweetening process during the colonial period. Kālī was domesticated to transform herself from a dangerous and violent goddess into a maternal goddess. See Rachel McDermott, *Mother of My Heart, Daughter of My Dreams: Transformations of Kālī and Umā in the Devotional Poetry of Bengal* (New York: Oxford University Press, 2001).

52. Kumar Dutta Gupta, "God as Love," in *Mother as Seen by Her Devotees*, edited by Gopinath Kaviraj (Varanasi: Shree Shree Anandamayee Sangha, 1967).

53. Dhingra, *Visages de Ma Anandamayi*, 52.

54. Atmananda, *Death Must Die*, 458.

55. Ibid., 170.

56. Dhingra, *Visages de Ma Anandamayi*, 51.

57. See David Kinsley, " 'Through the Looking Glass': Divine Madness in the Hindu Religious Tradition," *History of Religions* 13, no. 4 (May 1974): 270–305.

58. June McDaniel, *The Madness of the Saint: Ecstatic Religion in Bengal* (Chicago: University of Chicago Press, 1989), 219. By "ordinary madness" we mean a madness that belongs to the world of the senses, to the terrestrial world, to attachment, as the saint Lakṣmī Mā affirms: "There is a difference between ordinary madness and divine madness. One who has seen Bhagavān and has

become a madman loses all sense and is not conscious of his belongings. One who becomes insane for other reasons always remains conscious of his belongings. And one who has become mad by seeing Bhagavān can be easily distinguished. He will not concentrate on any worldly objects. He will forget even his close relatives and think only about God."

59. Mā Ānandamayī, *Matri Vani*, Vol. 2, translated by Atmananda, (Calcutta: Shree Shree Anandamayee Charitable Society, 1982), 152.

60. Catherine Clément and Sudhir Kakar, *La Folle et le saint* (Paris: Seuil, 1993), 100.

61. Marine Carrin, "Saintes des villes et saintes des champs: La Spécificité féminine de la sainteté en Inde," *Terrain*, no. 24 (March 1995): 117; Maya Warrier, "Processes of Secularization in Contemporary India: Guru Faith in the Mata Amritanandamayi Mission," *Modern Asian Studies* 37, no. 1 (February 2003): 232. In this regard, it is interesting to note that Mā's devotees similarly tend to deny a conscious choosing of Mā. This possibility of choosing seems to be present in other religious traditions, like the Sufi tradition, where the seeker has the possibility to choose among various different Sufi saints. On this, see A. R. Saiyed, "Saints and Dargahs in the Indian Subcontinent: A Review," in *Muslim Shrines in India: Their Character, History and Significance*, edited by Christian W. Troll (New Delhi: Oxford University Press, 2003), 244.

62. Brian Hutchinson, "The Divine-Human Figure in the Transmission of Religious Tradition," in *A Sacred Thread: Modern Transmission of Hindu Traditions in India and Abroad*, edited by Raymond Brady Williams (Chambersburg, PA: Anima, 1992), 108.

63. Desjardins, *Ashrams*, 82.

64. Madou, *A la rencontre de Ma Anandamayi: Entretiens avec Atmananda*, http://www.anandamayi.org/ashram/french/frmad1.htm.

65. Hugh Van Skyhawk, "A Note on Death and the Holy Man in South Asia," in *Ways of Dying: Death and Its Meanings in South Asia*, edited by Claus Peter Zoller and Elisabeth Schömbucher (New Delhi: Manohar, 1999), 193; Landell Samuel Mills, "The Hardware of Sanctity: Anthropomorphic Objects in Bangladeshi Sufism," in *Embodying Charisma: Modernity, Locality and the Performance of Emotion in Sufi Cults*, edited by Pnina Werbner and Helene Basu (London: Routledge, 1998), 39; and Katherine Ewing, "A Majzub and His Mother: The Place of Sainthood in a Family's Emotional Memory," in Werbner and Basu, eds., *Embodying Charisma*.

66. The word *samādhi* (tomb) is actually an abridged version of *samādhisthāna*, the place (*sthāna*) where an ascetic who is claimed to have attained the highest state of meditation (*samādhi*) is buried.

67. Translated as "The Postmortem Cult of Saints in the Hindu Tradition: Religious Experiences and Institutionalization of the Cult of Mā Ānandamayī (1896–1982)."

68. Andrée Fortin, "L'Observation participante: Au cœur de l'altérité," in *Les Méthodes de la recherche qualitative*, edited by Jean-Pierre Deslauriers (Québec: Presses de l'Université du Québec, 1988), 23–33.

69. The Varanasi ashram also maintains Mā's school for young girls, "Kaṇyapīṭha," which surely represents the first school in India to educate female students up to *śāstri*, that is to say the traditional studies in Sanskrit and religious sciences.

70. Laurence Bardin, *L'Analyse de contenu* (Paris: Presses Universitaires de France, 1977).

71. Charles Lindholm, "Prophets and *Pirs*: Charismatic Islam in the Middle East and South Asia," in Werbner and Basu, eds., *Embodying Charisma*.

72. If the state of *jīvanmukta* is generally recognized in the Hindu tradition, as in the *Advaita Vedānta* of Shankaracharya (see Andrew Fort, "Introduction," in *Living Liberation in Hindu Thought*, edited by Andrew Fort and Patricia Y. Mumme [Albany: State University of New York Press, 1996], as well as Lance E. Nelson, "Living Liberation in Śankara and Classical Advaita," in ibid.), some religious traditions do not however admit its existence, refusing this state of perfection in the terrestrial world. These schools of thought like the doctrine of Ramanuja (*viśiṣṭādvaita*) do not envisage liberation until after death (see Kim Skoog, "Is the *Jīvanmukti* State Possible? Ramanuja's Perspective," in Fort and Mumme, eds., *Living Liberation in Hindu Thought*).

73. Pierre Centlivres and Anne-Marie Losonczy, "Introduction," in *Saints, sainteté et martyre: La Fabrication de l'exemplarité*, Actes du colloque de Neuchâtel, 27–28 November 1997 (Paris: Editions de la Maison des Sciences de l'Homme, 2001), 11. Richard Kieckhefer and George Bond also examine the application of this term with Christian connotations to other traditions like Hinduism in *Sainthood: Its Manifestations in World Religions* (Berkeley and Los Angeles: University of California Press, 1988), pp. vii–xii; see also Françoise Mallison, "Introduction," in *Constructions hagiographiques dans le monde indien: Entre mythe et histoire* (Paris: Librairie Honoré Champion, 2001), pp. x–xi; and Katherine Young, "Introduction," in *Women Saints in World Religions*, edited by Arvind Sharma (Albany: State University of New York Press, 2000), 5–6.

74. Lynn Teskey Denton, *Female Ascetics in Hinduism* (Albany: State University of New York Press, 2004), 140–141.

75. France Bhattacharya, "La Construction de la figure de l'homme-dieu selon les deux principales hagiographies bengalies de Śrī Kṛṣṇa Caitanya," in *Constructions hagiographiques dans le monde indien: Entre mythe et histoire*, edited by Françoise Mallison (Paris: Librairie Honoré Champion, 2001), 185.

76. Jean Rivière, *Lettres de Bénarès* (Paris: Albin Michel, 1982), 171.

77. Jean Filliozat and Louis Renou, *L'Inde classique: Manuel des études indiennes*, Vol. 1, (Paris: Payot, 1985), 661; Louis Dumont, "Le Renoncement dans les religions de l'Inde," *Archives de Sociologie des Religions* 7, no. 7 (January–June 1959): 64.

78. Ursula M. Sharma, "The Immortal Cowherd and the Saintly Carrier: An Essay in the Study of Cults," in *Sociology of Religion in India: Themes in Indian Sociology*, Vol. 3, edited by Rowena Robinson (New Delhi: Sage Publications, 2004), 150.

79. Warrier, "Processes of Secularization in Contemporary India," 247; id., *Hindu Selves in a Modern World*, 14.

80. Swami Vivekananda, *Les Yogas pratiques* (Paris: Albin Michel, 2005), 138.

81. Swami Vijayananda, *Un français dans l'Himalaya: Itinéraire avec Mâ Ananda Môyî* (Lyon: Terre du Ciel, 1997), 157.

82. Charlotte Vaudeville, "*Sant Mat*: Santism as the Universal Path to Sanctity," in *The Sants: Studies in a Devotional Tradition of India*, edited by Karine Schomer and W. H. McLeod (Delhi: Motilal Banarsidass, 1987), 27; see also Wendy D. O'Flaherty, "The Interaction of *Saguṇa* and *Nirguṇa* Images of Deity," in Schomer and McLeod, eds., *The Sants*, 47.

83. Vivekananda, *Les Yogas pratiques*, 255.

84. Hallstrom, *Mother of Bliss*.

85. One can refer, for instance, to Talal Asad, who argues that secularism was used as a tool to enforce some sort of colonial Christianity in most parts of the world.

86. On *Yā tā*, one may refer to Swami Kedarnath's book *An Introduction to Sri Anandamayi Ma's Philosophy of Absolute Cognition* (Indore: Om Ma Sri Sri Mata Anandamayi Peeth Trust, 2012).

87. Interview Arnaud Desjardins, part IV, http://www.youtube.com/watch?v=32J9B8hNzKM.

88. Interview Arnaud Desjardins, part V, http://www.youtube.com/watch?v=Mjz1xyDzR2I.

CHAPTER 1

1. Atmananda, *Death Must Die: A Western Woman's Life-Long Spiritual Quest in India with Sri Anandamayee Ma*, edited by Ram Alexander (Delhi: Indica Books, 2000), 161.

2. Jackie Assayag, *Au Confluent de deux rivières: Musulmans et hindous dans le sud de l'Inde* (Paris: École Française d'Extrême Orient, 1995), 84.

3. Alexander Lipski, *Life and Teaching of Śrī Ānandamayī Mā* (Delhi: Motilal Banarsidass, 2005), 22.

4. Assayag, *Au confluent de deux rivières*, 90.

5. Joachim Wach, *Sociologie de la religion* (Paris: Payot, 1995), 338.

6. Denis Vidal, "Des dieux face à leurs spécialistes: Conditions de la prêtrise en Himachal Pradesh," in *Prêtrise, pouvoirs et autorité en Himalaya*, edited by Véronique Bouiller and Gérard Toffin (Paris: École des Hautes Études en Sciences Sociales, 1989), 66.

7. On Indira Gandhi and her relationship with Mā Ānandamayī and other gurus, see Christophe Jaffrelot, "The Political Guru: The Guru as Éminence Grise," in *The Guru in South Asia: New Interdisciplinary Perspectives*, edited by Jacob Copeman and Aya Ikegame (London and New York: Routledge, 2012), 80–96. Through the case of Indira Gandhi, Jaffrelot explores the role of gurus as political counselors to politicians in the postcolonial India and shows how gurus can legitimize or delegitimize the latter.

8. Gopinath Kaviraj was a devotee of Mā Ānandamayī but was also in contact with a female guru in Benares called Shobama, who was considered as an incarnation of Kṛṣṇa. See Catherine Clémentin-Ojha, *La Divinité conquise: Carrière d'une Sainte* (Nanterre: Société d'Ethnologie, 1990).

9. Atmananda, *Death Must Die*, 23.

10. Lawrence A. Babb, "Sathya Sai Baba's Saintly Play," in *Saints and Virtues*, edited by John Stratton Hawley (Berkeley and Los Angeles: University of California Press, 1988), 170.

11. Marc Gaborieau, "The Cult of Saints among the Muslims of Nepal and Northern India," in *Saints and their Cults: Studies in Religious Sociology, Folklore and History*, edited by Stephen Wilson (Cambridge: Cambridge University Press, 1983), 303.

12. Lisa L. Hallstrom, *Mother of Bliss: Ānandamayī Mā (1896–1982)* (New York: Oxford University Press, 1999).

13. For example, *Aux Sources de la joie: Mâ Ananda Moyî*, translated by Jean Herbert (Paris: Albin Michel, 1996), a collection of Mā's sayings translated into French by Herbert from a book of Roy and Joshi, was first edited in 1943.

14. Atmananda was also the editor in chief of *Ananda Varta*, a sort of chronicle of Mā published since 1952.

15. Charles Lindholm, *Charisma* (Cambridge, MA: Basil Blackwell, 1990), 82. On disenchantment, see Jean-Louis Schlegel, "Le Réenchantement du monde et la quête du sens de la vie dans les nouveaux mouvements religieux," in *Les Spiritualités au carrefour du monde moderne* (Paris: Centurion, 1994), 98.

16. Jürgen Habermas, *The Theory of Communicative Action: The Critique of Functionalist Reason*, Vol. 2 (Oxford: Blackwell, 1987).

17. Mā affirmed that all relations generally came from a past life. See Amulya K. D. Gupta, *In Association with Sri Sri Ma Anandamayi*, Vol. 1 (Calcutta: Shree Shree Anandamayee Charitable Society, 1987), 45.

18. Jacques Vigne, *L'Inde intérieure* (Gordes: Editions du Relié, 2007), 154.

19. Surinder M. Bhardwaj, *Hindu Places of Pilgrimage in India* (Berkeley and Los Angeles: University of California Press, 1973), 150.

20. Henri Chambert-Loir and Claude Guillot, "Indonésie," in *Le Culte des saints dans le monde musulman*, edited by Henri Chambert-Loir and Claude Guillot (Paris: École Française d'Extrême Orient, 1995), 251.

21. On *tīrtha*, see André Padoux, *Comprendre le tantrisme* (Paris: Albin Michel, 2010), 233 and 243.

22. Pascale Chaput, "Equivalences et equivoques: Le Culte des saints catholiques au Kerala," in *Altérité et identité,* edited by Jackie Assayag and Gille Tarabout (Paris: École des Hautes Études en Sciences Sociales, 1997), 188.

23. Glenn E. Yocum, "The Coronation of a Guru: Charisma, Politics, and Philosophy in Contemporary India," *A Sacred Thread: Modern Transmission of Hindu Traditions in India and Abroad,* edited by Raymond Brady Williams (Chambersburg, PA: Anima, 1992), 84.

24. Quoted in Babb, "Sathya Sai Baba's Saintly Play," 178.

25. Pnina Werbner, "*Langar:* Pilgrimage, Sacred Exchange and Perpetual Sacrifice in a Sufi Saint's Lodge," in *Embodying Charisma: Modernity, Locality and the Performance of Emotion in Sufi Cults,* edited by Pnina Werbner and Helene Basu (London: Routledge, 1998), 111.

26. Lawrence A. Babb, "Glancing: Visual Interaction in Hinduism," *Journal of Anthropological Research* 37, no. 4 (Winter 1981): 397.

27. Tulasi Srinivas, "Articles of Faith: Material Piety, Devotional Aesthetics and the Construction of a Moral Economy in the Transnational Sathya Sai Movement," *Visual Anthropology* 25 (July 2012): 281.

28. Victor W. Turner, *Le Phénomène rituel: Structure et anti-structure* (Paris: Presses Universitaires de France, 1969).

29. Surinder M. Bhardwaj, *Hindu Places of Pilgrimage in India* (Berkeley and Los Angeles: University of California Press, 1973), 162.

30. Kathleen M. Erndl, *Victory to the Mother: The Hindu Goddess of Northwest India in Myth, Ritual, and Symbol* (New York: Oxford University Press, 1993), 69.

31. Peter Brown, *Le Culte des saints: Son essor et sa fonction dans la chrétienté latine* (Paris: Cerf, 1996), 114.

32. Pierre Bourdieu, "Le Langage autorisé: Note sur les conditions sociales de l'efficacité du discours rituel," *Actes de recherche en Sciences Sociales* 1, nos. 5–6 (November 1975): 188; François Isambert, *Rite et efficacité symbolique: Essai d'anthropologie sociologique* (Paris: Cerf, 1979), 20.

33. Roger Caillois, *L'Homme et le sacré* (Paris: Gallimard, 1950), 212.

34. Frits Staal, "The Meaningless of Ritual," *Numen* 26, no. 1 (June 1979): 11.

35. Danièle Hervieu-Léger, *Le Pèlerin et le converti* (Paris: Flammarion, 1999), 67.

36. Werner Gephart, "Memory and the Sacred: The Cult of Anniversaries and Commemorative Rituals in the Light of the Elementary Forms," in *On Durkheim's Elementary Forms of Religious Life,* edited by N. J. Allen, W. S. F. Pickering, and W. Watts Miller (London: Routledge, 1998), 131.

37. See Raymond Jamous, "Faire, défaire et refaire les saints: Les *Pir* chez les Meo d'Inde du Nord," *Terrain,* no. 24 (March 1995): 43–56.

38. C. J. Fuller, *The Camphor Flame: Popular Hinduism and Society in India* (Princeton: Princeton University Press, 2004), 73.

39. Thara Bhai, "Emergence of Shrines in Rural Tamil Nadu: A Study of Little Traditions," *Sociology of Religion in India: Themes in Indian Sociology,* Vol. 3, edited by Rowena Robinson (New Delhi: Sage Publications, 2004), 170.

40. John A. Subhan, *Sufism: Its Saints and Shrines* (Lucknow: Lucknow Publishing House, 1960), 1.

41. *Jay Ma*, no. 45, http://www.anandamayi.org/ashram/french/frdocs1.htm.

42. Swami Vijayananda, "Un chemin de joie," unpublished.

43. Raimon Panikkar, *L'Expérience de Dieu* (Paris: Albin Michel, 1998), 189.

44. *Rakṣabandhan*, the celebration of brothers and sisters, corresponds to one of the most popular celebrations in the Hindu tradition and continues to be celebrated in Mā's ashrams today despite her departure. From the time that Mā was still present in her body, she placed in the hands of her disciples a bracelet in asking them to protect her, defining herself through this act as their little sister. Today, this religious tradition continues and Mā's disciples continue to place a bracelet in the hands of their spiritual sisters, making them their *gurubahin*.

45. Ululation is mostly practiced in the Eastern parts of India, such as Bengal. During Hindu temple rituals and celebrations, women roll their tongues to produce this special sound called the "ulu."

46. Hugh Van Skyhawk, "A Note on Death and the Holy Man in South Asia," in *Ways of Dying: Death and Its Meanings in South Asia* (New Delhi: Manohar, 1999), 196.

47. Marc Gaborieau, "A Nineteenth-Century Indian 'Wahhabi' Tract against the Cult of Muslim Saints: *Al-Balagh al-Mubin*," in *Muslim Shrines in India: Their Character, History and Significance*, edited by Christian W. Troll (New Delhi: Oxford University Press, 2003), 210.

48. Pinto S. J. Desiderio, "The Mystery of the Nizamuddin Dargah," in Troll, ed., *Muslim Shrines in India*, 123.

49. Arnaud Desjardins, *Ashrams*, France, Alizé Diffusion, 2006, Dvd 35 + 20mn.

50. The *Kumbhamelā* is one of the biggest pilgrimages in the world. In its biggest form (*Mahākumbhamelā*), it takes place every twelve years and in the four following sacred locations Prāyāga (the Hindu name for Allahabad), Uttaranchal, Hardwar (Uttar Pradesh), Ujjain (Madhya Pradesh), and Nasik (Maharashtra). The *saṅgha* of Mā is not present in the *Kumbhamelā* of Ujjain and Prāyāga.

51. *Nāga Bābās* are a shivaït sect of warrior ascetics. As indicated by their name, they usually do not wear clothes, as the monks jaïna *digambara* (nonviolent). Contrary to other *sādhus*, they tend to be vindictive and to get into conflict with other sects. They even fought militarily against the Muslims and the British. The *Nāgas* are often armed, though in a more symbolic way, with lances and trident, a sign of Śiva.

52. Phyllis Granoff and Koichi Shinohara, eds., "Introduction," in *Images in Asian Religions: Texts and Contexts* (Vancouver, BC: UBC Press, 2004), 4; Richard H. Davis, "Introduction: Miracles as Social Acts," in *Images, Miracles, and Authority in Asian Religious Traditions* (Boulder, CO: Westview Press, 1998), 16.

53. Jean Filliozat and Louis Renou, *L'Inde classique, manuel des études indiennes*, Vol. 1 (Paris: Payot, 1985), 575; see also André Padoux, *Comprendre le tantrisme: Les Sources hindoues* (Paris: Albin Michel, 2010), 250–251.

54. Gérard Colas, "The Competing Hermeneutics of Image Worship in Hinduism," in Granoff and Shinohara, eds., *Images in Asian Religions*, 167.

55. Phyllis Granoff, "Images and Their Ritual Use in Medieval India," in Granoff and Shinohara, eds., *Images in Asian Religions*, 22.

56. François Chenet, "L'Hindouisme, mystique des images ou traversée de l'image?" in *L'Image divine: Culte et méditation dans l'hindouisme: Etudes rassemblées par André Padoux* (Paris: Editions du CNRS, 1990), 166.

57. Diana Eck, *Darśan: Seeing the Divine in India* (Chambersburg, PA: Anima Books, 1985), 45; see also Alain Daniélou, *Mythes et Dieux de l'Inde: Le Polythéisme hindou* (Paris: Flammarion, 2001), 542.

58. Eck, *Darśan*, 45.

59. Catherine Clémentin-Ojha, "Image animée, image vivante: L'Image du culte hindou," in *L'Image divine*, 116.

60. Swami Nikhilananda (trans.) and Swami Adiswarananda (ed.), *Sri Sarada Devi: The Holy Mother* (Woodstock, VT, Skylight Paths Publishing, 2004), 146–147. On the belief that the living presence of Ramakrishna may be experienced through photographs of him, see also Gwilym Beckerlegge, *The Ramakrishna Mission: The Making of a Modern Hindu Movement* (New Delhi: Oxford University Press, 2000), 127.

61. Daniel Gold, *The Lord as Guru: Hindi Sants in North Indian Tradition* (New York: Oxford University Press, 1987), 179; Babb, *Redemptive Encounters*, 16.

62. Desjardins, *Ashrams*, 81.

63. Jean-Claude Schmitt, "Les Reliques et les images," in *Les Reliques, objets, cultes, symbols: Actes du Colloque International de l'Université du Littoral-Côte d'Opale* (Turnhout, Belgium: Brepols, 1999), 152.

64. William Mazzarella, "Internet X-ray: E-Governance, Transparency, and the Politics of Immediation in India," *Public Culture*, no. 18 (2006): 496.

65. *Gri gri* is a kind of voodoo amulet, or talisman, which is believed to protect the wearer from evil and to bring luck.

66. Gilles Tarabout, "Theology as History: Divine Images, Imagination, and Rituals in India," in Granoff and Shinohara, eds., *Images in Asian Religions*, 58.

67. In a very recent translation of Bhaiji's journal, *Mother Reveals Herself*, Mā narrates that Didimā was actually not present at her birth. Referring to Mā's *Prakāsh* (revelation), it is written that only Khurimā, the paternal aunt of Mā's grandmother, was present at Mā's birth, see *Mother Reveals Herself* (Varanasi: Pilgrims Publishing, 2010), 4.

CHAPTER 2

1. Patrick Geary, *Furta Sacra: Thefts of Relics in the Central Middle Ages* (Princeton: Princeton University Press, 1978), 32.

2. Gerardus Van Der Leeuw, *La Religion dans son essence et ses manifestations* (Paris: Payot, 1955), 232.

3. Peter Brown, *Le Culte des saints: Son essor et sa fonction dans la chrétienté latine* (Paris: Cerf, 1996); André Vauchez, *La Sainteté en Occident aux derniers siècles du Moyen Âge d'après les procès de canonisation et les documents hagiographiques* (Rome-Paris: École française de Rome, 1988).

4. Lindholm addresses the dilemma within Islam concerning the presence of charismatic beings, gifted with superhuman powers. While, in theory, there is no space in the egalitarian and individualistic religion of Islam for such beings, in practice, there are charismatic beings who are considered endowed with such powers and who are venerated. See Charles Lindholm, "Prophets and *Pirs*: Charismatic Islam in the Middle East and South Asia," in *Embodying Charisma: Modernity, Locality and the Performance of Emotion in Sufi Cults*, edited by Pnina Werbner and Helene Basu (London: Routledge, 1998), 209–233.

5. Catherine Servan-Schreiber, "Partage de sites et partage de textes: Un modèle d'acculturation de l'Islam au Bihar," in *Altérité et Identité: Islam et Christianisme en Inde*, edited by Jackie Assayag and Gille Tarabout (Paris: École des Hautes Études en Sciences Sociales, 1997), 163.

6. Nicole Hermann-Mascard, *Les Reliques des saints: Formation coutumière d'un droit*, Société d'histoire du droit collection d'histoire institutionnelle et social (Paris: Klincksieck, 1975), 42, cited in Pascale Chaput, "Equivalences et equivoques: Le Culte des saints catholiques au Kerala," in Assayag and Tarabout, eds., *Altérité et Identité*, 191.

7. Philippe George, "Les Reliques des saints: Un nouvel objet historique," in *Les Reliques, objets, cultes, symboles* (Turnhout, Belgium: Brepols, 1999), 230.

8. Kevin Trainor, *Relics, Ritual and Representation in Buddhism* (Cambridge: Cambridge University Press, 1997), 89.

9. Tulasi Srivinas, "Relics of Faith: Fleshly Desires, Ascetic Disciplines and Devotional Affect in the Transnational Sathya Sai Movement," in *Handbook of Body Studies*, edited by Bryan S. Turner (London: Routledge Press, 2012), 292–293; and Tulasi Srivinas, *Winged Faith: Rethinking Globalisation and Religious Pluralism through the Sathya Sai Movement* (New York: Columbia University Press, 2010), 314–315.

10. Jean Przylusky, "Le Partage des reliques du Buddha," *Mélanges chinois et bouddhiques* (1935–1936), 353–354, cited in John S. Strong, *Relics of the Buddha* (Princeton: Princeton University Press, 2004), 15.

11. Charles Malamoud, "Les Morts sans visage: Remarques sur l'idéologie funéraire dans le Brahmanisme," in *La Mort, les morts dans les sociétés anciennes*, edited by Gherardo Gnoli and Jean-Pierre Vernant (Cambridge: Cambridge University Press; Paris: Editions de La Maison des Sciences de l'Homme, 1982), 441.

12. Monier Monier-Williams, *Buddhism in its Connexion with Brahmanism and Hinduism and in Its Contrast with Christianity* (Varanasi: Chowkhamba Sanskrit Series office, 1964), 495–496, cited in Strong, *Relics of the Buddha*, 15.

13. Agehananda Bharati, "Pilgrimage in the Indian Tradition," *History of Religions* 3, no. 1 (Summer 1963): 152.

14. Johannes Bronkhorst, "Les Reliques dans les religions de l'Inde," unpublished. Regarding the movement of the *śramaṇa*, the author specifies that this name can lead to confusion: "a *śramaṇa* is an ascetic, while all those who belong to the *śramaṇa* movement were not. The expression is however useful to designate the circles from which certain types of ascetics, including Buddhists, Jains, and others, came from."

15. Ibid.

16. R. L. Mishra, *The Mortuary Monuments in Ancient and Medieval India* (Delhi: B. R. Pub. Corp, 1991), p. xiv.

17. On this subject, see Véronique Bouiller, "*Samādhi et Dargāh*," in *De l'Arabie à l'Himalaya*, edited by Véronique Bouiller and Catherine Servan-Schreiber (Paris: Maisonneuve & Larose, 2004), 251–271.

18. Dominique-Sila Khan, "La Tradition de Rāmdev Pīr au Rajasthan: Acculturation et syncrétisme," in Assayag and Tarabout, eds., *Altérité et identité*, 122.

19. There was a dispute between the Muslim devotees of Shirdi Sai Baba and his Hindu devotees concerning his burial's place in Shirdi. Although Muslims wanted his body to be buried in an open piece of land, it was interred in a Hindu devotee's building with a Kṛṣṇa image, completing the "Hinduization of the saint." On this see Antonio Rigopoulos, *The Life and Teachings of Sai Baba of Shirdi* (Albany: State University of New York Press, 1993), 241. Despite this Hinduization, there is still however a rich Sufi tradition surrounding Shirdi Sai Baba.

20. The Sathya Sai Movement situates itself within the saintly traditions coming from Hindu-Muslim syncretism. See Srivinas, *Winged Faith*, 117.

21. Jean-Claude Schmitt, "La Fabrique des saints," *Annales* 39, no. 2 (March–April 1984): 291.

22. L. S. S. O'Malley, *Popular Hinduism: The Religion of the Masses* (Varanasi: Pilgrims Publishing, 2000), 171–178.

23. Mircea Eliade, *Images et symboles* (Paris: Gallimard, 1979), 55; Roger Caillois, *L'Homme et le sacré* (Paris: Gallimard, 1950), 69.

24. Brown, *Le Culte des saints*, 113.

25. Saligrama K. Ramachandra Rao, *The Indian Temple: It's [sic] Meaning* (Bangalore: IBH Prakashana, 1979), 15. One can also refer to Haberman's excellent book on tree worship in India, David L. Haberman, *People Trees: Worship of Trees in Northern India* (New York: Oxford University Press, 2013).

26. Ibid., 78.

27. Jean-Claude Marol, *La Saturée de joie Anandamayi* (Paris: Dervy, 2001), 88.

28. Bharati Dhingra, *Visages de Ma Anandamayi* (Paris: Cerf, 1981), 72.

29. Christian Lee Novetzke, *Religion and Public Memory* (New York: Columbia University Press, 2008), 143–144. Eknath stands for renewal in Marathi

literature and religious history. As Lee Novetzke writes, this is an initiation of physical site and text as *loci* of public memory.

30. Mircea Eliade, *L'Inde* (Paris: Editions de l'Herne, 1988), 155.

31. Ibid., 150.

32. Madeleine Biardeau, *L'Hindouisme: L'Anthropologie d'une civilisation* (Paris: Flammarion, 1995), 55.

33. *Ucchiṣṭa* usually means the leftovers, the food remnants. On *ucchiṣṭa*, see Hugh B. Urban, *The Power of Tantra: Religion, Sexuality, and the Politics of South Asian Studies* (London: I. B. Tauris, 2010), 112–113.

34. Mircea Eliade, *Le Yoga: Immortalité et liberté* (Paris: Payot, 1983), 304.

35. The *Upaniṣad* affirms that the *prāṇa* does not leave the saint's body on their death. During the saint's *mahāsamādhi* the *prāṇa* merges into the *sahaśrāṇa chakra* and does not leave the body. The case of Swami Nityananda, guru of Swami Muktananda, from the line of *Siddha*, was said to be subjected to such a phenomenon. Regarding this topic, see Swami Muktananda, *Est-ce que la mort existe réellement?* (Paris: Saraswati, 1984), 45–46 and 50.

36. Arthur B. Keith, *The Religion and Philosophy of the Veda and Upanishads* (Cambridge, MA: Harvard University Press, 1925), 417.

37. See Pandurang Vaman Kane, *History of Dharmaśastra* (Poona: Bhandarkar Oriental Research Institute, 1973).

38. Keith, *Religion and Philosophy of the Veda and Upanishads*, 417.

39. Kathleen Iva Koppedrayer, *The Sacred Presence of the Guru: The Velala Lineages of Tiruvavatuturai, Dharmapuram, and Tiruppanantal* (Ottawa: National Library of Canada, 1991), 21.

40. See Catherine Weinberger-Thomas, *Cendres d'immortalité* (Paris: Seuil, 1996); Stuart H. Blackburn, "Death and Deification: Folk Cults in Hinduism," *History of Religions* 24, no. 3 (February 1985): 255–274. On *satī*, see also Arvind Sharma, *Sati: Historical and Phenomenological Essays* (Delhi: Motilal Banarsidass, 2001).

41. C. J. Fuller, *The Camphor Flame: Popular Hinduism and Society in India* (Princeton: Princeton University Press, 2004), 49; Weinberger-Thomas, *Cendres d'immortalité*, 89; Paul Courtright, "Satī, Sacrifice, and Marriage," in *From the Margins of Hindu Marriage: Essays on Gender, Religion, and Culture*, edited by Lindsey Harlan and Paul B. Courtright (New York: Oxford University Press, 1995), 185. The Liberation Tigers of Tamoul Eelam of Sri Lanka (LTTE), who appropriated the practice of interring their dead from the ascetics (looking to elevate their partisans to the level of saints and establishing them in popular memory as "martyrs"), are included within the *vīra*'s group. See Cristiana Natali, "Ériger des cimetières, construire l'identité: Pratiques funéraires et discours nationalistes chez les Tigres tamouls du Sri Lanka," *Frontières* 18, no. 2 (Spring 2006): 19.

42. Swarajya Gupta, *Disposal of the Dead and Physical Types in Ancient India* (Delhi: Oriental Publishers, 1972), 11; Max-Jean Zins, "Rites publics et deuil patriotique: Les Funérailles de la guerre indo-pakistanaise de 1999," *Archives de Sciences Sociales des Religions*, nos. 131–132 (July–December 2005): 84.

43. Kirin Narayan, *Storytellers, Saints, and Scoundrels: Folk Narrative in Hindu Religious Teaching* (Philadelphia: University of Pennsylvania Press, 1989), 184 and 186. Van der Veer, however, specifies that renouncers do not all perform their own death rites, contrary to the belief of the popular Hindu imagination. See Peter Van der Veer, *Gods on Earth: The Management of Religious Experience and Identity in a North Indian Pilgrimage Centre* (London: Athlone Press, 1988).

44. In the case of Mā, who was not officially a *saṃnyāsini*, her burial, though, cannot be explained in this way. Marcelle Saindon, "Le Rituel hindou de la crémation," in id., *Cérémonies funéraires et post funéraires en Inde: La tradition derrière les rites* (Sainte-Foy: Presses de l'Université Laval, 2000), 92.

45. Charles Malamoud, *Cooking the World: Ritual and Thought in Ancient India* (New Delhi: Oxford University Press, 1996), 47–48.

46. Malamoud, "Les Morts sans visage," 447; T. N. Madan, *A l'opposé du renoncement: Perplexités de la vie quotidienne hindoue* (Paris: Editions de La Maison des Sciences de l'Homme, 1990), 157. As Copeman notes, cremation actually represents some sort of "last-ditch renunciation," substituting for householders' failure to follow the last stage of life (*āśrama*). According to this brahmanic concept, one should renounce social life toward the end of life and become a wandering ascetic. See Jacob Copeman, "Cadaver Donation as Ascetic Practice in India," *Social Analysis* 50, no. 1 (Spring 2006): 103–126.

47. Malamoud, "Les Morts sans visage," 447–448. According to Abbé Dubbois, there exist beliefs that bits of coconut cracked on a dead *sannyāsīn*'s skull can make barren women bear children. See Abbé J. A. Dubbois, *Hindu Manners, Customs and Ceremonies* (Delhi: Oxford University Press, [1906] 1978), 538–541.

48. Michel Hulin, *La Face cachée du temps* (Paris: Fayard, 1985), 395.

49. Gian Giuseppe Filippi, *Mṛtyu: Concept of Death in Indian Tradition— Transformation of the Body & Funeral Rite* (New Delhi: Printworld, 1996), 173.

50. Mark Juergensmeyer, "Saint Gandhi," in *Saints and Virtues*, edited by John Stratton Hawley (Berkeley and Los Angeles: University of California Press, 1988), 189.

51. Iqtidar H. Siddiqui, "The Early Chishti Dargahs," in *Muslim Shrines in India: Their Character, History and Significance*, edited by Christian W. Troll (New Delhi: Oxford University Press, 2003), 13.

52. Geary, *Furta Sacra*, 33–34.

53. Gregory Schopen, "Burial 'ad sanctos' and the Physical Presence of the Buddha in Early Indian Buddhism: A Study in the Archaeology of Religions," *Religion* 17, no. 3 (1987): 193.

54. Richard Nolane notes this on the subject of vampirism in Central Europe: "to present an occasional resistance to decomposition was the best way to see your body dismembered, decapitated and burned" (cited in id., *Les Saints et leurs reliques: Une histoire mouvementée* [Beauport: Publications MNH; Paris: Anthropos, 2000], 90).

55. Sofia Boesch Gajano, "Reliques et pouvoirs," in *Les Reliques, objets, cultes, symboles* (Turnhout, Belgium: Brepols, 1999), 260.

56. See P. S. Rayanna, *St Francis Xavier and His Shrine* (Ranchi, India: Catholic Press, 1964).

57. Jonathan Parry, "Sacrificial Death and the Necrophagous Ascetic," in *Death and the Regeneration of Life*, edited by Maurice Bloch and Jonathan Parry (Cambridge: Cambridge University Press, 1982), 96–97; Jonathan Parry, *Death in Banaras* (Cambridge: Cambridge University Press, 1994), 260–261.

58. Alexandra David-Neel, *L'Inde où j'ai vécu* (Paris: Pocket, 1985), 248.

59. Satprem, *Mother or the Divine Materialism* (Paris: Institut de recherches évolutives, 1979), 3–4.

60. Jacques Vigne gives supplementary specifications on the subject of the death of Swami Ramatirtha: "It is interesting to note that, being a vedantin and reformist, and thus fairly critical of rituals, he perished because of a ritual. Essentially, the bath in the Ganges is one of the fundamental rituals of Hinduism. Must we see a type of 'return of karma'?" "A week later his body was seen floating in the Ganges, next to a place where he had meditated, Shimalasu Udhyan, a name which means 'the garden of the Black one', that is to say Kali. 'Mother Ganges returns her great follower, Râm's body, to the people so that they may give him the last rites. One claims with stupor that this body was intact. It was seated in the position of samâdhi—in the lotus position—the two hands placed on the feet one over the other, the back and the neck straight, the eyes closed and the mouth open in a way that evoked the pronunciation of the Om [this reminds us of the end of Zen master, who, in general, maintains the lotus position while dying],'" cited by Jacques Vigne, trans., *Râmatîrtha: Le Soleil du soi* (Paris: Accarias–L'originel, 2005), 39.

61. David-Neel, *L'Inde où j'ai vécu*, 247.

62. Régis Debray, *Le Feu sacré: Fonction du religieux* (Paris: Gallimard, 2005), 300.

63. Van Der Leeuw, *La Religion dans son essence et ses manifestations*, 231.

64. Catherine Grémion, "Les Saintes, victimes de leurs interprètes," in *Des Saints, des justes*, edited by Henriette Levillain (Paris: Autrement, 2000), 121.

65. Jean Przyluski, *Le Paranirvana et les funérailles du Buddha* (Paris: Imprimerie nationale, 1920), 179–180, cited in Strong, *Relics of the Buddha*, 17.

66. Jürgen W. Frembgen, "The *Majzub* Mama Ji Sarkar: A Friend of God Moves from One House to Another," in *Embodying Charisma: Modernity, Locality and the Performance of Emotion in Sufi Cults*, edited by Pnina Werbner and Helene Basu (London: Routledge, 1998), 145.

67. Leona M. Anderson, "Women in Hindu Tradition," in *Women and Religious Traditions*, edited by Leona M. Anderson and Pamela Dickey Young (Don Mills, ON: Oxford University Press, 2004), 226.

68. Ibid. On female Hindu asceticism, one can also look at Antoinette DeNapoli, "Beyond Brahmanical Asceticism: Recent and Emerging Models of Female Hindu Asceticisms in South Asia," *Religion Compass* 3, no. 5 (2009): 857–875, where she discusses the text-based structural studies on asceticism and introduces the recent scholarship on female Hindu asceticism that challenges the brahminical textual model. From the same author, see as well "By the Sweetness of the Tongue," *Asian Ethnology* 68, no. 1 (2009): 81–109, which examines the narratives themes that female Hindu *sādhus* emphasize in the construction of their personal narratives and shows how they validate their identity as female sādhus within what is viewed as a male-dominated tradition of renunciation. Finally, one can also refer to the works of Clémentin-Ojha, Denton, Kandelwal, Pechilis.

69. Vasudha Narayanan, "Brimming with *Bhakti*, Embodiments of *Shakti*: Devotees, Deities, Performers, Reformers, and Other Women of Power in Hindu Tradition," in *Feminism and World Religions*, edited by Arvind Sharma and Katherine K. Young (Albany: State University of New York Press, 1999), 37; see also Anant Altekar, "Ideal and Position of Indian Women in Social Life," in *Great Women of India*, edited by Swami Madhavananda and Ramesh C. Majumdar (Calcutta: Advaita Ashrama, 1997), 35.

70. Dennis Hudson, "Āṇṭāḷ Āḷvār: A Developing Hagiography," *Journal of Vaisnava Studies* 1, no. 2 (1993): 28.

71. See Catherine Clémentin-Ojha, *La Divinité conquise: Carrière d'une sainte* (Nanterre, France: Société d'Ethnologie, 1990); and id., "The Tradition of Female Gurus," *Manushi*, no. 31 (November–December 1985): 2–8.

72. Karen Pechilis, "Introduction: Hindu Female Gurus in Historical and Philosophical Context," in *The Graceful Guru: Hindu Female Gurus in India and the United States* (New York: Oxford University Press, 2004), 5–6; see also "The Female Guru: Guru, Gender, and the Path of Personal Experience," in *The Guru in South Asia: New Interdisciplinary Perspectives*, edited by Jacob Copeman and Aya Ikegame (London: Routledge, 2012), 114.

73. In the Advaitic tradition, liberation was generally destined for male Brahmin *saṃnyāsins*. Regarding this, see Andrew Fort, *Jīvanmukti in Transformation: Embodied Liberation in Advaita and Neo-Vedanta* (Albany: State University of New York Press, 19980, 3.

74. This anecdote is not in the English edition of Bhaiji's book, *Mother as Revealed to Me*; it has not been translated into English. One can find this story, however, in the Hindi version of Bhaiji's book, *Matri Darshan* (Calcutta: Shree Shree Anandamayee Charitable Society, 1983).

75. Madhu Kishwar, "Introduction," in *Manushi*, Tenth Anniversary Issue, Women Bhakta Poets, nos. 50-52 (1989): 6.

76. Nancy E. Falk, "*Shakti* Ascending: Hindu Women, Politics, and Religious Leadership during the Nineteenth and Twentieth Centuries," in *Religion in Modern India*, edited by Robert D. Baird (Delhi: Manohar, 2001), 298.

77. See David Kinsley, *Tantric Visions of the Divine Feminine: The Ten Mahavidyas* (Berkeley and Los Angeles: University of California Press, 1997). It is interesting to note that Aurobindo mentioned, in one of his letters, that Mirra Alfassa (the Mother) was none other than his complementary side, his counterpart, "Mother and I are one but in two bodies." See Satprem, *Mother or the Divine Materialism*, 1.

78. A. R. Natarajan, *Bhagavan Ramana & Mother* (Bangalore: Ramana Maharshi Center for Learning, 2002), 40–51; David M. Miller, "Karma, Rebirth and the Contemporary Guru," in *Karma and Rebirth*, edited by Ronald. W. Neufeldt (Albany: State University of New York Press, 1986), 75. In this regard, the mother of Sathya Sai Baba, Eashwaramma, was also buried and her *samādhi* is now a place of worship of the Divine Mother for devotees of Sathya Sai Baba. The *samādhi* of her son, however, is not located next to her Mother's. See Srivinas, *Winged Faith*, 352; and Smriti Srivinas, *In the Presence of Sai Baba: Body, City and Memory in a Global Religious Movement* (Hyderabad: Orient Longman Private Limited, 2008), 171.

79. Shashi B. Das Gupta, "Evolution of Mother Worship in India," in *Great Women of India*, edited by Swami Madhavananda and Ramesh C. Majumdar (Calcutta: Advaita Ashrama, 1997), 76. On *śakti pīṭha*, see also André Padoux, *Comprendre le tantrisme: Les Sources hindoues* (Paris: Albin Michel, 2010), 234–235; as well as Urban, *Power of Tantra*, 31–37.

80. Thomas B. Coburn, "Consort of None, Śakti of All: The Vision of the *Devī-Māhātmya*," in *The Divine Consort: Rādhā and the Goddesses of India*, edited by John Stratton Hawley and Donna M. Wulff (Berkeley and Los Angeles: University of California Press, 1982), 154.

81. Roxanne K. Gupta, "Kālī Māyī: Myth and Reality in a Banaras Ghetto," in *Encountering Kālī: In the Margins, at the Center, in the West*, edited by Rachel Fell McDermott and Jeffrey J. Kripal (Berkeley and Los Angeles: University of California Press, 2003), 139.

82. Fuller, *The Camphor Flame*, 46.

83. Frédérique Apfell Marglin, "Female Sexuality in the Hindu World," in *Immaculate and Powerful: The Female in Sacred Image and Social Reality* (Boston: Beacon Press, 1985), 55, cited in John Stratton Hawley, "Prologue: The Goddess in India," in *Devī: Goddesses of India*, edited by John Stratton Hawley and Donna M. Wulff (Berkeley and Los Angeles: University of California Press, 1996), 14.

84. Jacob N. Kinnard, "The Field of the Buddha's Presence," *Embodying the Dharma: Buddhist Relic Veneration in Asia*, edited by David Germano and Kevin Trainor (Albany: State University of New York Press, 2004), 117.

85. Assayag, *Au confluent de deux rivières*, 65; Lukas Werth, "The Saint Who Disappeared," in *Modernity, Locality and the Performance of Emotion in Sufi Cults*, edited by Pnina Werbner and Helene Basu (London: Routledge, 1998), 80.

86. Thomas Head, personal communication, 1995, cited in John Strong, "Buddhist Relics in Comparative Perspective: Beyond the Parallels," in Germano and Trainor, eds., *Embodying the Dharma*, 32.

87. Trainor, *Relics, Ritual and Representation in Buddhism*, 129.

88. André Bareau, "La Construction et le culte des stūpa d'après les Vinayapiṭaka," *Bulletin de l'École Française d'Extrême-Orient* 50 (1962): 269, cited in Bronkhorst, "Les Reliques dans les religions de l'Inde."

89. Strong, *Relics of the Buddha*, 4; on this subject, see also C. F. Keyes, "Death of Two Buddhist Saints in Thailand," in *Charisma and Sacred Biography*, edited by M. A. Williams (Chico, CA: Scholars Press, 1982), 172.

90. Elisabeth Schömbucher and Claus Peter Zoller, "Death and its Meaning in South Asia," in id., eds., *Ways of Dying: Death and its Meanings in South Asia* (New Delhi: Manohar Publishers and Distributors, 1999), 20.

91. Swami Narasimha, *Life of Sai Baba*, Vol. 1 (Madras: All India Sai Samaj, 1976), see the book's back cover.

92. Melita Maschmann, *Encountering Bliss: My Journey through India with Ānandamayī Mā* (Delhi: Motilal Banarsidass, 2002), 9; see also Amulya K. D. Gupta, *In Association with Sri Sri Ma Anandamayi*, Vol. 1 (Calcutta: Shree Shree Anandamayee Charitable Society, 1987), 15.

93. Madou, *A la rencontre de Ma Anandamayi: Entretiens avec Atmananda*, http://www.anandamayi.org/ashram/french/frmad1.htm.

94. Swami Vijayananda, *Un français dans l'Himalaya: Itinéraire avec Mâ Ananda Môyî* (Lyon: Terre du Ciel, 1997), 132.

95. Mircea Eliade, *Traité d'Histoire des Religions* (Paris: Payot, 1968), 374–375.

96. Testimony by Martine Quentric-Seguy, *Jay Ma*, no. 45.

97. Pnina Werbner and Helene Basu, "The Embodiment of Charisma," in Werbner and Basu, eds., *Embodying Charisma*, 9.

98. Madou, *A la rencontre de Ma Anandamayi*; Jean-Claude Marol, *En tout et pour tout*, (Thionville: Le Fennec, 1994), 15.

99. Hugh B. Urban, *Tantra: Sex, Secrecy, Politics, and Power in the Study of Religion* (Berkeley and Los Angeles: University of California Press, 2003), 251–252; Rachel McDermott, "Kālī's New Frontiers: A Hindu Goddess on the Internet," in McDermott and Kripal, eds., *Encountering Kālī*, 30. On guruship and media technologies, see also Jacob Copeman and Aya Ikegame, "The Multifarious Guru," in Copeman and Ikegame, eds., *Guru in South Asia*, 20, concerning the guru's "betrayal" by the same technologies that had facilitated the proliferation of his "presence."

100. On the concept of *śakti*, see Padoux, *Comprendre le tantrisme*; and Urban, *Power of Tantra*, 21–22.

101. Marc Gaborieau, "Pouvoir et autorité des soufis dans l'Himalaya," in *Prêtrise, pouvoirs et autorité en Himalaya,* edited by Véronique Bouiller and Gérard Toffin (Paris: École des Hautes Études en Sciences Sociales, 1989), 220 and 229.

102. Peter Brown, *La Société et le sacré dans l'Antiquité tardive* (Paris: Seuil, 1985), 96.

103. Charles White, "Swāmi Muktānanda and the Enlightenment through Śakti-pāt," *History of Religions* 13, no. 4 (May 1974): 318.

104. Jacques Vigne, *L'Inde intérieure: Aspects du yoga, de l'hindouisme et du bouddhisme* (Gordes: Editions du Relié, 2007), 153.

105. Caillois, *L'Homme et le sacré,* 58.

106. Cited in Bernard Faure, *La Mort dans les religions d'Asie* (Paris: Flammarion, 1994), 91.

107. Assayag, *Au confluent de deux rivières,* 165.

108. Pierre Bourdieu, "Genèse et structure du champ religieux," *Revue française de sociologie* 12, no. 3 (July–September 1971): 304.

109. James Frazer, *The Golden Bough: A Study in Magic and Religion* (New York: Touchstone Press, 1995), 9.

110. Mary Douglas, *Purity and Danger: An Analysis of Concepts of Pollution and Taboo* (London: Routledge & Kegan Paul, 1966), 112.

111. Eric Geoffroy, "Proche-Orient," in *Le Culte des saints dans le monde musulman,* edited by Henri Chambert-Loir and Claude Guillot (Paris: École Française d'Extrême Orient, 1995), 47.

112. Speaking on *dargahs,* Flueckiger notes that, in these environments, terms are easily interchanged. The *pir* becomes a guru and Viśnu is seen as an early prophet before Mohammad. See Joyce Flueckiger, *In Amma's Healing Room: Gender and Vernacular Islam in South Asia* (Bloomington: Indiana University Press, 2006).

113. Landell Samuel Mills, "The Hardware of Sanctity: Anthropomorphic Objects in Bangladeshi Sufism," in Werbner and Basu, eds., *Embodying Charisma,* 35 and 32.

114. Hugh Van Skyhawk, "A Note on Death and the Holy Man in South Asia," in *Ways of Dying: Death and Its Meanings in South Asia* (New Delhi: Manohar, 1999), 196.

115. Strong, "Buddhist Relics in Comparative Perspective," 38.

116. Marc Gaborieau, "Inde," in Chambert-Loir and Guillot, eds., *Le Culte des saints dans le monde musulman,* 202.

117. Brown, *Le Culte des saints,* 105; Schmitt, "La Fabrique des saints," 289.

118. Caillois, *L'Homme et le sacré,* 28.

119. Brown, *Le Culte des saints,* 105.

120. Bernard Faure, "Buddhist Relics and Japanese Regalia," in Germano and Trainor, eds., *Embodying the Dharma,* 97.

121. Mark Juergensmeyer, "The Radhasoami Revival of the Sant Tradition," in *The Sants: Studies in a Devotional Tradition of India,* edited by Karine Schomer and W. H. McLeod (Delhi: Motilal Banarsidass, 1987), 342; Lawrence A. Babb,

Redemptive Encounters: Three Modern Styles in the Hindu Tradition (Berkeley and Los Angeles: University of California Press, 1986), 33.

122. Michel Kaplan, "De la dépouille à la relique: Formation du culte des saints à Byzance du Vè au XIIè siècle," in *Les Reliques, objets, cultes, symboles* (Turnhout, Belgium: Brepols, 1999), 23.

123. Leo Schneiderman, "Ramakrishna: Personality and Social Factors in the Growth of a Religious Movement," *Journal for the Scientific Study of Religion* 8, no. 1 (Spring 1969): 68.

124. Henri Platelle, "Guibert de Nogent et le *De pignoribus sanctorum*: Richesses et limites d'une critique médiévale des reliques," in *Les Reliques, objets, cultes, symboles* (Turnhout, Belgium: Brepols, 1999), 117.

125. Lawrence Babb, "Sathya Sai Baba's Magic," *Anthropological Quarterly* 56 (1983): 116–123.

126. Assayag, *Au confluent de deux rivières*, 84.

127. Tulasi Srivinas, "Articles of Faith: Material Piety, Devotional Aesthetics and the Construction of a Moral Economy in the Transnational Sathya Sai Movement," *Visual Anthropology* 25 (July 2012): 290.

128. Kevin Trainor, "Introduction: Beyond Superstition," in Germano and Trainor, eds., *Embodying the Dharma*, 14.

129. Roger Bastide, *Eléments de sociologie religieuse* (Paris: Editions Stock, 1997), 97.

130. Caillois, *L'Homme et le sacré*, 25.

131. Jean-Claude Schmitt, "Les Reliques et les images," in *Les Reliques, objets, cultes, symbols*, 149.

132. Faure, *La Mort dans les religions d'Asie*, 97.

133. David Kinsley, "'The Death That Conquers Death': Dying to the World in Medieval Hinduism," in *Religious Encounters with Death*, edited by Frank E. Reynolds and Earle H. Waugh (University Park: Pennsylvania State University Press, 1977), 102.

134. Mathieu Boisvert, "Bouddhisme, contemplation et mort," *Frontières* 7, no. 3 (Winter 1995): 34. This also reminds us of the *Chōd* Tibetan practice, known as "cutting through the ego," in which the adept symbolically offers the flesh of his or her body in a form of *gaṇacakra* or tantric feast.

135. Purushottam Singh, *Burial Practices in Ancient India* (Varanasi: Prithivi Prakashan, 1970), 178.

136. Schmitt, "Les Reliques et les images," 150.

137. Weinberger-Thomas, *Cendres d'immortalité*, 130.

138. Edgar Morin, *L'Homme et la mort* (Paris: Seuil, 1970), 33.

139. Jackie Assayag, "Le Cadavre divin: Célébration de la mort chez les Liṅgāyat-Vīraśaiva," *L'Homme* 27, no. 103 (July–September 1987): 107–108.

140. Michel Meslin, *L'Expérience humaine du divin* (Paris: Cerf, 1988), 338.

141. Trainor, *Relics, Ritual and Representation in Buddhism*, 27.

142. Maurice Bloch and Jonathan Parry, *Death and the Regeneration of Life* (Cambridge: Cambridge University Press, 1982), 36.

143. I should however specify that a cult of ancestors does exist and non-renunciants are memorialized at family altars through portraits and photos.

144. Malamoud, "Les Morts sans visage," 446.

145. Ibid., 448.

146. Ibid., 449.

147. Mère Meera, *Mère Meera: Réponses*, Vol. 1, Edition Adilakshmi (n.d). Mother Meera is somehow situated in the tradition of Sri Aurobindo. She teaches mainly through silence. On Mother Meera, see Catherine Cornille, "Mother Meera, Avatar," *The Graceful Guru: Hindu Female Gurus in India and the United States*, edited by Karen Pechilis (New York: Oxford University Press, 2004), 129–147.

148. Danièle Hervieu-Léger, *La Religion pour mémoire* (Paris: Cerf, 1993), 108.

149. Jack Goody, *Representations and Contradictions: Ambivalence towards Images, Theatre, Fiction, Relics and Sexuality* (Oxford: Blackwell, 1997), 83, cited in Strong, *Relics of the Buddha*, 18.

150. Alain Daniélou, *Approche de l'hindouisme* (Paris: Kailash, 2005), 21.

151. David Kinsley, "Kālī," *Encountering Kālī: In the Margins, at the Center, in the West*, edited by Rachel Fell McDermott and Jeffrey J. Kripal (Berkeley and Los Angeles: University of California Press, 2003), 32; David Kinsley, "Kālī, Blood and Death out of Place," *Devī: Goddesses of India*, edited by John Stratton Hawley and Donna M. Wulff (Berkeley and Los Angeles: University of California Press, 1996), 82.

152. David Kinsley, "Freedom from Death in the Worship of Kālī," *Numen* 22, no. 3 (December 1975): 201; David Kinsley, *The Sword and the Flute: Kālī and Kṛṣṇa* (Berkeley and Los Angeles: University of California Press, 1975), 114; Urban, *Tantra*, 76–77.

153. Pierre Feuga, *Cinq visages de la déesse* (Paris: Le Mail, 1989), 119.

154. Shyam Ghosh, *Hindu Concept of Life and Death* (New Delhi: Munshiram Manoharlal, 2002), 3; see also Bruce J. Long, "Death as a Necessity and a Gift in Hindu Mythology," in *Religious Encounters with Death*, edited by Frank E. Reynolds and Earle H. Waugh (University Park: Pennsylvania State University Press, 1977), 73–96.

155. From a psychoanalytical perspective, this reminds us of Spratt, who considers Kālī's decapitating role as a return for the male devotee to an identification with the mother and, ultimately, to a mystical *regressus ad uterum*. On this, see Philip Spratt, *Hindu Culture and Personality: A Psychoanalytic Study* (Bombay: Manaktalas, 1966). See also Jeffrey J. Kripal, "Re-membering a Presence of Mythological Proportions: Psychoanalysis and Hinduism," in *Religion and Psychology: Mapping the Terrain*, edited by Diane Jonte-Pace and William B. Parsons (London: Routledge, 2001).

156. See Mircea Eliade, *Initiation, rites et sociétés secrètes* (Paris: Gallimard, 1959); and Mircea Eliade, *Le Sacré et le profane* (Paris: Gallimard, 1965), 161.

157. Otto Rank, *Le Traumatisme de la naissance*, cited in Morin, *L'Homme et la mort*, 143–144.

158. Ysé Tardan-Masquelier, *L'Hindouisme* (Paris: Bayard, 1999), 205.

159. Filippi, *Mṛtyu*, 7–8.

160. The archetype of the Mother contains many aspects of a bipolar structure in both a negative and positive sense. See David M. Wulff, "Prolegomenon to a Psychology of the Goddess," in *The Divine Consort: Rādhā and the Goddesses of India*, edited by John Stratton Hawley and Donna Marie Wulff (Berkeley and Los Angeles: University of California Press, 1982), 293.

161. Padoux, *Comprendre le tantrisme*, 246.

162. Madeleine Biardeau, "Devi: The Goddess in India," in *Asian Mythologies*, compiled by Yves Bonnefoy and translated by Wendy Doniger (Chicago: University of Chicago Press, 1993), 95.

CHAPTER 3

1. See Shree Shree Anandamayee Charitable Society, *I Am Ever with You: Matri Lila*, Vol. 2 (Calcutta: Shree Shree Anandamayee Charitable Society, 1991), 57.

2. "Mataji Amara Vani," *Ananda Varta* 4, no. 4 (1956): 314.

3. Bithika Mukerji, *Life and Teaching of Sri Ma Anandamayi (A Bird on the Wing)* (Delhi: Sri Satguru Publications, 1998), 192; Bithika Mukerji, *My Days with Sri Ma Anandamayi* (Varanasi: Indica Books, 2002), 85; Narayan Chaudhuri, *That Compassionate Touch of Ma Anandamayee* (Delhi: Motilal Banarsidass, 1988), 114.

4. Jean Herbert and Josette Herbert, trans., *L'Enseignement de Mâ Ananda Moyî* (Paris : Albin Michel, 1988), 326.

5. Swami Ramdas, *Présence de Ram* (Paris: Albin Michel, 1997), 321.

6. Arthur Osborne, *Ramana Maharshi and the Path of Self-Knowledge* (London: Rider, 1992), 185.

7. Jean-Claude Marol, *Ma Anandamoyi: Vie en jeu* (Paris: Accarias–L'Originel, 1995), 118.

8. Bhaiji, *Mother as Revealed to Me* (Kankhal: Shree Shree Anandamayee Sangha, 2004), 91.

9. Anil Ganguli, *Anandamayi Ma's Inscrutable Kheyāl* (Calcutta: Shree Shree Anandamayi Charitable Society, 1980), 24.

10. *The Bhagavadgītā* (ch. 2, 19–20), translated by S. Radhakrishnan (London: George Allen & Unwin Ltd, 1971), 107.

11. *The Complete Works of Swami Vivekenanda*, Vol. 1 (Calcutta: Advaita Ashrama, 1964), 421, cited in George M. Williams, "Swami Vivekananda's Conception of Karma and Rebirth," in *Karma and Rebirth: Post Classical Developments*, edited by Ronald W. Neufeldt (Albany: State University of New York Press, 1986), 48.

12. Atmananda, *Death Must Die: A Western Woman's Life-Long Spiritual Quest in India with Sri Anandamayee Ma*, edited by Ram Alexander (Delhi: Indica Books, 2000), 496.

13. Anil Ganguli, *Anandamayi Ma: The Mother Bliss-Incarnate* (Calcutta: Eureka, 1983), 170.

14. Atmananda, *Death Must Die*, 383.

15. Madou, *A la rencontre de Ma Anandamayi: Entretiens avec Atmananda*, http://www.anandamayi.org/ashram/french/frmad1.htm. This illusion of Mā's body is also found in the comments of Gopinath Kaviraj: "Mother's body is no body and Her mind is no mind in the ordinary connotation of terms. They are only apparent and exist for the ignorant who are under *māyā* and unable to see behind the veil." See Gopinath Kaviraj, "Mother," in *Selected Writings of M. M. Gopinath Kaviraj*, edited by Gopinath Kaviraj (Varanasi: M. M. Gopinath Kaviraj Centenary Celebrations Committee, 1990), 192.

16. *The Bṛhadāraṇyaka Upaniṣad*, with the commentary of Śaṅkarācārya (4, 4, 19–20) (Calcutta: Advaita Ashrama, 1965), 744–745.

17. Jean Herbert, *Spiritualité hindoue* (Paris: Albin Michel, 1972), 389.

18. Ananda K. Coomaraswamy, *Hinduism and Buddhism* (New York: Philosophical Library, n.d.), 30.

19. Kirin Narayan, *Storytellers, Saints, and Scoundrels: Folk Narrative in Hindu Religious Teaching* (Philadelphia: University of Pennsylvania Press, 1989), 185.

20. Arthur Osborne, *Ramana Maharshi and the Path of Self-Knowledge* (London: Rider, 1992), 184.

21. To express the death of the saint, one can also say that the saint "*took samādhi*" (*samādhi liyā*). See Narayan, *Storytellers, Saints, and Scoundrels*, 185.

22. Mircea Eliade, *Images et symboles* (Paris: Gallimard, 1979), 125 and 127.

23. A. R. Natarajan, *Bhagavan Ramana & Mother* (Bangalore: Ramana Maharshi Center for Learning, 2002), 40.

24. Jackie Assayag, "Le cadavre divin: Célébration de la mort chez les Liṅgāyat-Vīraśaiva (Inde du Sud)." *L'Homme* 27, no. 103 (July–September 1987): 106.

25. Madou, *A la rencontre de Ma Anandamayi*.

26. Ibid.

27. Ibid.

28. Ibid. Regarding Mā's progressive retreat before her death, see Mukerji, *My Days with Sri Ma Anandamayi*, 356.

29. Madou, *A la rencontre de Ma Anandamayi*.

30. Swami Mangalananda, "The Passing of a Saint: Sri Kishori Mataji," unpublished.

31. Jeffrey J. Kripal, *Kālī's Child: The Mystical and the Erotic in the Life and Teachings of Ramakrishna* (Chicago: University of Chicago Press, 1998), 261.

32. See Arnold Van Gennep, *Les Rites de passage* (New York: Johnson Reprint, 1969).

33. Madou, *A la rencontre de Ma Anandamayi*.

34. Edgar Morin, *L'Homme et la mort* (Paris: Seuil, 1970), 72–73.

35. *Śriśrirāmakṛṣṇa Paramahamsadever Jivanavṛttānta*, 144.

36. Kripal, *Kālī's Child*, 254.

37. Madou, *A la rencontre de Ma Anandamayi*.

38. *Pensée de l'Himalaya*, http://www.anandamayi.org.

39. Nanda Mookerjee, *Sri Sarada Devi: Consort of Sri Ramakrishna* (Calcutta: Firma KLM, 1978), 57.

40. On this subject, see Pnina Werbner and Helene Basu, "The Embodiment of Charisma," in *Embodying Charisma: Modernity, Locality and the Performance of Emotion in Sufi Cults*, edited by Pnina Werbner and Helene Basu (London: Routledge, 1998), 10.

41. André Rousseau, "Rites et discours religieux comme pratiques sociales," *Maison-Dieu*, no. 129 (1977): 118.

42. *Jay Ma*, no. 44.

43. See Van Gennep, *Les Rites de passage*.

44. Robert Hertz, *Death and the Right Hand* (London: Cohen & West, 2004), 81–82.

45. *Pensée de l'Himalaya*.

46. Vijayananda, "Un chemin de joie: Témoignages et réponses d'un disciple français de Mâ Anandamayi," unpublished.

47. Ibid.

48. Amulya K. D. Gupta, *In Association with Sri Sri Ma Anandamayi*, Vol. 3 (Calcutta: Shree Shree Anandamayee Charitable Society, 1987), 89–90.

49. June McDaniel, "Fusion of the Soul: Jayashri Ma and the Primordial Mother," in *The Graceful Guru: Hindu Females Gurus in India and the United States*, edited by Karen Pechilis (New York: Oxford University Press, 2004), 122.

50. Mookerjee, *Sri Sarada Devi*, appendix 3.

51. D. A. Swallow, "Ashes and Powers: Myth, Rite and Miracle in an Indian God-Man's Cult," *Modern Asian Studies* 16, no. 1 (1982): 135. Devotees of Shirdi Sai Baba, however, do not necessarily recognize Sathya Sai Baba as the reincarnation of Shirdi Sai Baba.

52. Tulasi Srivinas, *Winged Faith: Rethinking Globalisation and Religious Pluralism through the Sathya Sai Movement* (New York: Columbia University Press, 2010), 67.

53. Rao P. D. Sham, *Five Contemporary Gurus in the Shirdi (Sai Baba) Tradition* (Madras: Christian Literature Society, 1972), 35.

54. Pierre Feuga, *Cinq visages de la déesse* (Paris: Le Mail, 1989), 103.

55. This simultaneous reference to the concepts of "individual soul" and "spiritual principle" can be a source of confusion, in that it reveals some interchangeability of concepts. As we have specified on the subject of sanctity in the Hindu tradition, the limit between the individual, who has a soul, and God is fluid. The human being can thus both possess a soul (*ātman*) and be inseparable from everything, the spiritual principle (*Brahman*).

56. Vijayananda, "Un chemin de joie."
57. Maya Warrier, *Hindu Selves in a Modern World: Guru Faith in the Mata Amritanandamayi Mission* (London: Routledge Curzon, 2005).
58. Atmananda, *Death Must Die*, 301.
59. *Words of Sri Anandamayi Ma*, 126–127.
60. Alexandra David-Neel, *L'Inde où j'ai vécu* (Paris: Pocket, 1985), 249. Along these lines, one can think of the guru-avatar Sathya Sai Baba, whose knee and hip surgery, a few years before his death, were questioned by his devotees. A debate took place whether a divine being like him actually needs such a surgery. See Srivinas, *Winged Faith*, 211–212. The same reaction took place among devotees at the time of his death. Devotees hoped that "Swami would cure himself," that he "would decide to remain," as in 1963, when he had a series of strokes, while taking on, he affirmed, the illness of a devotee. See Tulasi Srivinas, "Relics of Faith: Fleshly Desires, Ascetic Disciplines and Devotional Affect in the Transnational Sathya Sai Movement." *Handbook of Body Studies*, edited by Bryan S. Turner (London: Routledge Press, 2012).
61. Narayan, *Storytellers, Saints, and Scoundrels*, 172, 178, and 184. This ability to predict one's own death is found in various religious traditions, such as Islam. On this, one can refer for example to the work of Katherine Ewing on Sufi saints in South Asia, "A Majzub and His Mother: The Place of Sainthood in a Family's Emotional Memory," in *Embodying Charisma: Modernity, Locality and the Performance of Emotion in Sufi Cults*, edited by Pnina Werbner and Helene Basu. (London: Routledge, 1998), 160–184.
62. Interview with one Indian devotee (Aymard, 2013).
63. Satprem, *Mother or the Divine Materialism* (Paris: Institut de recherches évolutives, 1979), 339.
64. W. J. Jackson, "A Life Becomes a Legend: Srī Tyāgarāja as Exemplar," *Journal of the American Academy of Religion* 60, no. 4 (Winter 1992): 732.
65. Jnaneshwar's physical death is considered in a narrative called "*samādhi*" to refer to the state of meditation the saint would maintain in his tomb in Alandi. See Christian Lee Novetzke, *Religion and Public Memory: A Cultural History of Saint Namdev in India* (New York: Columbia University Press, 2008), 42. On Jnaneshwar' *samādhi*, see as well Narayan, *Storytellers, Saints, and Scoundrels*, 185; and R. D. Ranade, *Mysticism in India: The Poet-Saints of Maharashtra* (Albany: State University of New York Press, 1983), 34–35 and 43–44.
66. Jean Herbert, "Karma et mort dans l'hindouisme," in *La Mort est une autre naissance*, edited by Marc de Smedt (Paris: Albin Michel, 1989), 226.
67. See Swami Purushottamananda, *Autobiography or the Story of Divine Compassion* (Vasishtha Guha, Tehri Garwal, Uttar Pradesh: Sri Purushottamananda Trust, n.d.), 275.
68. Thara L. Bhai, 2004. "Emergence of Shrines in Rural Tamil Nadu: A Study of Little Traditions," in *Sociology of Religion in India: Themes in Indian*

Sociology, Vol. 3, edited by Rowena Robinson (New Delhi: Sage Publications, 2004), 167.

69. Marol, *Ma Anandamoyi: Vie en jeu*, 110 (published in Hari Ram Joshi, *Mā Ānandamayī Līlā: Memoirs of Sri Hari Ram Joshi* [Calcutta: Shree Shree Anandamayee Charitable Society, 1981]).

70. Marol, *Ma Anandamoyi: Vie en jeu*, 109–110.

71. A Siddha (*Siddha* meaning perfect in Sanskrit) is one who has attained the supreme goal and who is endowed with supernatural powers (*siddhis*). Siddha also means the follower of *Śiva* in the Deccan, the alchemist of Tamil Nadu (Sittar), the tantric Buddhist in Bengal (Mahasiddha and Siddhācārya), the alchemists of medieval India (Rasa Siddha), and the Nath Siddha in North India.

72. David Gordon White, "The Exemplary Life of Mastnāth: The Encapsulation of Seven Hundred Years of Nāth Siddha Hagiography," in *Constructions hagiographiques dans le monde indien: Entre mythe et histoire*, edited by Françoise Mallison (Paris: Librairie Honoré Champion, 2001), 140. See also Véronique Bouiller, "Des prêtres du pouvoir: Les Yogis et la fonction royale," in *Prêtrise, pouvoirs et autorité en Himalaya*, edited by Véronique Bouiller and Gérard Toffin (Paris: École des Hautes Études en Sciences Sociales, 1989).

73. "Mataji Amara Vani," *Ananda Varta*, 313.

74. Helmuth Von Glasenapp, *Immortality and Salvation in Indian Religions* (Calcutta: Susil Gupta India, 1963), 10.

75. See Paramahansa Yogananda, *Autobiography of a Yogi* (Los Angeles: Self-Realization Fellowship, 1997).

76. Antonio Rigopoulos, *The Life and Teachings of Sai Baba of Shirdi* (Albany: State University of New York Press, 1993), 93.

77. Jacques Vigne, *Râmatîrtha: Le Soleil du soi*, translated by Jacques Vigne (Paris: Accarias–L'Originel, 2005), 79–80.

78. Jean M. Rivière, *Lettres de Bénarès* (Paris: Albin Michel, 1982), 176.

79. Satprem, *Mother or the Divine Materialism*, 331–332.

80. Madou, *A la rencontre de Ma Anandamayi*.

81. Christopher Isherwood, *Ramakrishna and His Disciples* (Calcutta: Advaita Ashrama, 1965), 298.

82. Madou, *A la rencontre de Ma Anandamayi*.

83. Kripal, *Kālī's Child*, 253.

84. Marol, *Ma Anandamoyi: Vie en jeu*, 39.

85. Catherine Clément and Sudhir Kakar, *La Folle et le saint* (Paris: Seuil, 1993), 145.

86. Ibid., 146.

87. Atmananda, *Death Must Die*, 215.

88. Satprem, *Mother or the Divine Materialism*, 337.

89. Madou, *A la rencontre de Ma Anandamayi*; on this subject, also see Gupta's, *In Association with Sri Sri Ma Anandamayi*, Vol. 1, 183, where Mā affirms to her disciples that her body cannot be maintained except in wishing it well.

90. Excerpt from Gurupriya Devī's *Sri Sri Ma Anandamayi*, Vol. 1 (Calcutta: Shree Shree Anandamayee Charitable Society, 1986): "Mâ sometimes says: Before this body appeared, my father had left his foyer. He had even slipped on his saffron robe for a while and spent his days and nights singing God's praise. This body appeared during this phase of renunciation," cited in Madou, *A la rencontre de Ma Anandamayi*.

91. Madou, *A la rencontre de Ma Anandamayi*.

92. By the terms *"Samyam Vratā,"* Atmananda is referring to *Samyam Saptah*, the retreat devoted to Mā that takes place every year.

93. Madou, *A la rencontre de Ma Anandamayi*.

94. Catherine Clémentin-Ojha, *La Divinité conquise: Carrière d'une sainte* (Nanterre, France: Société d'Ethnologie, 1990), 181–182.

95. Ibid.

96. David M. Miller, "Karma, Rebirth and the Contemporary Guru," in *Karma and Rebirth: Post Classical Developments*, edited by Ronald. W. Neufeldt (Albany: State University of New York Press, 1986), 67.

97. Lisa L. Hallstrom, *Mother of Bliss: Ānandamayī Mā (1896–1982)* (New York: Oxford University Press, 1999), 117.

98. Arnaud Desjardins, *Ashrams: Grands maîtres de l'Inde* (Paris: Albin Michel, 1982), 90–91.

99. Bharati Dhingra, *Visages de Ma Anandamayi* (Paris: Cerf, 1981), 54–55.

100. Madou, *A la rencontre de Ma Anandamayi*.

101. Atmananda, *Death Must Die*, 474.

102. Swami Nikhilananda, trans., and Swami Adiswarananda, eds., *Sri Sarada Devi: The Holy Mother, Her Teachings and Conversations* (New York : Ramakrishna-Vivekananda Center of New York and Skylight Paths Publishing, 2004), 23.

CHAPTER 4

1. Daniel Gold, *The Lord as Guru: Hindi Sants in North Indian Tradition* (New York: Oxford University Press, 1987), 108 and 159; Daniel Gold, *Comprehending the Guru: Toward a Grammar of Religious Perception* (Atlanta, GA: Scholars Press, 1988), 60.

2. Charlotte Vaudeville, *"Sant Mat*: Santism as the Universal Path to Sanctity," in *The Sants: Studies in a Devotional Tradition of India*, edited by Karine Schomer and W. H. McLeod (New Delhi: Motilal Banarsidass, 1987), 33–34.

3. Guy Bugault, "La Relation maître disciple en Inde," in *Maître et disciples dans les traditions religieuses*, edited by Michel Meslin (Paris: Cerf, 1990), 34.

4. David M. Miller, "The Divine Life Society Movement," in *Religion in Modern India*, edited by Robert D. Baird (Delhi: Manohar, 2001), 86.

5. Jacques Vigne, *Le Maître et le thérapeute* (Paris: Albin Michel, 1991), 138.

6. Jacques Vigne, *L'Inde intérieure: Aspects du yoga, de l'hindouisme et du bouddhisme* (Gordes: Editions du Relié, 2007), 221.

7. *Muṇḍaka Upaniṣad* (I.2.12), translated by Swami Muni Narayana Prasad (New Delhi, DK: Printworld, 1998), 39.

8. Swami Ramdas, *Entretiens de Hadeyah* (Paris: Albin Michel, 1957), 204.

9. *Words of Sri Anandamayi Ma*, translated by Atmananda (Kankhal: Shree Shree Anandamayee Sangha, 2001), 14; on the necessity of the guru, see also Amulya K. D. Gupta, *In Association with Sri Sri Ma Anandamayi*, Vol. 3 (Calcutta: Shree Shree Anandamayee Charitable Society, 1987), 54, where Mā affirms that the presence of a guru is indispensable for the person who wants to be guided on the path toward realization.

10. Bharati Dhingra, *Visages de Ma Anandamayi* (Paris: Cerf, 1981), 147.

11. Swami Vijayānanda, "Un chemin de joie. Témoignages et réponses d'un disciple français de Mâ Anandamayi" (n.d.).

12. René Guénon, *Initiation et réalisation spirituelle* (Paris: Editions Traditionnelles, 1982), 189.

13. Jacques Vigne, *La Mystique du silence* (Paris: Albin Michel, 2003), 25.

14. Jean M. Rivière, *Lettres de Bénarès* (Paris: Albin Michel, 1982), 182.

15. "Mataji Amara Vani," *Ananda Varta* 4, no. 4 (1956): 315.

16. Atmananda, *Death Must Die: A Western Woman's Life-Long Spiritual Quest in India with Sri Anandamayee Ma*, edited by Ram Alexander (Delhi: Indica Books, 2000), 507; on the absence of the guru's death, also see Mā's words in Gupta, *In Association with Sri Sri Ma Anandamayi*, Vol. 3, 193, where Mā affirms that the guru cannot die, and that in this, the successive initiations of the disciple can take place despite the physical absence of the guru.

17. Jean Herbert and Josette Herbert, trans., *L'Enseignement de Mâ Ananda Moyî* (Paris: Albin Michel, 1988), 44.

18. Jean Herbert, *Spiritualité hindoue* (Paris: Albin Michel, 1972), 447.

19. Vijayānanda, "Un chemin de joie."

20. Ibid., 19; see also Swami Vijayānanda, *Un français dans l'Himalaya: Itinéraire avec Mâ Ananda Môyî* (Lyon: Terre du Ciel, 1997), 55.

21. Atmananda, *Death Must Die*, 452–453.

22. *Muṇḍaka Upaniṣad* (III.2.8), 123.

23. Vijayānanda, "Un chemin de joie."

24. Jürgen W. Frembgen, "The *Majzub* Mama Ji Sarkar: A Friend of God Moves from One House to Another," in *Embodying Charisma: Modernity, Locality and the Performance of Emotion in Sufi Cults*, edited by Pnina Werbner and Helene Basu (London: Routledge, 1998), 156.

25. *Sad Vani: A Collection of the Teaching of Sri Anandamayi Ma as Reported by Bhaiji* (Calcutta: Shree Shree Anandamayee Charitable Society, 2000), 53; see also Jean Herbert, trans., *Aux sources de la joie: Mâ Ananda Moyî* (Paris: Albin Michel, 1996), 79.

26. Dhingra, *Visages de Ma Anandamayi*, 102–103.

27. David Gordon White, "Ashes to Nectar: Death and Regeneration among the Rasa Siddhas and Nāth Siddhas," in *The Living and the Dead: Social Dimensions of Death in South Asian Religions*, edited by Liz Wilson (Albany: State University of New York Press, 2003), 13.

28. Atmananda, *Death Must Die*, 26.

29. Dhingra, *Visages de Ma Anandamayi*, 86.

30. Ramdas, *Entretiens de Hadeyah*, 105.

31. Gold, *The Lord as Guru*, 152–156.

32. Vijayānanda, "Un chemin de joie."

33. Vigne, *L'Inde intérieure*, 154.

34. Jeremy Carrette, "Passionate Belief: William James, Emotion and Religious Experience," in id., ed., *William James and the Varieties of Religious Experience: A Centenary Celebration* (London: Routledge, 2005), 85.

35. Charles Taylor, *La Diversité de l'expérience religieuse aujourd'hui: William James revisité* (Saint-Laurent, QC: Bellarmin, 2003), 13; Jeremy Carrette, "William James," in *The Oxford Handbook of Religion and Emotion*, edited by John Corrigan (New York: Oxford University Press, 2008), 422 and 432.

36. Carrette, "Passionate Belief," 80.

37. Raimon Panikkar, *L'Expérience de Dieu* (Paris: Albin Michel, 1998), 39–40.

38. Arnaud Desjardins, *Ashrams: Grands maîtres de l'Inde* (Paris: Albin Michel, 1982), 78.

39. On *darśana* and religious experience, see June McDaniel, "Religious Experience in Hindu Tradition," *Religion Compass* 3, no. 1 (2009): 100–101.

40. Françoise Champion and Danièle Hervieu-Léger, *De l'émotion en religion: Renouveaux et traditions* (Paris: Le Centurion, 1990), 37.

41. William James, *L'Expérience religieuse: Essai de psychologie descriptive* (Paris: La Bibliothèque de l'Homme, 1999), 103; see also Carrette, "William James," 430.

42. André Godin, *Psychologie des expériences religieuses: Le Désir et la réalité* (Paris: Le Centurion, 1986), 140–141.

43. Mircea Eliade, *La Nostalgie des origines* (Paris: Gallimard, 1971), 216.

44. François Isambert, *Rite et efficacité symbolique: Essai d'anthropologie sociologique* (Paris: Cerf, 1979), 156.

45. Atmananda, *Death Must Die*, 430.

46. Antoine Vergote, *Religion, Belief and Unbelief: A Psychological Study* (Leuven: Leuven University Press, 1996), 137.

47. Carrette observed, though, that James also believed to some extent that "mystical states" are actually separated from "definite sensible images." See Carrette, "Passionate Belief," 86.

48. Panikkar, *L'Expérience de Dieu*, 214.

49. Sabino Samele Acquaviva, *La Sociologie des religions: Problèmes et perspectives* (Paris: Cerf, 1994), 98.

50. Marcel Gauchet, *Le Désenchantement du monde* (Paris: Gallimard, 1985), 399.

51. Jean-Claude Marol, *La Saturée de joie Anandamayi* (Paris: Dervy, 2001), 56.

52. David Kinsley, "Kālī, Blood and Death out of Place," in *Devī: Goddesses of India*, edited by John Stratton Hawley and Donna M. Wulff (Berkeley and Los Angeles: University of California Press, 1996), 81.

53. Marol, *La Saturée de joie Anandamayi*, 150.

54. On this topic, see Dominique Bourdin, "Psychanalyse et religion: La Pensée de Freud," in *La Religion: Unité et diversité*, edited by Laurent Testot and Jean-François Dortier (Auxerre: Sciences humaines éditions, 2005), 36.

55. Acquaviva, *La Sociologie des religions*, 97.

56. Antoine Vergote, *Religion, foi, incroyance: Étude psychologique* (Brussels: Mardaga Pierre, 1995), 126.

57. Panikkar, *L'Expérience de Dieu*, 204.

58. Champion and Hervieu-Léger, *De l'émotion en religion*, 36. « *Emotion* or *émotion* » ?

59. Panikkar, *L'Expérience de Dieu*, 109–110.

60. Rudolf Otto, *Le Sacré: L'Élément non rationnel dans l'idée du divin et sa relation avec le rationnel* (Paris: Payot, 2001), 16.

61. William James, *The Varieties of Religious Experience* (Oxford: Oxford University Press, 2012), 306.

62. Otto, *Le Sacré*, 56.

63. Panikkar, *L'Expérience de Dieu*, 190.

64. Desjardins, *Ashrams*, 190.

65. W. Doniger O'Flaherty, *Dreams, Illusion and Other Realities* (Chicago: University of Chicago Press, 1984).

66. Sudhir Kakar, *Shamans, Mystics and Doctors: A Psychological Inquiry into India and its Healing Traditions* (New York: Knopf, 1982), 48.

67. Lawrence A. Babb, "Glancing: Visual Interaction in Hinduism," *Journal of Anthropological Research* 37, no. 4 (Winter 1981): 388.

68. The day after his death, Shirdi Sai Baba is said to have appeared in a dream to one of his disciples, telling him: "Jog thinks I am dead. I am alive. Go and perform my morning *ārati*," cited in Mani Sahukar, *Sai Baba: The Saint of Shirdi* (Bombay: Somaiya Publications, 1971), 72.

69. Catherine Weinberger-Thomas, *Cendres d'immortalité: La Crémation des veuves en Inde* (Paris: Seuil, 1996), 110.

70. Smriti Srinivas, "The Advent of the Avatar: The Urban Following of Sathya Sai Baba and its Construction of Tradition," in *Charisma and Canon: The Formation of Religious Identity in South Asia*, edited by V. Dalmia, A. Malinar, and M. Christof-Fuechsle (Delhi: Oxford University Press, 2001), 303; Antonio Rigopoulos, *The Life and Teachings of Sai Baba of Shirdi* (Albany: State University of New York Press, 1993), 243–244; Charles White, "Swāmi Muktānanda and the Enlightenment through Śakti-pāt," *History of Religions* 13, no. 4 (May 1974): 307.

71. In her study on Mā Anandāmayī, Lisa Hallstrom notes that, in the course of her interviews with disciples who had known Mā in her lifetime, a number of cases mentioned her apparition in dreams after Mā's death. See Lisa Hallstrom, *Mother of Bliss: Ānandamayī Mā (1896–1982)* (New York: Oxford University Press, 1999), 123.

72. Dhingra, *Visages de Ma Anandamayi*, 140.

73. Swami Nirvedananda, "The Holy Mother," in *Great Women of India*, edited by Swami Madhavananda and Ramesh C. Majumdar (Calcutta: Advaita Ashrama, 1997), 502–503.

74. Dilip Kumar Roy and Indira Devi, *Pilgrims of the Stars* (Porthill, ID: Timeless Books, 1985), 359.

75. Vasudha Narayanan, "Gurus and Goddesses, Deities and Devotees," in *The Graceful Guru: Hindu Females Gurus in India and the United States*, edited by Karen Pechilis (New York: Oxford University Press, 2004), 157.

76. Swami Chandra, *L'Art de la réalisation* (Paris: Albin Michel, 1985), 15.

77. Sahukar, *Sai Baba: The Saint of Shirdi*, 73.

78. Dhingra, *Visages de Ma Anandamayi*, 16.

79. Shrî Aurobindo, *Métaphysique et psychologie* (Paris: Albin Michel, 1988), 243.

80. Loriliai Biernacki, "Shree Maa of Kamakkya," in Pechilis, ed., *The Graceful Guru*, 187.

81. Maya Warrier, "Processes of Secularization in Contemporary India: Guru Faith in the Mata Amritanandamayi Mission," *Modern Asian Studies* 37, no. 1 (February 2003): 235; and Maya Warrier, *Hindu Selves in a Modern World: Guru Faith in the Mata Amritanandamayi Mission* (London: Routledge Curzon, 2005), 104.

CHAPTER 5

1. Max Weber, *Economy and Society*, Vol. 1 (New York: Bedminster Press, 1968), 241.
   The Weberian concept of charisma, however, differs from Durkheim's. Although the latter one never used the word "charisma" itself, "charisma," according to his view, only appears in states of collective effervescence, where the individual ego is dissolved into the group. Unlike Weber, charisma here is not so much related to leadership, as Durkheim considers the charismatic leader to be more like a representative of the collective ecstatic effervescence, of the energy of the group. As for Freud, charisma has a more negative aspect compared to Weber and Durkheim, as it is related both to hatred and attraction. In his understanding, followers are not only bound by love.

2. Pierre Bourdieu, "Une interprétation de la théorie de la religion selon Max Weber," *Archives Européenne de Sociologie* 12, no. 1 (1971): 15; Charles Lindholm, *Charisma* (Cambridge, MA: Basil Blackwell, 1990), 25.

3. Pierre Bourdieu, "Le Langage autorisé: Note sur les conditions sociales de l'efficacité du discours rituel," *Actes de recherche en Sciences Sociales* 1, nos. 5–6 (November): 186–187.

4. Charles Lindholm, "Culture, Charisma, and Consciousness: The Case of the Rajneeshee." *Ethos* 30, no. 4 (2002): 358.

5. Marcel Gauchet, *Le Désenchantement du monde* (Paris: Gallimard, 1985), 230. In a similar way, one can draw a parallel with legitimate objects given by charismatic beings, to the extent that the most important thing for the devotee is not the object itself, but what it means. See Charles White, "The Sāi Bābā Movement: Approaches to the Study of Indian Saints," *Journal of Asian Studies* 31, no. 4 (August 1972): 874.

6. Jean Séguy, "Max Weber et la sociologie historique des religions," *Archives Sociologiques des Religions*, no. 33 (January–June, 1972): 96; Lindholm, "Culture, Charisma, and Consciousness," 358.

7. Weber, *Economy and Society*, Vol. 1, 326.

8. Danièle Hervieu-Léger and Jean-Paul Willaime, "Max Weber," in *Sociologies et religion* (Paris: Presses Universitaires de France, 2001), 73.

9. Max Weber, *Sociologie des religions* (Paris: Gallimard, 1996), 251–252, cited in Hervieu-Léger and Willaime, "Max Weber," 73.

10. Julien Freund, "Le Charisme selon Max Weber," *Social Compass* 23, no. 4 (1976): 391.

11. Lindholm, "Culture, Charisma, and Consciousness," 359.

12. Roger Bastide, *Les Amériques noires* (Paris: Payot, 1967), 133.

13. Henri Desroche, "Retour à Durkheim? D'un texte peu connu à quelques thèses méconnues," *Archives de Sociologie des Religions* 27 (1969): 79–88, cited in Françoise Champion and Danièle Hervieu-Léger, *De l'émotion en religion: Renouveaux et traditions* (Paris: Le Centurion, 1990), 221.

14. Henri Bergson, *Les Deux Sources de la morale et de la religion* (Paris: Presses Universitaires de France, 1946).

15. Charles Taylor, *La Diversité de l'expérience religieuse aujourd'hui: William James revisité* (Saint-Laurent, QB Bellarmin, 2003), 11.

16. Françoise Champion and Danièle Hervieu-Léger, *De l'émotion en religion: Renouveaux et traditions* (Paris: Le Centurion, 1990), 9.

17. Schmuel Trigano, *Qu'est-ce que la religion?* (Paris: Flammarion, 2001), 110.

18. Cited in Paul Brunton, *A Search in Secret India* (London: Rider, 2003), 49–50.

19. In this regard, see Irvin H. Collins, "The 'Routinization of Charisma' and the Charismatic," in *The Hare Krishna Movement: The Postcharismatic Fate of a Religious Transplant*, edited by Edwin F. Bryant and Maria L. Ekstrand (New York: Columbia University Press, 2004), 217.

20. E. A. Mann, "Religion, Money and Status: The Competition for Resources at the Shrine of Shah Jamal, Aligarh," in *Muslim Shrines in India*, edited by Christian W. Troll (New Delhi: Oxford University Press, 2003), 145.

21. Heinrich Von Stietencron, "Charisma and Canon: The Dynamics of Legitimization and Innovation in Indian Religions," in *Charisma and Canon: Essays on the Religious History of the Indian Subcontinent*, edited by V. Dalmia, A. Malinar, and M. Christof (New York: Oxford University Press, 2001), 25.

    On this subject, see Jacob Copeman, "The Mimetic Guru: Tracing the Real in Sikh-Dera Sacha Sauda Relations," in *The Guru in South Asia: New Interdisciplinary Perspectives*, edited by Jacob Copeman and Aya Ikegame (London: Routledge, 2012), where he explores the controversy in 2007 surrounding the alleged act of imitation by one guru of the DSS devotional order (Dera Sacha Sauda) of Guru Govind Singh, the last living Sikh Guru. Although the Sikh tradition strictly forbids new *dehdari* (living gurus), the DSS proclaimed himself the successor of Guru Govind Singh, provoking a scandal among the orthodox Sikhs.

    Regarding the true/fake guru, Hinduism does not possess a recognized decision-making body capable of differentiating between a true guru and a false one. There are no rules on the matter permitting such a distinction, which makes the process of differentiation between a true guru and a charlatan complex, as Meena Kandelwal affirms. According to Copeman, however, one should be cautious that the "really real gurus" may act in a fake way and pretend they are the charlatans!

    See Meena Kandelwal, *Women in Ochre Robes* (Albany: State University of New York Press, 2004), 141. On the true guru and charlatans, Copeman, "The Mimetic Guru," 175. See also Kirin Narayan's observations on stories of fake gurus told by one who is himself a guru in *Storytellers, Saints, and Scoundrels: Folk Narrative in Hindu Religious Teaching* (Philadelphia: University of Pennsylvania Press, 1989).

22. Alexandra David-Neel, *L'Inde où j'ai vécu* (Paris: Pocket, 1985), 245. This also returns us to the *smārta* community at Sringeri that sees in the present *jagadguru* (guru of the world) an incarnation of Shankaracharya. In this respect, see William Cenkner, *A Tradition of Teachers: Śankara and the Jagadgurus Today* (Delhi: Motilal Banarsidass, 1983); see also Yoshitsugu Sawai, *The Faith of Ascetics and Lays Smārtas* (Delhi: Motilal Banarsidass, 1992), 107.

23. We note that the *Governing Body* includes among its members a number of women. It gathers together three times a year, and elects its president by majority. For a while, this was Govind Narain, an important Indian civil servant who was dispatched by the pandit Nehru in 1956 to negotiate the return of Pondicherry to India, a return that occurred peaceably.

24. Maya Warrier, *Hindu Selves in a Modern World: Guru Faith in the Mata Amritanandamayi Mission* (London: Routledge Curzon, 2005), 37.

25. Regarding the sum of money Mā left to her monks, we do not know if this concerns all of her monks or only some of them, that is to say her closest disciples. As we do not have supplementary information on this matter, we

similarly do not know if there were tensions appearing between monks due to this money.

26. The creation of the Indore ashram is imparted to a spontaneous revelation a saint had while he was accompanying Swami Kedarnath in Indore. Pointing to the future place of the Indore ashram (the land was actually belonging to the India Legal court at that time), the saint would have told Swami Kedarnath that an ashram dedicated to Mā should be started on that plot, as it was "written in the higher worlds already."

27. Mā came to Omkareshwar in 1940 and a small temple was constructed at the place where she stayed. On the Ānandamayī Mā Omkareshwar Ashram School, see http://www.youtube.com/watch?v=vnfE_w2MVQY.

28. Swami Kedarnath wrote several books on Mā, especially eight volumes on her teaching, titled *Mā Ānandamayī Vachamāmrit* (The Immortal Teachings of *Mā Ānandamayī*) (Indore: Om Ma Śri Śri Mātā Ānandamayī Peeth Trust). He started the book series in 2004 and continued through 2012. The other books (from the same publisher) include *Sri Sri Ma Anandamayi: A Guide to Meditation and Understanding* (2009); *Sri Sri Ma Anandamayi: Divinity in Our Midst* (2009); and *An Epilogue to Reality: The Autobiography of a Pilgrim Soul* (which describes Swami Kedarnath's realization experience after he met Mā) (1985).

29. Jürgen Habermas, *The Structural Transformation of the Public Sphere* (Cambridge, MA: MIT Press, 1991).

30. Trigano, *Qu'est-ce que la religion?* 179.

31. Parita Mukta, *Upholding the Common Life: The Community of Mirabai* (Delhi: Oxford University Press, 1989), 30.

32. Charles Taylor, *Varieties of Religion Today: William James Revisited* (Cambridge, MA: Harvard University Press, 2002), 24.

33. Gerardus Van Der Leeuw, *La Religion dans son essence et ses manifestations: Phénoménologie de la religion* (Paris: Payot, 1955), 208.

34. George M. Williams, "The Ramakrishna Movement: A Study in Religious Change," in *Religion in Modern India*, edited by Robert D. Baird (Delhi: Manohar, 2001), 59.

35. David M. Miller and Dorothy C. Wertz, *Hindu Monastic Life* (Montreal, QC: McGill-Queen's University Press, 1976), 195–196.

36. It should be clarified that anyone can actually enter the Kankhal ashram (the *samādhi*, the book store, etc.) but large parts of the ashram are strictly forbidden to Westerners because of orthodox brahmin rules. For this reason, foreigners are not allowed to eat and sleep there, so as to avoid polluting the place.

37. David-Neel, *L'Inde où j'ai vécu*, 253.

38. Dilip Kumar Roy and Indira Devi, *The Flute Calls Still* (Bombay: Bharatiya Vidya Bhavan, 1982), 9.

39. Swami Vijayānanda, "Un chemin de joie: Témoignages et réponses d'un disciple français de Mâ Anandamayi."

40. Bharati Dhingra, *Visages de Ma Anandamayi* (Paris: Cerf, 1981), 31.

41. Mā said this to Khan Bahadur Nazir-ud-din Alimed (Dacca University). See Raj Sahib Akshoy Kumar Datta Gupta, "God as Love," in *Mother as Seen by Her Devotees* (Varanasi: Shree Shree Anandamayee Sangha, 1967).

42. Arnaud Desjardins, *Ashrams: Grands maîtres de l'Inde* (Paris: Albin Michel, 1982), 184.

43. Katherine Young and Lily Miller, "Sacred Biography and the Restructuring of Society: A Study of Anandamayi Ma, Lady-Saint of Modern Hinduism," *Boeings and Bullock-Carts*, Vol. 2, edited by Dhirendra K. Vajpeyi (Delhi: Chanakya Publications, 1990), 136–137.

44. *The Ramakrishna Math and Mission Convention—1926*, Belur, The Math, 1926, 31, cited in Williams, "The Ramakrishna Movement," 70–71.

45. On a more esoteric level, Brahmins believe that these ancient rules regarding rituals and caste purity, such as food restrictions (i.e., strict vegetarianism), absence of contact with dirt (and consequently with foreigners who are considered to be polluting agents), conduct of specific meditation practice and rituals, are meant to sustain the subtle energy field, the spiritual vibrations of the Indian land, so as to lead them to liberation. See Atmananda, *Death Must Die: A Western Woman's Life-Long Spiritual Quest in India with Sri Anandamayee Ma*, edited by Ram Alexander (Delhi: Indica Books, 2000), 232.

46. *Vijayananda: Some Aspects of Ma Anandamayi's Teachings* (texts collected and presented by Dr. Jacques Vigne), http://www.anandamayi.org/devotees/jvv2.htm.

47. Alexander Lipski, *Life and Teaching of Śrī Ānandamayī Mā* (Delhi: Motilal Banarsidass, 2005), 58; Atmananda, *Death Must Die*, 255.

48. Atmananda, *Death Must Die*, 256.

49. Jean-Claude Marol, *La Saturée de joie Anandamayi* (Paris: Dervy, 2001), 90.

50. Atmananda, *Death Must Die*, 243.

51. Melita Maschmann, *Encountering Bliss: My Journey through India with Ānandamayī Mā* (Delhi: Motilal Banarsidass, 2002), 227.

52. On this subject, see also the testimony of Daniel Roumanoff, where Mā affirms to Roumanoff that for her, there are no foreigners and that there is only the *Self*, in "A Tragic Passion," *What is Enlightenment*, no. 10 (Autumn–Winter 1996): 56.

53. Atmananda, *Death Must Die*, 504.

54. Ibid., 505.

55. Desjardins, *Ashrams*, 76–77.

56. Madou, *A la rencontre de Ma Anandamayi: Entretiens avec Atmananda*, http://www.anandamayi.org/ashram/french/frmadı.htm.

57. Atmananda, *Death Must Die*, 242.

58. Ibid., 254–255

59. Ibid., 257.

60. Ibid., 348.

61. Ibid., 259.

62. Jacques Vigne, *L'Inde intérieure: Aspects du yoga, de l'hindouisme et du bouddhisme* (Gordes: Editions du Relié, 2007), 360.

63. Jacob Copeman and Aya Ikegame, "Guru Logics," *HAU: Journal of Ethnographic Theory* 2, no. 1 (2012): 312.

64. The lack of reference of lower castes within Mā's ashrams is not due to any neglect on our part, but stems from the absence of information on this subject. As Indian devotees are usually assembled without distinction in Mā's ashrams, notably during mealtimes, it is difficult for us to take account of the place of the lower castes with regard to Brahmins.

65. Regarding brahminism and purity rules, we are reminded of Copeman's work, who argues that organ donation is an opportunity to challenge Brahmanism and its belief that all bodies need to be cremated. See Jacob Copeman and Deepa S. Reddy, "The Didactic Death: Publicity, Instruction, and Body Donation," *HAU: Journal of Ethnographic Theory* 2, no. 2 (2012): 59–83.

66. Mary Douglas, *Purity and Danger: An Analysis of Concepts of Pollution and Taboo* (London: Routledge & Kegan Paul, 1966), 113.

67. Madou, *A la rencontre de Ma Anandamayi.*

68. Jean-Pierre Albert, "Hagio-graphiques: L'Écriture qui sanctifie," *Terrain*, no. 24 (March 1995): 76.

69. Bruce B. Lawrence, "The Chishtiya of Sultanate India: A Case Study of Biographical Complexities in South Asia Islam," in *Charisma and Sacred Biography*, edited by M. A. Williams (Chico, CA: Scholars Press, 1982), 55; see also David N. Lorenzen, "The Life of Śaṅkarācārya," *The Biographical Process: Studies in the History and Psychology of Religion*, edited by Frank E. Reynolds and Donald Capps (La Hague: Mouton, 1976), 87.

70. Steven J. Rosen, "Introduction," *Journal of Vaiṣṇava Studies* 1, no. 2 (1993): p. i.

71. Frank E. Reynolds and Donald Capps, "Introduction," in *The Biographical Process*, 4.

72. T. K. Stewart, "When Biographical Narratives Disagree: The Death of Kṛṣṇa Caitanya," *Numen* 38, no. 2 (December 1991): 232.

73. See Karl H. Potter, "Śamkarācārya: The Myth and the Man," in *Charisma and Sacred Biography*; as well as Robin Rinehart, *One Lifetime, Many Lives: The Experience of Modern Hindu Hagiography* (New York: Oxford University Press, 1999).

74. R. Puligandla, *Fundamentals of Indian Philosophy* (Nashville: Abingdon Press, 1975), 247, cited in W. J. Jackson, "A Life Becomes a Legend: Srī Tyāgarāja as Exemplar," *Journal of the American Academy of Religion* 60, no. 4 (Winter 1992): 722.

75. Jonathan Bader, *Conquest of the Four Quarters* (New Delhi: Aditya Prakashan, 2000), 7.

76. S. G. Tulpule, "Hagiography in Medieval Marathi Literature," in *According to Tradition: Hagiographical Writing in India*, edited by W. M. Callewaert and R. Snell (Wiesbaden: Harrassowitz, 1994), 166.

77. Stephen Wilson, *Saints & their Cults: Studies in Religious Sociology, Folklore & History* (Cambridge: Cambridge University Press, 1983), 16; Rinehart, *One Lifetime, Many Lives*, 12.

78. Françoise Mallison, "Le 'Genre' hagiographique dans la Bhakti médiévale de l'Inde occidentale," in *Genre Littéraires en Inde*, edited by Nalini Balbir (Paris: Presses de la Sorbonne Nouvelle, 1994), 326.

79. John A. Colesman, "Conclusion: After Sainthood," in *Saints and Virtues*, edited by John Stratton Hawley (Berkeley and Los Angeles: University of California Press, 1988), 367.

80. Stephen Wilson, "Introduction," in id., *Saints & their Cults: Studies in Religious Sociology, Folklore & History* (Cambridge: Cambridge University Press, 1983), 31; Patrick Geary, "Saints, Scholars, and Society: The Elusive Goal," in *Saints: Studies in Hagiography*, edited by Sandro Sticca (Binghamton, NY: Medieval and Renaissance Texts and Studies, 1996), 15; Père H. Delehaye, *The Legends of the Saints* (London: University of Notre Dame Press, 1961), 2.

81. Phyllis Granoff, "Scholars and Wonder-Workers: Some Remarks on the Role of the Supernatural in Philosophical Contests in Vedānta Hagiographies," *Journal of the American Oriental Society* 105, no. 3 (July–September 1985): 462; Phyllis Granoff, "Holy Warriors: A Preliminary Study of Some Biographies of Saints and Kings in the Classical Indian Tradition," *Journal of Indian Philosophy* 12, no. 3 (September 1984): 291–292 and 296.

82. Bader, *Conquest of the Four Quarters*, 15.

83. See Miller and Young, "Sacred Biography and the Restructuring of Society."

84. A new translation (November 2010) of the journal of Mā's very close disciple, Bhaiji, even speaks of Mā's *prakāsh*, i.e., Mā's revelation, mentioning the absence of Mā's biological mother Didimā at her birth. Similarly to statues, stones, etc., Mā then appears as a self-manifested being for some of her devotees. See *Mother Reveals Herself*, 4.

85. Hari Ram Joshi, *Mā Ānandamayī Līlā: Memoirs of Sri Hari Ram Joshi* (Calcutta: Shree Shree Anandamayee Charitable Society, 1981), 6.

86. Edward C. Dimock, "On Impersonality and Bengali Religious Biography," in *Sanskrit and India Studies: Essays in Honour of Daniel H. H. Ingalls*, edited by M. Nagatomi (Dordrecht: D. Reidel Publishing Co., 1980), 238; on the subject of the recognition of the avatar, see also France Bhattacharya, "La Construction de la figure de l'homme-dieu selon les deux principales hagiographies bengalies de Śrī Kṛṣṇa Caitanya," *Constructions Hagiographiques dans le Monde Indien: Entre mythe et histoire*, edited by Françoise Mallison (Paris: Champion, 2001), 187.

87. Denis Matringue, "Pakistan," in *Le Culte des saints dans le monde musulman,* edited by Henri Chambert-Loir and Claude Guillot (Paris: École Française d'Extrême Orient, 1995), 174.

88. Rinehart, *One Lifetime, Many Lives,* 54.

89. *Revue Nouvelles Clés,* 2000, cited in Vigne, *L'Inde Intérieure,* 357.

90. Stewart, "When Biographical Narratives Disagree," 231; T. K. Stewart, *The Final Word: The Caitanya Caritāmṛta and the Grammar of Religious Tradition* (New York: Oxford University Press, 2010), 46, 56, 123.

91. Parita Mukta, *Upholding the Common Life: The Community of Mirabai* (Delhi: Oxford University Press, 1989), 227.

92. Véronique Bouiller, "Un 'bricolage' hagiographique: *Siddha* Ratannath du monastère de Caughera (Népal)," *Constructions hagiographiques dans le Monde Indien,* edited by Françoise Mallison (Paris: Librairie Honoré Champion, 2001), 134.

93. Edward C. Dimock, "Religious Biography in India: The 'Nectar of the Acts' of Caitanya," in *The Biographical Process,* 109.

94. Jean Filliozat and Louis Renou, *L'Inde classique: Manuel des études indiennes,* Vol. 1 (Paris: Payot, 1985), 478; see also Narayan, *Storytellers, Saints, and Scoundrels,* 185.

95. Katherine Young, "Introduction," in *Women Saints in World Religions,* edited by Arvind Sharma (Albany: State University of New York Press, 2000), 4; Christian Lee Novetzke, *Religion and Public Memory: A Cultural History of Saint Namdev in India* (New York: Columbia University Press, 2008), 262. A number of scholars have argued that Janabai is a contemporary of the sixteenth-century Brahmin poet Vishnudas Nama, and hence she is writing about the fourteenth Namdev some centuries after he lived. As for Namdev, there are numerous debates about the place of his death. Three places were selected by scholars, where memorials and other physical sites are present. See Lee Novetzke, *Religion and Public Memory,* 49, which relates the cultural history of Namdev with Maharashtrian public memory. On Janabai, see also Rajeshwari V. Pandharipande, "Janabai," in *Women Saints in World Religions.*

96. As Stewart notes, the tradition tends not to recognize Chaitanya's death, adopting the more theologically sound return to heaven, merging with one of the temple images of Jagannātha, or disappearing. See Stewart, *The Final Word,* 46 and 256.

97. Govind Narain, "Shree Shree Mā Anandamayee: The Eternal Flame," in *Ma Anandamayee: Embodiment of India's Spiritual and Cultural Heritage* (Kankhal, Hardwar, India: Shree Shree Anandamayee Sangha, 2005), 37.

98. Swami Mangalananda, *Om Ma. Anandamayi Ma: A Short Life Sketch* (Omkareshwar, India: Mata Anandamayi Ashram, 2004), 55.

99. Koshelya Walli, "Mata Anandamayee's Contribution to Cultural and Spiritual Heritage of India," in *Ma Anandamayee: Embodiment of India's Spiritual and Cultural Heritage,* 54.

100. See *I am ever with you: Matri Lila*, Vols. 1 and 2 (Calcutta: Shree Shree Anandamayee Charitable Society, 1985 and 1991).
101. Prasanna Madhava, *Ma Anandamayee: The Divine Mother Showers Grace on Us* (Meerut, India: Sohan Printing Press, 2004), 93.
102. See the back cover of Jean-Claude Marol's book, *Une fois Ma Anandamayi* (Paris: Le Courrier du Livre, 1995).
103. Filliozat and Renou, *L'Inde classique*, 351.
104. Yvan Amar, "Introduction: La Transmission de la conscience," in *La Transmission Spirituelle* (Gordes: Éditions du Relié, 2003), 8.
105. On initiation in Mā's time, one can also refer to Lisa Hallstrom's work, *Mother of Bliss: Ānandamayī Mā (1896–1982)* (New York: Oxford University Press, 1999), 137–147.
106. Gupta, *In Association with Sri Sri Ma Anandamayi*, vol. 3, 17.
107. "Pensée de l'Himalaya: Entretiens avec Swami Nirgunananda," http://www.anandamayi.org.
108. In this regard, some devotees refer to Mā as the *paramguru*, which, in a way, corresponds to the "grandmother guru," as the role of the guru may be held by a swami of Mā's *saṅgha*.
109. Swami Sarasvati Chandrasekhara, *The Guru Tradition: Voice of the Guru* (Bombay: Bharatiya Vidya Bhavan, 1991), 40.
110. Vijayānanda, "Un Chemin de Joie."
111. Alexandra David-Néel, *Initiations et Initiés au Tibet* (London: Rider, 1973), 47.
112. The affirmation which holds that the saint, even dead, can conduct an initiation in a dream is common in the Hindu tradition, as in Sai Baba's movement. See White, "The Sāi Bābā Movement," 874.
113. According to Swami Nirgunānanda, an early disciple, Mā however affirmed the importance of verifying the authenticity of the mantra: "I was witness to many interviews with Mā where the seeker told Her that they had received a mantra in a dream. In almost all cases, Mā asked the person to address himself to his guru, so as to authenticate and sanctify the mantra or, in the physical absence of the guru, to address himself to a competent person of the same line" (Swami Nirgunananda, Extraits de "Self-dialogue on Japa," 2005, see http://www.anandamayi.org).
114. A. R. Natarajan, *Ramana Maharshi: The Living Guru* (Bangalore: Ramana Maharshi Centre for Learning, 2000), 9–10.
115. Madou, *A la rencontre de Ma Anandamayi*.

CONCLUSION

1. Arnaud Desjardins, *Les Chemins de La Sagesse* (Paris: La Table Ronde, 1999), 96.
2. Jürgen Habermas, *Communication and the Evolution of Society* (Boston: Beacon Press, 1974), 178–206.

3. Estimates of the total number of Sathya Sai Baba devotees around the world vary between 10 and 70 million.

4. On Thursday, April 8, i.e. two days after Swami's Vijayānanda's departure, Swami Bhaskarānanda also left his body in Bhimpura ashram on the banks of the Narmada River in Gujarat. He was 94 year old. Swami Bhaskarānanda and Swami Vijayānanda came to Mā around the same time and were both very close to her. Another great Swami of Mā, Swami Śivānanda, also left his body four days after Swami Vijayānanda's departure, Friday, April 9. He had been hospitalized two days earlier.

5. See Gene R. Thursby, "Siddha Yoga: Swami Muktananda and the Seat of Power," in *When Prophets Die: The Postcharismatic Fate of New Religious Movements*, edited by Timothy Miller (Albany: State University of New York Press, 1991), 165–181; Steven Gelberg, "The Call of the Lotus-Eyed Lord: The Fate of Krishna Consciousness in the West," in Miller, ed., *When Prophets Die*, 149–164; and Gordon Melton, "Introduction: When Prophets Die," in Miller, ed., *When Prophets Die*, 1–12.

6. See Timothy Miller, "Afterword," in id., *When Prophets Die*, 195.

7. William James, *The Varieties of Religious Experience* (Oxford: Oxford University Press, 2012), 258.

8. Pierre Bourdieu, "Genèse et structure du champ religieux," *Revue française de sociologie* 12, no. 3 (July–September 1971): 319.

9. The new scriptures/liturgies include the Mā Chaleesa; the *Śri Śri Mātā Ānandamayī Lilāmṛta* (which is a story of Mā's life to be sung in four different ragas like the Ramayana).

10. Charles Lindholm, "Culture, Charisma, and Consciousness: The Case of the Rajneeshee," *Ethos* 30, no. 4 (2002).

11. Maya Warrier, *Hindu Selves in a Modern World: Guru Faith in the Mata Amritanandamayi Mission* (London: Routledge Curzon, 2005), 142.

12. There was some resistance from a part of the ashram. Some conservative people in Kankhal also demonstrated to oppose the construction of a *samādhi* for Swami Vijayānanda in the village. Here we refer especially to the *sādhus* connected to the *Dakśa* temple, the *Mahanirvanī akhāḍa* and a group of *pāndās* (pilgrimage's priests). For more information, see Jacques Vigne, "Swami Vijayânanda: The Last Days," unpublished, http://www.anandamayi.org/devotees/Vijayanandaeng.htm.

13. Some devotees of Swami Vijayānanda believe that the eruption of the Eyjafjallajokull volcano, one of Iceland's largest volcanoes, on April 14, 2010, took place to purify the atmosphere for the transport of Swami Vijayānanda's body from India to Paris. This explosion sent clouds of ash soaring as high as 11,000 meters, disrupting air traffic in Europe.

14. See Gwilym Beckerlegge, *The Ramakrishna Mission: The Making of a Modern Hindu Movement* (New Delhi: Oxford University Press, 2000), about the "Making" of the Ramakrishna movement, more specifically the promotion, presentation, and rejection of the movement.

Glossary

Advaita Doctrine of the "One without second," of non-duality.

Akhāḍa Ascetic order.

Ānanda Bliss, joy without object.

Antaryāmin Interior master.

Ārati Ceremony during which lights are placed before the image of the divinity.

Ashram Institution where the guru and his or her community reside.

Ātman The Self.

Avatar "Descent" of the divine; divine incarnation.

Bhagavan God.

Bhajana Religious chant.

Bhakta Devotee, adorer, he or she who progresses on the path of *bhakti*.

Bhakti Devotion, love for the Divine.

Bhaktiyoga Way of devotion.

Bhāva State of being, interior disposition.

Brahmacārin (fem. ini) He or she who takes the vows of *brahmacārya*.

Brahmacārya First stage of brahmanic life; celibacy, chastity.

Brahman The absolute, the One.

Chakra Wheel, circle; name given to the subtle centers of the body.

Dargah Cult space where the tomb of a Muslim saint is located in India.

Darśana The vision of a sage, of a divinity.

Devī Goddess.

Dharma The "order of the world"; the traditional laws of classical Hinduism.

Dīkṣā Initiation completed by a guru.

Duḥkha Suffering, pain.

Dvandvatita Beyond opposing pairs.

Guṇa Quality or attribute of the phenomenal world.

Gurubahin Spiritual sister.

Gurubhai Spiritual brother.

Gurupūrṇimā Hindu celebration in honor of the guru that takes place on the day of the full moon in July.

Iṣṭā Divinity to which the adorer feels particularly drawn (literally, the beloved).

Janmabhūmi Place of birth.

Jāpa "Repetition"; devotional practice consisting in indefinitely repeating a mantra or the name of a divinity.

Jāti Birth.

Jaya "Victory to."

Jīva Life.

Jīvanmukta Sage who has attained Liberation while retaining his or her human body.

Jīvanmukti The state of liberation of a soul in a living body.

Jñāna Literally knowledge.

Jhuṭā Literally that which is dirty, impure. Designating the traditional rules of purity.

Karma Action, result of action; law of cause and effect.

Kheyāla Thought or sudden and unexpected desire; applied to Mā Ānandamayī, this means a spontaneous impulse of the Divine Will.

Kīrtana Collective religious chant.

Līlā The game of God.

Līnga Representation of the deity Śiva used for worship in Hindu temples.

Liṅgayāt Śivaite sect of the Deccan, which is distinguished by the bearing of an individual *liṅga*.

Loka World.

Mahāsamādhi Literally "great *samādhi*," death of the saint, of the guru.

Mandira Temple.

Manhush The awakened man, conscious of himself.

Mantra Sacred words, words of power.

Māṭha Monastery.

Mauna Silence.

Mohā Illusion, attachment.

Mokṣa Liberation.

Mṛtyu Death, another name of Yama.

Mukti Liberation.

Mūrti Statue.

Nirguṇa Without *guṇa*, or attributes; without qualifications (opposite: *saguṇa*).

Nirvāṇa Dissolution of the ego, liberation.

Para Superior, supreme.

Parabhakti Supreme *bhakti*, or divine love.

Paramguru Grandfather or grandmother guru.

Prakṛti "Nature," opposed to the Mind, "*puruṣa*."

Pranāma Prostration as a sign of obedience and humility.

Prāṇapratiṣṭhā Process of establishing the breath in the statue or in an image of the divinity.

Prasāda Food offered to a divinity or to a sage and redistributed to devotees.

Prema Supreme love.

Pūjā "Adoration"; ritual Hindu ceremony.

Pūjāri Specialist of *pūjā*.

Puruṣa Mind, essential, immutable and conscious element of the person.

Satcitānanda Existence-consciousness-bliss.

Sadguru The perfect guru who leads to knowledge of Reality.

Sādhaka A person who practices asceticism, the *sādhanā*.

Sādhanā Spiritual discipline, asceticism.

Sādhu Wandering ascetic.

Saguṇa With attributes (opposite: *nirguṇa*); manifested God.

Śakta Worshipper of *Śakti*.

Śakti Divine "power" or "energy." Active aspect of God, considered to be feminine as opposed to its non-affected and immutable aspect; the Divine Mother.

Śaktipāta Initiating transmission.

Samādhi Technical yogic term that designates the highest form of mystic gathering. The *samādhi* can be *savikalpa* (with content) or *nirvikalpa* (without content). *Samādhi* also means the tomb of a renunciant.

Saṃnyāsa Complete renunciation of life in the world; also the last stage of human life, in which man should renounce his family, his possessions, his caste, and so on.

Saṃnyāsin (fem. *ini*) Renunciant; also individual who has attained the fourth and last stage of existence.

Sampradāya Spiritual line.

Saṃsāra "Transmigration," indefinite circle of deaths and rebirths; opposite of *mokṣa*.

Saṃskāra Results of impressions and of past karma that are found in our being.

Samyam Saptah One week retreat.

Sanātana Eternal.

Saṅgha Community.

Satī The perfect woman, faithful to her husband; secondarily the wife who throws herself onto her husband's funerary pyre.

Satsaṅga The society or company of saints and sages.

Siddhi Occult, supernatural power.

Śiṣya Disciple.

Śraddha Funerary rites.

Śūdra Last of the Hindu castes (*varṇa*).

Śukṣuma Subtle connection.

Svarūpa The true Being; Brahman.

Swami Member of a Hindu religious order.

Tapasya Austerities practiced for spiritual development.

Tīrtha Place of pilgrimage.

Ucchiṣṭa That which remains, which was sullied.

Upaguru Secondary guru.

Vairāgya Detachment and indifference toward the world.

Varṇa Caste.

Vedānta One of the most important *darśana* (schools) of traditional Hinduism.

Vīra "Hero." Initiated tantric practitioner.

Viśiṣṭādvaita "Qualified" non-dualism.

Vrata Vow.

Yajñā Sacrifice.

Bibliography

Acquaviva, Sabino Samele. 1994. *La Sociologie des religions: Problèmes et perspectives.* Paris: Cerf.

Albert, Jean-Pierre. 1995. "Hagio-graphiques: L'Écriture qui sanctifie." *Terrain,* no. 24 (March): 75–82.

Altekar, Anant S. 1997. "Ideal and Position of Indian Women in Social Life." In *Great Women of India,* edited by Swami Madhavananda and Ramesh C. Majumdar, 26–48. Calcutta: Advaita Ashrama.

Amar, Yvan. 2003. "Introduction: La Transmission de la conscience." In id., *La Transmission spirituelle,* 7–17. Gordes: Editions du Relié.

Ānandamayī, Mā. 1982. *Matri Vani,* Vol. 2. Translated by Atmananda. India: Shree Shree Anandamayee Sangha.

———. 2001. *Words of Sri Anandamayi Ma.* Translated by Atmananda. Kankhal: Shree Shree Anandamayee Sangha.

Ananda Varta. 1956. "Mataji Amara Vani." *Ananda Varta* 4, no. 4: 312–317.

Anderson, Leona M. 2004. "Women in Hindu Tradition." In *Women and Religious Traditions,* edited by Leona M. Anderson and Pamela Dickey Young, 1–44. Don Mills, ON and New York: Oxford University Press.

Assayag, Jackie. 1987. "Le Cadavre divin: Célébration de la mort chez les Liṅgāyat-Vīraśaiva (Inde du Sud)." *L'Homme* 27, no. 103 (July–September): 93–112.

———. 1995. *Au confluent de deux rivières: Musulmans et hindous dans le sud de l'Inde.* Paris: École Française d'Extrême Orient.

Atmananda. 2000. *Death Must Die: A Western Woman's Life-Long Spiritual Quest in India with Sri Anandamayee Ma.* Edited by Ram Alexander. Delhi: Indica Books.

Aurobindo, Shrî. 1988. *Métaphysique et psychologie.* Paris: Albin Michel.

Babb, Lawrence A. 1981. "Glancing: Visual Interaction in Hinduism." *Journal of Anthropological Research* 37, no. 4 (Winter): 387–401.

———. 1983. "Sathya Sai Baba's Magic." *Anthropological Quarterly* 56: 116–123.

———. 1986. *Redemptive Encounters: Three Modern Styles in the Hindu Tradition.* Berkeley and Los Angeles: University of California Press.

——. 1988. "Sathya Sai Baba's Saintly Play." In *Saints and Virtues*, edited by John Stratton Hawley, 168–186. Berkeley and Los Angeles: University of California Press.

Bader, Jonathan. 2000. *Conquest of the Four Quarters: Traditional Accounts of the Life of Śankara*. New Delhi: Aditya Prakashan.

Bardin, Laurence. 1977. *L'Analyse de contenu*. Paris: Presses Universitaires de France.

Bastide, Roger. 1967. *Les Amériques noires*. Paris: Payot.

——. 1997. *Eléments de sociologie religieuse*. Paris: Editions Stock.

Beckerlegge, Gwilym. 2000. *The Ramakrishna Mission: The Making of a Modern Hindu Movement*. New Delhi: Oxford University Press.

Bergson, Henri. 1946. *Les Deux Sources de la morale et de la religion*. Paris: Presses Universitaires de France.

Bhagavadgītā. 1971. Translated by S. Radhakrishnan. London: George Allen & Unwin Ltd.

Bhai, Thara L. 2004. "Emergence of Shrines in Rural Tamil Nadu: A Study of Little Traditions." In *Sociology of Religion in India: Themes in Indian Sociology*, Vol. 3, edited by Rowena Robinson, 165–173. New Delhi: Sage Publications.

Bhaiji (ed.). 2000. *Sad Vani: A Collection of the Teaching of Sri Anandamayi Ma as Reported by Bhaiji*. Calcutta: Shree Shree Anandamayee Charitable Society.

——. 2004. *Mother as Revealed to Me*. Kankhal: Shree Shree Anandamayee Sangha.

——. 2010. *Mother Reveals Herself*. Varanasi: Pilgrims Publishing.

Bharati, Agehananda. 1963. "Pilgrimage in the Indian Tradition." *History of Religions* 3, no. 1 (Summer): 135–167.

Bhardwaj, Surinder M. 1973. *Hindu Places of Pilgrimage in India: A Study in Cultural Geography*. Berkeley and Los Angeles: University of California Press.

Bhattacharya, France. 2001. "La Construction de la figure de l'homme-dieu selon les deux principales hagiographies bengalies de Śrī Kṛṣṇa Caitanya." In *Constructions hagiographiques dans le monde indien: Entre mythe et histoire*, edited by Françoise Mallison, 183–203. Paris: Librairie Honoré Champion.

Biardeau, Madeleine. 1993. "Devi: The Goddess in India." In *Asian Mythologies*, compiled by Yves Bonnefoy and translated under the direction of Wendy Doniger, 95–98. Chicago: University of Chicago Press.

——. 1995. *L'Hindouisme: L'Anthropologie d'une civilisation*. Paris: Flammarion.

Biernacki, Loriliai. 2004. "Shree Maa of Kamakkya." In *The Graceful Guru: Hindu Females Gurus in India and the United States*, edited by Karen Pechilis, 179–202. New York: Oxford University Press.

Blackburn, Stuart H. 1985. "Death and Deification: Folk Cults in Hinduism." *History of Religions* 24, no. 3 (February): 255–274.

Bloch, Maurice, and Jonathan Parry (eds.). 1982. *Death and the Regeneration of Life*. Cambridge: Cambridge University Press.

Boisvert, Mathieu. 1995. "Bouddhisme, contemplation et mort." *Frontières* 7, no. 3 (Winter): 32–37.

Bouiller, Véronique. 1989. "Des prêtres du pouvoir: Les Yogis et la fonction royale." In *Prêtrise, pouvoirs et autorité en Himalaya,* edited by Véronique Bouiller and Gérard Toffin, 193–213. Paris: École des Hautes Études en Sciences Sociales.

———. 2001. "Un 'bricolage' hagiographique: *Siddha* Ratannath du monastère de Caughera (Népal)." In *Constructions hagiographiques dans le monde indien: Entre mythe et histoire,* edited by Françoise Mallison, 123–138. Paris: Librairie Honoré Champion.

———. 2004. "Samādhi et Dargāh: Hindouisme et islam dans la Shekhavati." *De l'Arabie à l'Himalaya,* edited by Véronique Bouiller and Catherine Servan-Schreiber, 251–271. Paris: Maisonneuve & Larose.

Bourdieu, Pierre. 1971. "Genèse et structure du champ religieux." *Revue française de sociologie* 12, no. 3 (July–September): 295–334.

———. 1971. "Une interprétation de la théorie de la religion selon Max Weber." *Archives Européennes de Sociologie* 12, no. 1: 3–21.

———. 1975. "Le Langage autorisé: Note sur les conditions sociales de l'efficacité du discours rituel." *Actes de recherche en Sciences Sociales* 1, nos. 5–6 (November): 183–190.

Bourdin, Dominique. 2005. "Psychanalyse et religion: La Pensée de Freud." *La Religion: Unité et diversité,* edited by Laurent Testot and Jean-François Dortier, 33–40. Auxerre: Sciences humaines éditions.

Bṛhadāranyaka Upaniṣad. 1965. With the commentary of Śankarācārya. Calcutta: Advaita Ashrama.

Bronkhorst, Johannes. n.d. "Les Reliques dans les religions de l'Inde." Université de Lausanne. Unpublished paper.

Brown, Peter. 1985. *La Société et le sacré dans l'antiquité tardive.* Paris: Seuil.

———. 1996. *Le Culte des saints: Son essor et sa fonction dans la chrétienté latine.* Paris: Cerf.

Brunton, Paul. 2003. *A Search in Secret India.* London: Rider.

Bugault, Guy. 1990. "La Relation maître disciple en Inde." In *Maître et disciples dans les traditions religieuses,* edited by Michel Meslin, 21–35. Paris: Cerf.

Caillois, Roger. 1950. *L'Homme et le sacré.* Paris: Gallimard.

Caldwell, Sarah. 2003. "Margins at the Center: Tracing Kālī through Time, Space, and Culture." In *Encountering Kālī: In the Margins, at the Center, in the West,* edited by Rachel Fell McDermott and Jeffrey J. Kripal, 249–272. Berkeley and Los Angeles: University of California Press.

Carrette, Jeremy. 2005. "Passionate Belief: William James, Emotion and Religious Experience." In *William James and the Varieties of Religious Experience: A Centenary Celebration,* edited by Jeremy Carrette, 79–93. London: Routledge.

———. 2008. "William James." In *The Oxford Handbook of Religion and Emotion,* edited by John Corrigan, 419–436. New York: Oxford University Press.

Carrin, Marine. 1995. "Saintes des villes et saintes des champs: La Spécificité féminine de la sainteté en Inde." *Terrain,* no. 24 (March): 107–118.

Cenkner, William. 1983. *A Tradition of Teachers: Śankara and the Jagadgurus Today.* Delhi: Motilal Banarsidass.

Centlivres, Pierre, and Anne-Marie Losonczy. 2001. "Introduction." In *Saints, sainteté et martyre: La Fabrication de l'exemplarité,* Actes du colloque de Neuchâtel, 27–28 November 1997, 7–14. Paris: Editions de la Maison des Sciences de l'Homme.

Champion, Françoise, and Danièle Hervieu-Léger. 1990. *De l'émotion en religion: Renouveaux et traditions.* Paris: Le Centurion.

Chandra, Swami. 1985. *L'Art de la réalisation.* Paris: Albin Michel.

Chandrasekhara Sarasvati, Swami. 1991. *The Guru Tradition: Voice of the Guru.* Bombay: Bharatiya Vidya Bhavan.

Chaput, Pascale. 1997. "Equivalences et equivoques: Le Culte des saints catholiques au Kerala." In *Altérité et identité: Islam et Christianisme en Inde,* edited by Jackie Assayag and Gille Tarabout, 171–196. Paris: École des Hautes Études en Sciences Sociales.

Charpentier, Marie-Thérèse. 2010. *Indian Female Gurus in Contemporary Hinduism: A Study of Central Aspects and Expressions of Their Religious Leadership.* Åbo: Åbo Akademi University Press.

Chattopadhyaya, R. 1975. "Sri Anandamayee Ma: Mother of Eternal Bliss." In *Gurus, Godmen and Good People,* edited by Khushwant Singh. Bombay: Orient Longman.

Chaudhuri, Narayan. 1998. *That Compassionate Touch of Ma Anandamayee.* Delhi: Motilal Banarsidass.

Chenet, François. 1990. "L'Hindouisme, mystique des images ou traversée de l'image?" *L'Image divine: Culte et méditation dans l'hindouisme,* 151–168. Paris: Editions du CNRS.

Clément, Catherine, and Sudhir Kakar. 1993. *La Folle et le saint.* Paris: Seuil.

Clémentin-Ojha, Catherine. 1985. "The Tradition of Female Gurus." *Manushi,* no. 31 (November–December): 2–8.

——. 1990. "Image animée, image vivante: L'Image du culte hindou." *L'Image divine: Culte et méditation dans l'hindouisme,* 115–132. Paris: Editions du CNRS.

——. 1990. *La Divinité conquise: Carrière d'une sainte.* Nanterre, France: Société d'Ethnologie.

Coburn, Thomas B. 1982. "Consort of None, *Śakti* of All: The Vision of the *Devī-Māhātmya.*" In *The Divine Consort: Rādhā and the Goddesses of India,* edited by John Stratton Hawley and Donna M. Wulff, 153–165. Berkeley and Los Angeles: University of California Press.

Colas, Gérard. 2004. "The Competing Hermeneutics of Image Worship in Hinduism." In *Images in Asian Religions: Texts and Contexts,* edited by Phyllis Granoff and Koichi Shinohara, 149–179. Vancouver, Canada: UBC Press.

Colesman, John A. 1988. "Conclusion: After Sainthood." In *Saints and Virtues,* edited by John Stratton Hawley, 205–225. Berkeley and Los Angeles: University of California Press.

Collins, Irvin H. 2004. "The 'Routinization of Charisma' and the Charismatic." In *The Hare Krishna Movement: The Postcharismatic Fate of a Religious Transplant,* edited by Edwin F. Bryant and Maria L. Ekstrand, 214–257. New York: Columbia University Press.

Coomaraswamy, Ananda K. n.d. *Hinduism and Buddhism.* New York: Philosophical Library.

Copeman, Jacob. 2006. "Cadaver Donation as Ascetic Practice in India." *Social Analysis* 50, no. 1 (Spring): 103–126.

—— (ed.). 2012. "The Mimetic Guru: Tracing the Real in Sikh-Dera Sacha Sauda Relations." In *The Guru in South Asia: New Interdisciplinary Perspectives,* edited by Jacob Copeman and Aya Ikegame, 156–180. London: Routledge.

Copeman, Jacob, and Aya Ikegame. 2012. "Guru Logics." *HAU: Journal of Ethnographic Theory* 2, no. 1: 289–336.

—— (eds.). 2012. "The Multifarious Guru: An Introduction." In *The Guru in South Asia: New Interdisciplinary Perspectives,* edited by Jacob Copeman and Aya Ikegame, 1–45. London: Routledge.

Copeman, Jacob, and Deepa S. Reddy. 2012. "The Didactic Death: Publicity, Instruction, and Body Donation." *HAU: Journal of Ethnographic Theory* 2, no. 2: 59–83.

Cornille, Catherine. 2004. "Mother Meera, Avatar." In *The Graceful Guru: Hindu Female Gurus in India and the United States,* edited by Karen Pechilis, 129–147. New York: Oxford University Press.

Courtright, Paul B. 1995. "Satī, Sacrifice, and Marriage: The Modernity of Tradition." In *From the Margins of Hindu Marriage: Essays on Gender, Religion, and Culture,* edited by Lindsey Harlan and Paul B. Courtright, 184–203. New York: Oxford University Press.

Couture, André. 2001. "La Geste krishnaïte et les études hagiographiques modernes." In *Constructions hagiographiques dans le monde indien: Entre mythe et histoire,* edited by Françoise Mallison, pp. vii–xxviii. Paris: Librairie Honoré Champion.

Daniélou, Alain. 2001. *Mythes et dieux de l'Inde: Le Polythéisme hindou.* Paris: Flammarion.

——. 2005. *Approche de l'hindouisme.* Paris: Editions Kailash.

Das Gupta, Shashi B. 1997. "Evolution of Mother Worship in India." In *Great Women of India,* edited by Swami Madhavananda and Ramesh C. Majumdar, 49–86. Calcutta: Advaita Ashrama.

David-Neel, Alexandra. 1973. *Initiations et initiés au Tibet.* London: Rider.

——. 1985. *L'Inde où j'ai vécu.* Paris: Pocket.

Davis, Richard H. (ed.). 1998. "Introduction: Miracles as Social Acts." In id., *Images, Miracles, and Authority in Asian Religious Traditions,* 1–22. Boulder, CO: Westview Press.

Debray, Régis. 2005. *Le Feu sacré: Fonction du religieux.* Paris: Gallimard.

Delehaye, Hippolyte. 1961. *The Legends of the Saints.* London: University of Notre Dame Press.

DeNapoli, Antoinette. 2009. "Beyond Brahmanical Asceticism: Recent and Emerging Models of Female Hindu Asceticisms in South Asia." *Religion Compass* 3, no. 5: 857–875.

———. 2009. "By the Sweetness of the Tongue." *Asian Ethnology* 68, no. 1: 81–109.

Denton, Lynn Teskey. 2004. *Female Ascetics in Hinduism.* Albany: State University of New York Press.

Desiderio, Pinto, S.J. 2003. "The Mystery of the Nizamuddin Dargah: The Accounts of Pilgrims." In *Muslim Shrines in India: Their Character, History and Significance,* edited by Christian W. Troll, 112–124. New Delhi: Oxford University Press.

Desjardins, Arnaud. 1982. *Ashrams: Grands maîtres de l'Inde.* Paris: Albin Michel.

———. 1999. *Les Chemins de La Sagesse.* Paris: La Table Ronde.

Devi, Gurupriya. 1986. *Sri Sri Ma Anandamayi,* Vol. 1. Calcutta: Shree Shree Anandamayee Charitable Society.

Dhingra, Bharati. 1981. *Visages de Ma Anandamayi.* Paris: Cerf.

Dimock, Edward C. 1976. "Religious Biography in India: The 'Nectar of the Acts' of Chaitanya." In *The Biographical Process: Studies in the History and Psychology of Religion,* edited by Frank E. Reynolds and Donald Capps, 109–118. La Hague: Mouton.

———. 1980. "On Impersonality and Bengali Religious Biography." *Sanskrit and India Studies: Essays in Honour of Daniel H. H. Ingalls,* edited by M. Nagatomi, 237–242. Dordrecht: D. Reidel Publishing Co.

Douglas, Mary. 1966. *Purity and Danger: An Analysis of Concepts of Pollution and Taboo.* London: Routledge & Kegan Paul.

Dubbois, Abbé J. A. [1906] 1978. *Hindu Manners, Customs and Ceremonies.* Delhi: Oxford University Press.

Dumont, Louis. 1959. "Le Renoncement dans les religions de l'Inde." *Archives de Sociologie des Religions* 7, no. 7 (January–June): 45–69.

Eck, Diana L. 1985. *Darśan: Seeing the Divine in India.* Chambersburg, PA: Anima Books.

Eliade, Mircea. 1959. *Initiation, rites et sociétés secrètes.* Paris: Gallimard.

———. 1965. *Le Sacré et le profane.* Paris: Gallimard.

———. 1968. *Traité d'histoire des religions.* Paris: Payot.

———. 1971. *La Nostalgie des origines.* Paris: Gallimard.

———. 1979. *Images et symboles.* Paris: Gallimard.

———. 1983. *Le Yoga: Immortalité et liberté.* Paris: Payot.

———. 1988. *L'Inde.* Paris: Editions de l'Herne.

Erndl, Kathleen M. 1993. *Victory to the Mother: The Hindu Goddess of Northwest India in Myth, Ritual, and Symbol.* New York: Oxford University Press.

Ewing, Katherine P. 1998. "A Majzub and His Mother: The Place of Sainthood in a Family's Emotional Memory." In *Embodying Charisma: Modernity, Locality and the Performance of Emotion in Sufi Cults,* edited by Pnina Werbner and Helene Basu, 160–184. London: Routledge.

Falk, Nancy E. 2001. "*Shakti* Ascending: Hindu Women, Politics, and Religious Leadership during the Nineteenth and Twentieth Centuries." *Religion in Modern India*, edited by Robert D. Baird, 298–334. Delhi: Manohar.

Faure, Bernard. 1994. *La Mort dans les religions d'Asie*. Paris: Flammarion.

———. 2004. "Buddhist Relics and Japanese Regalia." In *Embodying the Dharma: Buddhist Relic Veneration in Asia*, edited by David Germano and Kevin Trainor, 93–116. Albany: State University of New York Press.

Feuga, Pierre. 1989. *Cinq visages de la déesse*. Paris: Le Mail.

Filippi, Gian Giuseppe. 1996. *Mṛtyu: Concept of Death in Indian Tradition— Transformation of the Body & Funeral Rite*. New Delhi: D. K. Printworld.

Filliozat, Jean, and Louis Renou. 1985. *L'Inde classique: Manuel des études indiennes*, Vol. 1. Paris: Payot.

Flueckiger, Joyce B. 2006. *In Amma's Healing Room: Gender and Vernacular Islam in South Asia*. Bloomington: Indiana University Press.

Fort, Andrew. 1996. "Introduction: Living Liberation in Hindu Thought." In *Living Liberation in Hindu Thought*, edited by Andrew Fort and Patricia Y. Mumme, 1–13. Albany: State University of New York Press.

———. 1998. *Jīvanmukti in Transformation: Embodied Liberation in Advaita and Neo-Vedanta*. Albany: State University of New York Press.

Fortin, Andrée. 1988. "L'Observation participante: Au cœur de l'altérité." In *Les Méthodes de la recherche qualitative*, edited by Jean-Pierre Deslauriers, 23–33. Québec: Presses de l'Université du Québec.

Frazer, G. James. 1995. *The Golden Bough: A Study in Magic and Religion*. New York: Touchstone Press.

Frembgen, Jürgen W. 1998. "The *Majzub* Mama Ji Sarkar: A Friend of God Moves from One House to Another." In *Embodying Charisma: Modernity, Locality and the Performance of Emotion in Sufi Cults*, edited by Pnina Werbner and Helene Basu, 140–159. London: Routledge.

Freund, Julien. 1976. "Le Charisme selon Max Weber." *Social Compass* 23, no. 4: 383–395.

Fuller, C. J. 2004. *The Camphor Flame: Popular Hinduism and Society in India*. Princeton: Princeton University Press.

Gaborieau, Marc. 1983. "The Cult of Saints among the Muslims of Nepal and Northern India." In *Saints and their Cults: Studies in Religious Sociology, Folklore and History*, edited by Stephen Wilson, 291–308. Cambridge: Cambridge University Press.

———. 1989. "Pouvoir et autorité des soufis dans l'Himalaya." In *Prêtrise, pouvoirs et autorité en Himalaya*, edited by Véronique Bouiller and Gérard Toffin, 215–238. Paris: École des Hautes Études en Sciences Sociales.

———. 1995. "Inde." In *Le Culte des saints dans le monde musulman*, edited by Henri Chambert-Loir and Claude Guillot, 198–210. Paris: École Française d'Extrême Orient.

———. 2003. "A Nineteenth-Century Indian 'Wahhabī' Tract against the Cult of Muslim Saints: *Al-Balagh al-Mubin*." In *Muslim Shrines in India: Their Character,*

History and Significance, edited by Christian W. Troll, 198–239. New Delhi: Oxford University Press.

Gajano, Sofia Boesch. 1999. "Reliques et pouvoirs." In *Les Reliques, objets, cultes, symboles*. Actes du Colloque International de l'Université du Littoral-Côte d'Opale, edited by Edina Bozoky and Anne-Marie Helvétius, 255–269. Turnhout, Belgium: Brepols.

Ganguli, Anil. 1980. *Anandamayi Ma's Inscrutable Kheyāl*. Calcutta: Shree Shree Anandamayi Charitable Society.

———. 1983. *Anandamayi Ma: The Mother Bliss-Incarnate*. Calcutta: Eureka.

Gardet, Louis, and Olivier Lacombe. 1981. *L'Expérience du soi*. Paris: Desclée de Brouwer.

Gauchet, Marcel. 1985. *Le Désenchantement du monde*. Paris: Gallimard.

Geary, Patrick. 1978. *Furta Sacra: Thefts of Relics in the Central Middle Ages*. Princeton: Princeton University Press.

———. 1996. "Saints, Scholars, and Society: The Elusive Goal." In *Saints: Studies in Hagiography*, edited by Sandro Sticca, 1–22. Binghamton: State University of New York Press.

Gelberg, Steven J. 1991. "The Call of the Lotus-Eyed Lord: The Fate of Krishna Consciousness in the West." In *When Prophets Die: The Postcharismatic Fate of New Religious Movements*, edited by Timothy Miller, 149–164. Albany: State University of New York Press.

Geoffroy, Eric. 1995. "Proche-Orient." In *Le Culte des saints dans le monde musulman*, edited by Henri Chambert-Loir and Claude Guillot, 33–56. Paris: École Française d'Extrême Orient.

George, Philippe. 1999. "Les Reliques des saints: Un nouvel objet historique." *Les reliques, objets, cultes, symboles*. Actes du Colloque International de l'Université du Littoral-Côte d'Opale, edited by Edina Bozoky and Anne-Marie Helvétius, 229–237. Turnhout, Belgium: Brepols.

Gephart, Werner. 1998. "Memory and the Sacred: The Cult of Anniversaries and Commemorative Rituals in the Light of the Elementary Forms." In *On Durkheim's Elementary Forms of Religious Life*, edited by N. J. Allen, W. S. F. Pickering, and W. Watts Miller, 127–135. London: Routledge.

Ghosh, Shyam. 2002. *Hindu Concept of Life and Death*. New Delhi: Manohar.

Godin, André. 1986. *Psychologie des expériences religieuses: Le Désir et la réalité*. Paris: Le Centurion.

Gold, Daniel. 1987. *The Lord as Guru: Hindi Sants in North Indian Tradition*. New York: Oxford University Press.

———. 1988. *Comprehending the Guru: Toward a Grammar of Religious Perception*. Atlanta, GA: Scholars Press.

Granoff, Phyllis. 1984. "Holy Warriors: A Preliminary Study of Some Biographies of Saints and Kings in the Classical Indian Tradition." *Journal of Indian Philosophy*, 12, no. 3 (September): 291–303.

———. 1985. "Scholars and Wonder-Workers: Some Remarks on the Role of the Supernatural in Philosophical Contests in Vedānta Hagiographies." *Journal of the American Oriental Society* 105, no. 3 (July–September): 459–467.

Granoff, Phyllis, and Koichi Shinohara (eds.). 2004. "Introduction." In id., *Images in Asian Religions: Texts and Contexts*, 1–15. Vancouver, BC: UBC Press.

———. 2004. "Images and Their Ritual Use in Medieval India: Hesitations and Contradictions." In id., *Images in Asian Religions: Texts and Contexts*, 19–55. Vancouver, BC: UBC Press.

Grémion, Catherine. 2000. "Les Saintes, victimes de leurs interprètes." *Des Saints, des justes*, edited by Henriette Levillain, 112–122. Paris: Autrement.

Guénon, René. 1982. *Initiation et réalisation spirituelle*. Paris: Editions Traditionnelles.

Guillot, Claude, and Henri Chambert-Loir (eds.). 1995. "Indonésie." In id., *Le Culte des saints dans le monde musulman*, 235–254. Paris: École Française d'Extrême Orient.

Gupta, Amulya K. D. 1987. *In Association with Sri Sri Ma Anandamayi*, Vols. 1 and 3. Calcutta: Shree Shree Anandamayee Charitable Society.

Gupta, Kumar Dutta. 1967. "God as Love." In *Mother as Seen by Her Devotees*, edited by Gopinath Kaviraj. Varanasi: Shree Shree Anandamayee Sangha.

Gupta, Roxanne K. 2003. "Kālī Māyī: Myth and Reality in a Banaras Ghetto." In *Encountering Kālī: In the Margins, at the Center, in the West*, edited by Rachel Fell McDermott and Jeffrey J. Kripal, 124–142. Berkeley and Los Angeles: University of California Press.

Gupta, Swarajya 1972. *Disposal of the Dead and Physical Types in Ancient India*. Delhi: Oriental Publishers.

Haberman, David L. *People Trees: Worship of Trees in Northern India*. New York: Oxford University Press, 2013.

Habermas, Jürgen. 1974. *Communication and the Evolution of Society*. Boston: Beacon Press.

———. 1987. *The Theory of Communicative Action: The Critique of Functionalist Reason*, Vol. 2. Oxford: Blackwell.

———. 1991. *The Structural Transformation of the Public Sphere: An Inquiry into a Category of Bourgeois Society*. Cambridge, MA: MIT Press.

Hallstrom, Lisa L. 1999. *Mother of Bliss: Ānandamayī Mā (1896–1982)*. New York: Oxford University Press.

———. 2004. "Anandamayi Ma, the Bliss-Filled Divine Mother." In *The Graceful Guru: Hindu Females Gurus in India and the United States*, edited by Karen Pechilis, 85–118. New York: Oxford University Press.

Hawley, John S. 1988. "Morality beyond Morality in the Lives of Three Hindu Saints." In id., *Saints and Virtues*, 52–72. Berkeley and Los Angeles: University of California Press.

———. 1996. "Prologue. The Goddess in India." In *Devī: Goddesses of India*, edited by John Stratton Hawley and Donna M. Wulff, 1–28. Berkeley and Los Angeles: University of California Press.

Herbert, Jean. 1972. *Spiritualité hindoue*. Paris: Albin Michel.

——. 1989. "Karma et mort dans l'hindouisme." In *La Mort est une autre naissance*, edited by Marc de Smedt, 220–253. Paris: Albin Michel.

—— (trans.). 1996. *Aux sources de la joie: Mâ Ananda Moyî*. Paris: Albin Michel.

Herbert, Jean, and Josette Herbert (trans.). 1988. *L'Enseignement de Mâ Ananda Moyî*. Paris: Albin Michel.

Hertz, Robert. 2004. *Death and the Right Hand*. London: Cohen & West.

Hervieu-Léger, Danièle. 1993. *La Religion pour mémoire*. Paris: Cerf.

——. 1999. *Le Pèlerin et le converti: La Religion en mouvement*. Paris: Flammarion.

Hervieu-Léger, Danièle, and Jean-Paul Willaime. 2001. "Max Weber." In id., *Sociologies et religion: Approches classiques*, 59–109. Paris: Presses Universitaires de France.

Hudson, Dennis D. 1993. "Āṇṭāḷ Āḻvār: A Developing Hagiography." *Journal of Vaishnava Studies* 1, no. 2: 27–61.

Hulin, Michel. 1985. *La Face cachée du temps*. Paris: Fayard.

Hutchinson, Brian. 1992. "The Divine-Human Figure in the Transmission of Religious Tradition." In *A Sacred Thread: Modern Transmission of Hindu Traditions in India and Abroad*, edited by Raymond Brady Williams, 92–124. Chambersburg, PA: Anima Books.

Isambert, François. 1979. *Rite et efficacité symbolique: Essai d'anthropologie sociologique*. Paris: Cerf.

Isherwood, Christopher. 1965. *Ramakrishna and His Disciples*. Calcutta: Advaita Ashrama.

Jackson, W. J. 1992. "A Life Becomes a Legend: Srī Tyāgarāja as Exemplar." *Journal of the American Academy of Religion* 60, no. 4 (Winter): 717–736.

Jaffrelot, Christophe. 2012. "The Political Guru: The Guru as Éminence Grise." In *The Guru in South Asia: New Interdisciplinary Perspectives*, edited by Jacob Copeman and Aya Ikegame, 80–96. London: Routledge.

James, William. 1999. *L'Expérience Religieuse: Essai de psychologie descriptive*. Paris: La Bibliothèque de l'Homme.

——. 2003. *The Varieties of Religious Experience*. New York: Signet Classic.

——. 2012. *The Varieties of Religious Experience*. Oxford: Oxford University Press.

Jamous, Raymond. 1995. "Faire, défaire et refaire les saints: Les *Pir* chez les Meo d'Inde du Nord." *Terrain*, no. 24 (March): 43–56.

Jay Ma, nos. 44, 45, http://www.anandamayi.org/ashram/french/frdocs1.htm.

Joshi, Hari Ram. 1981. *Mā Ānandamayī Līlā: Memoirs of Sri Hari Ram Joshi*. Calcutta: Shree Shree Anandamayee Charitable Society.

Juergensmeyer, Mark. 1987. "The Radhasoami Revival of the Sant Tradition." In *The Sants: Studies in a Devotional Tradition of India*, edited by Karine Schomer and W. H. McLeod, 329–355. Delhi: Motilal Banarsidass.

——. 1988. "Saint Gandhi." In *Saints and Virtues*, edited by John Stratton Hawley, 187–203. Berkeley and Los Angeles: University of California Press.

Kakar, Sudhir. 1982. *Shamans, Mystics and Doctors: A Psychological Inquiry into India and its Healing Traditions.* New York: Knopf.

Kandelwal, Meena. 2004. *Women in Ochre Robes: Gendering Hindu Renunciation.* Albany: State University of New York Press.

Kaplan, Michel. 1999. "De la dépouille à la relique: Formation du culte des saints à Byzance du Vè au XIIè siècle." *Les Reliques, objets, cultes, symboles.* Actes du Colloque International de l'Université du Littoral-Côte d'Opale, edited by Edina Bozoky and Anne-Marie Helvétius, 19–38. Turnhout, Belgium: Brepols.

Kaviraj, Gopinath. 1967. "Mother Anandamayi." In *Mother as Seen by Her Devotees.* Varanasi: Shree Shree Anandamayee Sangha.

———. 1990. "Mother." In *Selected Writings of M. M. Gopinath Kaviraj*, edited by Gopinath Kaviraj, 180–205. Varanasi: M. M. Gopinath Kaviraj Centenary Celebrations Committee.

Kedarnath, Swami. 2012. *An Introduction to Sri Anandamayi Ma's Philosophy of Absolute Cognition.* Indore: Om Ma Sri Sri Mata Anandamayi Peeth Trust.

Keith, Arthur B. 1925. *The Religion and Philosophy of the Veda and Upanishads.* Cambridge, MA: Harvard University Press.

Keyes, C. F. 1982. "Charisma: From Social Life to Sacred Biography." In *Charisma and Sacred Biography*, edited by M. A. Williams, 1–22. Chico, CA: Scholars Press.

———. 1982. "Death of Two Buddhist Saints in Thailand." In *Charisma and Sacred Biography*, edited by M. A. Williams, 149–180. Chico, CA: Scholars Press.

Khan, Dominique-Sila. 1997. "La Tradition de Rāmdev Pīr au Rajasthan: Acculturation et syncrétisme." In *Altérité et identité: Islam et Christianisme en Inde*, edited by Jackie Assayag and Gille Tarabout, 121–140. Paris: École des Hautes Études en Sciences Sociales.

Kieckhefer, Richard, and George Bond (eds.). 1988. "Preface." In id., *Sainthood: Its Manifestations in World Religions*, pp. vii–xii. Berkeley and Los Angeles: University of California Press.

Kinnard, Jacob N. 2004. "The Field of the Buddha's Presence." In *Embodying the Dharma: Buddhist Relic Veneration in Asia*, edited by David Germano and Kevin Trainor, 117–143. Albany: State University of New York Press.

Kinsley, David. 1974. "'Through the Looking Glass': Divine Madness in the Hindu Religious Tradition." *History of Religions* 13, no. 4 (May): 270–305.

———. 1975. "Freedom from Death in the Worship of Kālī." *Numen* 22, no. 3 (December): 183–207.

———. 1975. *The Sword and the Flute: Kālī and Kṛṣṇa, Dark Visions of the Terrible and the Sublime in Hindu Mythology.* Berkeley and Los Angeles: University of California Press.

———. 1977. "'The Death That Conquers Death': Dying to the World in Medieval Hinduism." In *Religious Encounters with Death*, edited by Frank E. Reynolds and Earle H. Waugh, 97–108. University Park: Pennsylvania State University Press.

——. 1996. "Kālī, Blood and Death out of Place." In *Devī: Goddesses of India*, edited by John Stratton Hawley and Donna M. Wulff, 77–86. Berkeley and Los Angeles: University of California Press.

——. 1997. *Tantric Visions of the Divine Feminine: The Ten Mahavidyas*. Berkeley and Los Angeles: University of California Press.

——. 2003. "Kālī." In *Encountering Kālī: In the Margins, at the Center, in the* West, edited by Rachel Fell McDermott and Jeffrey J. Kripal, 23–38. Berkeley and Los Angeles: University of California Press.

Kishwar, Madhu. 1989. "Introduction." *Manushi. Tenth Anniversary Issue. Women Bhakta Poets*, nos. 50–52: 3–8.

Koppedrayer, Kathleen Iva. 1991. *The Sacred Presence of the Guru: The Velala Lineages of Tiruvavatuturai, Dharmapuram, and Tiruppanantal*. Ottawa, ON: National Library of Canada.

Kripal, Jeffrey J. 1998. *Kālī's Child: The Mystical and the Erotic in the Life and Teachings of Ramakrishna*. Chicago: University of Chicago Press.

——. 2001. "Re-membering a Presence of Mythological Proportions: Psychoanalysis and Hinduism." In *Religion and Psychology: Mapping the Terrain*, edited by Diane Jonte-Pace and William B. Parsons, 254–279. London: Routledge.

——. 2003. "Why the Tāntrika Is a Hero: Kali in the Psychoanalytic Tradition." In *Encountering Kali: In the Margins, at the Center, in the* West, edited by Rachel Fell McDermott and Jeffrey J. Kripal, 196–222. Berkeley and Los Angeles: University of California Press.

Kripal, Jeffrey J., and Rachel F. McDermott (eds.). 2003. "Introducing Kālī Studies." In id., *Encountering Kālī: In the Margins, at the Center, in the West*, 1–19. Berkeley and Los Angeles: University of California Press.

Lannoy, Richard. 1996. *Anandamayi: Her Life and Wisdom*. Rockport, MA: Element Books Ltd.

Lawrence, Bruce B. 1982. "The Chishtiya of Sultanate India: A Case Study of Biographical Complexities in South Asia Islam." In *Charisma and Sacred Biography*, edited by M. A. Williams, 47–67. Chico, CA: Scholars Press.

Lee Novetzke, Christian. 2008. *Religion and Public Memory: A Cultural History of Saint Namdev in India*. New York: Columbia University Press.

Lindholm, Charles. 1990. *Charisma*. Cambridge, MA: Basil Blackwell.

——. 1998. "Prophets and *Pirs*: Charismatic Islam in the Middle East and South Asia." In *Embodying Charisma: Modernity, Locality and the Performance of Emotion in Sufi Cults*, edited by Pnina Werbner and Helene Basu, 209–233. London: Routledge.

——. 2002. "Culture, Charisma, and Consciousness: The Case of the Rajneeshee." *Ethos* 30, no. 4: 357–375.

Lipski, Alexander. 2005. *Life and Teaching of Śrī Ānandamayī Mā*. Delhi: Motilal Banarsidass.

Long, J. Bruce. 1977. "Death as a Necessity and a Gift in Hindu Mythology." *Religious Encounters with Death*, edited by Frank E. Reynolds and Earle H. Waugh, 73–96. University Park: Pennsylvania State University Press.

Lorenzen, David N. 1976. "The Life of Śaṅkarācārya." In *The Biographical Process: Studies in the History and Psychology of Religion*, edited by Frank E. Reynolds and Donald Capps, 87–107. La Hague: Mouton.

Madan, T. N. 1990. *A l'opposé du renoncement: Perplexités de la vie quotidienne hindoue*. Paris: Editions de La Maison des Sciences de l'Homme.

Madhava, Prasanna. 2004. *Ma Anandamayee: The Divine Mother Showers Grace on Us*. Meerut, India: Sohan Printing Press.

Madou. *A la rencontre de Ma Anandamayi: Entretiens avec Atmananda*, http://www.anandamayi.org/ashram/french/frmad1.htm.

Malamoud, Charles. 1982. "Les Morts sans visage: Remarques sur l'idéologie funéraire dans le brâhmanisme." In *La Mort, les morts dans les sociétés anciennes*, edited by Gherardo Gnoli and Jean-Pierre Vernant, 441–453. Cambridge: Cambridge University Press; Paris: Editions de La Maison des Sciences de l'Homme.

———. 1996. *Cooking the World: Ritual and Thought in Ancient India*. New Delhi: Oxford University Press.

Mallison, Françoise. 1994. "Le 'Genre' hagiographique dans la *bhakti* médiévale de l'Inde occidentale." In *Genre Littéraires en Inde*, edited by Nalini Balbir, 325–338. Paris: Presses de la Sorbonne Nouvelle.

——— (ed.). 2001. "Introduction." In id., *Constructions hagiographiques dans le monde indien: Entre mythe et histoire*, pp. vii–xxviii. Paris: Librairie Honoré Champion.

Mangalananda, Swami. 2004. *Om Ma. Anandamayi Ma: A Short Life Sketch*. Omkareshwar, India: Mata Anandamayi Ashram.

———. n.d. "The Passing of a Saint: Sri Kishori Mataji." Unpublished paper.

Mann, E. A. 2003. "Religion, Money and Status: The Competition for Resources at the Shrine of Shah Jamal, Aligarh." In *Muslim Shrines in India: Their Character, History and Significance*, edited by Christian W. Troll, 145–171. New Delhi: Oxford University Press.

Marol, Jean-Claude. 1994. *En tout et pour tout*. Thionville: Le Fennec.

———. 1995. *Une fois Ma Anandamayi*. Paris: Le Courrier du Livre.

———. 1995. *Ma Anandamoyi: Vie en jeu*. Paris: Accarias–L'Originel.

———. 2001. *La Saturée de joie Anandamayi*. Paris: Dervy.

Maschmann, Melita. 2002. *Encountering Bliss: My Journey through India with Ānandamayī Mā*. Delhi: Motilal Banarsidass.

Matringue, Denis. 1995. "Pakistan." In *Le Culte des saints dans le monde musulman*, edited by Henri Chambert-Loir and Claude Guillot, 167–191. Paris: École Française d'Extrême Orient.

Mazzarella, William. 2006. "Internet X-ray: E-Governance, Transparency, and the Politics of Immediation in India." *Public Culture*, no. 18: 473–505.

McDaniel, June. 1989. *The Madness of the Saints: Ecstatic Religion in Bengal*. Chicago: University of Chicago Press.

——. 2004. "Fusion of the Soul: Jayashri Ma and the Primordial Mother." In *The Graceful Guru: Hindu Females Gurus in India and the United States*, edited by Karen Pechilis, 119–128. New York: Oxford University Press.

——. 2009. "Religious Experience in Hindu Tradition." *Religion Compass* 3, no. 1: 99–115.

McDermott, Rachel F. 1996. "Epilogue: The Western Kālī." In *Devī: Goddesses of India*, edited by John Stratton Hawley and Donna M. Wulff, 281–313. Berkeley and Los Angeles: University of California Press.

——. 2001. *Mother of My Heart, Daughter of My Dreams: Transformations of Kālī and Umā in the Devotional Poetry of Bengal*. New York: Oxford University Press.

——. 2003. "Kālī's New Frontiers: A Hindu Goddess on the Internet." In *Encountering Kālī: In the Margins, at the Center, in the* West, edited by Rachel Fell McDermott and Jeffrey J. Kripal, 273–295. Berkeley and Los Angeles: University of California Press.

Meera, Mère. n.d. *Mère Meera. Réponses*, Vol. 1. n.p.: Edition Adilakshmi.

Melton, Goldon J. 1991. "Introduction. When Prophets Die: The Succession Crisis in New Religions." In *When Prophets Die: The Postcharismatic Fate of New Religious Movements*, edited by Timothy Miller, 1–12. Albany: State University of New York Press.

Meslin, Michel. 1988. *L'Expérience humaine du divin: Fondements d'une anthropologie religieuse*. Paris: Cerf.

Miller, David. 1986. "Karma, Rebirth and the Contemporary Guru." In *Karma and Rebirth: Post Classical Developments*, edited by Ronald. W. Neufeldt, 61–81. Albany: State University of New York Press.

——. 2001. "The Divine Life Society Movement." In *Religion in Modern India*, edited by Robert D. Baird, 86–117. Delhi: Manohar.

Miller, David M., and Dorothy C. Wertz. 1976. *Hindu Monastic Life: The Monks and Monasteries of Bhubaneswar*. Montréal, QC: McGill-Queen's University Press.

Miller, Timothy (ed.). 1991. "Afterword." In id., *When Prophets Die: The Postcharismatic Fate of New Religious Movements*. Albany: State University of New York Press.

Mills, Landell Samuel. 1998. "The Hardware of Sanctity: Anthropomorphic Objects in Bangladeshi Sufism." In *Embodying Charisma: Modernity, Locality and the Performance of Emotion in Sufi Cults*, edited by Pnina Werbner and Helene Basu, 31–54. London: Routledge.

Mishra, R. L. 1991. *The Mortuary Monuments in Ancient and Medieval India*. Delhi: B.R. Pub. Corp.

Mlecko, Joel D. 1982. "The Guru in Hindu Tradition." *Numen* 29, no. 1 (July): 33–61.

Mookerjee, Nanda. 1978. *Sri Sarada Devi: Consort of Sri Ramakrishna*. Calcutta: Firma KLM.

Morin, Edgar. 1970. *L'Homme et la mort*. Paris: Seuil.

Mukerji, Bithika. 1998. *Life and Teaching of Sri Ma Anandamayi (A Bird on the Wing).* Delhi: Sri Satguru Publications.

———. 2002. *My Days with Sri Ma Anandamayi.* Varanasi: Indica Books.

Mukta, Parita. 1989. *Upholding the Common Life: The Community of Mirabai.* Delhi: Oxford University Press.

Muktananda, Swami. 1984. *Est ce que la mort existe réellement?* Paris: Saraswati.

Muṇḍaka Upaniṣad. 1998. Translated by Swami Muni Narayana Prasad. New Delhi: DK. Printworld.

Narain, Govind. 2005. "Shree Shree Ma Anandamayee: The Eternal Flame." In *Ma Anandamayee: Embodiment of India's Spiritual and Cultural Heritage,* 37–44. Kankhal, Hardwar, India: Shree Shree Anandamayee Sangha.

Narasimha, Swami B.V. 1976. *Life of Sai Baba.* Madras: All India Sai Samaj.

Narayan, Kirin. 1989. *Storytellers, Saints, and Scoundrels: Folk Narrative in Hindu Religious Teaching.* Philadelphia: University of Pennsylvania Press.

Narayanan, Vasudha. 1999. "Brimming with *Bhakti,* Embodiments of Shakti: Devotees, Deities, Performers, Reformers, and Other Women of Power in Hindu Tradition." In *Feminism and World Religions,* edited by Arvind Sharma and Katherine K. Young, 25–77. Albany: State University of New York Press.

———. 2004. "Gurus and Goddesses, Deities and Devotees." In *The Graceful Guru: Hindu Females Gurus in India and the United States,* edited by Karen Pechilis, 149–178. New York: Oxford University Press.

Natali, Cristiana. 2006. "Ériger des cimetières, construire l'identité: Pratiques funéraires et discours nationalistes chez les Tigres tamouls du Sri Lanka." *Frontières* 18, no. 2 (Spring): 15–20.

Natarajan, A. R. 2000. *Ramana Maharshi: The Living Guru.* Bangalore: Ramana Maharshi Center for Learning.

———. 2002. *Bhagavan Ramana & Mother.* Bangalore: Ramana Maharshi Center for Learning.

Nelson, Lance E. 1996. "Living Liberation in Śankara and Classical Advaita." In *Living Liberation in Hindu Thought,* edited by Andrew Fort and Patricia Y. Mumme, 17–62. Albany: State University of New York Press.

Nikhilananda, Swami (trans.), and Swami Adiswarananda (eds.). 2004. *Sri Sarada Devi. The Holy Mother: Her Teachings and Conversations.* New York: Ramakrishna-Vivekananda Center of New York and Skylight Paths Publishing.

Nirgunananda, Swami. 2005. Extraits de "Self-dialogue on Japa," http://www.anandamayi.org.

———. "Pensée de l'Himalaya: Entretiens avec Swami Nirgunananda," http://www.anandamayi.org.

Nirvedananda, Swami. 1997. "The Holy Mother." In *Great Women of India,* edited by Swami Madhavananda and Ramesh C. Majumdar, 464–539. Calcutta: Advaita Ashrama.

Nolane, Richard D. 2000. *Les Saints et leurs reliques: Une histoire mouvementée.* Beauport: Publications MNH; Paris: Anthropos.

O'Flaherty, Wendy D. 1984. *Dreams, Illusion and Other Realities.* Chicago: University of Chicago Press.

———. 1987. "The Interaction of *Saguṇa* and *Nirguṇa* Images of Deity." In *The Sants: Studies in a Devotional Tradition of India,* edited by Karine Schomer and W. H. McLeod, 47–52. Delhi: Motilal Banarsidass.

O'Malley, L. S. S. 2000. *Popular Hinduism: The Religion of the Masses.* Varanasi: Pilgrims Publishing.

Osborne, Arthur. 1992. *Ramana Maharshi and the Path of Self-Knowledge.* London: Rider.

Otto, Rudolf. 2001. *Le Sacré: L'Élément non rationnel dans l'idée du divin et sa relation avec le rationnel.* Paris: Payot.

Padoux, André. 1991. "Le Sage hindou: Renonçant ou surhomme?" In *Les Sagesses du Monde,* edited by Gilbert Gadoffre, 113–114. Paris: Editions Universitaires.

———. 2010. *Comprendre le tantrisme: Les Sources hindoues.* Paris: Albin Michel.

Pandharipande, Rajeshwari V. 2000. "Janabai: A Woman Saint of India." In *Women Saints in World Religions,* edited by Arvind Sharma, 145–179. Albany: State University of New York Press.

Panikkar, Raimon. 1998. *L'Expérience de Dieu.* Paris: Albin Michel.

Parry, Jonathan. 1982. "Sacrificial Death and the Necrophagous Ascetic." In *Death and the Regeneration of Life,* edited by Maurice Bloch and Jonathan Parry, 74–110. Cambridge: Cambridge University Press.

———. 1994. *Death in Banaras.* Cambridge: Cambridge University Press.

Pechilis, Karen (ed.). 2004. "Introduction: Hindu Female Gurus in Historical and Philosophical Context." In id., *The Graceful Guru: Hindu Female Gurus in India and the United States,* 3–49. New York: Oxford University Press.

——— (ed.). 2004. "Gurumayi, the Play of Sakti and Guru." In id., *The Graceful Guru: Hindu Female Gurus in India and the United States,* 219–243. New York: Oxford University Press.

———. 2012. "The Female Guru: Guru, Gender, and the Path of Personal Experience." In *The Guru in South Asia: New Interdisciplinary Perspectives,* edited by Jacob Copeman and Aya Ikegame, 113–132. London: Routledge.

Platelle, Henri. 1999. "Guibert de Nogent et le *De pignoribus sanctorum*: Richesses et limites d'une critique médiévale des reliques." In *Les Reliques, objets, cultes, symboles.* Actes du Colloque International de l'Université du Littoral-Côte d'Opale, edited by Edina Bozoky and Anne-Marie Helvétius, 109–121. Turnhout, Belgium: Brepols.

Potter, Karl H. 1982. "Śamkarācārya: The Myth and the Man." In *Charisma and Sacred Biography,* edited by M. A. Williams, 111–123. Chico, CA: Scholars Press.

Purushottamananda, Swami. n.d. *Autobiography or the Story of Divine Compassion.* Vasishtha Guha, Tehri Garwal, Uttar Pradesh: Sri Purushottamananda Trust.

Raj, Selva J. "Ammachi, The Mother of Compassion." In *The Graceful Guru: Hindu Female Gurus in India and the United States,* edited by Karen Pechilis, 203–218. New York: Oxford University Press, 2004.

Ramachandra Rao, Saligrama Krishna. 1979. *The Indian Temple. It's [sic] Meaning.* Bangalore: IBH Prakashana.

Ramdas, Swami. 1957. *Entretiens de Hadeyah.* Paris: Albin Michel.

———. 1997. *Présence de Ram.* Paris: Albin Michel.

Ranade, R. D. 1983. *Mysticism in India: The Poet-Saints of Maharashtra.* Albany: State University of New York Press.

Rayanna, P. S. 1964. *St Francis Xavier and His Shrine.* Ranchi, India: Catholic Press.

Reynolds, Frank E., and Donald Capps (eds.). 1976. "Introduction." In id., *The Biographical Process: Studies in the History and Psychology of Religion,* 1–33. La Hague: Mouton.

Rigopoulos, Antonio. 1993. *The Life and Teachings of Sai Baba of Shirdi.* Albany: State University of New York Press.

Rinehart, Robin. 1999. *One Lifetime, Many Lives: The Experience of Modern Hindu Hagiography.* New York: Oxford University Press.

Rivière, Jean M. 1982. *Lettres de Bénarès.* Paris: Albin Michel.

Rosen, Steven J. 1993. "Introduction." *Journal of Vaiṣṇava Studies* 1, no. 2: i–iv.

Roumanoff, Daniel. 1996. "A Tragic Passion." *What is Enlightenment?* no. 10 (Fall–Winter), 52–58.

Rousseau, André. 1977. "Rites et discours religieux comme pratiques sociales." *Maison-Dieu,* no. 129: 117–130.

Roy, Dilip Kumar, and Indira Devi. 1982. *The Flute Calls Still.* Bombay: Bharatiya Vidya Bhavan.

———. 1985. *Pilgrims of the Stars.* Porthill, ID: Timeless Books.

Sahukar, Mani. 1971. *Sai Baba: The Saint of Shirdi.* Bombay: Somaiya Publications.

Saindon, Marcelle. 2000. "Le Rituel hindou de la crémation: À la jonction du sacrifice védique et des rites de perfectionnement." In id., *Cérémonies funéraires et post funéraires en Inde: La Tradition derrière les rites,* 79–93. Sainte-Foy: Presses de l'Université Laval.

Saiyed, A. R. 2003. "Saints and Dargahs in the Indian Subcontinent: A Review." In *Muslim Shrines in India: Their Character, History and Significance,* edited by Christian W. Troll, 240–256. New Delhi: Oxford University Press.

Satprem. 1979. *Mother or the Divine Materialism.* Paris: Institut de recherches évolutives.

Sawai, Yoshitsugu. 1992. *The Faith of Ascetics and Lays Smārtas: A Study of the Śaṅkaran Tradition of Śṛṅgeri.* Delhi: Motilal Banarsidass.

Schlegel, Jean-Louis. 1994. "Le Réenchantement du monde et la quête du sens de la vie dans les nouveaux mouvements religieux." In *Les Spiritualités au carrefour du monde moderne: Traditions, transitions, transmissions,* edited by Ysé Tardan-Masquelier, 85–102. Paris: Le Centurion.

Schmitt, Jean-Claude. 1984. "La Fabrique des saints." *Annales* 39, no. 2 (March–April): 286–300.

———. 1999. "Les Reliques et les images." In *Les Reliques, objets, cultes, symboles.* Actes du Colloque International de l'Université du Littoral-Côte d'Opale, edited by Edina Bozoky and Anne-Marie Helvétius, 145–167. Turnhout, Belgium: Brepols.

Schneiderman, Leo. 1969. "Ramakrishna: Personality and Social Factors in the Growth of a Religious Movement." *Journal for the Scientific Study of Religion* 8, no. 1 (Spring): 60–71.

Schömbucher, Elisabeth, and Claus Peter Zoller. 1999. "Death and its Meaning in South Asia." In id., *Ways of Dying: Death and its Meanings in South Asia,* 1–5. New Delhi: Manohar.

Schopen, Gregory. 1987. "Burial 'ad sanctos' and the Physical Presence of the Buddha in Early Indian Buddhism: A Study in the Archaeology of Religions." *Religion* 17, no. 3: 193–225.

Séguy, Jean. 1972. "Max Weber et la sociologie historique des religions." *Archives des Sciences Sociales des Religions,* no. 33 (January–June): 71–103.

Servan-Schreiber, Catherine. 1997. "Partage de sites et partage de textes: Un modèle d'acculturation de l'Islam au Bihar." In *Altérité et identité: Islam et Christianisme en Inde,* edited by Jackie Assayag and Gille Tarabout, 143–170. Paris: École des Hautes Études en Sciences Sociales.

Sham Rao, P. D. 1972. *Five Contemporary Gurus in the Shirdi (Sai Baba) Tradition.* Madras: Christian Literature Society.

Sharma, Arvind. 2001. *Sati: Historical and Phenomenological Essays.* Delhi: Motilal Banarsidass.

Sharma, Ursula M. 2004. "The Immortal Cowherd and the Saintly Carrier: An Essay in the Study of Cults." In *Sociology of Religion in India: Themes in Indian Sociology,* Vol. 3, edited by Rowena Robinson, 149–164. New Delhi: Sage Publications.

Shree Shree Anandamayee Charitable Society. 1985 and 1991. *I Am Ever with You: Matri Lila,* Vols. 1 and 2. Calcutta: Shree Shree Anandamayee Charitable Society.

Siddiqui, Iqtidar Husain. 2003. "The Early Chishti Dargahs." In *Muslim Shrines in India: Their Character, History and Significance,* edited by Christian W. Troll, 1–23. New Delhi: Oxford University Press.

Singh, Purushottam. 1970. *Burial Practices in Ancient India.* Varanasi: Prithivi Prakashan.

Skoog, Kim. 1996. "Is the *Jīvanmukti* State Possible? Ramanuja's Perspective." In *Living Liberation in Hindu Thought,* edited by Andrew Fort and Patricia Y. Mumme, 63–90. Albany: State University of New York Press.

Spratt, Philip. 1966. *Hindu Culture and Personality: A Psychoanalytic Study.* Bombay: Manaktalas.

Srinivas, Smriti. 2001. "The Advent of the Avatar: The Urban Following of Sathya Sai Baba and its Construction of Tradition." In *Charisma and Canon: The Formation of Religious Identity in South Asia*, edited by V. Dalmia, A. Malinar, and M. Christof-Fuechsle, 293–309. Delhi: Oxford University Press.

———. 2008. *In the Presence of Sai Baba: Body, City and Memory in a Global Religious Movement*. Hyderabad: Orient Longman Private Limited.

Srivinas, Tulasi. 2010. *Winged Faith: Rethinking Globalisation and Religious Pluralism through the Sathya Sai Movement*. New York: Columbia University Press.

———. 2012. "Articles of Faith: Material Piety, Devotional Aesthetics and the Construction of a Moral Economy in the Transnational Sathya Sai Movement." *Visual Anthropology* 25 (July): 270–302.

———. 2012. "Relics of Faith: Fleshly Desires, Ascetic Disciplines and Devotional Affect in the Transnational Sathya Sai Movement." In *Handbook of Body Studies*, edited by Bryan S. Turner, 185–205. London: Routledge Press.

Staal, Frits. 1979. "The Meaningless of Ritual." *Numen* 26, no. 1 (June): 1–22.

Stewart, T. K. 1991. "When Biographical Narratives Disagree: The Death of Kṛṣṇa Caitanya." *Numen* 38, no. 2 (December): 231–260.

———. 2010. *The Final Word: The Caitanya Caritāmṛta and the Grammar of Religious Tradition*. New York: Oxford University Press.

Strong, John S. 2004. "Buddhist Relics in Comparative Perspective: Beyond the Parallels." In *Embodying the Dharma: Buddhist Relic Veneration in Asia*, edited by David Germano and Kevin Trainor, 27–49. Albany: State University of New York Press.

———. 2004. *Relics of the Buddha*. Princeton: Princeton University Press.

Subhan, John A. 1960. *Sufism: Its Saints and Shrines*. Lucknow: Lucknow Publishing House.

Swallow, D. A. 1982. "Ashes and Powers: Myth, Rite and Miracle in an Indian God-Man's Cult." *Modern Asian Studies* 16, no. 1: 123–158.

Tarabout, Gilles. 2004. "Theology as History: Divine Images, Imagination, and Rituals in India." In *Images in Asian Religions: Texts and Contexts*, edited by Phyllis Granoff and Koichi Shinohara, 56–84. Vancouver, BC: UBC Press.

Tardan-Masquelier, Ysé. 1999. *L'Hindouisme: Des Origines védiques aux courants contemporains*. Paris: Bayard.

Taylor, Charles. 2002. *Varieties of Religion Today: William James Revisited*. Cambridge, MA: Harvard University Press.

———. 2003. *La Diversité de l'expérience religieuse aujourd'hui: William James revisité*. Saint-Laurent, QC: Bellarmin.

Thursby, Gene R. 1991. "Siddha Yoga: Swami Muktananda and the Seat of Power." In *When Prophets Die: The Postcharismatic Fate of New Religious Movements*, edited by Timothy Miller, 165–181. Albany: State University of New York Press.

Trainor, Kevin. 1997. *Relics, Ritual and Representation in Buddhism: Rematerializing the Sri Lankan Theravāda Tradition*. Cambridge: Cambridge University Press.

———. 2004. "Introduction: Beyond Superstition." In *Embodying the Dharma: Buddhist Relic Veneration in Asia*, edited by David Germano and Kevin Trainor, 1–26. Albany: State University of New York Press.

Trigano, Schmuel. 2001. *Qu'est-ce que la religion?* Paris: Flammarion.

Tulpule, S. G. 1994. "Hagiography in Medieval Marathi Literature." In *According to Tradition: Hagiographical Writing in India*, edited by W. M. Callewaert and R. Snell, 159–167. Wiesbaden: Harrassowitz.

Turner, Victor W. 1969. *Le Phénomène ritual: Structure et anti-structure*. Paris: Presses Universitaires de France.

Urban, Hugh B. 2003. *Tantra: Sex, Secrecy, Politics, and Power in the Study of Religion*. Berkeley and Los Angeles: University of California Press.

———. 2010. *The Power of Tantra: Religion, Sexuality, and the Politics of South Asian Studies*. London: I. B. Tauris.

Van der Leeuw, Gerardus. 1955. *La Religion dans son essence et ses manifestations: Phénoménologie de la religion*. Paris: Payot.

Van der Veer, Peter. 1988. *Gods on Earth: The Management of Religious Experience and Identity in a North Indian Pilgrimage Centre*. London: Athlone Press.

Van Gennep, Arnold. 1969. *Les Rites de passage*. New York: Johnson Reprint.

Van Skyhawk, Hugh. 1999. "A Note on Death and the Holy Man in South Asia." In *Ways of Dying: Death and Its Meanings in South Asia*, edited by Elisabeth Schömbucher and Claus Peter Zoller, 190–202. New Delhi: Manohar.

Vauchez, André. 1988. *La Sainteté en Occident aux derniers siècles du Moyen Âge d'après les procès de canonisation et les documents hagiographiques*. Rome-Paris: École française de Rome.

Vaudeville, Charlotte. 1987. "*Sant Mat*: Santism as the Universal Path to Sanctity." In *The Sants: Studies in a Devotional Tradition of India*, edited by Karine Schomer and W. H. McLeod, 21–40. New Delhi: Motilal Banarsidass.

Vergote, Antoine. 1995. *Religion, foi, incroyance: Étude psychologique*. Brussels: Mardaga Pierre.

———. 1996. *Religion, Belief and Unbelief: A Psychological Study*. Leuven: Leuven University Press.

Vidal, Denis. 1989. "Des dieux face à leurs specialists: Conditions de la prêtrise en Himachal Pradesh." In *Prêtrise, pouvoirs et autorité en Himalaya*, edited by Véronique Bouiller and Gérard Toffin, 61–78. Paris: École des Hautes Études en Sciences Sociales.

Vigne, Jacques. 1991. *Le Maître et le thérapeute*. Paris: Albin Michel.

———. 2003. *La Mystique du silence*. Paris: Albin Michel.

———. 2005. *Râmatîrtha: Le Soleil du soi*. Translated by Jacques Vigne. Paris: Accarias–L'Originel.

———. 2007. *L'Inde intérieure: Aspects du yoga, de l'hindouisme et du bouddhisme*. Gordes: Editions du Relié.

———. 2010. "Swami Vijayânanda: The Last Days," http://www.anandamayi.org/devotees/Vijayanandaeng.htm.

Vijayānanda, Swami. 1997. *Un français dans l'Himalaya: Itinéraire avec Mâ Ananda Môyî*. Lyon: Terre du Ciel.

———. n.d. "Un chemin de joie: Témoignages et réponses d'un disciple français de Mâ Anandamayi." Unpublished paper.

Vivekananda, Swami. 2005. *Les Yogas pratiques*. Paris: Albin Michel.

Von Glasenapp, Helmuth. 1963. *Immortality and Salvation in Indian Religions*. Calcutta: Susil Gupta India.

Von Stietencron, Heinrich. 2001. "Charisma and Canon: The Dynamics of Legitimization and Innovation in Indian Religions." In *Charisma and Canon: Essays on the Religious History of the Indian Subcontinent*, edited by V. Dalmia, A. Malinar, and M. Christof, 14–38. New York: Oxford University Press.

Wach, Joachim. 1955. *Sociologie de la religion*. Paris: Payot.

Walli, Koshelya. 2005. "Mata Anandamayee's Contribution to Cultural and Spiritual Heritage of India." In *Ma Anandamayee: Embodiment of India's Spiritual and Cultural Heritage*, 49–55. Kankhal, Hardwar, India: Shree Shree Anandamayee Sangha.

Warrier, Maya. 2003. "Processes of Secularization in Contemporary India: Guru Faith in the Mata Amritanandamayi Mission," *Modern Asian Studies* 37, no. 1 (February): 213–253.

———. 2005. *Hindu Selves in a Modern World: Guru Faith in the Mata Amritanandamayi Mission*. London: Routledge Curzon.

Weber, Max. 1968. *Economy and Society*, Vol. 1. New York: Bedminster Press.

Weinberger-Thomas, Catherine. 1996. *Cendres d'immortalité: La Crémation des veuves en Inde*. Paris: Seuil.

Werbner, Pnina. 1998. "*Langar*: Pilgrimage, Sacred Exchange and Perpetual Sacrifice in a Sufi Saint's Lodge." In *Embodying Charisma: Modernity, Locality and the Performance of Emotion in Sufi Cults*, edited by Pnina Werbner and Helene Basu, 95–116. London: Routledge.

Werbner, Pnina, and Helene Basu. 1998. "The Embodiment of Charisma." In *Embodying Charisma: Modernity, Locality and the Performance of Emotion in Sufi Cults*, edited by Pnina Werbner and Helene Basu, 3–27. London: Routledge.

Werth, Lukas. 1998. "The Saint Who Disappeared." In *Embodying Charisma: Modernity, Locality and the Performance of Emotion in Sufi Cults*, edited by Pnina Werbner and Helene Basu, 77–91. London: Routledge.

White, Charles, S.J. 1972. "The Sāi Bābā Movement: Approaches to the Study of Indian Saints." *Journal of Asian Studies* 31, no. 4 (August): 863–878.

———. 1974. "Swāmi Muktānanda and the Enlightenment through Śakti-pāt." *History of Religions* 13, no. 4 (May): 306–322.

White, David Gordon. 2001. "The Exemplary Life of Mastnāth: The Encapsulation of Seven Hundred Years of Nāth Siddha Hagiography." In *Constructions hagiographiques dans le monde indien: Entre mythe et histoire*, edited by Françoise Mallison, 139–161. Paris: Librairie Honoré Champion.

———. 2003. "Ashes to Nectar: Death and Regeneration among the Rasa Siddhas and Nāth Siddhas." In *The Living and the Dead: Social Dimensions of Death in*

South Asian Religions, edited by Liz Wilson, 13–27. Albany: State University of New York Press.

Williams, George M. 1986. "Swami Vivekananda's Conception of Karma and Rebirth." In *Karma and Rebirth: Post Classical Developments,* edited by Ronald W. Neufeldt, 41–60. Albany: State University of New York Press.

———. 2001. "The Ramakrishna Movement: A Study in Religious Change." *Religion in Modern India,* edited by Robert D. Baird, 55–85. Delhi: Manohar.

Wilson, Stephen. 1983. "Introduction." In id., *Saints & their Cults: Studies in Religious Sociology, Folklore & History,* 1–53. Cambridge: Cambridge University Press.

Wulff, David M. 1982. "Prolegomenon to a Psychology of the Goddess." In *The Divine Consort: Rādhā and the Goddesses of India,* edited by John Stratton Hawley and Donna Marie Wulff, 283–297. Berkeley and Los Angeles: University of California Press.

Yocum, Glenn E. 1992. "The Coronation of a Guru: Charisma, Politics, and Philosophy in Contemporary India." In *A Sacred Thread: Modern Transmission of Hindu Traditions in India and Abroad,* edited by Raymond Brady Williams, 68–91. Chambersburg, PA: Anima Books.

Yogananda, Paramahansa. 1997. *Autobiography of a Yogi.* Los Angeles: Self-Realization Fellowship.

Young, Katherine. 2000. "Introduction." In *Women Saints in World Religions,* edited by Arvind Sharma, 1–38. Albany: State University of New York Press.

Young, Katherine, and Lily Miller. 1990. "Sacred Biography and the Restructuring of Society: A Study of Anandamayi Ma, Lady-Saint of Modern Hinduism." *Boeings and Bullock-Carts,* Vol. 2, edited by Dhirendra K. Vajpeyi, 112–147. Delhi: Chanakya Publications.

Zins, Max-Jean. 2005. "Rites publics et deuil patriotique: Les Funérailles de la guerre indo-pakistanaise de 1999." *Archives de Sciences Sociales des Religions,* nos. 131–132 (July–December): 63–85.

DVD

Desjardins, Arnaud. 2006. *Ashrams.* France: Alizé Diffusion. Dvd 35 + 20 mn.

WEBSITES

http://www.anandamayi.org

http://www.srianandamayima.org

http://www.youtube.com/watch?v=vnfE_w2MVQY (The Anandamayi Ma Omkareshwar Ashram School)

http://www.youtube.com/watch?v=eMF0qInjohk (interview "Arnaud Desjardins talks about his experiences with Ma Anandamayi")

http://www.youtube.com/watch?v=32J9B8hNzKM (interview Arnaud Desjardins, part IV)

http://www.youtube.com/watch?v=Mjz1xyDzR2I (interview Arnaud Desjardins, part V)

Index